Mediamorphosis

Mediamorphosis

Kafka and the Moving Image

EDITED BY
Shai Biderman and Ido Lewit

WALLFLOWER PRESS
LONDON & NEW YORK

A Wallflower Press Book

Wallflower Press is an imprint of
Columbia University Press
publishers since 1893
New York

Copyright © 2016 Shai Biderman and Ido Lewit
All rights reserved

Wallflower Press® is a registered trademark of Columbia University Press

A complete CIP record is available from the Library of Congress

ISBN 978-0-231-17644-6 (cloth)
ISBN 978-0-231-17645-3 (pbk.)
ISBN 978-0-231-85089-6 (e-book)

Cover image: Copyright © Piotr Dumała / source: Filmoteka Narodowa

CONTENTS

Acknowledgments   vii
Notes on Contributors   ix

  Introduction   1
  Ido Lewit and Shai Biderman

PART ONE: THE CINEMATIC KAFKA

  Kafka, Rumour, Early Cinema: Archaic Moving Pictures   29
  Paul North

  Sebald Goes to the Movies: Reading Kafka as Cinematography   53
  Nimrod Matan

  The Ghost is Clear: The POV of the Daydreamer   68
  Laurence A. Rickels

  Moving Pictures – Visual Pleasures: Kafka's Cinematic Writing   81
  Peter Beicken

  To Move as the Image Moves: The Rule of Rhythmic Presence and Absence in Kafka's *The Man Who Disappeared*   97
  Tobias Kuehne

  Noises Off: Cinematic Sound in Kafka's 'The Burrow'   111
  Kata Gellen

  Gesture, Wardrobe, Backdrop and Prop in Franz Kafka's *The Man Who Disappeared* and Peter Weir's *The Truman Show*   130
  Idit Alphandary

  The Possibility of the Cinematic in 'The Metamorphosis' and 'The Burrow'   163
  Kevin W. Sweeney

PART TWO: THE KAFKAESQUE CINEMA

'The essential is sufficient': The Kafka Adaptations of Orson Welles, Straub-Huillet and Michael Haneke   181
Martin Brady and Helen Hughes

K., the Tramp, and the Cinematic Vision: The Kafkaesque Chaplin   198
Shai Biderman

'The Medium is the Message': Cronenberg 'Outkafkas' Kafka   210
Iris Bruce

The Absurdity of Human Existence: 'The Metamorphosis' and *The Fly*   236
William J. Devlin & Angel M. Cooper

'This is not Nothing': Viewing the Coen Brothers Through the Lens of Kafka   258
Ido Lewit

The Face: K. and Keaton   279
Omri Ben-Yehuda

Translating Kafka into Italian: Kafkaesque Themes in Eilo Petri's Films   295
Fernando Gabriel Pagnoni Berns & Leonardo Acosta Lando

EPILOGUE: A PERSONAL QUEST INTO THE CINEMATIC KAFKAESQUE

Magic, Mystery and Miracle: Re-spiralling Marker and Kafka   309
Dan Geva

Transcribing Kafka into Film: A Tortuous Love-Story   329
Henry Sussman

Index   349

ACKNOWLEDGEMENTS

Mediamorphosis: Kafka and the Moving Image was made possible by a huge collaborative effort. Both editors would like to thank the contributors, whose diligence and insights helped to create this volume. Special words of gratitude are owed to Idit Alphandary, Iris Bruce, Kata Gellen and Henry Sussman for their wonderful advice and suggestions. Our sincere thanks to everyone at Wallflower Press – especially Commissioning Editor Yoram Allon, whose undying support has made this book possible. We also wish to thank Ami Asher and Alana Sobelman for their professional assistance. Last but not least, our deepest gratitude to Marc Caplan, Stanley Corngold and Michael Weinman for their help and guidance.

Shai would also like to thank his family for their loving support, especially his parents, Shlomo and Israela; his wife, Yael; and his children, Tal, Amir and Yuval.

Ido would like to thank his family – Haim, Michal, Noa and Sara – for their boundless love and encouragement.

Shai Biderman and Ido Lewit
January 2016

NOTES ON CONTRIBUTORS

IDIT ALPHANDARY is Senior Lecturer of Comparative Literature in the Interdisciplinary Program of the Arts at Tel Aviv University. She is the editor of *Writing in Progress: The Aesthetics and Politics of Contemporary Interdisciplinary Studies of Gender and Feminism* (Hakibutz Hameuchad, 2016), and has published numerous articles on Kristeva, Godard, Lévinas, Arendt and psychoanalysis in journals such as *Philosophy Today*, *The New Centennial Review* and *Culture Unbound*.

PETER BEICKEN is Professor at the University of Maryland, College Park. Amongst many other publications, his works on Kafka include *Franz Kafka: Eine kritische Einführung in die Forschung* (Fischer Athenäum, 1974), *Franz Kafka. "Die Verwandlung": Dokumente und Erläuterungen* (Reclam, 1983), *Franz Kafka: Leben und Werk* (Klett, 1986) and *Franz Kafka: "Der Process": Interpretation* (Oldenbourg, 1995).

OMRI BEN YEHUDA is a PhD candidate at the Centre for German Studies in the Hebrew University of Jerusalem. His doctoral dissertation focuses on speech acts in the work of Franz Kafka and Shmuel Yosef Agnon. He has published numerous essays and op-eds in journals and magazines like Haaretz and Der Freitag.

SHAI BIDERMAN is Senior Lecturer of film and philosophy at Tel Aviv University and at Beit-Berl College, Israel. He is the co-editor (with William J. Devlin) of *The Philosophy of David Lynch* (University Press of Kentucky, 2011), and has published numerous articles in journals such as *Film and Philosophy* and *Cinema: Journal of Philosophy and the Moving Image*, and in various edited anthologies.

MARTIN BRADY is Lecturer in the German and Film Studies Departments at King's College London. He is the co-author (with Joanne Leal) of *Wim Wenders and Peter Handke: Collaboration, Adaption, Recomposition* (Rodopi, 2011). He has written (with Helen Hughes) a chapter on Kafka and film for the *Cambridge Companion to Kafka* (Cambridge University Press, 2002), as well as various articles and book chapters on Straub-Huillet, Michael Haneke, Robert Bresson, experimental film, literary adaptation, GDR documentary, Brechtian cinema and Jewish exile architects.

IRIS BRUCE is Associate Professor in the Department of Linguistics and Languages and in the Department of English and Cultural Studies at McMaster University in Hamilton, Ontario. She is the author of *Kafka and Cultural Zionism: Dates in Palestine* (University of Wisconsin Press, 2007) and has also published many articles on Kafka and Yiddish literature, Jewish folklore, Zionism and Kafka in popular culture.

ANGEL M. COOPER is Adjunct Professor at Bridgewater State University. Her research includes existentialism, Friedrich Nietzsche, ethics (especially Aristotelian virtue ethics), philosophy of popular culture, and video games and philosophy.

WILLIAM J. DEVLIN is Associate Professor at Bridgewater State University and summer lecturer at University of Wyoming. He is the co-editor (with Shai Biderman) of *The Philosophy of David Lynch* (University Press of Kentucky, 2011). He teaches classes in philosophy of science, existentialism, nineteenth-century philosophy, Nietzsche, logic, and philosophy and film.

KATA GELLEN is Assistant Professor of German at Duke University. She is currently completing a manuscript entitled *Kafka and Noise: The Discovery of Cinematic Sound in Literary Modernism*. She has published articles on various topics in German literary modernism, German-Jewish writing and Weimar Cinema in such journals as *Germanic Review*, *Modernism/Modernity* and *The Journal of Austrian Literature*.

DAN GEVA is a documentarian and theoretician. He has made over 25 full-length documentaries, including the international award-winning *What I Saw in Hebron* (1999) and *Description of a Memory* (2006). He is also a senior lecturer at Beit-Berl College, Israel and gives masterclasses at academic institutions such as IFS, Köln; Hunter College, NY; RIDM, Canada and FOCAL, Switzerland.

HELEN HUGHES is Senior Lecturer in Film Studies at the University of Surrey. She is the author of *Green Documentary: Environmental Documentary in the 21st*

Century (Intellect, 2014) and co-editor (with Martin Brady) of *Deutschland im Spiegel seiner Filme* (CILT, 2000). She has also published many articles and chapters on West German cinema, Austrian experimental film, Kafka adaptations, and GDR and New Austrian documentary.

TOBIAS KUEHNE is a PhD candidate at Yale University's Department of Germanic Languages and Literatures and a JD candidate at Yale Law School. His essay on *Kafka's Letter to His Father* appears in the 2014/15 issue of the *Journal of the Kafka Society of America*.

LEONAREDO ACOSTA LANDO graduated from the Universidad de Buenos Aires (UBA) – Facultad de Psicología (Argentina). He teaches psychoanalysis, horror cinema and popular culture.

IDO LEWIT is a PhD candidate in the Film and Television Department at Tel Aviv University, where he also teaches film narratology and film theory. He has published on the subject of Kafka and cinema in the *Journal of the Kafka Society of America*.

NIMROD MATAN heads the Department of Theoretical Studies at the Faculty of Arts at Beit-Berl College, Israel. He is the author of *Al Pi*, a collection of poems (Bialik Institute, 2014) as well as a translator (to Hebrew) of Wittgenstein's *Blue and Brown Books* (Resling Publishing, 2006) and 'Photography and the Supernatural in Wittgenstein' (Am Oved, 2013).

FERNANDO GABRIEL PAGNONI BERNS is a graduate teaching assistant of at the Universidad de Buenos Aires (UBA). He has published articles on Argentinian and international cinema and drama in *Imagofagia, Stichomythia, Anagnórisis, Lindes* and *UpStage Journal* among others.

PAUL NORTH is Professor of German at Yale University. He is the author of *The Problem of Distraction* (Stanford University Press, 2012) and *The Yield: Kafka's Atheological Reformation* (Stanford University Press, 2015) and the editor of *Messianic Thought Outside Theology* (Fordham University Press, 2014).

LAURENCE A. RICKELS is Professor of Art and Theory at the Academy of Fine Arts, Karlsruhe and Professor Emeritus of German and Comparative Literature at the University of California, Santa Barbara. Amongst many publications, he is the author of *The Vampire Lectures* (University of Minnesota Press 1999), *Nazi*

Psychoanalysis (University of Minnesota Press, 2002), *Ulrike Ottinger: The Autobiography of Art Cinema* (University of Minnesota Press, 2008), *The Devil Notebooks* (University of Minnesota Press, 2008), and *I Think I Am: Philip K. Dick* (University of Minnesota Press, 2010).

HENRY SUSSMAN is Visiting Professor at the Department of Germanic Languages and Literatures at Yale University. He is the author of *The Hegelian Aftermath* (Johns Hopkins University Press, 1982), *High Resolution: Critical Theory and the Problem of Literacy* (Oxford University Press, 1989), *Afterimages of Modernity* (Johns Hopkins University Press, 1990), *The Aesthetic Contract* (Stanford University Press, 1997), *The Task of the Critic* (Fordham University Press, 2005) and *Around the Book: Systems and Literacy* (Fordham University Press, 2011).

KEVIN W. SWEENEY is Professor Emeritus of Philosophy at the University of Tampa. He has published essays on film theory, Hollywood silent comedy and philosophical themes in literary works. An article on Kafka's *The Metamorphosis* was selected for inclusion in the Norton Critical Edition of *The Metamorphosis* (1996) and republished in Harold Bloom's *Franz Kafka's The Metamorphosis*, New Edition (2008). A recent essay on Kafka was published in *Philosophy and Kafka* (Lexington Books, 2013).

INTRODUCTION

IDO LEWIT AND SHAI BIDERMAN

> His thinking, as his wonderful diary shows, was generally done in the form of images.
>
> – Max Brod (1995: 52)

In his introduction to *The Kafka Problem*, one of the first collections of essays in the English language dedicated to Franz Kafka and his work, Angel Flores recalls an anecdote according to which Thomas Mann once lent his friend Albert Einstein a book by Kafka. It is said that Einstein returned the book with the comment: 'I couldn't read it, the human mind isn't complicated enough' (1946: ix). Indeed, Kafka's world has often been seen, perhaps by design, as an unresolved (and probably irresolvable) mystery, a paradox which defeats all possible commentary to the point of 'the commentators' despair', a frustratingly Sisyphean task in which 'each sentence says "interpret me", and none will permit it' (Adorno 1981: 246).

This aspect of Kafka's work has been commonly understood as bound to his unique employment of style and language (see Walser 1961; Corngold 1973; Sandbank 1981); a style of constant retraction and a language that refers to its own incapacitation. In other words, the *medium* as employed by Kafka is, prior to anything else, a way of 'performing' its own demise, a way that executes in the core of Kafka's art his beautiful aphorism: 'There is a goal, but no way; what we call a way is hesitation' (1991: 23).

Given this crucial implementation of the medium in Kafka's work, the declared task of the current volume – to think Kafka through the moving image – may seem counter-intuitive for the very reason that it is directed towards a different medium. The fact that there is not a single explicit appearance of cinema in Kafka's fictions (see Zischler 2003: 58, 107) would also seem to counteract this ambition. Given the unveiling of a strong cinematic inclination in his thinking and creative impetus, however, Kafka's reliance on the literary medium and ambivalence towards visual media (see Goebel 2000: 13; Duttlinger 2007: 5) are interpreted here not as an impediment but rather as a new arena for the reappraisal of the various perspectives on his unique art. Indeed, our point is to suggest a cross-medium methodology, a media *crossbreed*, or a *mediamorphosis*, as a novel and prolific means of facilitating new understandings of Kafka's literary world as well as opening new perspectives on the cinematic medium.

Kafka and the Moving Image

Franz Kafka's friend, biographer and literary executor Max Brod recalls a ritual in the Kafka family home: for his parents' birthdays, little Franz used to write plays that were staged in the family circle by his sisters (see 1995: 14). One of those plays, writes Brod, animated the family photographs that stood on the console table; it was called 'The Photographs Speak'. At about the same time that young Franz animated the photographs of his family,[1] public showings of animated (though not yet speaking) photographs created a stir as crowds flocked to witness the inventions of Thomas A. Edison (Kinetoscope) and Auguste and Louis Lumière (Cinematograph). Incorporating scripted stories into the technological novelties of Edison and the Lumière Brothers, pioneers of narrative film such as Edwin Porter and George Méliès gave birth to the new form of storytelling that we now know as cinema. While the proximity between the Kafka family ritual and the emergence of cinema may be accidental, young Franz's 'photoplays' indicate a unique and characteristic quality in Kafka's creative work: his imagistic thinking.[2]

The imagistic, or pictorial, may not be the kind of expression commonly associated with the master of the word, the writer who designated himself as a word-writing-entity – *Schriftstellersein*, a term coined by Kafka to name his 'literary being' (see Corngold 2009: 1–2). But evidently, Kafka's imagistic inclination, his incorporation of the visual media into his work, can be traced throughout his oeuvre. Indeed, one aspect of Kafka's work that has been rather neglected in the literature is his preoccupation with drawing, an aspect whose significance is highlighted by their inclusion next to his writings in his famous 'last request' of Brod.[3]

One of the scarce scholarly discussions of Kafka's drawings is Claude Gandelman's 'Kafka as an Expressionist Draughtsman', which places the author's drawings within the contemporary expressionist movement. Gandelman's appreciation and contextualisation of the drawings within the history of art is of minor significance to our current discussion. It is rather the aspect of 'pure motion' in Gandelman's description of Kafka's graphic work (1974: 258) that is relevant to our focus on Kafka's visual articulation.

Similarly, movement is the dominant feature attributed to Kafka's drawings by his friend Gustav Janouch, who remembers his first impression of the drawings as 'strange minute sketches, in which only the abstraction of movement was emphasized' (1971: 35). Gandelman's and Janouch's descriptions thus suggest an affinity between Kafka's drawings and animation, an affinity further amplified by Kafka's own contemplations on his drawings, as recounted by Janouch:

> Everything in the human world is a picture that has come to life. When the Eskimos want to set fire to a piece of wood, they draw a few wavy lines on it. That is the magical picture of fire which they'll bring to life by rubbing their fire-sticks together. That's what I do. Through my drawings I want to come to terms with the shapes which I perceive. (1971: 36)

Comparing the drawings to a 'picture that has come to life' weaves a subtle thread between little Franz's 'speaking photographs' and the motion-drawings of the adult Kafka. In the latter case, however, the aim 'to come to terms with the shapes which I perceive' is not achieved, as Kafka continues to testify:

> But my figures don't take fire. Perhaps I don't use the right material. Perhaps my pencil doesn't have the right powers. It's also possible that it's only myself, and nothing else, that lacks the necessary powers. (Ibid.)

Kafka's failed attempts to revive his drawings are highly reminiscent of the failed attempt of Karl Rossmann, the protagonist of his first novel *Der Verschollene* (*Amerika: The Man Who Disappeared*),[4] first published in 1927, to make his father's image 'more alive' (2004: 67) by changing the position of a family photograph to the light of a candle, a scene which in turn resonates with little Franz's ambition to animate the family photographs. Kafka suggests, with characteristic self-deprecation, that it might be he who lacks the necessary powers for his figures to 'take fire'; but before turning to question himself, Kafka questions the technical apparatus at his disposal, suggesting that he might not be using 'the right material'. Like Rossmann's apparatus – a single photograph and a candle – Kafka's pencil 'doesn't have the right powers' to conjure up motion. Do those failed attempts at animation disclose a wish for a means of representing movement that would better come to terms with 'pictures that come to life'?

The answer to that notwithstanding, it certainly seems that Kafka's 'imagistic thinking' can be extended to 'cinematic thinking'. The above-mentioned study of Kafka's drawings implicitly supports this notion: Gandelman does not mention cinema, but in relating Kafka's drawings to expressionism he invokes a cinematic trope which he finds in many of Kafka's drawings – the close-up.

> Close-up effect can be seen in the image of the gigantic bearded figure which sits before a shrunken black man, in the legs of the 'Mad Runner', which are indeed gigantic in relationship to his body, or in the head of the 'Drinker' which appears to dwarf the hand and body of the character. (1974: 260)

The drawings' use of features such as movement, animation and close-up suggests considering the same cinematic inclinations in Kafka's literary output. In fact, Gandelman extends his discussion of the 'expressionist close-up effect' (1974: 259) to several of Kafka's stories.[5] To demonstrate this effect he recalls a scene from 'Die Verwandlung' ('The Metamorphosis', 1915), in which the father 'lifted his feet uncommonly high, and Gregor was dumbfounded at the enormous size of his shoe soles' (1971: 121). Here the close-up effect is created by 'the violent approach, close to the eye of the observer, of one element of the antagonistic body of the opponent' (Gandelman 1974: 259).

The theoretical benefit of considering a cinematic inclination in Kafka's literary output is further supported by a second temporal proximity between Kafka's biography and the history of cinema: that between the creation of the bulk of his literary output and the wide distribution and public acceptance of the feature-length narrative film between the early 1910s and early 1920s.

Kafka was fascinated by cinema at its early stages (see Brod 1995: 102–3), and from 1908 to 1913 was an avid moviegoer. In *Kafka Goes to the Movies* Hanns Zischler scrutinises his writings about movies (mostly in diaries and letters). His study presents Kafka's relation to the cinema as ambivalent: on the one hand, Kafka is moved to tears by films, daydreams about memorable scenes, drags his sisters and friends with great enthusiasm to watch his favourite films, and knows the weekly screening schedules by heart (2003: 5, 34, 42, 77). At the same time, however, he is unsettled by cinema's automatic agitation of images and space-time distortion. Zischler elaborates on this point by contrasting Brod's and Kafka's understandings of the medium:

> Brod takes what he has seen in the cinema and expands on it in his imagination; the enthusiastic viewer turns into an extravagant (script) writer. He understands cinema as an extension of literature, a process of assemblage. For Kafka, by contrast, the almost demonic technological element challenges the way we have learned to see, confronts the author's powers of sight and writing with very great, agonizing demands. (2003: 16)

The disturbing effect that moving images had on Kafka seems to stem from his inability to fully explore the imaginary space under the assault of rapidly changing images. This unsettling dynamic is the reason, he writes to Felice Bauer in 1913, why he no longer visits the cinema frequently (1999: 132; see also Goebel 2000: 13). According to Zischler, Kafka's 'Archimedean point of rejection of cinematography' (2003: 28) may be found in a diary entry in which he recalls a visit to a *Kaiserpanorama* in Friedland in February 1911:[6]

> The pictures [are] more alive than in the cinema because they offer the eye all the repose of reality. The cinema communicates the restlessness of its motion to the things pictured in it; the repose would seem to be more important. The smooth floors of the cathedrals at the tip of our tongues. Why can't they combine the cinema and stereoscope in this way? (1992: 430)

In his interpretation of this diary entry, Zischler summarises Kafka's claim against the cinema: 'The three-dimensional standstill of stereoscopic photography' stands in sharp contrast to 'the automatic agitation of the cinematic image' (2003: 27, 28). Cinema thus 'infects the viewer with this movement, automates him', generating 'less a living than a mechanical reality, an automated unease' (2003: 28). This interpretation resonates with Kafka's own statements on the cinematic medium,[7] as recalled by Janouch:

> Franz Kafka always gave a look of surprise when I told him I had been to the cinema. Once I reacted to this change of expression by asking: 'Don't you like the cinema?' After a moment's thought Kafka replied: 'As a matter of fact I've never thought about it. Of course it is a marvelous toy. But I cannot bear it, because perhaps I am too "optical" by nature. I am an "Eye-man". But the cinema disturbs one's vision. The speed of the movement and the rapid change of images force men to look continually from one to another. Sight does not master the pictures, it is the pictures which master one's sight. They flood one's consciousness. The cinema involves putting the eye into uniform, when before it was naked.' 'That is a terrible statement,' I said. 'The eye is the window of the soul, a Czech proverb says.' Kafka nodded. 'Films are iron shutters.' (1971: 160)

Clearly, cinema preoccupies Kafka. Both his enthusiasm for it and his rejection of it betray intense emotional involvement. While reconciling Kafka's ambivalence towards cinema is beyond the scope of this discussion, one possible direction for such reconciliation may be outlined by assessing the congruity between Kafka's position or positions towards cinema and the nature of his fictional worlds. Such congruity is not hard to find. Indeed, some of Kafka's descriptions of the cinematic experience – 'disturbance of vision', 'blindness to reality', 'mechanised beings' – are part and parcel of his alien literary worlds and the characters that populate them.

More specifically, Peter Beicken's discussion of the imaginary in some of Kafka's early stories is astonishingly consistent with Kafka's complex position of fascination and trepidation with the visual experience of cinema:

> In the remarkable text 'On the Tram' ('Der Fahrgast', 1908), the flâneur is voyeuristically engaged in the city spectacle [...]. The intensity of the city gazer reveals a self in crisis which is marked by existential angst and panic vis-à-vis the threats emanating from the visible world. Kafka's characters engage in a look that is both fascinated by the frenzy of the visual experience and pained by the sights of objects, things, and people which, although screened with voyeuristic desire, dare the gazer to the core. The anxiety of Kafka's imperfect flâneur mirrors the challenge to the city gazer, and threatens him with loss of independence, to succumb to the rush of the world. (2000: 4–5)

Beicken's description supports the supposition that Kafka's trepidation with cinema is in fact incorporated within his fiction. Moreover, Rolf J. Goebel explicitly suggests reading Kafka's 'Beschreibung eines Kampfes' ('Description of a Struggle', 1912) – which predates Kafka's theoretical comment on cinema by almost a decade – as 'a poetic anticipation and elaboration of his cinematic skepticism' (2000: 13). Goebel reads Kafka's story as a narrative that 'records urban reality in the unsettlingly mechanic and hectic manner that Kafka abhorred in early film's subversion of the "calmness of the real"' (ibid.).

W. G. Sebald presents a similar argument in an essay on Zischler's *Kafka Goes to the Movies*. He suggests an affinity between Kafka's uncanny literary worlds and the vague horror Kafka felt 'at the impending mutations of mankind' (2006: 163) in the age of mechanical reproduction, which culminated with cinema:

> The freedom of movement of the heroes of his novels and stories, which is not great to begin with, steadily undergoes further restrictions in the course of the action, while figures already called to life by an inscrutable series of laws take over, characters such as the court functionaries, the two idiotic assistants and the three lodgers in 'The Metamorphosis', executives and officials whose purely functional, amoral nature is obviously better suited to this new state of affairs. In the Romantic period the doppelgänger, which first aroused a fear of mechanical appliances, was still a haunting and exceptional phenomenon; now it is everywhere. (2006: 163–4)

Beicken, Goebel and Sebald situate the existential anxiety in Kafka's stories within a visual context that overlaps Kafka's experience of cinema and his relation towards it. These correlations between Kafka's fiction and his understanding of cinema help position Kafka's rejection of and trepidation toward cinema as a complement, rather than a contradiction, to his overt enthusiasm with the medium. Much more important to this volume, however, is that these correlations can help position cinema itself as a fundamental force in Kafka's creative work.

The Kafkan and the Cinematic[8]

Many leading commentators on twentieth-century art and culture have detected cinematic qualities in Kafka's work. Theodor Adorno, for one, claims that Kafka's texts agitate the reader's feelings to the point that 'he fears that the narrative will shoot towards him like a locomotive in a three-dimensional film' (1981: 246). Adorno uses this dramatic metaphor to emphasise the 'aggressive physical proximity' (ibid.) between Kafka's texts and their readers, but at the same time the comparison alludes to a popular anecdote about the early days of cinema. Reportedly, on the first screening of the Lumière Brothers' *L'Arrivée d'un train en gare de La Ciotat* (*The Arrival of a Train at La Ciotat Station*, 1895), the audience was so overwhelmed by the image of a life-sized train driving directly at them that people stampeded to the back of the room (see Cook 1990: 11). Adorno's decision to compare the impact of Kafka's texts to that of a three-dimensional film rather than the common two-dimensional format is especially intriguing given that a three-dimensional version of *L'Arrivée d'un train en gare de La Ciotat* was in fact produced and screened by the Lumières around 1903 (see Zone 2007: 141–2), thus satisfying Kafka's aforementioned wish for a combination of cinema and the stereoscope.

Adorno's comparison, as well as the Lumières' two- and three-dimensional film versions, suggest that the 'shock of the new' discourse of modernity, with its origins in 'notions of collision, battle, "thrill" and speed' (Armstrong 2000: 60) was applied to the emergence of both Kafka's work and cinema. The report on Kafka's public reading of 'In der Strafkolonie' ('In the Penal Colony', 1919) in Munich from 1916, according to which three women fainted and many people left the hall (see Pohland 2000: 54; Corngold 2004: 70), further supports this shared application.

Walter Benjamin explicitly ties together the impact of Kafka's texts and that of cinema as aspects of modernity. Benjamin finds a correlation between the Kafkan human condition and that of the subject of modernity, represented by cinema. Cinema, according to Benjamin, 'detaches the reproduced object from the sphere of tradition' and devalues its 'here and now' (2011: 233, 232); it is therefore emblematic of modern social alienation. In 'Kafka: On the Tenth Anniversary of his Death', Benjamin presents Kafka's work as cinematic in the sense that it produces the same self-alienation effect as that of a subject who 'does not recognize his own walk on the screen or his own voice on the phonograph' (2007: 137).

Benjamin develops his theory of the self-alienated film subject in 'The Work of Art in the Age of its Technological Reproducibility'. Here Benjamin contends that cinematic alienation has the potential of empowering film audiences with a new kind of political competence. The fact that the cinematic image of a person becomes detached from the person photographed and is transported to the masses enhances their authority and control and can thus offer a political advantage (2011: 240–1). While it is unclear whether Benjamin finds the same political potential in Kafka, his contemporary, Siegfried Kracauer, seems to point to precisely such a correspondence. In 'Photography', an essay published in 1927, Kracauer discusses the built-in alienation effect of photography, one that, according to Miriam Hansen, 'ruptures the ostensible coherence of dominant publicity and reflects the disintegrated fragments of nature as detritus and disorder' (1993: 456). Echoing Benjamin's view, Kracauer suggests that photography's alienation effect 'assists consciousness in pointing up the "provisional status of all given configurations ... the suspension of every habitual relationship among the elements of nature"' (ibid.). This redemptive potential is even stronger in film, due to its 'capacity to stir up the elements of nature' and to combine 'parts and segments to create strange constructs' (Kracauer 1993: 436).

For Kracauer, Kafka's work is the model for this utopian dimension of film, since in those texts 'a liberated consciousness absolves itself of this responsibility [for establishing the provisional status of all given configurations] by destroying natural reality and jumbling the fragments against each other' (ibid.). However, this is not the only instance in which Kracauer turns to Kafka in his speculations on the phenomenological and political potential of film. Hansen notes that on the top of the first page of his 'Tentative Outline of a Book on Film Aesthetics', Kracauer had written in pencil: 'Kafka's Sancho Panza aphorism to be applied to the film' (1993: 451, n20). In order to shed some light on this obscure note, we could turn to Kracauer's elaborations on Kafka's short segment 'Die Wahrheit über Sancho Pansa' ('The Truth about Sancho Panza', 1931) in his essay on Kafka's posthumous works:

> According to Kafka, Don Quixote was actually Sancho Panza's devil, who knew, however, how to render this devil harmless by distracting him from himself. Thus, the devil incessantly performed the craziest deeds, and Sancho

Panza, who followed him out of a certain sense of responsibility, 'derived from them a great and useful entertainment to the end of his days'. In just the same way, Kafka wards off the reasonableness that is impotent despite its logical power, and accompanies it through the thicket of human conditions. (1995: 273–4)

How does cinema 'ward off reasonableness', and how exactly is that advantageous? Hansen provides further elucidation on how Kafka provided Kracauer a model for film's involvement in the process of ideological demythologisation:

[In Kracauer's Marseille notebooks] the term *dégonflage* (letting the air out, deflating) is often coupled with the shorthand of 'Sancho Panza', referring to the Cervantes character through the lens of Kafka's 'The Truth on Sancho Panza': 'Insofar as film, by representing materiality, promotes the work of disenchantment, it can be called the Sancho Panza who exposes the Donquichoteries of ideologies and intentional constructions.' (1997: xl, n35)

Adorno, Benjamin and Kracauer seem to suggest that the cinematic and the Kafkan share fundamental qualities, but evidently these commentators' notes have remained quite undeveloped. More recent studies take on the task of looking more rigorously into the Kafka-cinema nexus.

In one such study, Peter Beicken develops the argument that Kafka's literary-visual method employs cinema as a model and structuring principle. Beicken concentrates on Kafka's unique use of 'mono-perspectival narrative perspective' and intermedial linking of cinematic and literary imagination. Beicken presents Kafka's strong visual inclination as directing his literary imaginary and grounding it in cinematic perception (2000: 6), a perception that, while remarkably predating his actual familiarity with film, is only intensified when he goes to the movies (2011: 173). Focusing on configurations of vision and space in Kafka's narratives, Beicken contends that Kafka's main characters' unique perspective 'functions as a narrative camera resembling the point-of-view vision of a cinematic figure' and 'corresponds to the look with which the film camera screens the visual field' (2000: 4). This cinematic look creates cinematic space configurations of 'carefully designed settings, clothes, lighting, figure expression, and movement' (2000: 6), which constitute Kafka's literary imaginary of visual conflict and incapacitation (2000: 10).

Beicken extends the discussion to reveal the various cinematic techniques Kafka uses in his unique observational mode. Montage, shifts of focus, gaze guidance, camera eye, moving camera, changing camera angles, zoom, sequencing and 'the positioning of a figure as narrative camera in portals and windows as well as stationing the character on moving objects such as a tram, train, a boat, etc' (2011: 173) – are all identified in a detailed study of Kafka's early stories and meditations:

> Kafka created a culture of seeing that enabled him to transform narration through the incorporation of cinema's intermediality into his narratives. Using his main characters as visual focalizers, he turned them into special perceivers that function as camera eyes. The mono-perspectival narrative perspective is unique to Kafka's work, and the intermediality of the visual method in his works exhibits a truly remarkable cinematic quality throughout. (2011: 174)[9]

A complementary study to Beicken's is Peter-André Alt's *Kafka und der Film: Über kinematographisches Erzählen* ('Kafka and Film: On Cinematic Narration', 2009). Alt provides a lengthy account of both structures and contents extracted from Kafka's stories that are specifically common to the films of his time. Detecting the stories' filmic organisation provides access to their inner logic; Alt finds filmic structures, for example, in the application of such cinematic effects as 'shifts in perspective', 'light effects' and 'snapshots' in Kafka's early stories (2009: 33–47; 191–2), while cinematic contents may be found, for instance, in his use of the doppelgänger motif prevalent in German cinema of the 1910s and 1920s in *Der Prozess* (*The Trial*, 1925) (2009: 116), as well as in his use of such recurring cinematic contents as flowing traffic, chase scenes and last-minute-rescue in *Amerika: The Man Who Disappeared* (2009: 80–97). Like Beicken, Alt concludes that Kafka's writing inhabits an emerging conception of vision shared and supported by cinema (2009: 194).

Kafkaesque Cinema

Cinematic adaptations of literary sources have been the subject of much debate: from bibliophilic approaches that privilege the literary source over its cinematic adaptation (see Smiley 2003) to those that point at the potential supremacy of cinematic rendition (see McFarlane 1996; Stam 2000); from purists advocating the unfilmability of literary texts to those who claim that 'everything is adaptable' (Welsh 2007: xv); and from striving for maximum fidelity to the source text to highlighting the 'chimera of fidelity' (Stam 2000: 54) and proposing dialogism and intertextuality as alternatives (see Metz 1993, 2007; Stam 2000).

While these and other contemporary debates on cinematic adaptations are of much relevance to the discussion of the (im)possibility of converting Kafka's narratives into moving images, they will serve our study of Kafkaesque cinema only to a certain extent, as our designation of Kafkaesque cinema aims at a broader notion. While our understanding of Kafkaesque cinema certainly does not exclude cinematic adaptations of Kafka's stories, it embraces any filmic practice or quality that reproduces, enhances or transforms a distinctive Kafkan or Kafkaesque property. This understanding, as we shall soon see, does not necessarily entail that Kafkaesque cinema is common, or even possible.

In *Intervista* (1987), Federico Fellini plays a film director who is busy adapting Kafka's *Amerika*. In one scene the director's assistant turns to a woman he spots on the subway and offers her a part in the film: 'We need faces for the characters of Kafka's *Amerika*. To make it into a film. Great idea, isn't it?' Well, it depends on whom you're asking. Given the realisation that Kafka's writing possesses cinematic qualities it would seem reasonable to adapt it to the screen; it could even be said that this would realise it by means unfortunately unavailable to the writer himself. One could suggest, on the other hand, that Kafka would have rejected visual renderings of his work based on his plea to avoid printing a picture of the vermin on the cover of 'The Metamorphosis', but evidently what Kafka rejected in that case was visualising the vermin itself, not the story as such.[10] Still, many have rejected the very idea of 'imaging' the Kafkaesque.

This rejection is largely based on the assumption that Kafka's unique style confines the essence of his writing to the realm of language. This argument is put forward by Günther Nicolin: 'It is easy to illustrate Kafka's text in the traditional way, i.e. to draw each image of that wonderfully clear prose … but nothing is gained by this, rather, attention is wrenched away from Kafka's diction' (quoted in Brady and Hughes 2002: 228). Martin Brady and Helen Hughes believe that 'adapting Kafka's works to the visual media [risks] the frustration of the loss that occurs in transit' (ibid.).[11]

A powerful argument in a similar vein is presented by Tuvia Ruebner (1982, 1996) in discussing Kafka's unique use of metaphor. Ruebner examines Kafka's dual-natured figures whose corporal appearance is unclear and whose existence is therefore confined to the signifying level of language. These include the lamb-cat, the monkey-academician, the dog-musicians and dog-researcher, the singer-mouse, travelling salesman-vermin and many more. Ruebner draws a parallel between those 'linguistic creatures', which exist as oppositions welded together, and Kafka's techniques of annulment, such as 'making statements and giving their immediate cancellation' (1996: 126). Ruebner refers here to Shimon Sandbank's study that showed how Kafka's rhetoric and choice of words avoid factual commitment (1981: 386–7).

Extending Sandbank's study to Kafka's use of metaphor enables Ruebner to view Kafka's stories as 'parables of being' that are at the same time 'parables of non-being' (1996: 128–9), parables in which the expressible holds within itself something which is inexpressible (1982: 21). Ruebner finds Kafka's singularity in his use of metaphor that points at itself as inadequate (1982: 22). His dual-natured figures are such flawed metaphors: metaphors of being and non-being, of figures that exist due to their incapacity to exist (ibid.). Ruebner presents Kafka's linguistic image as founded on this ontological paradox, existing in the interlacing of being and not-being; an interlacing that Ruebner claims can only be disclosed by language – only language, metaphorically improper, with its silences and contradictions, can express that (1982: 11, 22; 1996: 132).

Similarly, Stanley Corngold's discussion of the metamorphosis of the metaphor in 'The Metamorphosis' suggests viewing Gregor Samsa as 'a mutilated metaphor, uprooted from familiar language' (1973: 12). Corngold reads the story as a 'conflict between ordinary language and a being having a character of an indecipherable word' (1973: 11). It literalises the metaphor 'this man is a vermin', but this literalisation is incomplete since Kafka shifts incessantly the relation between Gregor's mind and body, thus shattering the solidity of the metaphor. As Kafka presents the absolute loss of all significance as a consequence of the loss of human form, it can be said that Samsa's body is 'the speech in which the impossibility of ordinary language expresses its own despair' (1973: 12).

Another example of Kafka's use of language to create ontological paradoxes is offered by Peter Benson. In his analysis of the opening sentences of Kafka's *Das Schloss* (*The Castle*, 1926), Benson describes Kafka's use of double negation in the phrase 'die scheinbare Leere' (1982: 7; translated by Mark Harman as 'seeming emptiness' (Kafka 1998: 1) and by Anthea Bell as 'what seemed to be void' (Kafka 2009b: 5)). Benson designates Kafka's striking phrase as 'a negative term further negated, an absence absented, an obscurity additionally veiled' (1993: 88).

It might seem therefore that the filmic image, by virtue of its indexical nature and the blunt presence it discloses, is essentially unable to reproduce the unstable ontology that informs Kafka's 'parables of non-being' (Ruebner), 'rhetoric of annulment' (Sandbank), 'metamorphosis of the metaphor' (Corngold) and 'double negation' (Benson).

Still other substantial arguments against filmic rendition of Kafka's work can be raised. Take movement: the impossibility of movement in both space and time is one of the hallmarks of Kafka's work (see Segal 2008). The unimaginable journey to the next village, the man waiting before the law, the messenger who will never deliver the imperial message, and the country doctor tramping through snowy waste on an everlasting journey home are only some examples of the Kafkan paralysis in space and time. In 'Kafka and his Precursors', Jorge Luis Borges associated this element with Zeno's paradoxes, suggesting that 'the arrow and Achilles are the first Kafkaesque characters in literature' (1999: 363).

Cinema, on the other hand, is all about the flow of time and motion. Since it constitutes 'the setting in motion of a series of photographic images … along the temporal axis' (Verstraten 2011: 13), cinema cannot exist without motion in time and space. It is therefore not unreasonable to ask whether a space-time-motion medium is able to produce the paralysis that is so fundamental to Kafka's oeuvre.

Some of the chapters in this volume are aimed exactly at challenging these and other claims that reject the possibility or productivity of a cinematic rendering of Kafka's output. Filmmakers, of course, did not wait for such theoretical vindications and have been adapting Kafka to the screen for some time.[12]

The first cinematic adaptation of Kafka's work is most likely Tomás Gutiérrez Alea and Néstor Almendros's short Cuban film *Una confusión cotidiana* (*An Everyday Confusion*, 1950) based on Kafka's 'Eine alltägliche Verwirrung' ('A Common Confusion', 1931). In 1954, Lorenza Mazzetti directed a short adaptation of 'The Metamorphosis' entitled *K*. Then in 1962 no less than three TV adaptations were produced: a West German teleplay, *Ein Bericht für eine Akademie* (*A Report to an Academy*), written by Willy Schmidt and based on the eponymous short story; a Norwegian TV movie, *Prosessen*, based on *The Trial*; and another TV movie – *Das Schloss*, a West German adaptation of *The Castle*.

These productions were marginal and local, and it was only a fourth production of that year which brought Kafka to the screen in full force: Orson Welles' *The Trial*. This was the first internationally distributed and big-budget feature film adaptation of a work by Kafka, and to this day it is probably the best known. The liberties Welles took in adapting Kafka have been critically received, however. His overemphasis on character psychology, the increasing defiance displayed by Joseph K. and, most of all, the omissions from and additions to the plot itself have earned the film such critical diatribes as 'horribly banal', a 'misreading of the character' and 'a dangerous forgery' (quoted in Scholz 2009: 8, 10, 11).[13]

Some critics did appreciate the film's achievements. Jeffrey Adams considers it 'one of the most compelling cinematic adaptations of Kafka' and 'the cinematic equivalent of that strange blend of nightmarish absurdity and theatrical farce that now goes by the name of Kafkaesque' (2002: 141). James Naremore praises it for using 'movie syntax as lucid and correct as Kafka's own prose' (1989: 204). Naremore also praises the film's rendering of space, as echoed by Gilles Deleuze, who points out Welles' success in rendering a sense of space similar to Kafka's, where 'spatially distant and chronologically separate regions were in touch with each other, at the bottom of a limitless time which made them contiguous' (1989: 111).[14]

While opinions on Welles' *The Trial* and its relation to Kafka's novel certainly differ, the film did pave the way for many more screen adaptations. Some of these have aimed at accurate rendition using special medial means to capture or emphasise essential aspects of the story. One is Jan Nemec's *Die Verwandlung*, an adaptation of 'The Metamorphosis' from 1975 which is presented mostly from Gregor Samsa's own perspective, thereby managing to visualise the story while respecting Kafka's wish to leave the metamorphosis itself invisible. Another is Koji Yamamura's anime rendition of 'Ein Landarzt' ('A Country Doctor', 1919) from 2007; as an animation, this adaptation evades the indexical pitfalls of photographic depiction and offers visual representations of indeterminate space, undifferentiated subjective and objective focalisations, and distortions of unified identity.

Other post-Wellesian 'Kafka films' do not aim at fidelity to one specific story but rather at rendering the Kafkaesque. These may be designated as free adaptations or films inspired by Kafka. The first is Pavel Juráček and Jan Schmidt's *Postava k podpírání* (*A Character in Need of Support*, also titled *Joseph Kilian*, 1963) which imports popularised characteristics of the Kafkaesque (narrow corridors, brick-blocked windows, immense archive storerooms, etc) into 1960s Prague to present the absurdity of everyday life under Communism, where people vanish, records are mysteriously erased and citizens wait in vain before closed doors of empty offices.

Martin Scorsese's *After Hours* (1985) also belongs to what may be called the Kafkaesque category. It depicts the surreal night of Paul Hackett in New York's Soho neighbourhood, and his Sisyphean search for Marcy, a young woman he met earlier in the evening. On the wild taxi ride downtown Paul's only cash, a $20 bill, flies out the window and so, after losing track of Marcy, he finds himself trapped in Soho. All his efforts to locate her, get back home, or even interact with other nocturnal Sohoans are futile, and he ends up being mistaken for a burglar and murderer. Finally, in order to hide from a raging mob, Paul finds shelter with a local artist who disguises him by wrapping him in plaster to resemble one of her papier-mâché sculptures.

The film explicitly alludes to Kafka in a scene where Paul engages in a dialogue from Kafka's parable 'Before the Law' (1915), with a bouncer at the entrance to a nightclub where he believes Marcy is waiting for him. But the film is strongly Kafkaesque regardless of this explicit allusion. The fruitless efforts towards a goal only exacerbate the character's difficulties and provide the film with a narrative structure similar to that of *The Trial*, *The Castle* and other stories. Moreover, the protagonist's gradual transformation from a free human agent into an inanimate object resonates with what Adorno recognised in Kafka as the process of becoming non-human (1981: 252), blurring the 'boundary between what is human and the world of things' (1981: 262).

Notably, *After Hours* conveys these themes by means of cinematic dynamics that may be said to execute Kafka's 'acts of sabotage' against 'the space-time continuum of "empirical realism'" (Adorno 1981: 261). The taxi ride to Soho is rendered using rapid editing, fast-forward motion, oblique camera angles, screeching sound effects and frantic movement of the taxi-cab to designate a passage 'across the river' to the 'underworld'. Its violation of conventional space-time continuity seems to duplicate the 'storming rush that … buffeted all my senses' (Kafka 1971: 221) in the flight of the two enormous horses that take the country doctor on his one-way journey. Like the immeasurable and unpredictable relations between 'the journey to' and 'the journey back from' in Kafka's 'A Country Doctor' or 'A Common Confusion', the effortless ride to Soho stands in sharp contrast to the impossibility of returning uptown, which is also informed by means of cinematic dynamics. Unlike the frantic ride downtown, the 'Before the Law' dialogue with the bouncer is between two stationary characters filmed with a stable camera, relatively long takes and straight camera angles. This transition culminates with a dimly-lit static shot of the papier-mâché sculpture that enwraps Paul at the end. Like the country doctor, Paul Hackett had answered the 'false alarm of the night bell only once, but the mistake cannot be made good, not ever' (Kafka 1971: 225).

Other prominent films in the Kafkaesque category are Woody Allen's *Shadows and Fog* (1991), Steven Soderbergh's *Kafka* (1991) and Zbigniew Rybczynski's *Kafka* (1992). Allen's film opens with the intrusion of men into the bedroom of Max Kleinman, who is later labelled a vermin and charged with a murder he did not commit. Allen's mystery/romantic comedy uses these blanket Kafka allusions as part of the backdrop of the film's discussion on existential alienation and uncertainty. *Shadows and Fog* executes its themes of existential angst by means of blocked and distorted vision: set in a foggy night and filmed using expressionist lighting and oblique camera angles, it presents a range of opacities, distortions and illusions, which constitutes visual correspondence with Kafkaesque indecipherability and unpredictable terror.

Soderbergh's *Kafka* is structured as a post-modern mix of thriller, science-fiction, German expressionism and film noir, with a narrative composed as a complex and seemingly random mosaic of bits and pieces from Kafka's stories, biography and diaries. Donna Hoffmeister comments that the film's meticulous style 'effectively visualizes Kafka's labyrinthine nightmare world' (1993: 14) and finds its rich intertextuality and reflexive filmic techniques to be 'analogous to Kafka's mix of realism and indeterminacy' (1993: 17). Adams also commends the film's style as suitable for rendering the Kafkaesque (2011: 29).

Like Soderbergh's, Rybczynski's experimental video-film *Kafka* blends multiple Kafka narratives into a single space-time continuum. It is notable for its innovative use of a computer-generated environment, extremely long takes and live actors on a virtual set. All team up to produce disorientation, claustrophobia and a strong sense of indeterminate movement. Rybczynski creates a virtual space that embodies Adorno's observation that all of Kafka's stories 'take place in the same spaceless space', and takes to an extreme Kafka's 'hermetic stance towards history' (1981: 256, 257). At the same time, the integration of live actors and virtual spaces outdoes Yamamura's animation when it comes to producing the Kafkan hybrid of realism and unworldliness.

Evidently, both Kafkan and Kafkaesque films, whether direct adaptations or films inspired by Kafka, explore original ways to convey Kafka's narratives, specific features of his works or general understandings of his cultural impact. Welles' rendition of distorted space; Nemec's use of restricted points of view; Scorsese's incorporation of dynamics; Allen's use of optical hindrances; Rybczynski's virtual oblivion; and Yamamura's rendition of indeterminate space and undifferentiated focalisation are only a sample of the vast potential of moving images to visually reproduce, enhance and transform Kafka.

Yet a third category of 'Kafka films' may be designated as Kafkaesque despite including no explicit allusion to Kafka. While thorough scholarly research on films in this group is particularly scarce,[15] several chapters in this volume explore intrinsic Kafkaesque attributes in the works of such prominent filmmakers as Buster Keaton, Charlie Chaplin, David Cronenberg, the Coen Brothers and Chris Marker.

***

The chapters that comprise this collection of essays present the work of leading as well as emerging scholars from diverse disciplinary affiliations: from Comparative Literature and German Studies to Philosophy, Cultural Studies and Film and Media Studies. The common ground of this interdisciplinary effort aims to unveil the dual nature of Kafka-cinema relations. Since such complementary relation generally goes in one of two directions – the impact that film had on Kafka's writing, and the impact that Kafka's writing had on film – this volume seeks to explore the two sides of this dichotomy in two complementary parts (followed by a residual epilogue).

Part I, *The Cinematic Kafka*, explores the notion of Kafka's writing being 'cinematic'. This section unfolds in two complementary ways: first, by re-evaluating such topics as vision, image, sound and movement, and by considering other cinematically-inflected sensory modes and technical methods at play in Kafka's works; and then, by aiming to further examine the applicability of this proposition to key relevant issues.

We begin with Paul North's 'Kafka, Rumour, Early Cinema: Archaic Moving Pictures'. North examines the depiction of film in Kafka's work in its archaic altered form: rumour. He explores this archaic Kafkan double of early cinema through a comprehensive discussion on Kafka's posthumously published fragment 'The Village Schoolmaster'.

Complementing North's identification of Kafka's archaic moving pictures is Nimrod Matan's recognition of a primitive configuration of a moving image through a comparative examination of the writings of W. G. Sebald and Kafka in 'Sebald Goes to the Movies: Reading Kafka as Cinematography'. Matan finds Kafka to be a model for Sebald's cinematographic conception of writing and identifies a process of re-conceptualisation of writing and imagery in Sebald that entails conditions for meaningfulness of images along their setting in motion, thus constituting an embryonic definition of the cinematographic medium: writing-as-cinematography.

Next, in 'The Ghost is Clear: The POV of the Daydreamer', Laurence A. Rickels reconstructs Kafka's narratives' unique 'way of seeing' through a theoretical integration of the nature of the continuity shot of film and the waking wish fantasy. This elaborates on this 'way of seeing' in Kafka as in Freud, presenting it as a medium so basic that it goes without specification or explicit thematisation.

In the next chapter, Peter Beicken's 'Moving Pictures – Visual Pleasures: Kafka's Cinematic Writing' shifts the discussion on proto-cinematic conceptions in Kafka's work, studied in the first three chapters, to distinct cinematic manifestations that can be detected throughout his oeuvre. This thorough study examines the multifaceted intermedial use of the cinematic in Kafka's writing, providing a complex sense of a visually dense imaginary as an integral way of understanding Kafka's filmic writing.

Beicken's study is followed by Tobias Kuehne's 'To Move as the Image Moves: The Rule of Rhythmic Presence and Absence in Kafka's *The Man Who Disappeared*' which illuminates Kafka's own view of the cinematic medium and its disparity from his contemporary film theorists. This is followed by a rigorous exploration of the way Kafka's unique approach to film is manifested in his first novel, enabling Kuehne to present Kafka's unique cinematic vision as realised within his writing.

After presenting various ways in which Kafka's work actualises cinematic conceptions, we move on to explore more specific issues, shedding light on the productivity of thinking Kafka through cinema from different angles. In Kata Gellen's 'Noises Off: Cinematic Sound in Kafka's "The Burrow"', the presence of sound in Kafka's unfinished story is explored. Gellen analyses this using concepts from the theory of film and of film sound, culminating in the recognition of an inherent contradiction regarding its source, a contradiction which illuminates Kafka's fictional world and narrative rhetoric, and which is indistinguishable without the appropriation of film-sound theories.

Next, Idit Alphandary's 'Gesture, Wardrobe, Backdrop and Prop in Kafka's *The Man Who Disappeared* and Peter Weir's *The Truman Show*' provides a meticulous comparison of the novel and film. Based on concepts and understandings from Walter Benjamin and Stanley Cavell, Alphandary shows how literary and cinematic employments of gesture, wardrobe, backdrop and prop are accountable for the self-realisation and social integration of the individual in the American sphere in the novel and the film.

Concluding Part I is Kevin W. Sweeney's 'The Possibility of the Cinematic: "The Metamorphosis" and "The Burrow"', which examines the theoretical hindrances and advantages of adapting Kafka's two stories to the screen, showing how sound and image can complement indeterminacies in Kafka's narrative.

In Part II, *The Kafkaesque Cinema*, we reverse the order, and examine the capacity of cinema to incorporate and express the unique qualities of Kafka's world. We proceed by examining cinematic adaptations of Kafka as well as particular films or filmmakers that can be described as exhibiting a Kafkaesque aura.

We begin with '"The essential is sufficient": The Kafka Adaptations of Orson Welles, Straub-Huillet and Michael Haneke', where Martin Brady and Helen Hughes examine the dialectical relationship between words and images in three cinematic adaptations: Orson Welles' *The Trial* (1962), Jean-Marie Straub and Danièle Huillet's *Klassenverhältnisse* (*Class Relations*, 1983) and Michael Haneke's *Das Schloss* (*The Castle*, 1997). While focusing on the ways by which Kafka's visual austerity and the meticulous attention to rhythm and metre is handled by these filmmakers, the authors confront the difficulties enrooted in adapting Kafka to the screen, and explore different resolutions of such attempts.

Following this, Shai Biderman shifts the discussion to films and filmmakers that, while they do not adapt a specific Kafka story, do manifest the notion of Kafkaesque cinema. In his chapter, 'K., the Tramp and the Cinematic Vision: The Kafkaesque Chaplin', he explores the notion that the world of the moving image can uniquely and exclusively employ, explore and embrace the experience of the Kafkaesque. This, according to Biderman, can be best exhibited in the superbly orchestrated world of Charlie Chaplin. In his numerous masterpieces, and while keeping with the distinctive features of the visual medium, Chaplin can be understood as transforming the linguistic aura of the Kafkaesque into a cinematic performance, thus painting a cinematic picture which is no less idiosyncratic than the original. For Biderman, this is indicative to the nature and tenacity of the cinematic version of the Kafkaesque.

Following this line of questioning, other filmmakers and cinematic masterpieces take central stage. Iris Bruce's '"The Medium is the Message": Cronenberg "Outkafkas" Kafka' explores Kafka's and Cronenberg's different representations of (early- and late-) twentieth-century societies, moving from Kafkaesque dreams and nightmares to Cronenbergian possible worlds of technological advancement. Through a comparison between Cronenberg's *Videodrome* (1983), *The Fly* (1986) and *Naked Lunch* (1991) and Kafka's 'The Metamorphosis' and 'A Country Doctor' Bruce focuses on the political implications of the different depictions of relations between metamorphosis, (sexual) violence, power and technology in the various texts and media.

This is followed by another Kafka/Cronenberg investigation. William J. Devlin and Angel M. Cooper's 'The Absurdity of Human Existence: 'The Metamorphosis' and *The Fly*' analyses depictions of absurdity and metamorphoses in Cronenberg's film and Kafka's novella as two variations on Albert Camus' understanding of the Absurd. In focusing on the different applications of narrator focalisation and character perspective and their relation to the metamorphosis in the respective media, Devlin and Cooper assess the relations between media and absurdity in Kafka and in Cronenberg.

Next, in '"This is not Nothing": Viewing the Coen Brothers through the Lens of Kafka', Ido Lewit presents two films by the Coen brothers, *A Serious Man* (2009) and *Inside Llewyn Davis* (2013), as two complementary cinematic renditions of Kafka's application of written language. Analysing the films from two understandings of Kafka's use of language – Referential Fallacies of a Codeless Message, and the Self-defeat of the Metalingul Function – Lewit contravenes the contention that these Kafkan practices are confined to the literary medium.

Next, Omri Ben-Yehuda's 'The Face: K. and Keaton' which compares the roles of face and body in Kafka and Keaton. Focusing on the descriptive aspects in 'The Metamorphosis', *The Trial* and *The Castle*, and on Kafka's and Keaton's utilisation of notions as 'action', 'reaction' and *gestus*, Ben-Yehuda examines the cinematic persona of 'The Great Stone-face' as a Kafkan figure.

Closing Part II is Fernando Gabriel Pagnoni Berns and Leonardo Acosta Lando's 'Translating Kafka into Italian: Kafkaesque Themes in Elio Petri's Films' which examines the influence of Kafka on Petri and points out the political, aesthetic and existential significance of the allusions to Kafka's work in the Italian director's various films.

Finally, on a somewhat poetic note, the book concludes with an epilogue, *A Personal Quest into the Cinematic Kafkaesque*, which is set as a personal journey. The two taking this journey are Dan Geva, an award-winning documentary filmmaker, and Henry Sussman, a leading Kafka scholar. While musing on their personal experiences, the authors disclose a creative and intellectual process that endures the cinematic Kafka.

Geva's 'Magic, Mystery and Miracle: Re-spiralling Marker and Kafka' engages three descriptions that weave together Kafka and cinema: the first,

Kafka's story, 'Description of a Struggle'; the second, Chris Marker's film-essay from 1960 named after Kafka's story; and the third, Geva's own film, *Description of a Memory* (2006), which revisits Marker's film. The interlacing of the three descriptions, the three periods and the various media used provides Geva with the opportunity to investigate the centrality of 'magic, mystery and miracle' in Kafka and in Marker.

Sussman's 'Transcribing Kafka into Film: A Tortuous Love-Story' is a personal meditation on the filmic Kafka, from the impact of Welles' *The Trial* and observations on the Kafkaesque aesthetic of French and Italian New-Wave to a comparative study of two of the most innovative cinematic renditions of Kafka: Aleksei Balabanov's and Michael Haneke's 1994 and 1997 adaptations of *The Castle*.

NOTES

1 According to Brod (1995: 14) this family ritual was frequently performed until the children reached adolescence, or around the mid-1890s.

2 Intriguingly, 'photoplay' was one of the early designations of cinema. Pioneering film theorist Hugo Münsterberg is known to have used it in *The Photoplay: A Psychological Study* (1916).

3 'Dearest Max, my last request: everything I leave behind me … in the way of diaries, manuscripts, letters … sketches [*Gezeichnetem*] and so on, to be burned unread; also all writings and sketches which you or others may possess; and ask those others for them in my name' (Brod 1968: 265–6).

4 The novel's title has been translated in different ways, most recently as *Amerika: The Missing Person* (Mark Harman).

5 Interestingly, Theodor Adorno finds that 'many decisive parts in Kafka read as though they had been written in imitation of expressionist paintings which should have been painted but never were' (1981: 264).

6 A *Kaiserpanorama* was a stereoscopic device for viewing still photos, creating a 3D effect.

7 While Kafka's impressions of specific films are frequent in his diaries and letters, explicit reflections on the cinematic medium as such are much scarcer.

8 The cultural term 'Kafkaesque' has long exceeded Kafka's literary output. 'Kafkaesque' commonly designates 'social alienation, the victimization by anonymous bureaucratic institutions, the irrational terror of metaphysical powers, or the conflict between a weak son and an overbearing father figure' and is often expressed by 'rhetorical strategies like paradox, irony, or sudden reversals in action' (Gray et al. 2005: 156). It is important to differentiate it from the more restrictive term 'Kafkan', which 'implies a

9   greater degree of similarity with, and/or the direct, attributable influence of, Kafka's actual works' (Lemon 2011: 207).
9   Beicken further develops this topic in his essay within this anthology.
10 In 1915 Kafka wrote to his publisher Kurt Wolff: 'The insect cannot be depicted. It cannot even be shown from a distance', and offered his own suggestion for a cover illustration: 'I would choose such scenes as the following: the parents and the head clerk in front of the locked door, or even better, the parents and the sister in the lighted room, with the door open upon the adjoining room that lies in darkness' (1977: 114–15).
11 This discussion is further elaborated by Brady and Hughes in their essay within this anthology.
12 In 2000 Brady and Hughes compiled a list of forty Kafka-films (2002: 240). Since then, according to the Internet Movie Database, 27 film adaptations of Kafka stories have been produced.
13 Anne-Marie Scholz (2009) offers a comprehensive review of the critical evaluation of Welles' *The Trial*. Note that even critics who praise *The Trial* as a filmic achievement conclude that relative to the literary original the film 'seems divided against itself' and 'lacks the 'authenticity' of the original' (Naremore 1989: 196, 203); 'could be seen as the triumph of … the Kafkaesque over Kafka himself' (Brady and Hughes 2002: 233); and is even 'betraying Kafka' (Adams 2002: 154).
14 Still other comments underscore the influence Welles' *The Trial* had on the visual understanding of the Kafkaesque. Jeffrey Adams suggests it has had a decisive influence on the aesthetic choices of later Kafka-films (2002: 141), while Ido Lewit (2015) suggests that scrutinising its two concluding scenes discloses that it is much closer to its literary source than might be apparent at first.
15 Iris Bruce's (1998) study of Woody Allen's *Zelig*, Ido Lewit's (2011) study of the Coen Brothers' *A Serious Man*, and Alan Nelson's (2013) study of David Lynch's *Mulholland Drive* are notable exceptions.

REFERENCES

Adams, Jeffrey (2002) 'Orson Welles' *The Trial*: Film Noir and the Kafkaesque', *College Literature*, 29, 3, 140–57.

_____ (2011) 'Soderbergh's Kafka: In Retrospect', *Post Script*, 30, 3, 26-39.

Adorno, Theodor W. (1981 [1953]) 'Notes on Kafka', *Prisms*, trans. Shierry Weber Nicholsen and Samuel Weber. Cambridge: MIT Press, 243–71.

Alt, Peter-André (2009) *Kafka und der Film: Über kinematographisches Erzählen*. Munich: Verlag C. H. Beck.

Armstrong, Tim (2000) 'Two types of shock in modernity', *Critical Quarterly*, 42, 1, 60–73.

Beicken, Peter (2000) 'Kafka's Mise-en-scéne: Literary and Cinematic Imaginary', *Journal of the Kafka Society of America*, 24, 1/2, 4–11.

_____ (2011) 'Kafka's Visual Method: The Gaze, the Cinematic, and the Intermedial', in Stanley Corngold and Ruth V. Gross (eds) *Kafka for the Twenty-First Century*. Rochester, NY: Camden House, 165–78.

Benjamin, Walter (2007 [1934]) 'Kafka: On the Tenth Anniversary of his Death', in *Illuminations*, trans. Harry Zohn. New York: Schocken, 111–40.

_____ (2011 [1935]) 'The Work of Art in the Age of its Technological Reproducibility (Second Version)', in Timothy Corrigan, Patricia White and Meta Mazaj (eds) *Critical Visions in Film Theory: Classic and Contemporary Readings*. Boston and New York: Bedford/St. Martin's, 229–52.

Benson, Peter (1993) 'Entering *The Castle*', *Journal of Narrative Technique*, 23, 2, 80–91.

Borges, Jorge Luis (1999) 'Kafka and his Precursors', *Selected Non-Fictions*, ed. Eliot Weinberger, trans. Esther Allen, Suzanne Jill Levine and Eliot Wein-berger. London and New York: Penguin, 363–4.

Brady, Martin and Helen Hughes (2002) 'Kafka Adapted to Film', in Julian Preece (ed.) *The Cambridge Companion to Kafka*. Cambridge: Cambridge University Press, 226–41.

Brod, Max (1968 [1925]) 'Epilogue' in Kafka, Franz *The Trial*, trans. Willa and Edwin Muir. New York: Schocken Books, 265–9.

_____ (1995 [1937]) *Franz Kafka Biography*, trans. G. Humphreys Roberts and Richard Winston. Boston: Da Capo Press.

Bruce, Iris (1998) 'Mysterious Illnesses of Human Commodities in Woody Allen and Franz Kafka', *Studies in 20th & 21st Century Literature*, 22, 1, Article 9; available at: http://dx.doi.org/10.4148/2334-4415.1438 (accessed 10 July 2015).

Cook, David (1990) *A History of Narrative Film*. New York: W. W. Norton.

Corngold, Stanley (1973) *The Commentators' Despair: The Interpretation of Kafka's Metamorphosis*. Port Washington, NY: Kennikat Press.

_____ (2004) *Lambent Traces: Franz Kafka*. Princeton, NJ: Princeton University Press.

_____ (2009) 'Kafka and the Ministry of Writing', in Stanley Corngold, Jack Greenberg and Benno Wagner (eds) *Franz Kafka: The Office Writings*. Princeton, NJ: Princeton University Press, 1–18.

Deleuze, Gilles (1989) *Cinema 2: The Time-Image*, trans. Hugh Tomlinson and Robert Galeta. Minneapolis, MN: University of Minnesota Press.

Duttlinger, Carolin (2007) *Kafka and Photography*. Oxford: Oxford University Press.

Flores, Angel (1946) 'Introduction', in Angel Flores (ed.) *The Kafka Problem*. New York: New Directions, ix–xii.

Gandelman, Claude (1974) 'Kafka as an Expressionist Draughtsman', *Neohelicon*, 2, 3/4, 237–77.

Goebel, Rolf J. (2000) 'Kafka's Cinemtic Gaze: Flanerie and Urban Discourse in

Beschreibung eines Kampfes', *Journal of the Kafka Society of America*, 24, 1/2, 13–16.

Gray, Richard T., Ruth V. Gross, Rolf J. Goebel and Clayton Koelb (2005) *A Franz Kafka Encyclopedia*. Westport, CT: Greenwood Press.

Hansen, Miriam (1993) '"With Skin and Hair": Kracauer's Theory of Film, Marseille 1940', *Critical Inquiry*, 19, 437–69.

_____ (1997) 'Introduction', Kracauer, Siegfried *Theory of Film: The Redemption of Physical Reality*. Princeton, NJ: Princeton University Press, vii–xlvi.

Hoffmeister, Donna (1993) 'Kafka Lite: Woody Allen and Steven Soderbergh on Kafka's Play-Ground', *Journal of the Kafka Society of America*, 17, 2, 13–21.

Janouch, Gustav (1971 [1951]) *Conversations with Kafka*, trans. Goronwy Rees. New York: New Directions.

Kafka, Franz (1971) *The Complete Stories*, ed. Nahum N. Glatzer. New York: Schocken Books.

_____ (1977 [1958]) *Letters to Friends, Family, and Editors*, ed. Nahum Glatzer, trans. Richard and Clara Winston. New York: Schocken.

_____ (1982 [1926]) *Das Schloss*. Frankfurt a.M.: S. Fischer Verlag.

_____ (1991 [1954]) *The Blue Octavo Notebooks*, ed. Max Brod, trans. Ernst Kaiser and Eithne Wilkins. Cambridge, MA: Exact Change.

_____ (1992 [1948]) *The Diaries of Franz Kafka 1910–23*, ed. Max Brod, trans. Joseph Kresh and Martin Greenberg, with Hannah Arendt. London: Minerva.

_____ (1998 [1926]) *The Castle*, trans. Mark Harman. New York: Schocken Books.

_____ (1999 [1937]) *Schriften, Tagebücher, Briefe: Kritische Ausgabe*. Frankfurt Am Main: S. Fischer.

_____ (2004 [1927]) *Amerika: The Man Who Disappeared*, trans. Michael Hofmann. New York: New Directions.

_____ (2008 [1927]) *Amerika: The Missing Person*, trans. Mark Harman. New York: Schocken.

_____ (2009a [1925]) *The Trial*, trans. Mike Mitchell. Oxford: Oxford University Press.

_____ (2009b [1926]) *The Castle*, trans. Anthea Bell. Oxford: Oxford University Press.

Kracauer, Siegfried (1993 [1927]) 'Photography', trans. Thomas Y. Levin. *Critical Inquiry*, 19, 3, 421–36.

_____ (1995) 'Franz Kafka: On his Posthumous Works', *The Mass Ornament: Weimer Essays*, ed. Thomas Y. Levin. Cambridge, MA: Harvard University Press, 267–78.

Lemon, Robert (2011) 'The Comfort of Strangeness: Correlating the Kafkaesque and the Kafkan in Kazuo Ishiguro's *The Unconsoled*', in Stanley Corngold and Ruth V. Gross (eds) *Kafka for the Twenty-First Century*. Rochester, NY: Camden House, 207–21.

Lewit, Ido (2011) 'The Kafkaesque Cinematic Language of The Coen Brothers' *A Serious Man*', *Journal of the Kafka Society of America*, 33/4, 29–38.

_____ (2015) 'Orson Welles's *The Trial* and the Problem of Interpretation after the Holocaust', *Journal of the Kafka Society of America*, 36/7, 115–26.

McFarlane, Brian (1996) *Novel to Film: An Introduction to the Theory of Adap-tation*.

Oxford: Clarendon Press.

Metz, Walter C. (1993) 'Pomp(ous) Sirk-imstances: Intertextuality, Adaptation, and *All That Heaven Allows*', *Journal of Film and Video*, 45, 4, 3–21.

_____ (2007) 'The Cold War's "Undigested Apple-Dumpling": Imaging *Moby-Dick* in 1956 and 2001', in James M. Welsh and Peter Lev (eds) *The Literature/Film Reader: Issues of Adaptation*. Lanham, MD: Scarecrow Press, 65–76.

Munsterberg, Hugo (2013 [1916]) *Hugo Munsterberg on Film: The Photoplay: A Psychological Study and Other Writings*, ed. Allan Langdale. New York and London: Routledge.

Naremore, James (1989 [1978]) 'The Trial', in *The Magic World of Orson Welles*. University Park, TX: Southern Methodist University Press, 195–214.

Nelsons, Alan (2013) 'Cowboy Rules: *Mulholland Drive*, Kafka, and Illusory Freedom', in Zina Giannopoulou (ed.) *Mulholland Drive*. New York: Rout-ledge, 38–52.

Pohland, Vera (2000) 'Trains of Traffic', *Journal of the Kafka Society of America*, 24, 1/2, 54–68.

Ruebner, Tuvia (1982) 'Can One Illustrate Kafka's Cockroach? (Remarks on Kafka's Metaphoric Language)', in David Hanegbi (ed.) *Kafka Symposium: A Study-Day, March 1981*. Tel Aviv: Sifriat Poalim, 7–26. [Hebrew]

_____ (1996) 'Some Remarks Concerning Kafka the Jew', in Hans-Jürgen Schrader, Elliott M. Simon and Charlotte Wardi (eds) *The Jewish Self-Portrait in European and American Literature, Vol. 15*. Berlin: Walter de Gruyter, 125–34.

Sandbank, Shimon (1981) 'Uncertainty as Style: Kafka's *Betrachtung*', *German Life and Letters* 34, 4, 385–97.

Sebald, W. G. (2006) *Campo Santo*, trans. Anthea Bell. London: Penguin.

Segal, Eyal (2008) *The Decisive Moment is Everlasting: Static Time in Kafka's Poetics*. Tel Aviv: Hakibbutz Hameuchad. [Hebrew]

Scholz, Anne-Marie (2009) '"Josef K von 1963…": Orson Welles' "Americanized" Version of *The Trial* and the Changing Functions of the Kafkaesque in Postwar West Germany', *European Journal of American Studies*, 1, 2–21.

Smiley, Robin H. (2003) *Books into Films: The Stuff That Dreams Are Made Of*. Santa Barbara, CA: Capra Press.

Stam, Robert (2000) 'Beyond Fidelity: The Dialogics of Adaptation', in James Naremore (ed.) *Film Adaptation*. New Brunswick, NJ: Rutgers University Press, 54–78.

Verstraten, Peter (2011) *Film Narratology*, trans. Stefan van der Lecq. Toronto: University of Toronto Press.

Walser, Martin (1961) *Beschreibung einer Form*. Munich: Carl Hanser.

Welsh, James M. (2007) 'Introduction', in James M. Welsh and Peter Lev (eds) *The Literature/Film Reader: Issues of Adaptation*. Lanham, MD: Scarecrow Press, xiii–xxviii.

Zischler, Hanns (2003) *Kafka Goes to the Movies*, trans. Susan H. Gillespie. Chicago:

Chicago University Press.

Zone, Ray (2007) *Stereoscopic Cinema and the Origin of 3-D Film, 1838–1952*. Lexington, KY: University Press of Kentucky.

PART ONE

THE CINEMATIC KAFKA

KAFKA, RUMOUR, EARLY CINEMA: ARCHAIC MOVING PICTURES

PAUL NORTH

I. THE INCIPIENCE OF THE ARCHAIC

Kafka loved archaic things. This is Walter Benjamin's theory, which takes the form of a technical term invented by him, *the unforgotten* (1968: 131–4). Now, this technical term has received much less attention than another word, *gesture*, and there may be reasons for this. Gesture seems to describe so much that is 'modern', the reported loss of the fullness of meaning, the alienation of the isolated social actor, and so forth, whereas it is hard to see the value of something that has been unforgotten, simply because it is no longer lost. Yet an archaising impulse is also quite pronounced in Kafka, even if its connection to his own era, or for that matter to ours, is not immediately apparent. The narrator of Kafka's story 'Beim Bau der Chinesischen Mauer' ('While Building the Chinese Wall', 1931) makes the archaic into something of a principle when he says: 'Battles from our most ancient history are only now being fought, and your neighbour, with a flushed face, stumbles into your house with the news' (2002b: 353–4; my translation). A lot hangs on how we understand the relationship between the ancient battles and the 'news' in this line. One thing is obvious, I think. It does not mean to say that those ancient battles are actually more current than our current battles, as if Kafka were practicing a mode of ideology critique, rolling back the curtains to expose modernity's hidden truth. Kafka's interest in the archaic is not exactly a critical interest. The relationship between old and new in this passage also does not mean, though, that the present is a stage in a preexisting historical development, that is, that rivers flowing out of the most distant past discharge their clear waters in the now. Kafka also does not understand the past as leading up to and producing the present.

Kafka loved archaic things – animals, legends, myth, the law, sovereignty – neither because the present is the past in disguise nor because the present is an effect of a chain of past causes. He loved the archaic, I think, in part because it could be so disturbing, so alien to the present, so disconnected, as Benjamin's formulation 'unforgotten' implies; but he also loved certain kinds of archaisms the most – these were, at least it seems to me, the nondetermining ones. Things like the CatLamb or the Jewish Bible offered mixed-up and hard to assimilate inheritances. Their kinds of lineages we can hardly identify with a single hidden truth or conflate with the roots of a tree of which we think we are the ripened fruit. These modes of history are much too orderly, for one thing. Court and castle, the hunter Gracchus, the ape that makes a report – these Kafkan figures gesture toward a past that is harder, not easier, to understand, insofar as it was more, shall we say, free for unholy amalgams of all sorts – as these examples demonstrate.

The new medium of film Kafka mentions occasionally in a letter or an early diary entry, naming a few particular films or planning trips to the cinema. But cinema makes no appearance in his fictions at all. To judge from depictions of the medium or references to films, the cinema had hardly any effect on Kafka's avocation. If we credit only what is represented by Kafka, however, we would miss entirely many of the forces that moved him. These forces often do not appear as depictions, yet they do appear, not as they are, but in altered form. And this may hint at Kafka's particular way of approaching contemporary culture. He tends to face his own culture through older doubles: movies in advertising placards, say. Or to take another example, whereas other intellectuals and writers of the time – Thomas Mann or Hermann Cohen; friends like Max Brod and Oskar Baum – addressed the conflicts and contradictions of *Judentum* and *Deutschtum* directly, Kafka almost always chose antiquated or primeval reflections, whether these were animals or medieval institutions, an odd spool of thread, a resistant loaf of bread, a benighted salesman, and so on.

Let us then combine these two facts about Kafka – his love for the archaic (and his displacement of current phenomena into out of date doubles) and the perfect absence of the cinema in his fictions[1] – and make a set of hypotheses. First, although cinemas and movies are not represented, other modes of mass communication are, especially from the period in which he was writing *Der Prozess* (*The Trial*, 2009a) and afterward. The characteristic traits of *Verleumdung*, slander – transmission through a conduit of low resistance, high fidelity of reception, wide dissemination – make it a potential double for other, more technological broadcast media. I won't say it is a predecessor. For Kafka, these are not causal chains that add up to something like progress. Yet archaic modes do allow us to say things about putatively modern ones that we wouldn't otherwise be able to articulate.

Slander enters Joseph K.'s bedroom at the start of *The Trial* in the strangest of figures: 'a man he had never seen in his room came in' (2009a, 7; translation modified). Like a phantasm of a later age, a stranger steps into Joseph K.'s bedroom and gives him the news. And it slowly dawns on Joseph K., although it takes the entire novel for it to happen, that a vast concealed network of signal relays enabled the stranger to appear there. *The Trial*, we could say, is an archaic displacement of a system like the television system, which, to be sure, Kafka did not live to experience. In the archaic system, nonetheless, communications are distributed among a geographically dispersed mass yet still function intimately, in an imitation of face-to-face encounters. Moreover, through the movement of slander, stealthy as it is and yet invasive, the law keeps itself distant while exercising its power over isolated individuals in the tightest economy. The network of distribution, the delivery by strangers, invasion of the most private sphere, all this increases rather than decreases the power of the slanderer. Something similar happens over the telephone system in *Das Schloss* (*The Castle*, 2009b), although the political configuration is somewhat different. In the later novel the technology is represented directly, but the medium, however modern, follows an archaic protocol. A phone call to the sovereign may or may not be answered, and if it is answered, it is never the sovereign himself on the end of the line. The old protocol is something like revelation, a primitive modality of authority to be sure, and yet the modern medium does nothing to improve its intentionally broken linkages and obviously deceptive tones. In fact the expectation to be able to talk to the one you have called, a telephonic expectation, exposes precisely the archaisms, theological ones, that still plague the modern medium that was supposed to have overcome them with its earthly pulses. And still, those you really want to call are not on the network.

A first hypothesis: modern communications media are addressed through archaic shills in Kafka's writing, especially after 1915. A second hypothesis: this displacing way of writing can have different objectives. It may show how the fundamental problems that shaped an older form of communication – in the case of the telephone, the archaic double would be prayer – persist in the medium, are intensified by it, or even reach a zenith in the new technological form. Or it may imply that the new medium operates in the very same way as the old, only that the context has been lost and so this, the very new, seems to have been born without purpose, a foundling or a miracle in search of a narrative in which it might become justified. Whatever the precise objective of the Kafkan displacement, as a general rule, whenever he turns to the archaic you can read it as an argument against the idea of progress. 'Believing in progress does not mean that there has been progress. That wouldn't be a belief', Kafka jots in a notebook in 1917 (2002c: 57; my translation). It is this belief – not progress itself, which of course only exists as an object of belief, an ideal or an idea – that he wants to eradicate, and showing the proximity of the most ancient past with the most contemporary present is his way of eradicating it. The proximity implies that, despite our rhetoric, nothing has yet happened. A third hypothesis: Kafka looks for the positive dialectical moments in the archaic forms. They are easier to see there because, looking back, we are not blinded either by the false light of progress or by the accompanying general assumption of the need for progress, in other words the conviction that, at this moment, things couldn't get any worse. If communications with the sovereign are assumed to be broken, arbitrary, or untrustworthy, even when there is a direct line to the royal chamber or a webcam in the throne room, one has to stop wishing and live with the dead line, the empty image, the blocked wish. And thus, if a phone call comes to be treated like its archaic sibling, like a prayer rather than like a telecommunication, Kafka will have achieved some part of his objective.

The example we haven't mentioned yet, the case of cinema, stands out from the others both because of the particular problems with communication that it seems to solve and in part to perpetuate, and because of the positive dialectical moment that it offers Kafka. This positive moment film inherits from its archaic double. Thus, a fourth and final hypothesis, a speculation really: cinema, if it appears in Kafka's fictions at all, appears through the archaic double, rumour, and Kafka treats rumour – a further speculative leap – in order to emphasise a radical political potential that may have been lost along the way, as cinema *qua* medium was received, its codes codified, its habits institutionalised. Let us note that it is early cinema and proto-cinema, the first instances of moving pictures, that echo in the double, rumour. As a mode of transmission, rumour spreads quickly; it knows really no resistance – the law doesn't recognise it and so legal measures cannot slow it, as they can and do to slander. Rumour flows through the entire land, and rather than isolating individuals into nodes of a network, it tends to bring them together in one place, into a type of theatre. Around the end of 1914 or the beginning of 1915 Kafka writes a story fragment, 'Der Dorfschullehrer' ('The Village Schoolteacher'), named and published after his death by Max Brod, that centres on a theatre of rumour.[2] What is playing in this theatre is a rumour about the existence of a giant mole. We should emphasise a crucial point: the story is about the rumour, not about the giant mole, and in order to highlight the benefits of rumour it also goes into great detail about contrasting media and modes of distribution – pedagogical texts, opinion pieces, city gossip, scientific studies – that are not nearly as effective. Rumour it portrays as the quickest, most explosive, epistemically suspect, and for this reason the most creative archaic mass medium for the communication of moving images. Rumour moves in several ways: it animates images, it disseminates them rapidly and widely, and it dynamises audiences politically. Rumour puts the polity into motion.

Perhaps this allowed Kafka, if my speculative hypothesis holds, to think through a few aspects of early cinema, although it leaves other aspects and later developments untouched. It does not allow him, or us, to think about cinema as an art form or even as a development in the history of culture. It does not help us to understand film as a development in ways of seeing, either as a new possibility for self-reflection or as an extension of nineteenth-century techniques for disciplining the senses.[3] Rather, in rumour, Kafka finds a phenomenon akin to what Tom Gunning in a well-known article from 1986 called the 'cinema of attractions'. Attraction means one thing for Gunning, and he is careful to distinguish it from another. It names a place to which people are drawn, an amusement park, an 'act of showing and exhibition' (1986: 64), and only secondarily does it imply a psychological state or sense stimulation. That is to say, Gunning's theory of early cinema as a version of the circus, the vaudeville act, the amusement park, the side show even, is a theory of film as a social or political phenomenon, not as a kind of psychology.

I want to single out, in this influential reading of early film, a Kafkan aspect that Gunning mentions but does not emphasise. While Gunning is focused on drawing a clear line between early moving pictures and later more narratively organised films, to label the mode of early cinema 'exhibition' and to identify the subject matter as 'actuality' or 'trick', he also inadvertently stumbles upon the for-whom of this medium, which we should not be astonished to find corresponds with the for-whom of rumour. Early cinema is for 'an audience not acculturated to the traditional arts' (1986: 66). Indeed, it is parasitic on the audience that attended burlesques, which became porn films, and sideshows and amusement parks, and so on, which became the trick film and the 'actuality' (1986: 64). The 'for-whom' of early cinema is not only a class of people, a political class; the class exhibits a very peculiar type of engagement with the political world and with cultural forms that one could only call apolitical and acultural. What do these uncultured marginal political figures get from cinema? Gunning emphasises the pleasure quotient. Attraction, he says, is 'direct stimulation' by sensational images. It may well be the case that the uncultured seek pure or mere sensual stimulation, but direct sense stimulation is, we have to add, as precarious and fleeting in the cinema as in the circus, or in the burlesque house. We should focus not only on the climax, so to speak, but also on the type of collective behaviour that the sensorial stimulation creates. We can imagine the political group drawn to Gunning's 'attractions' as what Kafka might call *die Unanständigen*, the indecent, immodest, the not respectable, those from whom you can't get a square deal and those who neither buy into nor benefit from the social contract as they are supposed to. R. W. Paul gives a wonderful illustration of this type of spectator in 1901 in *The Countryman and the Cinematograph*, although the film survives only in fragments. A 'yokel' watches a motion picture for the first time, standing beside a movie screen and reacting to different effects. To a dancer dancing he leaps and laughs and slaps his knees, a train speeds toward him and he throws up his hands 'stop' and when it doesn't he flees off screen, when he returns a romance between two lovers touches his heart, and there the fragment breaks off. The yokel sees the cinema not as art but as a depiction of events to which he ought to respond. Undoubtedly it is not these fairly quotidian events that do this, but the medium itself and its power to astonish, which is largely due to its newness. He reacts because these mundane happenings are depicted in a film. Elsewhere Kafka is fascinated by the way the force of an art form changes, in the moment when its cultural status declines;[4] here he is similarly fascinated by the effects a cultural form can have at a certain stage in its social life, the 'temporal character', we might call it. Film had this power to attract yokels in the moment of astonishment. Yokel or not, spectators became yokels through early film's ability to make quotidian happenings astonishing. No one is a yokel with respect to moving pictures anymore. To be honest, by 1901, by the time such a clown could be shown on the screen, as he was in Paul's film, the audience already will have transformed. It was already impossible to be the 'yokel', only possible to remember him.

Rumour is a medium, if it is a medium, that maintains the incipience of a new medium. It is always new, untrustworthy, historyless, without support from a tradition or an industry or a regime of truth. Its 'temporal character' is to be always newborn, simultaneously needy and threatening, and highly attractive. And thus it is only incipient cinema that can be called rumour's double. 'Early cinema' means a medium that carries rumour's temporal character, for a brief time, along with its political potential and its dangers. No one ever confused rumour with art. A rumour is effective insofar as no one can come to trust it as a form of truth; in the same way early cinema may cause effects completely out of proportion with its social or epistemic status, and it may draw to it the *Unanständigen*, the yokels, for the brief moment in which it itself is still indecent and untrustworthy. Who trusts the untrustworthy? Or rather, who is at home in a milieu in which trust is not the prerequisite? These are the figures attracted by this indecent attraction. Here we can quote one of those rare notes about the medium of film. Kafka jotted this in his travel diary in February, 1911: 'The cinematograph gives the seen object [*dem Angeschauten*] the restlessness of its movement' (2002c: 937; my translation).

What was the 'attraction' of incipient cinema? Before the 'actuality' or the 'trick' that Gunning highlights, it was undoubtedly in part at least the new attraction of movement itself, the movement of images, or rather – not to confuse technical details with cinematic experience – the movement of what is shown in images. The Lumiéres' *L'Arrivée d'un train en gare de La Ciotat* (*The Arrival of a Train at La Ciotat Station*, 1895) is obviously 'about' locomotion. It exhibits locomotion, you could say, and this caused, or so the legend goes, a reaction in the audience – they reportedly ran away. Kafka is also thinking of movement, of the power to astonish when something suddenly can be moved that has not previously been moved. In this diary entry he records the experience of viewing the moving pictures of a *Kaiserpanorama*. I quote here only part of a passage that has been discussed before:[5]

> Kaiserpanorama. Only amusement in Friedland. [...] An old man at a little lighted table reading a volume of the *Illustrierte Welt* was in charge of everything. After a while he let the Ariston [a music automat] play for me ... the pictures more alive than in the cinematograph because they allow the gaze reality's restfulness. The cinematograph gives the seen object the restlessness of its movement, but rest for the eye seems more important. The smooth floors of the cathedrals before our tongues. Why is there no combination of cinema and stereoscope in this way? (2002c: 937)

Here Kafka is lamenting a loss in the transition from the peepshow type of viewing experience to the cinematic one, from a panorama where the viewpoint is held steady and the images revolve placidly before it, to a different effect on the viewer, which he calls restlessness. At least according to this note, one of the very few about cinematic things, Kafka was not interested in the speed or mechanicity of the projected film, and not even in the depiction of motion that was so ubiquitous in early films – trains arriving, people walking, car accidents, and so forth. His interest lies in the ability or not to rest, which is not so much an aesthetic interest, and certainly not a technical issue alone, but more importantly a social and political interest. Doubtless a change in opinion took place between 1911 and 1915. The movement of the spectator that Kafka in 1911 seems to want to squelch, he reevaluates in the story fragment of 1915 about the rumour of a giant mole, where he finds a political use for the restlessness and unculturedness of the yokel.

II. A BRIEF RUMOUROLOGY

A rumour is a delicate creature, easily suffocated; the wrong kind of attention takes away its breathing room. It depends for its existence on an exact balance of attitudes. It is not precisely belief, the attitude with which one first embraces a rumour – unless you can imagine a belief that does not presume the existence of its object. In the epistemic sense, belief posits the existence of a being or state of affairs and through this posit secures the truth of statements about it. You may of course believe that some set of sentences or images is false, that its objects do not exist as portrayed, but disbelieving something is at the same time an assertion of the truth of that falsity and the assertion of a different state of affairs that could be represented truthfully. Disbelief is a species of belief.

At first it seems as if rumour would require either assent in the mode of belief or dissent in the mode of disbelief. You 'believe' or 'disbelieve' a rumour and you find out later whether it was true or false. In other words, it seems as though rumour is an alethic phenomenon, however displaced its confirmation may be in time. And perhaps at some point in its life a rumour does become an alethic matter, and yet its truth-status is at first derived from a more primary issue. For rumour to be rumour, and not fact or a vehicle for belief, it must present an exact balance between truth and falsity. If completely true, it is no longer rumour but fact; if completely false it is no longer rumour but illusion, error or deception. Rumour lives in the abeyance of the alethic. The attitude in which one becomes susceptible to rumour, then, is first an ability, maybe even a desire, to make no alethic commitment at all. For rumour truth is really a secondary or tertiary matter. Rumour is the ad-hoc way in which we receive a configuration of things, before the configuration has been institutionalised in a form about which we could, post-hoc, assert belief. A similar sentiment appears in one of Joseph Joubert's earliest notebook entries, from the portentous year 1789: 'It is not facts, but rumors that cause emotions among the people.' Then he adds: 'What is believed creates everything' (2005: 11).[6] Here belief means something different – a belief that is not a belief in the truth of something's existence; Joubert's belief is analethic. Instead of a commitment to the truth of something on the basis of the absurd (in the manner of Kierkegaard), rumour demands perfect ambivalence, or, said a different way, it first demands a commitment to something other than truth. Most likely Joubert's note is a response to the events of the Great Fear. In these scant sentences, however, he begins to conceptualise a mode of mass communication that, like Leviathan, precedes creation and continues to move through it, ignoring what has already been created – that which could be affirmed as true. Joubert's rumour, like Kafka's, is a relation to what does not seem to exist or to that for which the question of existence is as of yet unimportant. In July 1789, unlanded peasants, deprived of grain and starving, revolted against local landowners and by association the King, acting on rumours of an aristocratic plot to buy up all available corn. This came to be called the Great Fear. According to Joubert, the belief that corresponds to rumour is creative; it is not revelatory of a world that has already been created. This does not quite describe the Great Fear, however. In view of a story of coming starvation, the peasants saw the extreme telos of what had been their social condition for decades – and responded to the fiction of injustice with all the righteousness that attends to truth. What had been true for some time, though, had not led to action.

We shouldn't say too much on rumour's behalf. When we represent rumour, when we become, in the words of the Salesman who narrates Kafka's fragment ('The Village Schoolteacher'), rumour's advocate (*Fürsprecher*), we supplant it, becoming an origin for the story and extinguishing its rather unique powers, which arise from the inability to locate a source by which you could either confirm or reject the story. This is what Kafka's narrator does not quite understand, though of course entire philosophies can be made out of the things that Kafka characters do not quite understand. In the fragment, the Salesman does not quite understand that speaking on behalf of rumour tears the tenuous tissue of relations that makes rumour rumour: when a plurality speaks authoritatively, together, at once, out of nowhere and with no proof, and without the authority to do so. Insofar as one takes up the case of rumour or seeks to substantiate a particular bit of hearsay, one substitutes real authority for the appearance of authority. And yet it was the mere appearance of authority, without grounds or proof, that afforded an image or a story its creativity, its movement – to recall Joubert. The word movement on which the analogy between rumour and cinema is based here does not refer to the movement of film through a projector, but rather the movement of films in political and cultural space.[7] No real authority could lead to such virtues as those of rumour, some of which are: speed, communicability and a capacity to produce action. Rumour inflates, spreads out, consumes, hurries, arrives before facts and prepares the ground for other activities and institutions. In a legal or bureaucratic lexicon in which advocacy would make sense, rumour's effects are squelched, and it is effects by which a rumour is primarily judged, not contents, sources, authority or style. Can it be that what is rumour-like in the cinema – not the auteur system, the star system, the studio system, the montage technique or the style of a particular movement or decade – is worth emphasising?

Rumour is not only an archaic mass medium, an older mode of moving images; it is also the medium that first pervaded all realms of human life – as screens are doing now. The experience of moving pictures, in all the forms in which it comes today, is still catching up with rumour, you could say. Newer video media have of course incorporated their medial antecedents, film and television, photography and opera. And further, so much of news broadcasts and YouTube sensations are still taken up with rumour-like contents. Indeed if you whispered the contents of a BuzzFeed headline it would be indistinguishable from rumour. What's more, these places and institutions – television, internet – exist themselves virtually only as rumours. They are rumour-like in their structures. Although it may not seem to be the case, the legal system has a fundamental rumour-like structure as well – many of Kafka's fictions, and before the fictions his legal writings, show this to be the case. Almost too many facets of the legal process have a rumour-like quality – all of the executive and procedural parts. And yet Kafka also makes a point to demonstrate that laws themselves are rumouresque. At the time when he wrote the 'Village Schoolteacher' fragment – in one night, on 18 December 1914 – Kafka was also writing *The Trial*, whose opening scene contains this exchange: '"That is not a law I am acquainted with," said K. "All the worse for you," said the guard. "I suspect it only exists inside your heads," said K' (2009a: 9).[8] The law, its existence and its character, is given in a rumour. A Kafkan argument would be that without rumour laws would have little or no effect.

A few days before writing the 'Village Schoolteacher' fragment, Kafka was working on the exegesis of what he calls in his diary 'Die Legende' (2002c: 707),[9] the short text that came to be titled 'Before the Law' when it was published separately in the journal *Selbstwehr* on 7 September 1915. A legend, let us say, is a rumour from the past that has (purportedly) lost its ability to produce action. This is a legend, however, about a very effective rumour. The man from the country, who comes to gain entry to the law, comes in response to a rumour, since the law itself has not called him; indeed 'the' Law cannot summon anyone. You might say rumour has to precede law in order to seduce us to accept its call. A recent description of rumour's structure of address belongs to Jean-Nöel Kapferer, a professor of marketing. Rumour is, to paraphrase Kapferer, a communication whose speaker is never its origin; a rumour's mouthpiece always heard it from someone else. More than this: in the form 'X told me' or 'I heard it from X', X themselves never had access to the fundamental source (Kapferer 1990: 67).[10] That is to say, it is not only the source that is not verifiable; the chain of transmission is constitutively broken. The one who comes before the law may understand in his last living moment what the reader could have already read in the logic of the legend, that the law gains its force from such a broken chain. Law is the socially legitimised discourse whose transmission cannot guarantee a connection to its origin. Law is fundamentally reported, a primary transmissive-projective technology. The locus of primal enunciation will have already receded and become inaccessible the moment it is accessed, indeed the moment before, although it is also always rumoured to be just a step away. In its essence law may be divine or natural, but in its existence and its real communicative structure it is equal to rumour.

The 'Village Schoolteacher' fragment doesn't concern the law. It is as if, in his novel, Kafka writes the exoteric version of that which here appears in the esoteric version. Law in *The Trial*, rumour in 'The Village Schoolteacher'. At the fragment's centre is a rumour whose delicacy and ephemerality is so severe that we endanger the topic just by speaking about it. The rumour is about a giant mole, but the story fragment, to reiterate, is about the precarious status of the rumour, once it gets into the hands of those who seek to advocate for it or explain it. Those who affirm rumour in another medium are its worst enemies. The Village Schoolteacher and the Salesman handle the rumour differently. Without any real reason to, the Salesman takes it upon himself to become the Schoolteacher's advocate in a case as disturbing as it is mundane. The Schoolteacher, who originally recorded the rumour in a 'little scripture' (*kleine Schrift*), seems to intuit the underlying problem with rumours. They cannot be advocated for. And so the Schoolteacher is annoyed by his self-appointed advocate. Annoyance at an advocate who takes your delicate writing and publicises it as something it is not is at the centre of the fragment onto which Max Brod appended the title 'Der Dorfschullehrer' when he published it as a story in the 1930s, without, we could say, the authority to do so. In addition to being unfinished, as are the majority of Kafka's fictions, the fragment is also unauthorised, and so it too is rumour-like. In it the Village Schoolteacher intuits, although he also doesn't fully understand, that the Salesman's crusade to 'speak on behalf of' is a violent defence against rumour's rejection of authorities external to itself.

The fragment is presented as a memoir in which the Salesman recounts the intentions and failures of the pamphlet he wrote in support of the Schoolteacher's little *Schrift* – 'scripture' – about the rumour. The Salesman's pamphlet is also called a *Schrift*. The struggle over the rumour and its rumour-character takes the form of a conflict between two *Schriften*: the Schoolteacher's original 'little scripture' and the Salesman's belated, derivative, advocating, new 'scripture'. To return to our initial hypotheses: Kafka's text presents a battle between two ways of modernising an archaic medial form. The two ways of writing down a rumour, of preparing it for a new public, are comic. The first is not archaic, just old fashioned, the teaching notes of a rustic pedagogue. The second is already outdated – as compared to the mass circulation newspaper and early cinema – a public endorsement written by a salesman. School lesson and marketing gimmick: one thing common to them both is their alethic unreliability.

Although Brod called the fragment 'Der Dorfschullehrer', this too is based upon a misunderstanding, similar to the one that leads the Salesman to take up and support the Schoolteacher's case. Neither the Salesman nor Brod are all that interested in the rumour that wafts through the fragment. The Salesman wants, rather, to save the honour, *Ehre*, of the Schoolteacher, to give him back his authority and his authorship. The rumour hardly shows up in the Salesman's account, and when it does, in oblique references, it is often concealed behind the hyperbolic name *Riesenmaulwurf*, 'mammoth mole', which emphasises size, implying that the wonder of the creature lies in the magnitude of its body. Instead of a text on the mole or on the original rumour, the Salesman publishes an *apologia* for the Village Schoolteacher's method, with a specific group of opponents in mind: the professors, whose attitude belittles schoolteachers, making them look silly and out of touch. Brod for his part wants to save Kafka's reputation, to advocate for his friend's authorship, to see his mole expand until it fills the literary firmament. There is a parallel between Brod and the Salesman: both repackage their ego-ideals, seeking to save them from oblivion and discredit, in order to make them fungible for a larger market, beyond the village and its immediate surroundings.

Kafka is keenly interested in the *Dorf* and its outer fringes, the peculiar anonymity that reigns there, the fecundity of the place for producing and disseminating rumours,[11] and its openness to a singular class or non-class, disenfranchised mendicant day-labourers, parallel to but different from the peasants who fuelled the French Revolution during the Great Fear.[12] In Kafka's own experience in the 1910s, there were frequent uprisings in rural Bohemia, and these soon became incorporated into the movement for Czech independence. The isolated village and its rural surroundings sound archaic, as does rumour's primarily aural/oral bailiwick, especially in a technological age. Yet as we have said it is not nostalgia that leads Kafka to investigate the rustic milieu and its antiquated medium. On the other side of the issue, Kafka seems keenly aware, in this fragment and elsewhere, of the dangers of living too close together, a situation here called 'city', *Stadt*, and whose communicative mode is idle talk, which promotes a very different political configuration. Rumour is definitively not gossip. A decade or so before Heidegger, Kafka recognises the levelling force of gossip, which the Schoolteacher in a monologue compares to *Zwitschern*, the sparrow's twitter: 'In the city, many people assemble immediately upon being summoned. What one is concerned with, the other immediate concerns himself with. With their breath they take each others' opinions away and appropriate them' (2002a: 210; translations modified). Unlike Heidegger, Kafka does not propose as a solution to *Zwitschern* – tweeting – a revivified, repotentised *Wissenschaft* (science) or a method with the power to 'speak being'. Rumour is nothing like idle talk and at the same time it is nothing like the transcendental speech of fundamental ontology. Nevertheless, it may accomplish at least one of that method's stated goals: rumour, if it is allowed to be rumour, has nothing for a ground. Idle talk appears grounded but in fact is not; it requires a philosophical intervention to modify it and lead everyday people toward philosophically grounded speech.[13]

Rumour ignores the question of ground altogether; it calls into question the very need for a foundation or origin for human things. It does this, paradoxically, not by levelling insight and understanding, but by exalting the lowest, the most sensational, and the most peculiar. What this fragment offers for discussion is an alternative to ground, which is always satisfied with sufficiency. It goes beyond the mere, flat sufficiency of ground, in a rhetorical *a priori* – rumour – that exceeds what is sufficient for any occasion, surpassing what is merely adequate to the production of an expected phenomenon. Grounding, as a form of transcendence and a *sine qua non* of the world and our understanding of it, one might add, may always have been based in rumour; there may have never been anything more than rumours of transcendence, and, we should note, these have often been more than enough to maintain the status quo – and they often produce the oddest aberrations, of course, as well.

A fairly rigorous theory of rumour *qua* mass communications medium is worked out in Kafka's fragment. The major questions he raises are: what is rumour, what can we hope from it; how do we avoid its obvious dangers; and what form can the logos of rumour take without suffocating its topic and ruining its effect? One answer to this last question – what form does a discussion of rumour take that does not elevate it into a kind of truth? – could well be early cinema. Cinema technologises rumour without abrogating its power. From one perspective, a negative one, the Schoolteacher fragment points out all the ways in which the breathing room for rumour can be violently taken away. One of these is the excess breath in the ceaseless exchange of opinion that is 'tweeting' (*Zwitschern*), which blows and blows and leaves nothing in its wake but a group assimilated to hot air. *Gerücht*, rumour, does not summon a subject to the law or call groups together; it brings together an uncollected group in common complaint. One of the great dangers of rumour is that it reduces distance in the empire to zero, such that king stands directly beside commoner, judge beside criminal. Anybody can accept a rumour. It thrives on distance, distance is its medium – it is an archaic tele-technology – but its effect is generally to nullify distance. Wherever rumour is, there is also the centre of everything. Rumour doesn't function well in cities. Its breathing room is also sucked away by machine-like labour, where there are no pauses or breaks. Another place it is squelched is in a scripture, a *Schrift*, that establishes the authority of the story or its bearer. Imagine how damaging it would have been to the authority of Moses if Aaron had circulated a legal brief establishing his brother's credibility as a lawgiver. The authority for the law cannot be authorised in a law. As the Schoolteacher warns, scripture takes away the groundlessness from rumour and lends it a source, a form, a place and a determinate size. A scientist tells the Schoolteacher that it is surely no surprise he saw a mammoth mole; naturally such a creature would thrive in the region's rich soil, because it is so full of nutrients. This implies an interesting modal difference. Science's objective is to prove the creature possible, based on conditions for its physical existence. In contrast, the Schoolteacher senses that rumour lives off the impossibility of its object. It is yet another sign of the Salesman's misunderstanding that he takes the side of science. The Salesman explains that in circulating a secondary and competing 'scripture' he had hoped to see the Schoolteacher's work on the giant mole become 'scientifically grounded' (Kafka 2002a: 213). He insists that 'the main issue [is] to have proven the existence of the mole' (2002a: 199) – 'completely and irrefutably' (2002a: 203). We can easily recognise in the Salesman's objective a complicated gesture that underlies both secular science and rational theology. In the latter, the existence of God is what is to be proved, in the former, what is to be proved is the nature of natural beings. In making the *sine qua non* of existence and essence 'proof', however, God and nature become dependent on the human activity of proving, which in addition to providing this awesome service to God and nature, has to be executed 'completely and irrefutably', as the salesman says.

And yet, efforts to prove this particular rumour true fail so miserably that rumour begins to grow back to its original size. Kafka holds back; he does not interrupt the process of failed justification; there is no analysis here, no winks at the reader; he lets the war of two scriptures become what it is: ludicrous. What's more, nothing of the contents of the Schoolteacher's original scripture is reproduced. The story of the mammoth mole is not repeated in the fragment. We could say that the Salesman's memoir of the failure of his supportive *Schrift* is the rich soil in which rumour gets released from the attempts to justify it by rhetoric and by proof, whereupon it returns to its enormity and *dörfisch* rampages. The Schoolteacher's resistance, the failure of the 'new testament' to salvage the old, the Salesman's lack of qualifications and authority to make statements about this sort of thing – all this buffoonery – helps restore rumour's powers. Less than credible, roundabout, even silly communications are the milieu in which rumour thrives.

Writing kills rumour in very specific ways, but cinema may rescue it. When it means to speak for it, to prove it, to turn it into knowledge, to give it a source and to name its effects instead of letting its effect happen, to erase the distance between rumour and truth in which effects surpass truth as the raison d'être of the medium – under these circumstances writing murders rumour. Films, on the other hand, seem to work more like rumours, especially in their technological dispersability. They seem able to travel anywhere, to bring the far near, and at the same time to sever any connection with the purported source. Like rumours, images are projected. Rumours, like images, are played, performed, re-performed, and are thus hard to contain with the usual means for containing stories, that is: between book covers, under literary commissions, within economic limitations, in libraries, behind the fiction of expertise, and so forth.

The fragment itself gives *Gerücht* an image – and another name that emphasises, instead of its alethic character, its hyperbolic tendency, refusal of social limits and potential for dissemination. The story fragment presents a reevaluation of a failed 'scripture' in support of a forgotten account of a rumour about the hyperbolic name and bloated shape of rumour, as perceived through attempts to negate its monstrosity, autonomy, speed and appetite. The giant mole is a rumour, and rumour, we also feel, is a giant mole.[14] Rumour is often described with animal metaphors: rumours fly, run, breed, are swift and insatiable (see Kapferer 1990: x). Furthermore, the fragment alludes to, without proving its existence, an archaic political order that worships this beast, rumour, and welcomes its frightening political potential. The mole cult would be like a proto-cinema cult – it would have to move around, be satisfied with fleeting glimpses, and view from a distance, without being able to engage in the action. The open philological secret of its name, *Maulwurf*, combines a savage ventriloquism with a wide disseminative scope. The mole is in effect a giant moving loudspeaker, a mouth that throws itself ever elsewhere – *werfen*, to throw; *Maul*, an animal mouth – speaking always in another place and from another position, and where its mouth lands it tears up the ground. Its image-language is the only ground, albeit a disturbed, provisional one. Who would want to be a spectator at this spectacle? The giant mole draws a special class, day workers, distant and local, toward the fringes of the village.

III. MOLE MIRACLE

Early in 1914 Kafka went to hear a public lecture, as was his wont – he went to hear a doctor speaking about pilgrims to a holy site in Lourdes, France, where, in 1858, a 14-year-old girl had been visited by a woman calling herself 'the immaculate conception'. By Kafka's day, the site had become one of the premier European spots for spiritual cures. Kafka notes in his diary at the end of January how French newspaper boys still sold papers by means of reports on the shrine: 'Superbe guérison de ce soir. Guérison affirmée!' ('Excellent healing tonight. Healing confirmed!') (2002c: 630). At the lecture, the doctor ranted about the flocks at the shrine for healing: 'It is time that German thoroughness and probity stand up to Latin charlatanism' (ibid.). But when Kafka reflects on Lourdes and the doctor's assessment a few days later, there is something about both German honesty and Latin charlatanism that stops him. He notes: 'Karlsbad,' a famous German spot for cures, 'is a bigger fraud than Lourdes and Lourdes has the advantage that one travels there on account of one's innermost belief.' Medicine is the worse belief, because it offers only 'pigheaded opinions with regard to operations, serum cures, vaccinations, drugs' (2002c: 632).

Kafka shows an interest here in beliefs, the obvious charlatanism of whose object is neither concealed nor naturalised by general opinion or by experts. The Lourdes miracle is a (still current) example of 'immaculate conception', which is a description of the kind of effect Kafka favours for rumours, an effect that contrasts with the dirty trickery of medicine, masquerading as truth. Rumours, in contrast to opinions, have Lourdes-like structures: they are miraculous births, fatherless children, and yet still conduits for the highest powers. More importantly, they are to be judged, as Kafka tries to do here, by their effects, not on their truth. If we allow ourselves to imagine an afterimage of Lourdes, with its messengers streaming to Paris, newspaper reports and incredulous doctors, we can see perhaps what happens when the holy mother is replaced by a mammoth mole. Its site is a shrine, its effects political rather than spiritual, what occurs there is something less sentimental than a religious revival and something much more radical than a trick of science. Indeed, the holy mole digs around in the soil of miracles; its fakery is transparent and its effects are for this reason all the stronger.

Who is attracted to it, who makes the pilgrimage to the mole's holy site and why? The Salesman's memoir points out the mole's belief in the opening lines:

> Those, and I am one of them, who find even a small ordinary-sized mole disgusting, would probably have died of aversion if they had seen the giant mole that a few years back was observed in the vicinity of a small village, and which because of this achieved some passing fame. (2002a: 194)

The phrase already has the tone and syntax of a rumour: 'if they had seen...', and this confirms the point. The movements of the mammoth *Maulwurf* report on, echo, conjure up the shape and movements of rumour. In contrast to the absolutism of Kierkegaard's 'faith' by virtue of 'the absurd', Kafka seeks a truly weak, intermittent and unappealing disposition, which does not take away the power of surprise with anything so certain and so steady as faith; the less the attraction, the more groundless the phenomenon appears, and the more widespread its effects can become. This is rumour's unholy ratio, and it is also why the affective relation to the mole is so important in the story. The narrator, being a Salesman, is not qualified to make scientific statements, but he can report on his feelings. The mole causes aversion. If rumour itself were seen, the sight of its hideous, misshapen hulk would provoke an aversion that almost no one could survive. Rumour does not attract; it repels. Yet there are those who are attracted by repulsion. They are those who already live in the medium of repulsion. The

Salesman calls them 'simple people, people whose habitual day's work hardly affords them a calm moment to exhale' (2002a: 194; my translation). Time to breathe, it seems, is what rumour affords, when it interrupts the breathless work of industrial labour and the ceaseless one upon another of days. Day labourers, those contractless workers whose next day's job is not guaranteed, abandon their mechanistic movements and obsessive time-keeping and struggle towards the 'vicinity' of the non-descript village. They come not only from nearby but also 'from far away, even from out of the country' (2002a: 194). A form of 'international' is clearly at issue here, though it is far from Communism that is implied, more like a loose mob of *Lumpen*.

Bigger than it should be, indeed bigger than it can be – hyperbolic, casting itself beyond its home turf, its true home, its land – at work not a geographically locatable place but merely in a 'vicinity', the mole meets the placeless in their exile. Excessive, but for that no less nimble, it consumes everything in its path and throws its mouth across great distances. Whatever is said about it the mole-rumour incorporates into itself. No account of it is safe from its voracious appetite; the mole absorbs all. The existence and operation of this beast can hardly be a fact; yet it goes on, it must keep moving, keep leaving its territory behind. The mole's medium is the ground, which it breaks up, and makes uncultivatable and precarious to stand on. The *Riesenmaulwurf* is *widerlich* in this way: the more strongly you reject it, the more likely it is to come up directly under your feet.

IV. *DIE UNANSTÄNDIGEN* – A COLLECTION OF YOKELS

Let us turn briefly to the original *Schrift* written by the Village Schoolteacher. It is not given, not even quoted, in the fragment – and so, true to the medium, readers have to operate almost totally on hearsay. The title of the Schoolteacher's original document, however, is quoted once by the salesman: 'A Mole, Bigger Than Anyone Has Ever Seen' (2002a: 199; my translation). No one has seen a mole of this size, and the title implies in its syntax that even with the Schoolteacher's scripture, no one will have seen it. Rumours of course don't have titles. The title, at the very least, is true, since it is not possible to capture the impossible in a pedagogical text. The first attempt to document the rumour had all the earmarks of a first testament, a revelation of something unheard of. It presented itself, hyperbolically, as the record of a *theriophany*, recorded by someone without training in classification or measurement, an 'anyone', in other words, whose specialty had been passing on other people's stories to begin with: the Schoolteacher. And this makes sense: if rumour is a god, as some in antiquity maintained, it is a god of whom no one should have direct experience, and as nobody, this one god can approach anybody, even non-believers.[15] Whoever catches rumour, whoever is caught by it, becomes its mouthpiece. To a certain extent the Village Schoolteacher betrays the rumour by writing about it, but at the same time, insofar as his scripture does not assimilate it to a higher or more coherent system, it preserves its hyperbolic character and contagious communicability. Natural science, according to the Salesman, does the opposite. 'Every discovery is immediately led into the totality of the sciences and with that it effectively stops being a discovery, it is absorbed into the whole and disappears, and one has to already have a glance schooled in science in order subsequently to recognize it' (2002a: 214). In the one-room schoolhouse in the village that has educated generations without reforming its methods or updating its textbooks, there is no whole, no standard. Everything there is sensational. With its capacity to remain sensational, thwart expectations, and exceed what is, rumour, unlike a scientific fact, maintains its phenomenality at all costs. A rumour has to survive and produce effects; a scientific fact has to be confirmable, but then it is free to disappear.

For the task of receiving rumour's effects, day labourers are more qualified than scientists. They journey to where the *Riesenmaulwurf* appears and give it its due. Perhaps this is because the mole is also an ad-hoc subsistence worker who labours without stopping, while hungering continually for its next meal. The creature is the ideal worker, constantly at its labours, its primary tool its mouth, in whose gape production and consumption are indistinguishable. It is pastoral, works the land, but it does so already so industriously that it is an industry unto itself; it has become a machine, and the machinic upgrade of rumour is going to be the cinema. Furthermore, the mole makes the perfect capitalist subject, whose work is consummately productive and yet what it produces never satisfies its own abyssal hunger. It is the ideal producer whose need for consumption increases in exact proportion to its production. In the city-dwelling Salesman's almost offhand remark about the main affect evoked by the creature – *Widerwille*, repugnance, aversion – there lies another rumourological principle. Those who accept it, those who are attracted to it, those who are comfortable with its semblance of unbelievability, decide for repulsion. They are drawn toward what repels and drives apart. 'Labourers of the world disunite!' may be the motto of this fragment, and the slogan of the Kafkan international. Here Kafka may be identifying a kind of economic and political warfare that is not the struggle of one class against another. Kafka seems to strengthen a tendency against revolution here; this rumour produces the antithesis of the Great Fear, which brings about a movement towards ultimate political unity behind a just cause.[16] It is certainly the antithesis of idle talk, that other mode which produces the *Aneignung*, assimilation, of the proletariat to itself. At a minimum, rumour communicates without making a group similar intellectually and without requiring full assent by anyone. Moreover, it 'convinces' without experts and so there is no intellectual hierarchy, no special knowledge that will bring about the good. It speaks with many voices, gives the naked image to the imagination, travels the nation and among nations, and is effective only so long as it addresses the most pressing concerns of those left out of rational public discourse. It draws the most distant figures close, though not into the centre of the village, only outward toward its fringes, and as such its grouping principle is more like diasporics than politics. The narrator emphasises that the scope of rumour extends beyond the nation, with an ideal less cosmopolitan than chaopolitan. Later in the fragment, when the salesman has convinced himself that he must recall all the copies of his failed new testament, the Schoolteacher teaches him a lesson about the people for whom rumour is the single principle. Their so-called simplicity consists in a refusal to assent or to assimilate to the most basic social conventions. They are unable to be, as he says, 'decent', and so they get no credit in a cosmopolitan milieu. They have 'no connections', 'keine Verbindungen', with their fellows. About the rumour, the Schoolteacher says: 'if a shabby farmer [*ein lumpiger Bauer*; a yokel] believes us and speaks out, that can't help us at all, since what a farmer does is always indecent, whether he says "the old village Schoolteacher is right" or in a somehow unsuitable way spits, both are the same in their effect' (2002a: 209). To the analethic mode of rumour there corresponds a not completely trustworthy, though also not completely mendacious political configuration: a gathering of the *Lumpen*. *Unanständig* is perhaps better translated in the context of our argument as 'not upstanding', which is not to say rebellious, just not prone to uphold habit, custom, opinion and law, when no one is around to look.[17] These blackguards are the heroes of Kafka's theo-political rehabilitation of rumour; they straggle out to the vicinity of the town to witness a phenomenon that neither they nor anyone else can accept, over which they have no influence, and whether they assent or dissent is essentially the same. Here is a truly impassive collective, and the more it grows the more impassive it becomes. The teacher concludes: 'and if instead of one farmer ten thousand stand up, the effect is still worse, if that is possible' (2002a: 209).

Although they might look to us like disadvantages, the advantages of this archaic mass medium are clear to Kafka. Rumour is good because of its analethic power; it produces effects that do not arise from states of affairs but rather are epiphenomena of a report whose truth or falsity is irrelevant to its effects. And, as a consequence, rumour gathers the *Lumpen*, those excluded from the regimes of knowledge, scientific and technical, and excluded also from the worker revolution, because they are unable to achieve class-consciousness. 'The whole indefinite disintegrated mass, thrown hither and thither', Marx calls them

(1963: 75). Let us hypothesise then that were Kafka to have written on cinema, it would have been because films also refuse questions about the sources for their images. When they are events, and they bring a bit of that indeterminate fringe of a country village into the centre of a city, they exhibit their political potential.[18] Like the Nature Theatre of Oklahoma, everyone is welcome in Kafka's cinema; this means, as it does in the novel *Der Verschollene* (which can be rendered as: 'The One Who Disappeared'),[19] that unlike other institutions in that ideal of democratic institutions that is 'Amerika', social status does not affect the welcome. Everyone is welcome means precisely that those who are not welcome elsewhere, such as the lump Karl Rossmann, fugitive European son of a dictatorial father, are invited.

Kafka thinks of modern things, politics, morals, beings and literary genres, in terms of archaic doubles. This may be what explains his love for tales and parables. It is no doubt what explains his fascination with the ambiguities of the law. What is archaic is ambiguous about its origins and its purposes, for two reasons. First of all, anything that old is so close to 'origins' as to be indistinguishable from them. The archaic either is its own origin or else it itself has no origin. The truly archaic is always incipient. That is to say that archaic things are beautifully exempt from speculation about grounds, influences, analogies, and so forth. Secondly, we are not talking about the archaic in some pristine historical setting. Battles of our oldest history are fought only now – their temporal character is 'now': the archaic enters the present and becomes there so ambiguous as to be useful politically. That is why the *Lumpen*, like Kafka's nomads – such as jackals, or the infamous 'northern tribes' in the Wall story – have such political potency. And so we could ask, has cinema born out the promise of its archaic double, the mass communication modality rumour? Did the giant mole, when it ate its way into urban centres and threw up its dark chambers, remain true to its early earth-shaking powers? On the model of rumour, a Kafkan cinema would happen when a plurality of those who cannot be collected into a group, the wretched and classless, straggles in, attracted to what has as of yet no cultural standing, without condensing into a recognisable political unit, in order to assent to an unheard of image, authoritatively, all together, at once, for a short time, out of nowhere and with no proof, to affirm or deny it, without the authority to do so.

NOTES

1   Hanns Zischler calls the mentions of the cinema in Kafka's non-fictional writings 'very scattered, occasionally curt and cryptic' (2003: 3). He also notes that express mentions of films cease almost completely at the end of 1913. Both Zischler's book,

and the later book by Peter-André Alt, *Kafka und der Film: Über kinematographisches Erzählen* (2009), share a method. They either reconstruct Kafka's personal attraction to film or make analogies between cinematic techniques and his fiction writing. The evidence for the personal attraction is drawn from letters, diary entries, and contemporary evidence about cinema in Prague and elsewhere. Evidence for the analogy between movie techniques and Kafka's writing techniques is drawn from his fictions, we could say, although the logic is rather circular. Alt promises to make 'the inner logic of [Kafka's] stories understandable through their filmic organization' (2009: 11; my translation). And yet only once you have understood the stories can they be shown to be 'filmic'. Whereas, if you approach them armed with structures from film, you will never know whether you have understood them. By filmic organisation Alt intends a mode of 'cinematographic seeing' (2009: 31; my translation) that cuts across Kafka's fictional production. This kind of seeing has three major components in Kafka's style: a succession of images, shifts in perspective that mimic a camera (angle of view, close up or wide view, a view that itself moves), and an external perspective different from that of psychology (these are the most salient out of the expanded list of eight 'indicators for Kafka's cinematographic writing' listed on pages 191–2).

2 The fragment is published in German in *Franz Kafka, Nachgelassene Schriften und Fragmente, I* (Frankfurt am Main: Fischer, 2002a). The English translation used here is by Willa and Edwin Muir (*Complete Stories*, 1971), who translated the fragment's title as 'The Village Schoolmaster'.

3 For a view of cinema as a mode of 'vision' in a broad phenomenological and semiological, not merely perceptual, sense of the word, see Casetti 2008. This book deals mainly with the developments in narrative film from the 1920s onward. Casetti sees film as the characteristic mode of self-understanding of its century; film is the 'gaze of its age,' as the title of Chapter One tells us.

4 To wit, the diary entries on 'small literature' written between 25 and 28 December 1911; see *Diaries, I* (1965: 191–5), *Tagebücher* (2002c: 312–26).

5 See Zischler 2003: 27–31; Alt 2009: 16, 145–6.

6 The so-called Great Fear, a peasant uprising started by rumours and motivated above all by famine, took place between 20 July and 6 August 1789.

7 Virgil paints the most vivid picture of rumour as what thrives only when moving. 'No other evil is swifter than she. Rumour's being is fuelled / By her mobility, gaining additional strength as she travels' (see Ahl 2007: 82).

8 The worry that the first communication of a law arrives as a rumour has surfaced before. A notable early occurrence of this worry is in Plato's Laws, about the rumour that precedes and contaminates the law; see Plato (1926: 952b7, 966c5).

9 'Exegese der Legende' (Kafka 2002c: 707).

10 It is not surprising that a marketing expert should understand rumour better than sociologists. According to Kapferer, they always arrive when it is too late (1990: 1–2).

His book also makes a strong case against the psychological studies of Gordon W. Allport and Leo Postman, who in their influential book (1947) consider rumour a type of degraded, unverified information. Kapferer notes the dangerous implication of this type of rumour research, that rumour always leads to error. Rather than to substitute for knowledge, a rumour exists in order to 'posit a reality' (1990: 3). Because it is important to capitalism that consumers 'take control', though only of consumption, the political element in rumour is rightly identified by Kapferer as a relationship to authority, a check on power by the people, who pass around information in the absence of an official version and thereby seize power (1990: 14). These 'spontaneous social productions' mobilise a whole group's attention suddenly (1990: 24), and always concerning events that can lead to 'sudden, important changes' (1990: 42). The measure of a rumour is not its truth but its capacity to produce a reaction (1990: 43).

11 Oskar Baum, a friend Kafka greatly admired, wrote a novel in 1913 about rumours in a small Bohemian town that lead to the downfall of an innocent figure: *Die böse Unschuld: ein jüdischer Kleinstadroman* (1913).

12 Georges Lefebvre, in *The Great Fear of 1789: Rural Panic in Revolutionary France*, debunks two myths about the event. First, it was not started by conspiracy, as was thought at the time; and second it did not start all at once, as was commonly thought by historians. Rumour started it, and given the uneven way rumour spreads, combined with its tendency to reinforce itself as events unfold, it began in several places at once (1973: 141). On the character of the rumour mongers, Lefebvre quotes the Duc de Gesvres: 'These rumors, so far as we can make out, were based on nothing more serious than a conversation between five or six strangers who were slightly drunk and who settled down for a rest near the corn they were supposed to have threatened to cut down, the farmer having refused to pay them what they wanted' (1973: 145).

13 See Heidegger on Rede and Gerede (1967: §34 and §35).

14 The allegorical mole has many antecedents in philosophy; the closest and most interesting with regard to political issues is Marx's mole that describes the speed and the concealment of sudden political change: 'we do recognize our brave friend, Robin Goodfellow, the old mole that can work in the earth so fast, that worthy pioneer – the Revolution' (Marx 2003: 656). For an opinion strangely in tune with Marx's, although judged in the opposite way – that is, negatively – see Harsin 2006. He argues that the media have become purveyors of rumour to the same extent that the government has become secretive, withholding information rather than disseminating it. Rumour, in Harsin's view, is detrimental to deliberative democracy. That is to say, he imagines a public sphere, once governments stop keeping secrets, that would have no need for rumour's particular powers.

15 Hesiod has it thus: 'Rumour is a dangerous thing, light and easy to pick up, but hard to support and difficult to get rid of. No rumour ever dies that many folk rumour. She too is somehow a goddess' (1988: 59). Rumour is somehow a god, yet not in the

way other gods are gods. The lightness and stickiness of rumour – easy to acquire, hard to get rid of – undoubtedly makes it a kind of model for a religion based on the attitude of faith. The two are epistemically similar. You have faith when you have heard about the object of faith but have never seen it. As Jesus says to Thomas in John: 'Blessed are those who have not seen and yet have come to believe' (20:29).

16 Lefebvre shows, however, that the situations that get started by rumour, as opposed to other forces – ideology, planning, revolt, etc – are much more fractious and even deleterious to the revolution itself. In the case of the Great Fear, the peasant uprisings threatened to interrupt the bourgeois revolution then underway; see Chapter 5 'The Peasant Revolts' (1973: 100–21).

17 Lefebvre: 'Most often the panic was spread by people with no official status of any kind' (1973: 148).

18 This potential may have returned to cinema through the new forms into which it has 'relocated', to use Francesco Casetti's term. Screens can now show up anywhere, and access to cinema has expanded well beyond even the yokel. Casetti shows how the dispersal of the theatre into screens increases the contingency and at the same time the transformative potential of cinematic experience. It may be that the temporal character of early cinema, incipience, is now the temporal character of screen culture per se; that is, it is fragile, sudden and fleeting (2015: 144); see especially the chapter on 'Hypertopia' (2015: 129–54).

19 The novel's title has been translated in different ways, most recently as *Amerika: The Missing Person* (Mark Harman).

BIBLIOGRAPHY

Ahl, Frederick (2007) *Virgil: Aeneid*, trans. Frederick Ahl. Oxford: Oxford University Press.

Allport, Gordon W. and Leo Postman (1947) *The Psychology of Rumor*. New York: Henry Holt.

Alt, Peter-André (2009) *Kafka und der Film. Über kinematographisches Erzählen*. Munich: Verlag C.H. Beck.

Baum, Oscar (1913) *Die böse Unschuld: ein jüdischer Kleinstadroman*. Frankfurt am Main: Rütten & Loening.

Benjamin, Walter (1968) 'Franz Kafka: On the Tenth Anniversary of his Death', *Illuminations*, trans. Harry Zohn. New York: Schocken.

Casetti, Francesco (2008) *Eye of the Century: Film, Experience, Modernity*. New York: Columbia University Press.

____ (2015) *The Lumière Galaxy: 7 Key Words for the Cinema to Come*. New York: Columbia University Press.

Gunning, Tom (1986) 'The Cinema of Attractions: Early Film, Its Spectator and the Avant-Garde', *Wide Angle*, 8, 3/4, 63–70.

Harsin, Jayson (2006) 'The Rumor Bomb: Theorising [sic] the Convergence of New and Old Trends in Mediated US Politics,' *Southern Review: Communication, Politics & Culture*, 39, 1, 84–110.

Heidegger, Martin (1967 [1927]) *Sein und Zeit*. Tübingen: Niemeyer.

Hesiod (1988) *Theogony and Works and Days*, trans. M. L. West. Oxford: Oxford University Press.

Joubert, Joseph (2005) *The Notebooks of Joseph Joubert*, trans. Paul Auster. New York: New York Review of Books.

Kafka, Franz (1915) 'Vor dem Gesetz', *Selbstwehr. Unabhängige jüdische Wochen-schrift*, ed. Siegmund Kaznelson, 9, 34, 2–3.

____ (1965) *Diaries, vols I and II*, ed. Max Brod. New York: Schocken.

____ (1971) 'The Village Schoolmaster,' *The Complete Stories* trans. Willa and Edwin Muir, ed. Nahum Glatzer. New York: Schocken, 168–82.

____ (2002a) *Nachgelassene Schriften und Fragmente I*, ed. Hans-Gerd Koch. Frankfurt am Main: Fischer.

____ (2002b) *Nachgelassene Schriften und Fragmente II*, ed. Hans-Gerd Koch. Frankfurt am Main: Fischer.

____ (2002c) *Tagebücher*, ed. Hans-Gerd Koch, Michael Müller and Malcolm Pasley. Frankfurt am Main: Fischer.

____ (2008 [1927]) *Amerika: The Missing Person*, trans. Mark Harman. New York: Schocken.

____ (2009a [1925]) *The Trial*, trans. Mike Mitchell. Oxford: Oxford University Press.

____ (2009b [1926]) *The Castle*, trans. Anthea Bell. Oxford: Oxford University Press.

Kapferer, Jean Noel (1990) *Rumors: Uses, Interpretations, and Images*. New Brunswick, NJ: Transaction.

Lefebvre, Georges (1973) *The Great Fear of 1789: Rural Panic in Revolutionary France*, trans. Joan White. New York: Pantheon Books.

Marx, Karl (1963) *The Eighteenth Brumaire of Louis Bonaparte*. New York: International Publishers.

____ (2003) 'Speech at the Anniversary of the People's Paper, 1856,' *Collected Works of Marx and Engels, Vol. 14*. Charlottesville, VA: InteLex Corporation; available at: http://pm.nlx.com/xtf/view?docId=marx/marx.14.xml;query=robin%20good fellow;brand=default;hit.rank=1#rank1 (accessed 25 June 2015).

Maronis, P. Vergili (1969) *Opera*, ed. R. A. B. Mynors. Oxford: Oxford University Press.

Plato (1926) *Plato: Laws*, trans. R. G. Bury. London: Heinemann.

Zischler, Hanns (2003) *Kafka Goes to the Movies*, trans. Susan H. Gillespie. Chicago: University of Chicago Press.

SEBALD GOES TO THE MOVIES: READING KAFKA AS CINEMATOGRAPHY

NIMROD MATAN

I. THE WITHDRAWAL OF THE IMAGE

The fourth and last miniature chapter of W. G. Sebald's unfinished novel about Corsica[1] opens with a description of a crisis, a genuine writer's block:

> After this picture[2] was sent to me last December, with a friendly request for me to think of something appropriate to say about it, it lay down on my desk for some weeks, and the longer it lay there and the more often I looked at it the further it seems to withdraw from me, until the task, in itself nothing worth mentioning, became an insuperable obstacle looming ahead. (2006a: 49)

The block appears quite literally in the form of a locked, impenetrable gate, or rather, as an *image* of one, whose opening becomes analogous to the prospect of overcoming the block. The image seems 'to withdraw' that is, to *move* away, and the writing task at hand 'became an insuperable obstacle'. But the block was eventually overcome: the text Sebald had been commissioned to write was completed and the gate was opened:

> Then one day, at the end of January, not a little to my relief, the picture suddenly disappeared from the place where it lay, and no one knew where it had gone. When some time had passed and I had almost entirely forgotten it, it unexpectedly returned, this time in a letter from Bonifacio, in which Mme Seraphine Aquaviva, with whom I had been corresponding since the summer before, told me that she would be interested to know how I had come by the

drawing enclosed without comment in my letter of 27 January, showing the yard of the old school in Porto Vecchio, which she had attended in the thirties. (2006a: 49–50)

The sort of writing that becomes possible on the other side of the closed gate is uniquely remote from any common conception of writing as expression, representation or communication. Before analysing the notion of writing that is achieved here and the method by which it is enabled, let me stress an important characteristic of the initial writing task, as conceived by Sebald here and elsewhere – the task whose completion is celebrated in this short text. Writing is conceived as paradigmatically attached to an image, related and responding to it. The question, 'how can one write?' therefore appears equivalent to the question, 'how can an image become meaningful?' This is the first and as yet undeveloped moment of what I take to be Sebald's cinematographic conception of writing, of which Kafka, in Sebald's eyes, I claim, is a model.

Overcoming the writer's block therefore involves re-conceptualisation not only of writing but also of imagery or imagination. It entails a new set of conditions for meaningfulness of images, whereby their setting-in-motion enables them to become meaningful. Resolving the twofold problem that triggered Sebald's text – how one can write, and how an image can become meaningful – may be said to involve a shift or a movement in three dimensions: (i) a shift in *time*, as what was eventually written about the gate image was a report of a childhood memory; (ii) a shift in *space*, as the school's gate story was about another, remote place; and (iii) a shift in *agency*, as the person whose writing experience recollection seals the text is someone else – other than the text's author. It is this description of a writing experience, that of Seraphine Aquaviva as a child in Corsica, in a classroom behind the school gate depicted in the image – that is ultimately the bearer of success in relation to the task at hand: '[W]henever our teacher … bent over my work he would say: *"Ce que tu écris mal, Séraphine! Comment veux-tu qu'on puisse te lire?"* ["How badly you write, Seraphine! How do you expect anyone to read that?"]' (2006a: 50–1).

Seen as a method to enable an image to become meaningful, this triple shift is initiated by the image's migration (i.e. movement) from its initial location: from Sebald's desk to Seraphine's, and back to Sebald's – from a blocked writer to another writer and back – and it is this movement that enables Sebald to become a successful writer. The image's physical shifting of positions serves as a medium enabling the metaphysical shift into the three above-mentioned dimensions. This enabling movement, I argue, is a primitive configuration of a moving-image. Its direct effect is a metaphysical shift of time, space and agency, which in turn creates the conditions for the image to become meaningful. Since this movement is a paradigm for writing, it can be seen as an embryonic definition of the cinematographic medium: writing through the setting-in-motion of images so as to enable their becoming meaningful. Note, though, that in the process, the gate remains, as it were, idle. What is set in motion is the *image* rather than what is seen in it. The three constituents of the circumstances of writing (time, space, agency) in fact constitute the surrounding world to which the image belongs. Its movement *in* the world (as represented by Sebald through the metaphor of correspondence – an almost literal form of exchanging meaning) generates a movement *of* the world: time elapses, locations change and agents switch the roles of writer and reader.

The Corsican teacher regards the writing enabled through this process as bad; so much so, in fact, that one cannot expect others to be able to read it. He must be referring to Seraphine's *hand*writing, but considered metaphysically his words can be seen as hinting at a new type of reading that writing (setting images in motion) calls for. Examining this value judgement closely reveals, first, that the truth conditions for the teacher's evaluation are set in the future, relative to the time of the writing and the evaluation itself. It is only when others are given the opportunity to read Seraphine's writing that the teacher's evaluation *will* be confirmed. Second, the writing's value (its 'badness') will not be met with disapproval, but rather will ensure that it will *not be read at all*. Its reading will be *blocked*, so to speak. In saying that Seraphine's writing is illegible rather than, say, contemptible, the teacher can be taken to mean – metaphysically – that what Seraphine writes is in fact not a text. Rather, it is a product of a new form of writing that has its own meaningfulness criteria – an instance of a new medium, a new art form, designed for activity that is essentially different from reading. In a word: cinema.

The immediate temptation is to conclude that since writing-as-cinematography is ill fit for reading, it is instead apt for viewing. This conclusion may be supported by the visual nature of Sebald's writing – which always integrates images – as well as the fact that the teacher bases his evaluation on a *view* of the (hand)writing rather than on a reading designed to elicit its meaning. However, I argue that the corresponding practice of the reader/viewer is not limited to an epistemological act but should also involve a shift – in addition to that of the moving image. It is a (non-mental, non-representational) act of *moving towards the image* that is characteristic of the reading of cinematographic writing, echoing Giorgio Agamben's maxim: 'man is a movie-going animal' (2002a: 313).[3] The image's movement – represented in the gate story by the image's withdrawal and then its misplacement in the letter sent to Seraphine – enables the reader's movement towards it, or the movement of the world surrounding it.

II. MOVING TOWARDS THE IMAGE

The foregoing analysis of the teacher's evaluation brings us closer to the understanding that Sebald identifies this new art form with Franz Kafka. Kafka's writings emerged into culture under impossible conditions of readability. The reader's encounter with them involves a halt akin to that experienced by writers – a *reader's block*. This *a priori* quality of Kafka's writings is first and foremost a result of their publication conditions, as they have been published in direct violation of the author's testament: 'Dearest Max, my last request: Everything I leave behind me … to be burned unread' (Brod 1969: 265).

Reading Kafka must then be conceived of metaphysically as reading that which *must not* be read; and to follow the imagery of burning to ashes, the attempt to read Kafka can moreover be seen, at least in the late writer's eyes, as reading that which *cannot* be read. The fragmentary nature of much of Kafka's corpus and the fact that none of his three novels was completed further reinforce these *a priori* conditions: the conditions dictated by his writings constitute an inherent obstacle, rendering any attempt at their reading an attempt to accomplish the impossible.

The solution to Sebald's writer's block – which as we have seen is akin to answering the question, 'how can an image become meaningful?' – thus corresponds further to the question, 'how can the unreadable be read?' How can writing, so bad that no-one can be expected to read it, become meaningful, if not by reading?

There are other hints in Sebald's writing suggesting that he associates Kafka with 'bad writing' of the kind that calls upon the reader to move towards an already moving image. One such hint may be found towards the end of Sebald's 'Kafka Goes to the Movies', a review of Hanns Zischler's book bearing the same title. The question of the image's possibility to become meaningful appears here in the course of Sebald's reflections on a scene from Leni Riefenstahl's *Triumph des Willens* (*Triumph of the Will*, 1935) which shows a view of a 'city of tents':

> There they are, stretching as far as the eye can see […]. At first, because of the unusual perspective, you do not see exactly what they are. Day is just dawning, and gradually, in the still twilit landscape, people come out of the tents alone or in twos and threes, all going the same way as if they had been called by name … a magical picture of those white tents lingers in mind. A people travelling through the desert. The Promised Land appears on the horizon. They will reach it together. (2006b: 172)

The image of the tent camp is meaningless in itself. It may be taken to depict either German youth in training or the people of Israel on their journey to the Promised Land: that is, it has the capacity for having two opposite meanings. Or to put it more accurately, the meaning of this already-*moving* image is undetermined as long as another movement has not yet been initiated: that of the reader/viewer towards it. Note that this indeterminacy is not due to lack of context, i.e. Sebald does not claim here that the image's meaning can be determined only by positioning it in a historical (or other) context. The movement of the reader/viewer towards the image that I take to be necessary to determine its meaning does not necessarily consist of an act of contextualisation. Moreover, the nature of the opposition between these two alternative meanings is not that of contradictory alternatives but rather of two opposed directions in which the image can, so to speak, travel. Its meaning's indeterminacy signifies its potential for *motion* in different directions.

To grasp the nature of this movement, the introduction of the tent camp image into Sebald's essay should be examined closely. The image enters the essay through an awkward textual gesture. First, after describing Kafka's visit to a Prague cinema to watch the Zionist documentary *Shivat Zion* (*Return to Zion*, 1920) on 23 October 1921 – of which Kafka writes succinctly in a diary note: 'Afternoon, Palestine film' (2006b: 168) – Sebald adds that Kafka 'did not go to the cinema very often afterwards' (2006b: 171), and comments: 'At least he was spared *Triumph of the Will*, though we may wonder what he would have thought if he had been obliged to watch all that marching' (ibid.). Next, he lists three films screened in Verona on 20 September 1913, when Kafka is reported by Zischler to have cried during a film, in what seems like an attempt to guess which film he had viewed, and then picks – with no apparent justification – one of the films on the list, in a gesture almost equivalent to a random zooming-in, only to conclude: '*La lezione dell'abisso* [*The Lesson of the Abyss*] was the precursor of the heroic Alpine genre in which Riefenstahl made her name two decades later. In 1935 Riefenstahl ... was shooting a film high among the snow-white, cloud-capped mountains of Bavaria' (ibid.).

This textual gesture does not comply with scholarly conventions: it is indifferent to criteria such as relevance or coherence. Kafka did not and could not have watched the 1935 film, which is only brought into the text and analysed under the pretext that Kafka did not live long enough to watch it. The connection between the two films – the one which Kafka may have watched in Verona and the one he did not live long enough to watch – is presented as that between a precursor and its successor. Analysing the future moment rather than the actual moment in Kafka's life can therefore be justified only in that by doing so Sebald is applying a distinct method for reading Kafka, and in particular his three-word diary entry: 'Afternoon, Palestine film.' Sebald refers to his methodological choice as follows: 'Let me be allowed one more discursion' (ibid.), that is, a movement, or a shift remarkably similar to the one identified above as the key enabler of meaningfulness of the Corsican gate image, and of the writing experience enabled in turn by its becoming meaningful: a shift in *time* from 1913 to 1921, to Kafka's posthumous future, in *place* from Prague/Verona to Bavaria, and in *agency* from Kafka to Sebald.

The writing act consisted in the surprising introduction of a seemingly irrelevant image – that of the 1935 tent camp – into an analysis of Kafka's relation to cinema as manifested in his reports of movie-going experiences in 1913 and 1921 is also an act of reading. Sebald reads Kafka's 1921 diary entry, 'Afternoon, Palestine film', by bringing in the 1935 image. To 'bring in' an image is to write. To do that in response to Kafka's otherwise not yet meaningful 1921 note is to move towards it – from the future, so to speak. Sebald takes the position of first a reader (of Kafka), then a viewer (of Riefenstahl) and then a writer – a correspondent, like Seraphine, whose successful writing experience brings the movement of the images at stake to a halt: both the tent camp image and the one depicted by Kafka's 1921 diary note, which is written, in fact, in a style resembling a scriptwriting convention (time, location). Moving towards the (moving) image, or going to the movies – in Agamben's terms – is thus a mode of reading: a response to an image by way of bringing oneself towards it – an event that occurs in what at the time of writing is the future, and in the domain of the reader's, rather than the writer's, biography.[4]

The meaning of images *per se* is undetermined. It is only through their setting in motion – which in turn entails the motion of their viewer – that the possibility of their becoming meaningful is established. The setting in motion of the image is therefore a method of writing. The response to the request that images make of us to move towards them is consequently a method of reading. Images, thus, have the capacity to reveal the urgency of this writing method's implementation because they manifest the metaphysical structure of meaningfulness as such: meaningfulness is bestowed through the interplay of writing and reading, through movement or – in short – through and *in* life. This can be seen as Sebald's metaphysical motive for insisting on including images in his writing and, more importantly, to write *in relation* to images such as the Corsican gate, or to use them as triggers for writing. Images reveal the impossibility of separating meaningfulness from life. Translating this insight into a writing method means realising that writing which is not also biography is impossible. Cinematography and biography seem now to be aspects of the same writing method: the former emphasises the first movement, that of the image as initiated by the writer, while the latter stresses the second, that of the reader towards the image. This means that to set an image in motion as a writer is to be ready to welcome life, to surrender to meaningfulness conditions that are entangled in life – first and foremost, the reader's.

III. SEEING ONESELF DIE

Let us return to the Corsican teacher who asked Seraphine, *'Comment veux-tu qu'on puisse te lire?',* which should, in my view, be more carefully translated as 'How do you expect anyone to read *you*?' To write means to set oneself as an object of reading as much as it means to produce a text. Meaningfulness that requires setting in motion to escape its initial indeterminacy applies also to human life, posing the biographical question, how can a person's life become meaningful? Reflecting on 'the German-Jewish symbiosis' in the pre-World War II era, Sebald writes:

> The overriding concept of those mirror-image identities is the myth of the Chosen People, to which Germans blindly subscribed at the times when their ideas of national emancipation were taking a wrong turn. Whereas Herzl may still have been trying to square the circle when he suggested that German would be the language spoken in Zion, Hitler (somewhere in his table talk, I think) came to a conclusion which he thought irrefutably justified the annihilation of the Jews: there could not be two Chosen Peoples. (2006b: 170)

The concept of a Chosen People suffers from the same indeterminacy of meaning as the image of the tent camp. In fact, the tent camp *is* an image of the Chosen People and so potentially refers to either the Germans or the Jews. The metaphysical problem of indeterminacy of meaning coincides here with the historical one materialised through the cataclysmic collision between Germans and Jews. Kafka's identity is undetermined in this same respect, and Sebald can be taken to see his premature death as a refusal to resolve this indeterminacy. Had Kafka lived through 1935 he would have had to choose – or have been made to choose – one determined meaning, one determined identity. The indeterminacy of meaning of Kafka's life cannot be resolved within the context of his own biography, but rather within that of his readers', through a shift in time, space and agency achieved by reading Kafka.

Herzl and Hitler each represent a failed attempt to determine the meaning of the Chosen People *a priori*, i.e. without applying Sebald's method. In other words, their failure lies in determining Kafka's identity through a literal rather than cinematographic reading, treating it as an idle object of contemplation without recognising that to become meaningful it must be set in motion. Herzl tried to synthetically determine its meaning by creating a hybrid, dialectical concept that would be able to contain the two meanings at the same time. Hitler's 'final solution' to the 'Jewish Problem' is read here as an attempt to annihilate one of the competing alternative meanings of the concept in question, so as to eliminate the indeterminacy altogether.

To solve the indeterminacy problem of the Chosen People in the context of reading Kafka is, therefore, to solve the indeterminacy problem of the meaning of Kafka's life. The question of how to read Kafka is thereby solved as well. Sebald directly associates the cinematographic writing and reading method I have described with Kafka's writings. Trying to explain Kafka's attraction to cinema, then in its early, 'still primitive' (Sebald 2006b: 160) evolutionary stage as an art form, Sebald invokes the fact that cinema is where 'fugitive images [are] running inexorably away like life itself', where you are allowed – as Zischler recognises – to 'see yourself die' (ibid.). The image, for Kafka, takes the position of that which one does not live to see. The image of one's own death is the paradigmatic case. Cinema's moving images offer a direct invitation to exercise the particular method of writing and reading described here. Craving the sight of one's own death means for a writer to acknowledge that he cannot live to see what he is called to write about, that he will not live long enough to fulfil his duties and complete his writing task. The literary form that best expresses this position is the unfinished text whose author did not live long enough to complete. This mode of writing is paralleled by a mode of reading that constitutes a completion of the incomplete text: a reading that moves towards the incomplete, still-undetermined-in-meaning text (or image, or concept, or life), brings its movement to a halt and determines its meaning, at a time that by definition is the future relatively to the writing.[5]

To this conception of writing (and reading) one could oppose a conception that would treat the text as a complete entity capable of providing its own meaningfulness conditions *a priori*. The reader is then left in the position of a receiver, or even consumer, while the writer becomes a professional capable of delivering meaning to his passive, idle audience. A striking example of such a fallacious idea of writing can be found in Kafka's *The Castle* (1926). K. arrives at the village at the foot of the castle with the illusionary conception that writing (here specifically a land survey) is a task that can be completed through the utilisation of professional tools and with the aid of assistants that are (always) yet-to-arrive. This is a writing that is alien to the land that is to be surveyed. At the outset K. conceives the task of writing to be self-sufficient. He then realises the fallacy of this conception, as I will describe later.

As described here along the lines of Sebald's reading, the writer's task is completely different: it enables the image's movement into its future and the reader's movement towards the moving image, so as to become a moviegoer. This configuration can be found, for example, in the relations between the cinematographic author (taking the position of a writer) and the cinema actor (reader of the script). To act would mean, quite literally, move or respond to the setting-in-motion of the image, generated by the scriptwriter. A merely written script remains unfulfilled, its meaning undetermined; and it is through its acting out that its meaning is determined. This is perhaps why Sebald takes Zischler's acting background as the source of his sensibility in identifying Kafka's cinematographic writing: 'Zischler, perhaps because he has been in front of the camera lens himself, knows all about the curiously mingled sense of identification and alienation felt when – in the extreme sense, but it is a frequent one in cinema – you can see yourself die' (2006b: 160). A description of a reading act of this sort seals Sebald's essay. The reader who acts or moves towards the image is a painter:

> Few people ever seem to have been much alone as Kafka appears in the last pictures of him, to which we may add one extrapolated from them, so to speak, and painted by Jan Peter Tripp. It shows Kafka as he might have looked had he lived eleven or twelve years longer. That would have been in 1935. The Reich party rally would have been held, just as Riefenstahl's film shows it. The race laws would have come into force, and Kafka, if he had had his photograph taken again, would have looked at us as he does from Tripp's ghostly picture – from beyond the grave. (2006b: 173)

Tripp the painter – like Zischler the actor – is also a reader of Kafka actively participating in the setting-in-motion of the image generated by Kafka's writing, so as to enable it to become meaningful. Painting Kafka as if 'from beyond the grave' means bridging the inherent gap between the moment of writing and the moment of its becoming meaningful – moving Kafka to its future. At the same time, it means ending the movement of the tent camp image towards its meaningfulness: it is Kafka, the German-writing Jew, who is now read as the dweller of tents. It is through this shift in time – of the tent camp image to its past, and of Kafka's image to its future – that they both coincide, in a montage, and become meaningful. Their meaningfulness conditions are provided by their mutual movement one towards the other, achieved only through the reader's movement towards them. Moving towards what is read – the image, Kafka – is clarified here an act of imagination. To move towards the image as it moves – to go to the movies – means to imagine the image viewed, to make an image of it that is already part of another person's life.

IV. DUTY AND LIFE INTERWOVEN

Let us return to Sebald's description of the locked gate: 'the more often I looked at it the further it seems to withdraw from me' (2006a: 49). The very act of viewing an image makes it move away from the viewer. This withdrawal calls for an opposite movement: reading that enables meaningful writing. In chapter five of Kafka's *The Castle* we find a remarkably metaphysical formulation of the fallacy of the conception of literature as profession and a hint to Kafka's cinematographic conception of literature, as the setting in motion of an image for its meaning to be capable of determination through a new form of *reading* involving *action* (rather than a mental activity) – a movement towards the moving image. It is experienced by K. as disillusion from a naïve conception of the relation between life and vocation:

> Nowhere before had K. ever seen official duties and life so closely interwoven, so much so that sometimes it almost seemed as if life and official duties had changed places. What was the meaning, for instance, of the power, so far only formal, that Klamm had over K.'s services compared with the power that Klamm really did exert in K.'s bedroom? It just showed how any carelessness in procedure or easygoing attitude was appropriate only in direct contact with the authorities, while elsewhere great caution was necessary, and you had to look round on all sides before taking any step. (2009: 55)

K. at the foot of the impenetrable castle gate, like Sebald facing the locked school gate, is experiencing a writer's block: he cannot fulfil his 'official duties'; he cannot write. His realisation that 'official duties and life' are 'so closely interwoven, so much so that sometimes it almost seemed as if life and official duties had changed places' means that it is *in life* that a writer should practice his 'official' skills. Life devoid of official ambition would be a paralysed, blocked life, where movement – even a single step – is impossible. Official duty separated from life would be a meaningless activity, that is, incapable of producing meaningful outcomes.

The conception of (official) duties as separated from life, the disillusionment from which is expressed by K., means that the meaningfulness conditions of what is produced by pursuing one's duties are independent of the context of their appearance in life, while in fact they are dependent of their potential for the step-by-step movement constitutive of life, of movement in (historical, biographical) time, space and agency. The notion of land survey is a brilliant example of a product whose meaning can only be determined through movement in the surveyed land rather than, say, contemplation of the surveyed land.

On 22 February 1918 Kafka writes: 'Contemplation and activity have their apparent truth; but only the activity radiated by contemplation, or rather, that which returns to it again, is truth' (1991: 49). It is not only that contemplation should inform action for it to become meaningful so as to raise the question of truth. Activity should return to contemplation, that is, interlace with it, so that the pretension of separating the domains can be abandoned. To be radiated by contemplation so as to return to it again means to move towards it, and not merely to stand in a so to speak projective, idle relation to it. It means that for life to be lived as meaningful, one cannot contemplate *on* life but should rather *return* to contemplation; one should *arrive* at contemplation through the motion consisted in living.

A few days later, Kafka writes in his diary of human life (and death) as a task one can accomplish only if one 'is erecting his life on … justifications' (1991: 52). He objects to the view that a person can provide himself with such justifications retrospectively. Such a retrospective act of signification is rejected as 'mirror-writing' (*Spiegelschrift*) and reading this writing would be mere psychology: 'laborious, and as regards the always correct result, it is richly informative; but nothing really happens' (1991: 53). To this method of reading he opposes another: 'We see every human being living his life (or dying his death). This achievement would not be possible without an inner justification; no human being can live an unjustified life' (1991: 52).

It is through an act of seeing human life that an alternative, non-psychological reading method is achieved. The writer who strives to justify his life in retrospect assumes the position of a reader. He tries to meet himself, so to speak, in his future, and move towards his mirror image so as to grant it meaning. But 'nothing really happens' this way, as the mirror only provides an illusion of motion. It is only if we see human life – that is, in principle, not our own – that our movement towards the image of the task at hand can be said to be something that 'really happens', that is, genuine motion.

The writer's responsibility is to render his life apt to real, non-reflective reading involving the readers' motion, that is, to erect it on an inner justification. The only possible justification for life – the only way to make it meaningful – is inner justification. Only thus can life be seen or read by others, and the achievement of living (and dying) accomplished meaningfully. Inner justification, for the writer, is distinguished from retrospective justification that would make the reader redundant (mirror-reading). For the reader, inner justification of (another person's) life means that he is called for real – not merely contemplative – action, movement towards the other.

V. THE PRIMACY OF THE WORLD

The protagonists of many of Kafka's stories and of his three unfinished novels often portray Kafka's position as a writer whose life is never long enough to complete his writing task. This metaphysical position is represented narratively in the form of late arrival.[6] In fact, K.'s realisation that official duties and life are 'so closely interwoven' can also be put this way: when conducting one's official tasks, one is always already acting, already part of a set-up designed in advance. Living is not exempt from official rules of conduct, inasmuch as official duties are not exempt from the rules of action governing life (not exempt from ethical judgement, one can say). A model for such being – within interwoven official duties and life – is that of the over-sleeper, awakening to a reality the defining conditions of which he had no part in forming, requiring him to respond immediately. So are Gregor Samsa, awakening to the reality of becoming a vermin in 'The Metamorphosis' (1915), K., who wakes up to the noise made by his prosecutors in the adjunct room in *The Trial* (1925) and K. on the inn's floor, waking up to find out that he has already entered the castle's domain. Similar to how Sebald's initial position as a writer is that of a witness to the image's withdrawal, thus enabling the reader's approach, so is *The Castle*'s K. always frustrated in his attempt to catch a glimpse of (the image of) Klamm that keeps eluding – just like the image of one's own death that is perpetually beyond the present.[7]

What comes for Kafka's protagonists as an uncanny realisation – almost always too late for them to be able to correct their conception of official duties/writing and successfully respond to – is part of cinema's ontological fabric. If we treat the human figure as it appears on the screen and its conduct towards fellow humans and in the world that surrounds him not as a representation but as another variation of our world, as a mode of appearance of life in the world, we may conclude that this form of conduct is typically characterised by late arrival or oversleeping. The people we see on screen always arrive at a scene already set in advance. This cinematic trait is at the heart of the art's strong sense of realism.[8] It has to do with the fact that, as opposed to a literary character's conduct, the cinematographic character is always obliged to respond, without having the privilege to set up or prepare for the world. He does not enter it like the theatrical figure enters the stage, but is already there. This inherently realistic nature of cinema can be stylistically mitigated, but an ontological gap is always there between *a priori* reality and human agency. The most basic and irreducible representation of this unbridgeable gap is the face of the actor portraying the character: the gap between the non-cinematographic reality of the actor's face and the cinematographic reality of the character's face.

The world is already designed to the minutest detail – from the physical laws of motion to the psychological laws of action – before the screen character takes 'any step'. To write is to accept this primacy of world over human agency. To struggle with it would render both life and literature meaningless. Accepting this primacy means setting the image or the object of writing in motion so as to invite a reader – never oneself, as this would mean psychology, not literature; mirror-writing, not pursuing one's vocation in life – to move towards this moving image.

In 1917, Kafka writes: 'In the struggle between yourself and the world, second the world' (1991: 29). 'To second' means to take the world's side over one's psychological own, or to accept the world's primacy over one's self. This famous aphorism can now be read as metaphysical stage directions for those interlaced in the realm of cinematography: writers and readers alike, inhabitants of the world, living their lives in it.

NOTES

1   Published posthumously in 2003 in the volume *Campo Santo*.
2   Sebald refers here to Quint Buchholz's painting *Die Befragung der Aussicht*, reproduced at the end of the chapter.
3   Note that the two aspects of movement are already encapsulated in Agamben's words: man goes – moves towards – the moving image.
4   A rough prefiguration of this gesture opens Sebald's essay, when he introduces Zischler by alluding to his own experience of going to the movies back in 1975 to watch Wim Wenders' *Kings of the Road*, in which Zischler played one of the two protagonists (2006b: 156).
5   It is not solely with Kafka that Sebald associates this reading method. The opening chapter of *The Rings of Saturn* (2002a), for example, features a reading of Rembrandt's painting *The Anatomy Lesson of Dr. Nicolaes Tulp* (1632) – in itself a depiction of a reading experience: the participants in the lesson read the anatomy book laid at the foot of the corpse. René Descartes, who Sebald claims witnessed the event depicted, represents for him the literal reader, whereas Thomas Browne stands for the cinematographic one. Rembrandt is the writer who sets the image in motion. Sebald's reading/writing gesture that reveals this set-up is a zoom-in into the hand of the patient, potentially the writing hand – one could speculate – of the deceased – a thief, who in Sebald's metaphysics can be seen as being synonymous to a writer (see Sebald's tip to writers: 'You must get the servants to work for you. You mustn't do all the work yourself. That is, you should ask other people for information, and steal ruthlessly from what they provide' [Lambert and McGill 2009: 9]). The meaning of the

hand image is undetermined in the sense that its direction – right or left – cannot be determined, as 'the exposed tendons, which ought to be those of the left palm, given the position of the thumb, are in fact those of the back of the right hand' (2002a: 16). This indeterminacy further affects the entire scene – either a scientific procedure or a punitive ritual. Browne is taken by Sebald to develop this indeterminacy into a writing method, characterised by an ongoing effort to overcome the world's resistance to his attempt to achieve a clear image thereof, and generate motion (a resistance that yields something akin to a block): 'Browne's writing can be held back by the force of gravitation, but when he does succeed in rising higher and higher through the circles of his spiralling prose, borne aloft like a glider on warm currents of air, even today the reader is overcome by a sense of levitation. The greater the distance, the clearer the view: one sees the tiniest details with the utmost clarity' (2002a: 19).

6   See, for example, the opening sentence of *The Castle*: 'It was late evening when K. arrived' (2009: 5).

7   In the third chapter of his first novel *Vertigo* (2002b), Sebald describes a scene which took place just one day after Kafka's 1913 movie-going experience, where Kafka pushed the notion of late arrival to its limit. He was expected on an official meeting in Desenzano, but avoided it by 'reclining on the grass down by the lake', enjoying the sight of his colleagues passing by without noticing his presence. So late was he that his colleagues eventually dispersed, disappointed. 'One of them is reported to have observed', Sebald concludes, 'that those with whom we invest our hopes only ever make their appearance when they are no longer needed' (2002b: 153-4).

8   Realism is taken here metaphysically, and not in the sense of a cinematographic genre or style.

BIBLIOGRAPHY

Agamben, Giorgio (2002a) 'Difference and Repetition: On Guy Debord's Films', in Tom McDonough (ed.) *Guy Debord and the Situationist International*. Cambridge, MA: MIT Press, 313–20.

Brod, Max (1969 [1925]) 'Postscript to First Edition', Franz Kafka, *The Trial*, trans. Willa and Edwin Muir. New York: Schocken Books.

Kafka, Franz (1991 [1954]) *The Blue Octavo Notebooks*, ed. Max Brod, trans. Ernst Kaiser and Eithne Wilkins. Cambridge, MA: Exact Change.

_____ (2009 [1926]) *The Castle*, trans. Anthea Bell. Oxford and New York: Oxford University Press.

_____ (2013 [1915]) *The Metamorphosis*, ed. and trans. Stanley Corngold. New York: Modern Library.

_____ (2009a [1925]) *The Trial*, trans. Mike Mitchell. Oxford: Oxford Univer-sity Press.

Lambert, David, and McGill, Robert (eds) (2009) 'The Collected "Maxims"', *Five Dials*, 5, 9; available at http://fivedials.com/portfolio/issue-5-dunthorne-sebald-translators (accessed 9 July 2015).

Sebald, W. G. (2002a) *The Rings of Saturn*, trans. Michael Hulse. London: Vintage.

―――― (2002b) *Vertigo*, trans. Michael Hulse. London: Vintage.

―――― (2006a) 'Le cour de l'ancienne école', *Campo Santo*, trans. Anthea Bell. London: Penguin, 49–52.

―――― (2006b) 'Kafka Goes to the Movies', *Campo Santo*, trans. Anthea Bell. London: Penguin, 156–73.

Zischler, Hanns (2002) *Kafka Goes to the Movies*, trans. Susan H. Gillespie. Chicago: University of Chicago Press.

THE GHOST IS CLEAR: THE POV OF THE DAYDREAMER

LAURENCE A. RICKELS

The phantasmagoria of Kafka's media relations has come under such close scrutiny since the 1970s that the genealogy of media by now counts as the clear text or context of Kafka scholarship. Many of the literary authors of Kafka's day symptomatised, thematised or otherwise included in their work the watershed of media changes since the mid-nineteenth century, notably through recourse to what Walter Benjamin called the optical unconscious, the breakthrough of Freud's psychic apparatus through all the channels of its shared mediatisation. The wrap of all these media mutations and their visualisation was, certainly for Benjamin, film. Surrealism in letters, for example, could be seen as the evoked or described visual mediatisation of a new frontier between the unconscious and conscious thought.

In the meantime, we've been captive audience to ever accelerating changes in the sensorium in the course of the digital revolution. One surprise result of this revolution is the recognition that film, for all the changes in editing, for instance, has remained unchanged by digital innovation. Film is more a setting, a milieu and a way of seeing than another finite or historical medium. While we know Kafka was an inveterate moviegoer, the film medium is not recognisably included in his works. While it's possible to argue that the torture-writing machine of Kafka's 'In der Strafkolonie' ('In the Penal Colony', 1919) is at once typewriter, telegraph, gramophone and telephone, a specifically cinematic feature would appear to be missing. And yet the colony as a whole, including the teahouse with the old commander's grave as well as the travelling POV crisscrossing it throughout, is, arguably, immersed in cinema. Freud's strict avoidance of reference to the film medium even as he pressed every other available technical medium into service as analogue with yet another feature or function of the psychic apparatus is the kind of absence that doubles as metonymy for his science's inseparability from it. Rather than rest, however, with Friedrich Kittler's conclusion that Freud kept his distance from film as the rival medium for figuring the doppelgänger (1986: 214ff), let's postulate instead that in Freud as in Kafka cinema provides a setting or foundation for the legibility of media so basic that it goes without specification or explicit thematisation.

Another feature of original psychoanalysis that has gone under in the receiving area is the all-important concept, in part dictated by the German language, of the wish (*der Wunsch*). There really is no word in German for 'desire'. One offshoot of the basic wish was Freud's exploration, in 'Der Dichter und das Phantasieren' ('The Poet and Daydreaming', 1908), of our second nature as daydreamers. What precedes the buffering of our sensorium through technical media and mass psychologisation is the immersion in waking fantasy or wish fulfilment in proximity to the omnipotence of thought. We have art or what Freud preferred to address as *Dichtung* (poetry) because omnipotence is too vital to surrender to the privacy of our daydream wish fantasies. The mere personalisation of narcissism in daydreaming is not only boring and embarrassing, in other words, inartistic, but even antisocial. 'The adult … is ashamed of his fantasies and hides them from others […]. As a rule he would rather confess his trespasses than impart his fantasies' (Freud 1941a: 215; my translation).

If the first poetry was the heroic saga, as Freud argues in *Massen Psychologie und Ich-Analyse* ('Mass Psychology and the Analysis of the Ego', 1908), then the first hero, certainly for the audience, was the poet himself, who had wrested omnipotence from a condemned site and given it a public form and forum (1941b: 152). But as Freud made explicit in 'The Poet and Daydreaming', before psychoanalysis came along one needed a poet without knowing it: our second nature wasn't recognised as such. Everyone felt alone with antisocial thoughts and wishes of one's own, as Freud observes of the daydream in the recent past prior to changes that psychoanalysis was bringing about. 'It may happen that for that reason he believes he is the only one who engages in such fantasying, and doesn't have a clue that quite similar creations are generally widespread' (1941a: 215–16; my translation).

Although daydreaming is heir to the pursuit in child's play of being big, unlike this acceptable content of playing, which remains out in the open, the antisocial daydream, which picks up in adolescence where child's play left off, requires privacy. Whereas the playing child moves through various realities, the fantasising teen, according to Freud, is less dependent on reality, which triggers the fantasy scenarios in what Anna O. famously called one's private theatre. Censorship brings night dreams closer to poetry and more available for retelling. By reducing them to wish fulfilment, however, the psychoanalytic interpretation made public a plain text that drives home the continuity between night dreams and daydreams. But daydreaming is so second nature it goes – it's gone – without saying. The continuity shot of film that traverses the sensorium without recognisably signing itself in or out is correlative to the second nature of the waking wish fantasy. Out of their silent partnership one might begin to reconstruct what has been referred to in the scholarship as the 'way of seeing' (Kobs 1970: 98ff) unique to Kafka's protagonists, a give and take in the stability of their POV. To return to the earlier comp among historical art forms responsive to the psychic emergency of media, the way of seeing of Kafka's protagonists doesn't disclose a surrealist world. What the protagonist wears on his sleeve and projectively encounters is not like a dream or a nightmare; it's like a daydream in the process of going public or withdrawing into oblivion (or both). My precursor in this consideration of Kafka's materials is Theodor Adorno, who identified among Kafka's special effects the daydream combination of déjà vu and the doppelgänger. When he lists a sampling of the eclectic figures populating Kafka's 'realm of déjà vu' (1953: 264; my translation), the doppelgänger is at the front of the line. 'Perhaps the secret aim of his writing in general was to make déjà vu available, technical, and collective' (1953: 263; my translation).

In *Der Prozess* (*The Trial*, 1925), the coherence and continuity that K. claims to recognise in Titorelli's court paintings he must first supply within a context or apparatus of seeing that animates that which it takes in. Like the cinematic apparatus which, according to Kafka, imposes onto the observed object, in place of the viewer's steady gaze, its own restlessly repeated motion (in Barthes 1980: §22), K. flexes a way of seeing by projecting an isolated instance as a series of stills. He wonders why the depicted fantasy figure (a knight in armour) remains standing and doesn't move closer.

> He illuminated the altar painting with the flashlight. The eternal light hovered disturbingly before it. [...] K., who for a long time now had not seen any paintings, contemplated the knight for some time, even though he had to blink his eyes constantly, since he could not endure the green light of the lamp. (1946: 216–17; my translation)

During K.'s scene of arrest in the book's opening, the guards shuffled through photographs but couldn't set them in order again. The photographs in disarray alone record the 'disturbance' introduced by the Court. Kafka, whose talent for projecting or forecasting the imminent future is legend, identified photography as an act of forgetting (see Binder 1976: 55–6). Now that every photograph is indeed already a found photograph that is oblivious to its object relation, we know that what looks like melancholia lasts like successful mourning.

In 'Mind and its Relation to the Psyche-Soma', D. W. Winnicott argued that basic mental functioning begins at birth as the bifurcation of memory with which we're familiar via Freud via Walter Benjamin. Already at birth, 'memorizing or cataloguing' is 'extremely active' (1992b: 248). Impingements that demand excessive reactions can be recorded exactly and in the correct order. This protective self-storage catalogue is a necessary and inevitable buffer zone; yet it is an encumbrance on the individual's continuity of being, which is constitutive of the self: 'this cataloguing type of mental functioning acts like a foreign body if it is associated with environmental adaptive failure that is beyond understanding or prediction' (ibid.). In analysis this record, which goes back to the birth experience, can play in that linear fashion with which the analyst is familiar: the boring client likes to 'fill in' the analyst on his or her week. In analysis, the foreign-body recording 'of the bit of psychic reality which was difficult to get at at the moment, but of which the patient so acutely needed to become aware' (1992b: 249), can be turned into remembering-to-forget. In 'Birth Memories, Birth Trauma, and Anxiety', Winnicott emphasises that the very linearity of the record insures and requires that the patient can deal with one impingement, experience or reaction at a time. 'The ego effort ... is an attempt to hold the impingements at bay by mental activity, so that the reactions to them can be allowed one at a time and without disruption of the psyche' (1992a: 192). Winnicott already underscored the down side, at least in the long run, namely that the intellect can, in relation to 'the border-line of intolerable reaction phases, [begin to work] as something distinct from the psyche' (1992a: 191). The intellect, as a recording or cataloguing function, helps defend the psyche against impingement and reaction. When the self-storage unit becomes too important the body no longer minds the psyche.

> It is as if the intellect collects together the impingements to which there had to be reaction, and holds them in exact detail and sequence, in this way protecting the psyche until there is a return of the continuing-to-exist state. In a rather more traumatic situation the intellect develops excessively and can even seem to become more important than the psyche, and subsequent to birth the intellect can continue to expect and even to go out to meet persecutions so as to collect them and hold them, still with the aim of preserving the psyche. The value of this defence is shown when the individual ultimately comes to analysis, for in the analytic setting we find that carefully collected primary persecutions can be remembered. Then, at long last, the patient can afford to forget them. (1992a: 191–2)

Cinema's externalisation of the physiology of seeing modifies the adaptive dialectic of remembering and forgetting to fit the basic recording service in mental functioning, which is as pervasive and fleeting as waking fantasy. From the archive of eyewitness accounts of the first impact of cinema Kittler selects as most salient the interpretation that the moviegoers react to the screen as to an externalised retina in long-distance connection with the brain (1986: 186). Kittler then summarises the consequence: 'Fragmentation or cut in the real, merger or flow in the imaginary – the entire history of the scientific study of cinema plays out nothing but this very paradox' (1986: 187). Benjamin tried to make the most of the paradox by transferring the admitted distraction to the test situation in front of the camera, which by identification establishes a techno culture of gadget-loving expertise. But preliminary to this in-group formation, the fact of cinema is that each viewer has to perform the act of seeing without the help of others, with his eyes only.

Along the periphery of isolated seeing, Victor Burgin, at once media artist and art theorist, assembled out of introspection, his own film experiences and media philosophy, a composite picture of the remembered film buoyed up by forgetting. He gives the rundown of his review of a scene he was struck by from the movie *Fire Down Below* (1957):

> The fragment I saw was all that was required to retrieve this narrative from the archive of the 'already seen.' But already, in memory, the obvious meaning of the film is giving way to obtuse meanings. The 'already seen' of the story hovers like an aura around the sequence of the farewell at the jetty, but already the narrative is fading. The jetty scene is itself decomposing into its component images. [...] What was once a film in a movie theatre ... is now a kernel of psychical representations, a fleeting association of discreet elements. [...] The more the film is distanced in memory, the more the binding effect of the narrative is loosened. The sequence breaks apart. The fragments go adrift and enter into new combinations, more or less transitory, in the eddies of memory: memories of other films, and memories of real events. (2004: 67–8)

Burgin allows that our eidetic memories often emerge out of the flux of forgetting or remembering movies. False memories, like the-android-is-us, could be pitched so successfully as our forecast in *Blade Runner* (1982) because it fit the bottom line of an indefatigably self-reflexive film.

Klaus Wyborny, the experimental filmmaker who is also a trained physicist, describes how forgetting washes/watches over us in the setting of film projection. Using the projector as model, Wyborny singles out the gate as the present tense of projection, the take-up reel as the past, and the feed reel as the future.

To illustrate the process between and within each tense he adds the metaphors: 'picture particle', 'pool of impressions' and 'raft'.

> Whenever a new shot gets into the gate, a 'picture particle' is ejected from there. Reaching the brain it hits the pool of impressions with a big splash. Doing this it hits the raft floating on top first. The raft (presenting our memory of the preceding shot) gets destroyed or it at least loses its distinctness, so that most of its structures disappear within a fraction of a second, while some remnants start sinking down. Meanwhile the present particle already works havoc in the memory-liquid, where it modifies and destroys a considerable amount of the impressions deposited there. [...] Having finished its destructive job ... the picture particle drifts up to the pool's surface, forming a new raft there, which now floats on a "sea of changed impressions," getting more and more structure within its remaining projection time – till the next picture particle will be in the gate, by which the present raft will also be destroyed and the pool modified anew. [...] Somehow a pool of those impressions vaguely remains and when the film is over, the remaining pool plus the impressions of the last shot ... is what you think you have seen, when you leave the cinema. (2014: n.p.)

In the close quarters of daydream, historical memory and achievement, imagined or actual, Wyborny spun an allegory of the film medium's proximity to forgetting in his 2002 film, *Sulla*. Based on the first chapter of his historical novel, also titled *Sulla*, Wyborny adopted as the adaptation's audio track what literature departments prefer to identify as stream of consciousness. However, whereas the literary stream tends to be subsumed in the receiving area by poetic prose and epiphany, in the movie *Sulla* we overhear the private reserve of daydream fantasy. A tension is thus upheld between our second nature of constant wishing at the speed of thought and the historical accomplishment of Sulla, which lies on the film's horizon. What we consider as Roman architecture, which came complete with the use of concrete, was first realised by the Roman general and consul Sulla. The film covers one afternoon in his life, which is suffused with the audio tracking of daydream. Among the projects he wishes or fantasises is a building in which he would commemorate his wish fantasy of sexual relations, fulfilled that afternoon only by proxy or masturbation. In this span of tension Wyborny makes public the private cinema of daydreaming.

What you see is what you forget. The intake of media follows the temporal paradox of daydreaming according to Freud's 1908 article. The waking wish fantasy is triggered in the present, but retains of this initiating contact only the *Zeitmarke*, the date mark. The arc of the fantasy Freud offers as his main example makes a wish that returns to an idealised absconded past but then jump cuts past the present tense (and the ongoing tensions carried forward in the present) into the future of its fantastic fulfilment. An orphan on his way to a job interview projects success all the way up, a fantastic mobility that makes him the boss's heir and son-in-law. At the same time the *Zeitmarke*, here the job interview, is not only the ticket to forgetting but the erogenous zone of the daydream. It represents what Winnicott refers to as 'the here-and-now fixity of any satisfaction that there can be in fantasying' (2002: 35). Winnicott argues that there is nothing to interpret in the daydream; it is about doing something, in other words, nothing at all. The night dream like art adds the symbolism that makes interpretation possible. In the analytic session, so-called free association is, paradoxically perhaps, the dissection of daydreaming that is kept from emerging. The component parts are reintegrated into the transferential process of analytic understanding, which occupies or cathects the border to the night-dream unconscious. Night dreams are in session the royal road to working on the transference.

The Happy End arc of Freud's daydream example is what the fantasy genre exploits along the lines of the ultimate fantasy, the fantasy that is, as J. R. R. Tolkien advises, at the same time true: the death of death, the redemption of every deposit or loss. But the fantasy leap to the other world would thus circumvent not only the present but also the volatile, inchoate process of our second nature as daydreamers. Hanns Sachs observes that although one might expect that it is the aggressive and death-wishing aspect that must be barred from art, 'the opposite is true. The "happy end" stories and plays are entertainment, which means they lose their grip on the audience as soon as they are over. […] A new supply of them is constantly needed' (1942: 23).

Is the daydreamer in training to render, like the child at play, his inchoate thoughts or feelings big and clear? That would certainly fit the range of fantasy fiction – a curtailed range or leap, as already noted. But isn't the excess in beauty and feeling in the fantasy genre, which critics stamp as kitsch, another way of saying that it is most repressed? It is the proximity to its often-disowned basis in daydream fantasy that comes under repression, even within the fantasy genre's understanding of itself. Tolkien chose 'fantasy' over 'fairy tale', for example, to name the genre he derived from folklore and heroic epics belonging to the era of transition from Paganism to Christianity. This choice dared name its synonym and significance, which Tolkien otherwise sought to circumvent.

Kafka commenced keeping a diary late in life, perhaps as delayed onset of adolescence; but certainly it was part of his adult decision to be a writer. A diary is like a website: it is a neutral structure that is completely content and production-value dependent. The teenager takes a first step in his journal writing out of the privacy of daydreaming toward publication (the open invitation to family and friends to violate his personal space and read the diary). In the medley that Kafka kept as his diary – including daily records, excerpts from letters and literature, night dream transcripts, drafts of stories, travelogues and impressions from movies watched and plays attended – we also find daydreams. On 8 December 1911, Kafka enters the following daydream: 'I have now and had this afternoon a great yearning to write my withdrawn state completely outside myself and even as it emerges out of the depths to write it into the depth of the paper or to write it down in such a way that I could absorb what is written fully inside myself' (1990: 286). What moved him to imagine merging with his writing at the instant that it emerged from him was 'no artistic desire', as he concludes the thought. This is one inartistic daydream, however, that did cross over into his literary work.

In his 1914 story, 'In the Penal Colony' (published in 1919), Kafka installed a travelling explorer as protagonist. By his POV, Kafka reversed but preserved the inartistic daydream, which the officer narrates as the fantastic inscription of the verdict. This internal narrative is in running contrast not only to the traveller's superficial mode of reading or touring, but also to the officer's fulfillment of the underlying daydream. When he enters the machine it breaks away from the discourse of its autonomous writing and carries out in its breakdown the inartistic merger/murder as p-unitive fantasy. The explorer's perspective circumvents the torture-writing machine, though only to the extent that this travelling shot crosses to that other side of shrift – shameful fleeing – where it must remain. In the diaries, however, Kafka participated in such cursory itinerant activity which, in the case of reading, amounted to 'flying over' a text (*überfliegen*), and in the case of travel could be a 'flight outwards' (*Ausflug*). Mapping out this flight trajectory in the diaries, we discern the coordinates and props of Kafka's preoccupation with his health. Kafka claimed that if he were wrong about the various 'nature cures' he pursued – including travel, nudism, vegetarianism and the agrarian praxis of Zionism – he would also be wrong about everything else. Turning away from conventional medicine to seek out nature cures, Kafka gave as his reason the deaths of his younger brothers Georg and Heinrich at the hands of incompetent physicians. His brothers had not, therefore, died of natural causes; as murder victims they retained the right to haunt.

On 6 December 1921, Kafka includes in his diary a citation from the newspaper. It is inserted below the extended reflection with which the entry opens. Kafka contemplates a metaphor used in a letter he received that day. It is by now one of the cornerstones of Kafka scholarship. In the posted metaphor Kafka sees reflected back constraints placed upon his writing. And yet he cannot help but evoke, by revoking it from the start, the possibility of writing's independence and autonomy. The adjective he uses, 'eigengesetzlich', declares independence while literally ascribing and inscribing the ability to proceed according to a Law

(*Gesetz*) of one's own. 'Metaphors are among the many things which lead me to despair over writing. Writing's lack of independence, its dependence on the maid who is heating the stove, on the cat warming itself by the stove, even on the poor old person who warms himself. All these are independent activities ruled by their own laws; only writing is helpless, does not dwell in itself, is a joke and a despair' (1990: 875; my translation).

The emphatic quality of this declaration is in contrast to the missing affect adequate to the news inserted below, which gives an inside view of Kafka's assault on metaphor. The report of premature burial doesn't suggest research or inspiration but seems rather the placeholder for waking fantasies that came and went at the speed of thought – like a memory that terminates the run of daydreaming. 'Two children, alone at home, climbed into a large trunk, the lid shut tight, they couldn't open it and suffocated' (Kafka 1990: 491; my translation). Newspapers have a wide open relationship to archivisation. The correlative of daydreaming, which, according to Melanie Klein (as summarised by her colleague and student Susan Isaacs), is the ongoing but fleeting metabolic record of instinctual reality, also represents a form of first contact with the ephemera lodged between inner and outer worlds. In *The Psychology of Daydreaming* (1921), J. Varendonck sought to develop waking fantasy as reality testing's parallel universal and secure for daydreaming the mode of hypothesis. But, example by example, we discern chains of thoughts pulling up short before memory. Although daydreaming in its dependence on and incompatibility with memory is largely a fitful process of stops, restarts and oblivion, it remains the first level of recording. What the bureaucratic record shows is the obsessive-compulsive obverse of these applications: its information gathering is preliminary to sorting out and selection. Before Kafka could assume his day job as insurance assessor he had to apply at the local police department for a certificate of good conduct. The officer wrote down a complete record that also registered his dead brothers.

While the sentencing of desire in the wish has been dropped from the foreground of psychoanalytic investigation, one wish had such a long run in Freud's thought that it can't be ignored. Freud considered the death wish both the first application of omnipotence of thoughts and the main ingredient in the untenable mix and mess of ambivalence. In his discussion of haunting in *Totem und Tabu* (*Totem and Taboo*, 1940), Freud argued that mixed feelings set up mourning's obstacle course, one that initially only projection can get around, because, once the fantasy goner in fact goes, the death wish cannot be admitted up close. The death wish opens up a long-distance relationship whereby the omnipotence flexed has to be shared with the goner, who thus returns.

Kafka aligned his *Schriftstellersein*, his 'being a writer' or, more literally, 'being the placing of script', with the flight-of-fantasy trajectory between the death wish and its ghost mediations. On 27 January 1922 he entered into his diary:

> The strange, mysterious, perhaps dangerous, perhaps saving comfort that there is in writing: it is a leap out of murderers' row; it is a seeing of what is really taking place. This occurs by a higher type of observation, a higher, not a keener type, and the higher it is and the less within reach of the 'row,' the more independent it becomes, the more obedient to its own laws of motion, the more incalculable, the more joyful, the more ascendant its course. (1990: 892)

Kafka wrote the first account in German letters of artificial flight. 'Die Aeroplane in Brescia' ('The Airplanes in Brescia', 1909) documents Kafka's visit to a flight show where, as he records it, D'Annunzio and Puccini were invited as the star guests. At the time Puccini wanted to work with D'Annunzio, who, however, decided to skip the opera-libretto assignment and proceed directly to film. For *Cabiria* (1914), often touted as the first modern film, he wrote the intertitles and invented the names of the characters. He was advertised upon the film's release as its 'creator'. Since flying with Wilbur Wright in 1908, D'Annunzio was obsessed with the new technology of flight, which he soon libidinised. He foresaw right away that mechanical flight would rise up as the techno fetish of a new world, the world of the future that the World War would deliver. Kafka described this new world, which he also glimpsed in Brescia, as one in which 'order and accident … were equally possible' (1974: 364; my translation). Kafka diagnosed acceleration as the dominating moment of this world, in which customary relations of control no longer held. In the New Introductory Lecture on *Weltanschauungen*, Freud interpreted the crossing of the English Channel as the true beginning of the World War, which was waged to draw new boundaries where the old ones no longer stood up to mechanical flight. Kafka writes: 'Now we see the apparatus with which Blériot crossed the Channel; no one said it, everyone knows it' (1974: 365; my translation). The way Kafka sees it, the pilot Blériot gives the advance preview of a techno-mutation, for which plane flight is rehearsal or repetition: 'one sees his upper body sitting straight up above the wings, his legs are stuck deep down as part of the machinery' (ibid.). But the fetishisation claims the pilot himself, who to the onlookers, also transformed in the shadow of flight, cannot signify as hero: 'a human being trapped inside a wooden contraption defends himself against the invisible danger he voluntarily took on. We, however, utterly pushed back and unreal, stand below watching this human being' (ibid.). Within the preview of a functioning chaos Kafka admits his own identification with flight: he sees the aviator Rougier sitting 'at his controls' 'like a gentleman at his desk' (1974: 366; my translation). This gentleman, however, who gets a rise out of Kafka's identification, doesn't rule, but engages in nomadic ascent. 'He ascends in small circles, flies beyond Blériot, makes him the viewer, and never ceases to ascend' (ibid.). As Kafka departs Brescia with his fellow travellers, the writing-flight of Rougier is without limit. 'Rougier appears so high up, that one believes his location can soon be calculated only according to the stars that will shortly appear in the night sky' (1974: 367; my translation).

Writing to Milena in March 1922, Kafka gives the clear text of his genealogy of media. He describes from the losing side of the finish line a race or contest: on the fast lane, transportation media, and, on the invisible, invincible track, media technologies:

> Mankind has invented the train, the car, the airplane in order to exclude to the extent possible that which is phantom-like between people ... but it will not help anymore. [...] The opposing side is so much calmer and stronger; after the postal service it invented the telegraph, the telephone, the radio-telegraph. (2004: 302)

Following the head starts that transportation takes, each advance in telecommunication encircles with a 'phantom hand' every new takeoff. As Kafka concludes: 'The phantoms will not starve, but we will be destroyed' (ibid.). From the start of his literary career Kafka had succeeded in inscribing the Oedipus complex within his fantasy rapport with ghosts. However menacing the opposing side might be, however frightening its inroads in ghost writing, the opposition is subsumed by the consumer protection of all the ghosts.

Georg, Kafka's mother's 'beautiful' son (see Hayman 1982: 10), who died at about age two, was engendered anew in 'Das Urteil' ('The Judgment', 1913), which Kafka described in his diary entry of 11 February 1913 as a 'birth' and the 'ghost of a single night'. Also noted: 'Thoughts of Freud of course.' In 'The Judgment', the mother, who has been dead for two years, appears never to have been properly mourned. This incapacity for proper mourning is ascribed to Georg's Russian friend, whose written condolence seemed to reflect nothing so much as the inability to grasp the magnitude of this grievous loss.

The 'birth' Kafka achieved with the writing of 'The Judgment' – it was his breakthrough literary achievement that marked the onset of work he could see through to publication – is conveyed within the story as Georg's creation of a phantom friend. The phantom friend embodies, according to Kafka's commentary in his diary, 'the connection between father and son' (1990: 491; my translation). This embodied connection is shadowed by the post – the friend is phantom to the extent that he exclusively inhabits a letter-writing relationship – just as it embodies the loss between father and son, the two-year-old loss of the mother.

The power a father exercises over his son takes the fantasy form, in 'The Judgment', of intercepting and derailing the son's rapport with a phantom. The father calls into question the existence of the letter-writing friend only to claim, ultimately, that he has all along been corresponding with the phantom, who obeys only the father's commands. Jürgen Kobs showed how every attempt in 'The Judgment' to assert an overview, in Georg's case against the pull of reverie, but equally so in regard to the father and his judgements, is dismantled and withdrawn into the equally untenable 'almost endless traffic' that closes the story. The non-artistic urge to retain the deep inscription or underside of one's own writing in ecstatic acceptance of penance or shrift lies on the other – though always reversible – side of the phantasm of writing as autonomous flight. Kafka makes the phantom connection last and lasting; it absorbs the Oedipal punitive fantasy in the alternation between rescue or flight signals and the 'comedy' of the father's command to jump. What Gilles Deleuze and Félix Guattari (1975) affirmed as anti-Oedipal deterritorialisation stops short of the daydream realm of haunting or cinema – in which a relentless relationality prior to adaptive responsibility runs the course of the death wish.

BIBLIOGRAPHY

Adorno, Theodor W. (1953) 'Aufzeichnungen zu Kafka', in Rolf Tiedemann, (ed.) *Gesammelte Schriften*, Volume X. Frankfurt am Main: Suhrkamp Verlag, 254–87.

Barthes, Roland (1980) *La Chambre Claire. Notes sur la photographie*. Paris: Gallimard.

Benjamin, Walter (1980 [1936]) 'Das Kunstwerk im Zeitalter seiner technischen Reproduzierbarkeit', in *Gesammelte Schriften* Volume I, eds. Rolf Tiedemann and Hermann Schweppenhäuser. Frankfurt am Main: Surhkamp, 471–508.

Binder, Hartmut (1976) *Kafka in neuer Sicht. Mimik, Gestik und Personengefüge als Darstellungsformen des Autobiographischen*. Stuttgart: Metzler.

Burgin, Victor (2004) *The Remembered Film*. London: Reaktion.

Deleuze, Gilles and Félix Guattari (1975) *Kafka. Pour une littérature mineure*. Paris: Edition de Minuit.

Freud, Sigmund (1940) *Totem und Tabu* in *Gesammelte Werke* (volume IX) Frankfurt: Fischer Verlag.

_____ (1941a [1908]) 'Der Dichter und das Phantasieren' in *Gesammelte Werke*, (volume VII) Frankfurt: Fischer Verlag.

_____ (1941b [1908]) *Massen Psychologie und Ich-Analyse* in *Gesammelte Werke*, (volume XIII) Frankfurt: Fischer Verlag, 73–161.

_____ (1944 [1932]) *Neue Folge der Vorlesungen zur EInführung in die Psycho-analyse* in *Gesammelte Werke* (volume XV) Frankfurt: Fischer Verlag.

Hayman, Ronald (1982) *Kafka: A Biography*. New York: Oxford University Press.

Isaacs, Susan (1948) 'The Nature and Function of Phantasy', *International Journal of Psychoanalysis*, 29, 73–97.

Kafka, Franz (1946) *Gesammelte Schriften*, ed. Max Brod. New York: Schocken.

―――― (1974 [1909]) 'Die Aeroplane in Brescia', in Max Brod, *Über Franz Kafka*. Frankfurt am Main: Fischer Taschenbuch Verlag, 364–7.

―――― (1990) *Tagebücher*, eds Hans-Gerd Koch, Michael Müller and Malcolm Pasley. Frankfurt am Main: S. Fischer.

―――― (2004) *Briefe an Milena. Erweiterte Neuausgabe*, eds Jürgen Born and Michael Müller. Frankfurt am Main: Fischer Taschenbuch Verlag.

Kittler, Friedrich (1986) *Grammophon, Film, Typewriter*. Berlin: Brinkmann & Bose.

Kobs, Jürgen (1970) *Kafka. Untersuchungen zu Bewusstsein und Sprache seiner Gestalten*, ed. Ursula Brech. Bad Homburg: Athenäum Verlag.

Sachs, Hanns (1942) *The Creative Unconsciou: Studies in the Psychoanalysis of Art*. Cambridge, MA: Sci-Art Publishers.

Tolkien J. R. R. (1983 [1947]) 'On Fairy-Stories', in Christopher Tolkien (ed.) *Monsters and the Critics and Other Essays*. London: George Allen & Unwin, 109–61.

Varendonck, J. (1921) *The Psychology of Daydreams*. London: George Allen & Unwin.

Winnicott, D. W. (1992a [1949]) 'Birth Memories, Birth Trauma, and Anxiety', in *Through Paediatrics to Psycho-Analysis: Collected Papers*. New York and London: Brunner-Routledge, 174–93.

―――― (1992b [1949]) 'Mind and its Relation to the Psyche-Soma', in *Through Paediatrics to Psycho-Analysis: Collected Papers*. New York and London: Brunner-Routledge, 243–54.

―――― (2002 [1982]) 'Dreaming, Fantasying, and Living: A Case-history describing a Primary Dissociation', in *Playing and Reality*. Hove and New York: Brunner-Routledge, 26–37.

Wyborny, Klaus (2014) 'Theoretical Physics and Film', transcript of a lecture at the Think: Film Congress (12 January 2014); www.thinkfilm.de

MOVING PICTURES – VISUAL PLEASURES: KAFKA'S CINEMATIC WRITING

PETER BEICKEN

I. KAFKA AS MOVIEGOER AND FILM AFICIONADO

The modes of observation, perception and representation in Kafka's works show a penchant for visual depiction and an affinity to cinema's visuality (see Jahn 1962, 1965; Augustin 1987; Beicken 1999a, 1999b, 2000, 2011; Alt 2009; Brabandt 2009; Duttlinger 2010). In addition, Kafka was fond of photography, although he stressed also its 'flaws' (Duttlinger 2007: 255). In his new and engaging visual method, Kafka reveals not only his closeness to the cinema and its mesmerising immediacy, he also uses elements of film that give his narratives a cinematic texture and feel (see Beicken 1999a). Kafka's visual method fascinates for the richness of its innovative and structural uses of the cinematic that, at times, appears to anticipate film concepts and techniques such as the moving camera, freeze frame and parallel action.

Kafka's passionate love of the motion pictures is well documented in his letters and diaries (see Zischler 2003). This fondness for films began early, though there is no evidence that Kafka attended 'ambulatory film showings', which were common in Prague from 1896 until they were joined in 1907 by regular cinemas (see Zischler 2003: 15). Kafka became an avid moviegoer, according to letters and Max Brod's recollections (see Brod 1960: 274). A card to Brod in August 1908 mentions 'The cinema' (Kafka 1977: 44), while a letter of December of the same year to Elsa Taussig Kafka recommends visiting the cinema 'Orient' (1977: 48f.). According to Hanns Zischler, Kafka enjoyed films: 'The entire spectrum of little trances of the moviegoer, the tears, the distraction, the boundless entertainment', although 'the affective traces that Kafka has conveyed only very sporadically in the sense of an actual description of scenes in his writing'

(2003: 10). Characteristically, without reference to any specific images, Kafka notes on 20 November 1913 in his diary: 'Was at the cinema. Cried' (1975: 238). Recording not the visual but the emotional impact, Kafka recalls figures or narrative situations that impressed him when watching three films. In *Lolotte* (1912), he noticed a good character, 'the good minister'; an object, 'the little bicycle'; and a family situation, 'the reconciliation of the parents' (1975: 238). The melodrama left him 'tremendously entertained' (ibid.), having seen the rather sad film *The Accident on the Dock* first and afterwards the funnier one, *Alone at Last*. But overall the viewing had a rather negative effect: 'Am entirely empty and insensible, the passing tram has more living feeling' (ibid.). Most likely Kafka experienced sensory excess (see Duttlinger 2010: 73), being left with a pervasive feeling of emptiness and senselessness that spoiled any cathartic reaction.

II. RESTLESS IMAGES AND THE NEED FOR A CALM LOOK

Essential to film is the passage of fleeting images. Kafka had plenty of opportunity to identify with melodramatic plots and tear-jerking effects, but he rarely described an image in detail. On one occasion he takes note of a specific picture: 'The millionaire in the motion picture *Slaves of Gold*. Must hold on to him. The calmness, the slow movement, right on target, a faster step when needed, a twitching of the arm' (1975: 222; translation modified). Here, Kafka dissects the film action by turning the sequence into a kind of slow motion of stills that allow him to dwell on the figure's appearance and body language as if he were contemplating single images in serial photography. The succession of individual gestures underscores the deliberateness of the movements, as each individual motion comes into focus. Emphasising the gestural in the Brecht-influenced concept of *gestus*, Walter Benjamin wrote: 'Kafka could understand things only in the form of a *gestus*' and he explicated the notion of *gestus* in discussing Kafka's portrayal of Abraham not as the biblical patriarch but as a willing-to-serve waiter (1999b: 808). The deliberate depiction of subservience in the *gestus* makes social class transparent. Similarly, Kafka concludes his observation of the figure of the millionaire: 'Rich, spoiled, lulled to sleep, but how he springs up like a servant and searches the room into which he was locked in the forest tavern' (1975: 223). Describing behaviour that conforms to the master-servant dynamic, Kafka reveals the figure of the self-assured and condescending rich man juxtaposed to the willing servant. Kafka uses *gestus* to reflect on the subaltern, as he often contrasts the powerful and the powerless in his narratives. The description of the sequenced film images is devoid of psychological explanation. Rather, Kafka's approach to cinematic images is transformative, as he treats them more like film stills or photographs than moving pictures.

In his approach to screen images, Kafka contemplates them as isolated from the rush of cinematic movements. Focusing on *gestus*, social power relations are made transparent. The preference of adapting and transforming existing images also reflects Kafka's dissatisfaction with cinema's fleeting pictures, which in early film amounted to a rapid, flickering stream of images. Despite his love of the movies and their emotional appeal, Kafka nevertheless had an ambivalent relationship to the cinema because he was sceptical about the viewing experience. Early cinema as an apparatus had many imperfections, aesthetically, structurally and technically. Kafka objected to the 'restlessness of its motion' as he preferred the 'calmness of the look' (1975: 430; translation modified). Kafka addresses here both the flickering projection modus and also the 'restlessness' of the film medium that reproduces accelerated movements in a constant flux of images. Distancing himself from the dual 'restlessness' of these technical and aesthetic dynamics, Kafka found stereoscopic images such as the ones he encountered in the 'Emperor's Panorama' (1975: 429) in Friedland much 'more alive' (1975: 430) than the 'flickering images' (Janouch 1971: 147) that frustrated his desire for close observation. Kafka, as an 'eye-person' (see Beicken 2011: 174; Janouch 1971: 160), was given to intense observation and favoured absorbing the richness of detail and distinction that still photos provide the contemplative gazer.

Having lamented the 'restlessness' of cinematic movement and motion, i.e. the representation of moving objects and film's quintessential rush of images, Kafka questions whether a joint medium that would 'combine the cinema and stereoscope' is possible (1975: 430). This combination is something that Kafka tries to achieve in a pivotal moment in *Der Prozess* (*The Trial*, 1925), as Josef K. shows Leni a picture of his 'sweetheart' Elsa who 'was caught at end of a whirling dance' (1968: 107). Intriguingly, the snapshot that shows Elsa in her fast, whirling movement resembles the dance of Lyduschka, a gypsy woman, on a table in a garden restaurant in Stellan Rye's *Der Student von Prag* (*The Student of Prague*), which was filmed and shown in Kafka's hometown in 1913. Possibly, Kafka was familiar with the film (see Alt 2009: 126), although it could be a mere coincidence that Elsa and Lyduschka's dances are similar (see the illustration in Diedrichs 1985: 4). Kafka employs his method of *gestus* by configuring the snapshot as the moment where the dancer is visually arrested in her spinning motion, 'her dress still swirling about her, her hands on her hips, looking off to the side and laughing, her throat taut; the person at whom her laughter was directed couldn't be seen in the picture' (1968: 107). Caught in her abandon, Elsa appears self-absorbed and fixed in her laughing, as her look, perhaps flirtatiously, seems to be fixed on a viewer outside the picture's frame. In portraying Elsa as seemingly still in motion and by connecting her look to a viewer/space outside the frame, Kafka attempts to combine film and photography, the medium of moving pictures and the other representing photographic stasis.

A corresponding image in *Das Schloss* (*The Castle*, 1926) that the landlady Gardena presents to K. depicts the messenger who summoned her to the official Klamm for sexual services (1974: 101). As the photograph is old, K. first believes the man is lying on a board. But urged to look more closely, he discovers that the image is a snapshot of a high jumper hovering in the air as he clears a rope. As a film still breaks the temporal continuum of the cinematic visual stream, the snapshot similarly fixes a moment and is comparable to the photographic stills Eadweard Muybridge used in his serial photography, creating a motion continuum through successive images (see Duttlinger 2007: 231). Again Kafka looks for a fusion of film and photography by using the still/snapshot as a common denominator. The attempted combination of the two media shows both a desire for synthesis and an effort to question established parameters. Kafka 'brings out the ambiguous, misleading nature of photographic representation, thus counteracting the cliché of the medium's immediacy' (Duttlinger 2007: 234). K.'s inability to see the image of the high jumper correctly at first sight indicates the author's insistence on a questioning look and prolonged study. Indeed, Kafka 'subjects both photographs and other spectacles of modern life to a disquieting second exposure, revealing their supposed stability and familiarity' (2007: 258).

As Kafka probes the media concepts of his time, he enhances his sense of perception and visual portrayal by exploring new avenues of pictorial representation in his texts. As early as 1927, in the afterword to the first edition of *Der Verschollene* (1927), Brod stated that some 'grotesque-comical scenes' (quoted in Alt 2009: 8) in Kafka's novel reminded him of Charlie Chaplin films adding, however, that these films came after Kafka had abandoned the novel. The topos of the Kafka-Chaplin affinity was adopted by Walter Benjamin in 1931 when he claimed that Chaplin was the 'real clue to the interpretation of Kafka' (ibid.), notably in the corresponding situations of being marginalised and dispossessed. In a December 1934 letter to Benjamin, Theodor W. Adorno confirmed Kafka's link to cinema describing his novels as 'the last and disappearing connecting texts of the silent film' (1999: 70).

Examining the influence of early cinema on Kafka independently, Wolfgang Jahn analysed film elements in the novel *Amerika* (1927). He focused on the author's preference for depicting images, the visual continuity in the narrative, the use of gestures, the emphasis on comical scenes, parallel action, and the use of 'interspersed images' ('Zwischenbilder') that are montaged into the narrative process (see Jahn 1965: 66ff.). The visual impressions are not plot-related in the sense of driving the narrative, but offer visual cutaways like film shots that are inserted into the action. While Jahn makes a case that Kafka's visual style and narration correspond to elements in film, Zischler rejected the assumption that the author's writing was impacted in terms of direct influence; he also dismissed one of Jahn's research findings because of a wrong attribution (2003: 126, n38). Altogether, Zischler characterises views of Kafka being influenced by film as 'speculations', pointing out that the Prague author never recorded or admitted to any influence of specific films on his writing (2003: 57). While he examines Kafka's reception of contemporary cinema extensively, Zischler nevertheless states categorically: 'In the prose, cinematography is not thematised either as a technique or as an image; it remains oddly excluded, as if Kafka, in distinct contrast to many writers of his generation, doubted its ability to be turned into literature' (2003: 107). While Zischler makes his case against the view of film influence on Kafka, he fails to recognise the author's writing in the cinematic mode.

Earlier, Bettina Augustin had differentiated the view of influence and pointed out that 'Kafka's special kind of visual perception' was not necessarily 'inspired' by the films he saw (1987: 38). Later, reviewing Peter-André Alt's study she critiqued his overuse of referencing individual films as sources of influence, renewing her case that the anticipatory function in Kafka's cinematic writing ought to be fully recognised (2009). Long before, she had referred to Kafka's 'sensibility regarding the need for new forms of representation to express the "modern consciousness" in his texts before film realises them in technique' (1987: 56). In addition, quoting from Benjamin's 'Little History of Photography', Augustin stressed the 'law that new advances are prefigured in older techniques' (1999a: 517), elucidating the at-times anticipatory dimension of Kafka's visual method (1987: 56). But the notion of Kafka's cinematic writing remained contested, as Oliver Jahraus (2008) also denied that film and cinema were of intermedial significance in the author's works, a claim that was rejected for overlooking the evidence of the cinematic in Kafka (see Alt 2009: 10; Beicken 2011: 165, 175 n7).

III. THE *FLÂNEUR* IN THE CITY: GAZING AT OBJECTS OF DESIRE

A closer look at Kafka's visual method reveals both the presence of cinematic elements and the foreshadowing aspect. His earliest work, 'Beschreibung eines Kampfes' ('Description of a Struggle'), in a first version written between 1902 and 1904, shows an intriguing relationship to film. Using the concept of the *flâneur* as delineated in Siegfried Kracauer's definition of the moviegoer, Rolf J. Goebel has pointed out that Kafka's first-person narrator in the story 'resembles the modern moviegoer/*flâneur*' who 'takes in the minute details of urban entertainment, people and architecture, combining camera-like, overly precise observation with the *flaneur*'s highly subjective intoxication with the phantasmagoric details of evanescent urban life' (2000: 13). Goebel considers Kafka's focus 'on the concrete visuality of ambiguous gestures' as a sign of his 'quasi-cinematic technique' (2000: 15). Also, he thinks that the dialogue between the narrator and his acquaintance 'imitates the filmic shot/reverse-shot technique' (2000: 14).

Inserted into the narrative about the nightly city stroll are several episodes with a cinematic feel that are characteristic of Kafka's *flâneur*-like vision. The *mise-en-scène* suggests paradigmatic situations or *Urszenen*, as the main figure serves as a narrative camera. One such *Urszene* concerns the narrator's look at a policeman, who as a self-absorbed skater happily is gliding and yodelling on the icy pavement. The disconnect in this scene between the self-enclosed event cantering on the policeman and the narrator's fear that his acquaintance could try to kill him enhances the film-like quality of the episode (see Kafka 1971: 17). In the second scene the intoxicated narrator slips on the ice. His fall attracts attention, and a fat woman exits from a wine tavern with a lantern to check what is happening in the street. While the woman cannot see the fallen narrator, a drunken man joins and accosts her. He exclaims that nothing happened, as he pulls her back into the tavern (1971: 18). While these episodes create a sense of slapstick, the third episode is an almost surreal *Urszene* concerning the narrator's odd behaviour, as he is making swimming movements in the air when crossing the Charles Bridge. Being pulled down to the ground again by the acquaintance after having encircled five statues, the narrator feels a pain in his knee, and this hurt prevents him from moving freely above ground (1971: 19). In all, Kafka's fantasy of unbound movement envisions the *flâneur* as a moving camera foreshadowing F. W. Murnau's 'unfettered camera' of the 1920s (see Augustin 1987: 56) and perfected later by crane shots that created an even freer filming method and cinematic vision.

Kafka's first, unfinished novel, 'Hochzeitsvorbereitungen auf dem Lande' ('Wedding Preparations in the Country'), written between 1905 and 1907, reveals a significant development in his cinematic writing. The main figure, Eduard Raban, serves as a distinct narrative camera (see Beicken 1999a). As a *flâneur*, Raban remains in the opening scene mainly in stasis, placed at a doorway overlooking the city-scape, a square with the hustle and bustle of urban traffic, both human and vehicular (see Beicken 2006). Raban gazes at the movements of 'many people walking in various rhythms' and 'carriages on delicate high wheels' that are 'drawn along by horses with arched necks' (Kafka 1971: 52). What makes the shot-by-shot recording of rhythmically moving, seemingly choreographed objects so filmic is the observer's focalised cinematic vision.

In studying the camera as narrative entity and theorising the filmic gaze, Norbert Grob recalls that Bela Balázs defined film and its language through the following triad: 'close-up, shot, and montage' (2003: 139). Thus, functioning as a narrative camera, Raban collects shot after shot, closes in on details, and his collected views provide a montage of the urban spectacle. The *flâneur*'s sense of superiority goes back to E. T. A. Hoffmann's 1823 novella *My Cousin's Corner Window*, where the gazer is superior, being placed high above the crowd in the market zooming in on single figures at will (see Beicken 2011: 171). However, the elevated stance and dominating position is missing in Raban's grounded setting. In addition, his sense of authority, control, and self is being challenged both in his viewing and in his situation at work. A lady whose look he interprets as a return of his gaze unnerves Raban. The challenge irritates him. In addition, he is being treated like a total stranger in the office, and he feels isolated, alienated and very insecure. As *flâneur*, Raban is rather 'immobilized, if not incapacitated' (Beicken 2011: 168).

Engaged to Betty, 'an oldish pretty girl' (Kafka 1971: 70), Raban is conflicted about the imminent marriage to her. At one point he expresses a desire not to have journeyed to the countryside, as he could 'spent an agreeable night at Elvy's' (1971: 68), a lover in the city that provides sexual pleasures. While travelling on the train, Raban continues his role as close observer and narrative camera. He eyes the other passengers, their faces, gestures and clothes. Then, disembarked at a station, he waits for a bus to take him to his final destination, a village, where his mother and fiancée await him. While Raban talks to an official about the rainy weather, he observes very closely a girl who is seated nearby. Kafka adds a sense of the extraordinary to this ordinary scene by simulating a shot on a film set: 'The official had put his right hand on his hip, and through the triangle formed by the arm and the body Raban saw the girl, who had now shut the parasol, on the seat where she sat' (ibid.). Raban's gaze is framed by the mask-like triangle that limits his field of vision while also focusing it on the girl, the object of desire. This filmic view affects Raban and points to his conflictedness, as the triangulation of the visual field corresponds to his sense of triangulated desire. Only a moment later does he wish to be with Elvy rather than joining his fiancée. The *mise-en-scéne*, i.e. Kafka's composition of the scene privileges Raban's focus on the girl. The male look triggers a desire that comes to the surface as a wish for the alternate relationship with Elsa. The longing for sex in the city is juxtaposed with marriage and conforming to social conventions. Raban's uneasy *flânerie* enhances the contrast between the urban pleasure seeker of modernity and the traditional hetero-normative society. Kafka's innovative use of a masked screen and the triangulation was ahead of the cinema of his time.

In 1908 Kafka published eight prose pieces that became part of his first book publication *Betrachtung* (1913), a title that can be rendered as observation, contemplation or meditation. Among them is 'Der Fahrgast', translated as 'On the Tram' (1971: 388–9) or 'The Passenger' (2007: 21–3), an intriguing text with a traditional narrative frame in which the first-person narrator reveals his complete insecurity within 'this world, in this town, in my family' (1971: 388). Then the narrator describes the scene: standing on the platform of a tram, being carried through the city where pedestrians cross the path of the tram, walk alongside it or 'stand gazing into shopwindows' (ibid.). The eye-catching shop windows indicate the modern urban consumer world. The gazing narrator differs from the traditional *flâneur*, as he is transported and turned into a moving camera that records sights of the city as passing images in the fleeting manner of film. The narrator then focuses on an everyday encounter that takes an unusual turn. As the passenger gazes at a girl in her finery ready to disembark, his male look objectifies her into an object of voyeuristic desire: 'She is as distinct to me as if I had run my hands over her' (1971: 388). The intrusive voyeur takes possession of the female, as her appearance is divided into anatomical parts to be absorbed visually like details of a statue: 'Her face is brown, her nose, slightly pinched at the sides, has a broad round tip. She has a lot of brown hair and little tendrils on the right temple' (1971: 389). This view of the face, initially descriptive and detached, reveals an erotic interest, if not obsession. The passenger's look becomes more intensified, as he focuses his gaze on just one particular part of her body: 'Her small ear is close-set, but since I am near her I can see the whole ridge of the whorl of her right ear and the shadow at the root of it' (ibid.). Now, the voyeuristic looker has zeroed in on his object of desire without regard for private space in a public arena. Coming from a male who had figuratively run his 'hands over her', the gaze is transgressive.

Alt believes that the gaze represents 'the end of an uncut camera movement' (2009: 40), with the narrator assuming the 'perspective of an imaginary camera' (2009: 42). Correcting Alt, Augustin (2009) points out that the moving camera was not yet part of film technique in 1908, but came more than a decade later. However, Augustin does not question whether Alt's concept of the 'uncut camera movement' can be applied here. The descriptive passages in Kafka's text suggest not a continuously moving camera, but a sequence of separate shots that are stitched together (see Beicken 2011: 170). In a similar way the author montaged the gestures in his description of the millionaire in the above-mentioned film *Slaves of Gold*. Alt also misreads the cinematic aspects of Kafka's 'Absent-minded Window-gazing', where the visual details/shots are sutured as well (see Beicken 2011: 170). Kafka gives each detail its relative independence pursuant with his concepts of close observation and contemplative approach.

IV. *URSZENEN* OF THE CINEMATIC GAZE IN *AMERIKA, THE CASTLE*

With Raban as focaliser, Kafka established a third-person narrative that privileges the mono-perspectival narrative, a narrative structure that became prevalent in his works. Raban as main figure also takes on the role of narrative camera. In *Amerika*, Karl Rossmann serves this function, as revealed in the opening paragraph. Karl has been sent across the ocean by his parents in Prague because a servant girl seduced him and got herself a child by him. As the ship that carries him is 'entering the harbour of New York, a sudden burst of sunshine seemed to illumine the Statue of Liberty, so that he saw it in a new light, although he had sighted it long before. The arm with the sword rose up as if newly stretched aloft, and round the figure blew the free winds of heaven' (1962: 3). Here, more so than the streetcar scene, Kafka's visual innovation creates an *Urszene* of the moving (narrative) camera. On deck of the slowly moving ship, Karl encounters the vista of the harbour and city of New York, an epitome of the modern metropolis. The panoramic establishing shot is enhanced by two aspects of cinematography, the guidance of the gaze (*Blickführung*) and the impressive lighting dynamics (*Lichtregie*) (see Beicken 1999a: 165, 158). The panoramic view is complemented by and visually contrasted with Karl's focus on the statue, which is entrancingly illuminated with the airs blowing freely around it. A sense of open space, grandeur and hope pervades this spectacle.

Cinematically speaking, there is, as with the sudden burst of sunlight, a distinct focal shift that alters the steady slow motion with a sense of the unexpected. While Karl as narrative camera had been training his eyesight on the statue for quite some time, the sudden burst of sunlight provides a startling new focus: the newly stretched arm with the sword. Kafka's liberty to replace the torch, the well-known attribute of the 'Statue of Liberty' (in German *Freiheitsstatue*) with a sword was criticised by Camill Hoffmann, a contemporary Viennese critic (see Beicken 1999a: 165). Also, the term *Freiheitsgöttin* (Kafka 1983: 7), literally a 'goddess of freedom', serves to re-mythologise the real Statue of Liberty. In allegorical representations, the sword is usually an attribute of Iustitia, the Goddess of Justice. Karl, penalised by his parents and packed off to America, is facing in the renamed and reconfigured Statue of Liberty a sword-carrying Goddess of Justice. This figure is not the beacon of freedom and hope that the Statue of Liberty represents in American popular myth, but an allusive reminder of Karl's recent punishment. It also is a veiled threat of possible continued punishment even as he is approaching the shores of the New World, where the American Dream is supposed to prevail, but where Karl will get lost, disappear.

Matthias Hurst points out that the notion of 'filmic writing' (1996: 253) came about in answer to 'the new sensory experiences' of the modern age: 'speed and dynamics, variety, simultaneity, and opaqueness shape the urban life, a fragmentation of reality' (1996: 257). The hectic and fragmenting dynamics of modern life play a role when Kafka heightens the cinematic moments by using inserted images. Images of the busy New York harbour are intercut, while Karl is in the Captain's cabin pleading for justice for the stoker. The images convey the sense of 'a movement without end, a restlessness transmitted from the restless element to helpless human beings and their works!' (1962: 17). Compared to this restlessness, Karl's initial cinematic impressions are calmer, though the image of the statue and the arm with the sword is clearly more intense than the moving panoramic camera view of the harbour. When the sword comes into sudden focus, it serves as a stark reminder of past troubles and an ominous threat to the protagonist's future, although the impact of the menacing picture is softened by the 'free winds of heaven'. Here, Kafka's cinematic art is to montage together two images that have opposing dynamics. While the panoramic harbour view is restful, the image of the statue and the intercut *Zwischenbilder* are both disquieting. The image of the statue comes within a particular *mise-en-scène*. Against the background of the panoramic view the appearance of the statue grows in definition as the *Lichtregie* makes a detail, the arm with the sword, the sole and startling focus of vision. The sudden illumination suggests an epiphany that forces the viewer, i.e. the reader as a virtual spectator of the cinematic moment, to focus on the close-up of the image and contemplate its neo-mythological message of misdeed, punishment and revenge. Karl is both a slow moving narrative camera that takes in the reassuring panoramic harbour view as well as a gazer that is forced to focus on the challenging, even shocking statue image. His past, presence and future configure in an ill-omened way. In this *Urszene* of the moving (narrative) camera, Kafka's writing expressively and effectively achieves the intermedial blending of the literary and the cinematic.

An *Urszene* of a different kind follows, when Karl's Uncle Jakob addresses his nephew's seduction in Prague by the family's servant girl. Although he claims he had 'no feelings' for the girl (1962: 27), Karl recalls the encounter vividly. Visiting the kitchen, where the servant works or writes letters, he notices her seeking eye contact and, without acknowledging, he seems to develop an interest in the woman. Sometimes she would pray in her tiny room next to the kitchen, leaving the door ajar with the following result: 'then Karl would feel shy if he passed by and caught a glimpse of her through the crack of the slightly open door' (1962: 29). The servant seems to be inviting to be looked at, and the 'shy' teenager does little to avoid looking at the woman. The situation puts Karl into the position of the male gazer, making this the more eroticised *Urszene* of voyeuristic gazing in Kafka. While the passenger on the tram ogles the young woman, as if looking at an art object, the erotic interest seems aestheticised. By comparison, Karl's gaze through the crack of the door at the female in moments of privacy and intimacy fits the pattern of male behaviour in peep shows prevalent in early cinema. The male gaze has been theorised in feminist film criticism as controlling (see Mulvey 1989), the peep-show syndrome privileges the male gazer in a superior position to the female, often a nude object of desire.

Judith Mayne reverses the *Urszene* of early cinema 'in which mostly men, but occasionally women, peek through keyholes, offering bold demonstrations of the voyeuristic pleasure that has been central to virtually every contemporary theory of cinema' (1990: 9). That women are 'situated on both sides of the keyhole', as Mayne asserts (ibid.), is confirmed by a scene in *The Castle* where Frieda, the barmaid, invites K. to see Klamm, her master and soon to be relinquished lover, through a peephole (Kafka 1974: 47). While Klamm appears in K.'s view 'as the sitter in a photographic studio' and K. seems to take on 'the role of the photographer looking through the aperture' (Duttlinger 2010: 242), the image of the inactive figure can also be seen as a film still. Although the reflection of the lighting on Klamm's pince-nez makes eye contact impossible adding to the opaqueness of the official's appearance, K. sees the immobile body as a peephole-privileged voyeur. He expects some movement, but Frieda is in the know and states that Klamm is asleep. While Kafka employs the *Urszene* of voyeurism, K. fails to have the controlling visual power, as he only gets an incomplete picture of the viewed figure. For K. there is no visual domination. As if in an opaque frozen frame, Klamm becomes an enigma. This confirms Kafka's preference for the parable in its inexplicable form, or as Benjamin observed, Kafka 'took all conceivable precautions against the interpretations of his writings' (1999a: 804).

While Karl's gaze through the crack in the door did not give him control, as he was ultimately seduced, K.'s visual power is diminished as well, although he was privileged in the *Urszene* of cinematic voyeurism. K. is incapable of reading and interpreting the freeze frame of Klamm correctly in a similar way that he misconceives the photograph of the high jumper. Kafka undercuts the 'optics of power' (Duttlinger 2007: 206). Frieda, however, has visual power. While she seems to be an 'unobtrusive little girl' at first, her 'striking look of conscious superiority' impresses K. (Kafka 1974: 47). Frieda closes the peephole with a pin, engages K. in intercourse, and gains agency when she responds defiantly to Klamm's 'deep, authoritative, impersonal voice' (1974: 54) that calls for her services. Clenching her fist and beating on the door she shouts that she is with the Land-Surveyor. Subverting the traditional *Urszene* of male voyeurism, Kafka reveals the innovative thrust of his cinematic writing.

V. THE SOCIAL GAZE OF SURVEILLANCE IN *THE TRIAL*

The Trial adds new dimensions to Kafka's visual method by creating the *Urszene* of surveillance. Upon waking up, Josef K. is the object of the gaze by the old lady, a neighbour across the street who stares at him with a curiosity unusual even for her. Subsequently, K. is confronted by the two warders and the inspector who tells him of his arrest. Regarding K.'s spatial movement, it takes him from his room through the one next door finally to a third room that belongs to Ms Bürstner. Intriguingly, the people across the street parallel K.'s movement through the rooms to see the inspector. As he proceeds, K. realises with dismay that he is being watched. This being-looked-at irritates K. so much that he, losing his cool in front of the inspector and the two warders, angrily shouts at the onlookers across to go away. Not only had the old lady followed him in a parallel movement reminiscent of parallel action in film, she also had gotten company, first by an older man and then by a younger bearded fellow to form a 'party of three' (1968: 13) or *Gesellschaft* (Kafka 1990: 20), i.e. society that subjects K. to a surveilling social gaze.

Although there are frequent cutaways to the other side, the social gazers do not get their own narrative agency unlike in parallel action in film where independent yet simultaneous events are connected by crosscutting and suture. Rather, K. experiences repeatedly the annoying spectators as 'officious, inconsiderate wretches!' (1968: 13) whose gazing is both inquisitive and controlling. K. senses an ominous threat from the representatives of the social hierarchy, as the two older figures configure a couple with the younger man appearing to be their son, suggesting a family icon. As such, the family icon group represents the hetero-normative hierarchy of the society that both surveills and marginalises K. Because of his homoerotic leanings, he stands for the antithesis of the given patriarchal social order.

K.'s shifting sexual identity and homosexual tendencies become evident in another *Urszene* that presents K.'s daydream of meeting with the court painter Titorelli. In his fantasy he experiences a transformation of identity, which occurs in a deleted part of the unfinished chapter 'The House' (1968: 245–50). As the court proceedings against him wear him down, K. seeks out Titorelli for help in his trial. Often he lies exhausted on a sofa in his office given to daydreams. In one of them his fellow lodgers stare at him as a 'closed group' and an 'accusing chorus' (1968: 247). Escaping this hostility, K. enters the court building and encounters in the antechamber a foreigner who is dressed like a 'bullfighter' (1968: 248). As part of the interior *flânerie*, K. focuses on the dance-like gait of the figure, moving around him, and 'gaping at him with wide-open eyes' (ibid.). K.'s voyeurism seems insatiable, as 'he couldn't see enough of it' (ibid.). K. bends low, circles around the bullfighter's lower torso, and his desiring gaze is fixed camera-like on the short dress with its elaborate lace and torn fringes, marvelling at the 'masquerades foreign countries provide' (ibid.). Ingeniously, the *mise-en-scène* is concentrated on the dizzying object of desire and the gaze of the swirling camera. With great efforts K. tears himself away from the exotic spectacle. The erotic appeal both entrances and tortures him: 'K. flung himself round on the sofa and pressed his face into the leather upholstery' (ibid.).

Continuing this *Urszene* of interior *flânerie*, K. engages in a daydream of meeting Titorelli that has been noted for its 'homosexual effusion' (Deleuze and Guattari 1986: 44) and its 'cinema of wishfulfillment' (Beicken 1999b: 13). Kafka crossed out this revealing passage that celebrates a male-male encounter with all the trappings of desire and flirtation, touching and affection, as K. woos the painter whose arms and cheeks K. caresses with passion and delight. Indicating his consent to K.'s wishes, Titorelli takes his hand, embraces him and, moving in flight along the stairs, upward and downward, effortlessly they glide in a lovely motion. Amazed, K. experiences an epiphany-like 'transformation' (1968: 249), as a bright light that had been behind them suddenly flows in a blinding stream toward them. At the moment of transformation, the light appears like the glare on a cinema screen, transfiguring K.'s metamorphosis. In this cinematic moment he fades out as it were, leaving behind his old embattled self (and Titorelli), while gaining a new gender-bending identity. This new identity-formation is indicated by K.'s shedding his old clothes in a heap. He now dons a dress that is new, long and dark, giving him the comfort of warmth and weight. These epithets are reminiscent of the garment the washerwoman wore, a 'coarse, heavy, dark dress' (1968: 56). At the end of K.'s homosexual fantasy with Titorelli follows the fulfilling daydream of a refuge from the dominant heteronormative society by being transgendered.

CONCLUSION: KAFKA THE CINEMATIC GAZER AND WRITER

Kafka's relationship to cinema is characterised by his love of film as spectacle providing intense emotional appeal and release, while his own cinematic writing created moving pictures and visual pleasures of its own. Although he disliked the 'restlessness' of early film, both the flawed projection modus and the rush of images of moving objects, Kafka favoured slow moving pictures and cinematic stills that engendered a contemplative approach. Kafka's mono-perspectival narration established the protagonist as focaliser, whose subjective perception functioned as narrative camera, particularly in the urban scene. Of the various cinematic paradigms Kafka created, five memorable *Urszenen* are: the male gazer or *flâneur* in the cityscape or cinematic *flânerie*; the moving camera; the peephole voyeurism; the social gaze and surveillance; and the interior *flânerie*. While scholars are conflicted regarding the influence of specific films on Kafka, his cinematic writing essentially appears to have been developed independently of any one film that he saw. Innovations such as the moving camera, parallel action, the surveilling gaze, the peephole view and cinematic daydreaming show that Kafka was independent of contemporary cinema in his visual concepts and practices at times foreshadowing future film techniques. Kafka's cinematic writing conveyed not only his love of moving pictures and visual pleasures, but also stamped his works with a remarkable visuality that is both fascinating and enigmatic, mysterious and captivating: a cinema of rapture for the reader's inner screen.

BIBLIOGRAPHY

Adorno, Theodor and Walter Benjamin (1999) *The Complete Correspondence 1928–1940*, ed. Henri Lonitz, trans, Nicholas Walker. Cambridge, MA: Harvard University Press.

Alt, Peter-André (2009) *Kafka und der Film. Über kinematographisches Erzählen*. Munich: C. H. Beck.

Augustin, Bettina (1987) 'Raban im Kino. Kafka und die zeitgenössische Kinematographie', *Schriftenreihe der Franz-Kafka-Gesellschaft* 2. Vienna: Braumüller, 38–69.

_____ (2009) 'Buch über Kafkas Prosa. Visionen eines Kinos der Zukunft', review of *Kafka und der Film. Über kinematographisches Erzählen*, by Peter-André Alt. *Frankfurter Rundschau*; available at: http://www.fr-online.de/literatur/buch-ueber-kafkas-prosa-visionen-eines-kinos-der-zukunft,1472266,3031516.html (accessed 6 August 2015).

Beicken, Peter (1999a) *Franz Kafka. Der Process. Oldenbourg Interpretationen*, second edition. Munich: Oldenbourg.

_____ (1999b) 'Kafka's Gays/Gaze', *Journal of the Kafka Society of America*, 23, 1/2, 3–22.

_____ (2000) 'Kafka's Mise-en-Scène: Literary and Cinematic Imaginary', *Journal of the Kafka Society of America*, 24, 1/2, 4–11.

_____ (2006) 'Le Flâneur de Kafka: Regard, Image, Vision Cinématographique', *europe. revue littéraire mensuelle*, 84, 923, 160–83.

_____ (2011) 'Kafka's Visual Method: The Gaze, the Cinematic, and the Intermedial', in Stanley Corngold and Ruth V. Gross (eds) *Kafka for the Twenty-First Century*. Rochester, NY: Camden House, 165–78.

Benjamin, Walter (1999a [1934]) 'Little History of Photography', *Selected Writings. Vol. 2, 1927–1934*, eds Michael W. Jennings, Howard Eiland and Gary Smith, trans.

Rodney Livingstone. Cambridge, MA and London: The Belknap Press of Harvard University Press, 507–30.

_____ (1999b [1931]) 'Franz Kafka. On the Tenth Anniversary of His Death', *Selected Writings. Vol. 2, 1927–1934*, eds Michael W. Jennings, Howard Eiland and Gary Smith, trans. Rodney Livingstone. Cambridge, MA: The Belknap Press of Harvard University Press, 794–818.

Brabandt, Anne (2009) *Franz Kafka und der Stummfilm. Eine intermediale Studie*. Munich: Meidenbauer Verlagsbuchhandlung.

Brod, Max (1960) *Streitbares Leben. Autobiographie*. Munich: Kindler.

Deleuze, Gilles and Félix Guattari (1986) *Kafka: Toward a Minor Literature*. Minneapolis, MN: University of Minnesota Press.

Diedrichs, Helmut H. (ed.) (1985) *Der Student von Prag. Einführung und Proto-koll*. Stuttgart: Focus Film-Texte.

Duttlinger, Carolin (2007) *Kafka and Photography*. Oxford and New York: Oxford University Press.

_____ (2010) 'Film und Fotografie', in Manfred Engel and Bernd Auerochs (eds) *Kafka-Handbuch. Leben, Werk, Wirkung*. Stuttgart and Weimar: Metzler, 72–9.

Goebel, Rolf J. (2000) 'Kafka's Cinematic Gaze: Flanery and Urban Discourse in *Beschreibung eines Kampfes*', *Journal of the Kafka Society of America*, 24, 1/2, 13–16.

Grob, Norbert (2003) 'Die Kamera als erzählerische Instanz. Zur Theorie des filmischen Blicks', *Zwischen Licht und Schatten. Essays zum Kino*, second edition. St. Augustin: Gardez! Verlag, 139–57.

Hurst, Matthias (1996) *Erzählsituationen in Literatur und Film. Ein Modell zur vergleichenden Analyse von literarischen Texten und filmischen Adaptionen*. Tübingen: Niemeyer.

Hoffmann, E. T. A (2000 [1822]) 'My Cousin's Corner Window', *The Golden Pot and Other Tales*, trans. Ritchie Robertson. Oxford and New York: Oxford University Press, 377–402.

Jahn, Wolfgang (1962) 'Kafka und die Anfänge des Kinos', *Jahrbuch der deutschen Schillergesellschaft*, 6, 353–68.

_____ (1965) *Kafkas Roman 'Der Verschollene' ('Amerika')*. Stuttgart: J. B. Metz-lerische Verlagsbuchhandlung.

Janouch, Gustav (1971) *Conversations with Kafka*, trans. Goronwy Rees, second edition. New York: New Directions.

Jahraus, Oliver (2008) 'Kafka und der Film', in Bettina von Jagow and Oliver Jahraus (eds) *Kafka-Handbuch. Leben, Werk, Wirkung*. Göttingen: Vandenhoeck & Ruprecht, 224–36.

Kafka, Franz (1962 [1927]) *Amerika*, trans. Willa and Edwin Muir. New York: Schocken.

_____ (1968 [1925]) *The Trial*. New York: Schocken.

_____ (1971) *The Complete Stories*, ed. Nahum N. Glatzer. New York: Schocken.

_____ (1974 [1926]) *The Castle*. New York: Schocken.

_____ (1975) *The Diaries 1910–1923*. New York: Schocken.

_____ (1977) *Letters to Friends, Family, and Editors*, trans. Richard and Clara Winston. New York: Schocken.

_____ (1983) *Der Verschollene*, ed. Jost Schillemeit. *Franz Kafka. Schriften, Tagebücher. Kritische Ausgabe*. Frankfurt: S. Fischer Verlag.

_____ (1990) *Der Proceß*, ed. Malcom Pasley. *Franz Kafka. Schriften, Tagebücher. Kritische Ausgabe*. Frankfurt: S. Fischer Verlag.

_____ (2007) *Metamorphosis and Other Stories*. New York: Penguin.

Mayne, Judith (1990) *The Woman at the Keyhole. Feminism and Women's Cinema*. Bloomington: Indiana University Press.

Mulvey, Laura (1989) *Visual and Other Pleasures*. Bloomington, IN: Indiana University Press.

Zischler, Hanns (2003) *Kafka Goes to the Movies*, trans. Susan H. Gillespie. Chicago: Chicago University Press.

TO MOVE AS THE IMAGE MOVES: THE RULE OF RHYTHMIC PRESENCE AND ABSENCE IN KAFKA'S *THE MAN WHO DISAPPEARED*

TOBIAS KUEHNE

I. GEISHAS AND THE MACHINE HALL

Soon after the first cinema theatre opened in Prague in 1907, Franz Kafka and Max Brod became frequent moviegoers (see Zischler 2003). While Brod was unequivocally enthusiastic about the artistic potential of the burgeoning medium, it alternately evoked tears, apathy and mystification from Kafka. Although he frequented the movies until 1913, his attitude toward cinema was ambivalent (see Brabandt 2009: 77). In a postcard from 22 August 1908, he wrote to Brod: 'The only thing that I convincingly discern from this is that we will have to watch the cinematograph, the machine hall and the geishas together often and for a long time until we understand the matter not just for us, but also for the world' (my translation).[1] Kafka's position towards the cinema in this passage is ambivalent, disoriented and undecided. The placement of 'together' in this sentence leaves it entirely ambiguous if it is referring to the collective grammatical subject 'we' (Kafka and Brod) or the grammatical object 'the cinematograph, the machine hall and the geishas'. Kafka calls on the support of a second gaze in the endeavour to collectively make sense of what can be seen, while he also invokes the impossible task of simultaneously examining the cinematic apparatus, looking around the theatre (the machine hall) and beholding the flitting, exotic images on the screen (the geishas). His gaze is fragmented and pulled into three different directions at once – toward the images, the locale where they are displayed and the machinery that projects them. His subjectivity is fragile and in need of an ally seeing what he sees. In his postcard to Brod, Kafka is unsure about his assessment of the cinema as he struggles to keep his impressions, thoughts and subjectivity together.

Although we have no records of Kafka offering an extended reflection on cinema, the young writer and Kafka admirer Gustav Janouch offers an anecdotal conversation in which Kafka has developed a firmer and more critical stance: 'I am an Eye-man. But the cinema disturbs one's vision. The speed of the movements and the rapid change of images force men to look continually from one to another. Sight does not master the pictures, it is the pictures which master one's sight' (1971: 160). In addition to his earlier recognition of the cinema's ability to disorient the gaze and undermine the subject's integrality, Kafka later grasped its capacity to entrap the subject in a structure of domination. The cinema, far from being merely an aesthetic diversion, raised epistemological and disciplinary problems for Kafka.

Kafka's view thus differed considerably from Brod's, whose 1909 essay 'Cinematographic Theatre' ('Kinematographentheater') was a panegyric on the new medium's visual effects and capabilities. The cinema sparked Brod's desire to create his own sequence of images for the cinematograph: 'Now on the way home, I turn into an inventor, devising new images for the biograph [sic]' (1992: 17; my translation). This wish came true with his contribution to Kurt Pinthus's 1913 compilation of literary writers' scripts for film scenes, the *Kinobuch*. In the preface to his scene, Brod mused that the technical possibilities of the cinema could enhance, and eventually surpass, the effects literature can create: 'By developing technical ideas, the cinematograph can achieve new artistic effects. [...] If someone cared to do so, it would thus eventually be possible to cinematographically perform a "writer at work." His inspirations emerge from the furniture, from the blotting paper' (Pinthus 1913: 71; my translation). Kafka's more reflective critical comments on the cinema show little of Brod's hopeful anticipation.

Around roughly 1910, the cinema began to draw attention from critics and intellectuals in Wilhelmine Germany and beyond. Systematic attempts at film theory were still lacking around the time, as Max Mack's *Die zappelnde Leinwand* (1916), *Kino-Debatte* (Kaes 1978) and *Prolog vor dem Film* (Schweinitz 1992) illustrate. Heinz-B. Heller comments: 'The fact cannot be overlooked: in contrast to the first post-war years … the high concentration of film theories published between 1924 and 1926 strikingly aimed at holistic accounts' (1985: 201; my translation).[2] While Brod became an active participant in the budding theoretical debate about film, Kafka refrained from such an involvement (see Brabandt 2009: 19). Nonetheless, Kafka's private glosses capture the debates' central conundrums much more aptly than Brod's public statements. Within the multitude of dissonant and often polemical voices, several problem clusters emerged, which mirror the issues that Kafka identified. Some critics emphasised the bewitching power of aggressive, rapid and exotic images that evoke an irresistible desire to watch ('*Schaulust*') (see Baeumler 1992; Hart 1992; Roland 1992; Serner 1992). The captivating images absorbed the viewer into their surface aesthetic, mesmerised her gaze and led her to surrender her autonomous individuality to the flow of non-causally connected images on the screen. Others expressed a fascination with, or fear of, the technical machinery that conditioned, sustained and explained the illusion of the projected moving images (see Lange 1992; von Molo 1992). Positions focusing on the machinery attempted to retrieve the captured gaze and look beyond the surface to the machine's logic that would explain the flurry of a-logically sequenced images. A third pole in the discussion focused on positive or adverse cognitive, educational and political effects on the moviegoing subject. In other words, this problem cluster revolved around the site and object of contention that was caught in the tension between image and machine.

The debate as a whole, though highly dispersed in focus, style agenda and outlook, oscillated between directing attention to the images, the apparatus and the spectating subject caught in the middle, just as Kafka's postcard to Brod shifts between the flitting geishas, the cinematograph and the machine hall between the two. The debates' underlying stakes of how the spectating subject was to engage with the moving images and defend its integrity vis-à-vis an enveloping and overpowering aesthetic-technological structure (csee Heller 1985: 3) resurface in Kafka's remarks to Janouch about the images' assault on the gaze. Kafka never entered the conversation on cinema, yet the pithy remarks he made in private show how finely attuned he was to the problems and dangers the new medium posed.

It has been convincingly argued that several of Kafka's writings, in particular *Der Verschollene* (*The Man Who Disappeared*, 1927) (whose creation between 1912 and 1914 fell into the heyday of Kafka's interest in film), are exponents of filmic writing and, by implication, steep the reader in an experience of filmic seeing. Wolfgang Jahn commented on the visuality of *The Man Who Disappeared* (1962: 357–8; 1965: 32–67) and Kafka's use of intermediate images ('*Zwischenbilder*'; 1965: 55) and parallel montage (1962: 359; 1965: 57). Peter-André Alt elaborated this position by giving a more expansive account of the novel's filmic tropes, such as the depiction of flowing traffic and gigantic cityscapes, chase scenes, last minute rescues, the rich uncle, grotesque figures, large props, as well as structural techniques of film, such as sequencing of images, surprising interventions and an episodic structure (2009a: 80–97; 2009b: 25–32). Anne Brabandt published another detailed study on this topic (2009). Through Kafka's filmic writing, the reader sees what the moviegoer sees and 'how' the moviegoer sees it.

While these observations are illuminating, enquiry should not stop here. Diagnosing filmic techniques and themes does not, by itself, elucidate how Kafka's writings do any more than what Max Brod was interested in, namely, adopting filmic means for an enhanced or altered aesthetic effect. Kafka's critical remarks on the cinema and his manifestly different position from Brod's, however, allow for a hypothesis that goes further. Kafka's *The Man Who Disappeared* goes beyond the emulation of a cinematic aesthetic and attempts to work through the problems that the new medium raised: the assaulting images' captivation of the gaze versus the viewer's technico-analytical push to penetrate to the machinery behind the image, questions of control and discipline, and the modern subject's uncertain position in the midst of those assaults. The crucial point of departure in understanding the ways in which the novel fragment grapples with these problems is the observation that there is another viewer of moving images besides the reader: Karl Rossmann, the protagonist of *The Man Who Disappeared*. He is the site on which these tensions are negotiated.

II. TRAINING IN MOVING IMAGES

Karl employs two heterogeneous modes of engaging with moving images. He oscillates between a mesmerised, unreflective, distracted absorption in moving images and an urge to critically pierce through their surface, understand their underlying mechanism and constructively intervene in them. When, in the first chapter, he finds himself in the office of the ship's captain, Karl fixes his gaze on the commotion he sees through the window in the New York harbour, which creates an 'endless movement, a restlessness communicated by the restless element to the helpless men and their works' (1996: 13). He becomes similarly distracted when staring down from his rich Uncle Jakob's balcony, where Karl is spellbound by the sight of moving traffic and a slew of sights and sounds 'that seemed so palpable to the confused eye that it was like a sheet of glass spread out over the street that was being continually and violently smashed' (1996: 29). Later, Karl's rapt attention on a judicial candidate's election rally under the balcony of the singer Brunelda's apartment causes her to remark: 'Look at the little chap [...]. He's forgotten where he is for looking' (1996: 171). Karl, like Kafka, is an 'Eye-man' whose gaze frequently falls under the sway of the overpowering image.

By the same token, however, Karl is equally fascinated with the hidden technical operations running underneath the image. The reader learns early on: 'I've always been terribly interested in machinery … and I'm sure I would have become an engineer' (1996: 5; also cf. 67, 96, 181, 213). Karl's dream job is that of a planner, arranger and controller of mechanisms that run underneath the polished surface of a technical object. Despite his stated lack of technical knowledge, he is interested in the marvellous construction of his desk, repeatedly asks his uncle to reveal the inner workings of his shipping company, is disappointed when he has only limited access to the machinery in operating the elevator in the Hotel Occidental and foregoes his secured position as an actor at the Nature Theater of Oklahoma in favour of a post as a low technical worker. Karl wants to work in the machine hall and take his proper place in it. At the same time, a spectacle of motion can easily bewitch his gaze like a geisha, holding him in mystified suspense.

Neither of Karl's two ways of engaging the moving image empowers him. Although he stands in static hypnosis when he stares at images of motion, he also loses control when he attempts to understand the machinery. Turning the crank on his desk is just as captivating to him as staring down his uncle's balcony, the noise in his uncle's company is 'bewildering' (1996: 34) and Karl immediately gets lost in the labyrinthine hull of the ship in the first chapter and the intricate corridors during his fateful visit to the mansion of his uncle's business partner, Pollunder. The reality that Karl inhabits is understandable neither by immersing oneself in the surface phenomena it offers, nor in attempting to come to an in-depth understanding of the intricate, multi-nodal networks that run underneath. Both approaches paralyse and disorient the subject when what is truly at stake is exactly to avoid such a fixation. The crucial task is to constantly stay in motion.

To sidestep the pitfalls of both viewing habits and to ensure that Karl is able to integrate himself into the vast disciplinary mechanisms of the new land in which he has arrived, the uncle envisions a more appropriate education for him. Karl receives instruction that requires rhythmic assimilation: music, the English language and horseback riding. Karl learns to play the piano by playing an old military song, and English through reciting poems. The uncle aids him by clapping the rhythm: 'in sympathy with the verse, he slowly and rhythmically clapped his hands' (1996: 32). Karl is expected to learn the art of proper timing, of proper response, of going through the motions of playing the piano, reciting poetry and riding a horse (Karl's last name, Rossmann, literally translates as 'horse man' or 'steed man'). The principle of his uncle's educative programme crystallises in the mantra: Karl 'was to absorb and examine everything, but not allow himself to be captured by it' (1996: 29), lest he slip into ruinous idleness. In order to stay in constant motion, Karl is to avoid both aesthetic and analytical enthrallment. Instead of forgetting himself in the stasis of aesthetic contemplation or technical analysis, he is supposed to be a natural actor, to become a millionaire's nephew by playing the part.[3] His task is not to watch moving images or critique their technical conditions, but to *become* a moving image, to act the part intuitively: to do the right thing at the right time.

Transforming Karl's viewing habits thus aligns and coincides with ushering him into a new disciplinary regime: not to remain fixated on an image or on the machine, but to move as the images move and to be in sync with their rapid rhythmic succession.[4] Instead of visiting the machine hall and looking at its procedures and products, Karl must go to work in it. It is a simple, but unforgiving, rule of rhythmic presence and absence. Against this backdrop, it becomes understandable that the uncle resorts to the drastic measure of casting Karl out when he visits Pollunder's mansion for an overnight stay. Missing his lessons the next day, Karl breaks the rhythm of being at his proper place at the assigned time. Since this rule of rhythmic presence and absence is itself the essential core of his education, Karl has flunked out by virtue of his absence. If the rhythm is broken once, it is broken in its entirety.

Karl's engagement with moving images can thus be read as a gauge for his assimilation into the disciplinary structure of his environment writ large. While cinema theatres and films are conspicuously absent in *The Man Who Disappeared*, the problem of how to engage with moving images is negotiated all the more forcefully in three encounters with photographs. They are static images that, if they are put into a proper mechanism of uniform succession, have the potential to evoke motion, but are prone to deny or resist the impression of motion when they are engaged singly or improperly. In his first encounter with a photograph – that of his parents – Karl is bound to fail at conjuring up motion because he is constrained to having only one picture at his disposal. A second photo exists, but it is absent: 'he hadn't been allowed to take that photograph with him on the journey' (1996: 69).[5] As a result, he can only engage with the one he has: 'The more minutely he now examined the one in front of him and tried to catch his father's gaze from various angles. But try as he might, even moving the candle to different points, his father refused to become any more alive' (ibid.). His engagement with the photograph is comically helpless. He attempts to make it more lively by changing its relative position to the candle, but fails, achieving only a series of exaggerated misrepresentations that are due to the static nature of the photo and the bad lighting. As he cannot conjure up motion by keeping the light source static and replacing images with one another (which he is, *qua* his material constraint to one, unable to do), he uselessly tries to achieve this effect by moving the angles from which he views a single, static image. He clings to it until he sinks into sleep.

A second set of images – the photographs he finds in the bedroom of the Hotel Occidental's Head Cook – fails to come to life for the opposite reason: his gaze moves over them like a stereoscopic panorama, but none of them rouse his interest: 'All these pictures probably came from Europe, you could probably read on the back just where, but Karl didn't want to pick them up' (1996: 92). Although he now has the opportunity to follow his uncle's advice and 'examine everything, but not allow himself to be captured by it' (1996: 29) by taking up one, focusing on it and letting it go for the next, he does not do it. Here, too, Karl does not interact with the images properly.

The next time Karl comes into contact with photographs is after he has found a position as a technical worker with the Theater of Oklahoma and has joined the celebratory banquet before the company's departure. At the banquet, images are passed around: 'anyone who didn't care to participate in the general conversation could look at pictures of the Theater of Oklahoma, which had been piled up at one end of the table, from where they were supposed to be *passed from hand to hand*' (1996: 215; emphasis added). Two motions have to develop in mutual dependence: each image is to physically move from hand to hand, and the proper sensation of motion before the eye is achieved if everyone (and only everyone) engages with those images in this way. Everyone has to grasp and let go of the image they receive in a synchronised manner. Everyone must play by the rule of rhythmic presence and absence of images, no one must become fixated on a single image lest the entire effect is lost.

Karl is again deprived of this effect, but not because of any fault of his own. Only a single image reaches him at the end of the table. It is important to note, however, that Karl's engagement with the image has changed. He is neither mesmerised by it, nor is he disengaged: 'Karl didn't forget to eat, but he often looked at the picture too, having put it next to his plate. He would have liked very much to see *at least one of the other pictures*, but didn't want to fetch it himself because a servant had his hand on the stack of them, and *some sequence had to be kept to*' (ibid.; emphasis added). Karl is aware that there is more than one image he should engage with. At the same time, he does not attempt to interfere in the malfunctioning mechanism. Karl's habits have changed. He has received the necessary training for handling the moving image according to the law of rhythmic presence and absence.

III. HAND IN HAND

The central mediator that emerges from studying Karl's engagement with moving images under the aegis of discipline is neither the eye nor the mind, i.e. neither the faculty for seeing nor the one for thinking, but the *hand*. Karl does not let go of his parents' photo, he does not want to take the Head Cook's photos into his hands and he witnesses, but refrains from disrupting, a manual mechanism of passing photos from hand to hand. It is thus the hand in all its polysemic ambiguity that silently demands a closer investigation in *The Man Who Disappeared*: while it flits by unnoticed on the textual surface at first, a shift in attention reveals that the word appears explicitly at least 218 times and is implied in many more mentionings of fists, fingers and arms.[6] The hand extends to a variety of semantic domains, and it can take on an ambiguous valence within each of them. As a symbol of both disciplinary authority and resistance to it, an establisher and severer of connections, a limb that grasps and lets go, a weapon that attacks and defends, a medium that communicates in silent gestures or loud clapping, an extremity that caresses and coerces, pushes and pulls, approves and threatens, bestows and seizes, indicates and misleads – with all these connotations, it offers a glimpse at the vast reach of the uncle's educational programme for Karl and the corresponding rules and expectations of proper behaviour in America. Indeed, it will become clear that the 'proper' active, tactile and rhythmic engagement with the moving image translates into, and becomes identical with, the expectations of the totalising disciplinary structure into which Karl must insert himself.

The sheer number of instances in which the word 'hand' occurs makes it impossible to give all of them their proper attention. However, a particularly striking and constantly recurring theme is the hand's use for rhythmic and machinic clapping. It happens, for example, when Karl's questionable companions Robinson and Delamarche devise rosy future plans on their march to Butterford and start to sing and clap for joy, in the sleeping room of the Hotel Occidental when the boys are having a sportive scuffle, in the audience's support of the judicial candidate and when the head of personnel of the Theater of Oklahoma introduces the newly admitted cohort to their overseer. Clapping appears in transitory states, when disarray and chaos loom on the fringes of a precarious order. When the judicial candidate interrupts his rhythmic performance to take a food break and organise entertainment for the audience, the rally gets out of hand – 'even the people in the buildings had been unable to resist the temptation to take a hand in the proceedings themselves' (1996: 172) – as the mass swells and becomes uncontrollable. Rhythmic order keeps gigantic mechanisms together, yet those mechanisms are extremely fragile for their dependence on the uncompromised maintenance of that rhythm. No one in the disciplinary machinery is exempt from its law of rhythmic presence and absence.

With a single violation of this rule, the mechanism as a whole begins to screech. One such violation leads to Karl's demise in his job as an elevator boy, which consists in being there when there are guests that need to be transported between floors. Although Karl seems to have made some progress in his training

– he breaks the rules by accelerating the elevator only when he is alone in it, while he is on point when he moves others around – he still does not grasp the *universality* of the rule of rhythmic presence and absence, which would make him a fully integrated cog in the machine hall. He does not have to be on point most of the time – he has to be on point every single time. As such, his two-minute absence seals his fate. The Head Porter summarily exclaims: 'You left your post without permission. Do you know what that means? It means dismissal. I want no excuses … for me the mere fact that you weren't there is quite enough' (1996: 115). However, Karl is not released. The scene continues for another fifteen pages, during which Karl's dismissal is announced four more times, while painstaking reconstructions of events, critical questionings and conflicting interpretations of facts collide with each other. A single slip-up in Karl's rhythmic performance of 'up and down' endangers the entire mechanism, which cannot re-establish its rhythm by simply expelling the disruptive element.

On his way out, Karl gets a last look at how seamlessly the Hotel's machinery usually runs: the two clerks manning the information desk speak without interruption, receive help without interruption and are replaced without so much as a split second interruption. The Head Porter summarises: 'We always stand in for each other here. Otherwise such a great enterprise would be impossible' (1996: 135). A presence must always be substituted by another presence – as soon as a pure absence is noticed, the surface reveals its surface character and prompts a long-winded and arresting process of critical investigation. Motion screeches to a halt if the discipline of a rhythmic presence and absence is broken for one instant.

Everything has to go hand in hand. The cogs in the machinery have to interlock 'just right' to run smoothly. They can neither grasp into thin air nor must they be jammed. The polysemy of the hand in *The Man Who Disappeared* thus expands from rhythmic clapping to properly timed grasping and releasing: the rhythm of hands consists in their synchronised coming together and moving apart on which a functioning machine depends. For the living cogs in the machine, this entails shedding the metaphysical assumption that there are surface phenomena to be contemplated and deeper processes to be inferred. In a properly timed presence, there is no meaningful distinction between a 'surficial' image and 'deeper' mechanism. One has to take up the image and let it go for the next. To properly move is to move as the images move. Otherwise, the fragile apparatus begins to sputter and the participants in it experience violent pushes and pulls: the grip tightens, and if a human element refuses to comply, it is painfully extricated and chucked out. The hand establishes and severs connections, caresses and coerces, pushes and pulls.

IV. THE SUBJECT'S DILEMMA

If rhythmic noncompliance entails expulsion, it is striking that, as Karl becomes better and better versed in his engagement with moving images, and as he manifests that training in an improving interaction with the system in which he finally secures a position – he disappears. The last few pages feature Karl looking at a nature scene from the window of a swiftly moving train. Karl is having a paradigmatically cinematic experience. The train takes him away, deep into the American heartland and Karl is half absorbed by, half driven into, the images he sees from his compartment. These images are 'so close that the chill breath of them made their faces shudder' (1996: 218). They already touch his face. On a note of dark foreboding, Karl disappears from view forever. He slips from Kafka's view as much as he does from ours in a long, gradual process of effacement. Indeed, as his instruction in the law of rhythmic presence and absence progresses, he simultaneously loses more and more of his individuality: his parents' photograph, his belongings and lastly, his name as it devolves into 'Negro', a marker of disenfranchisement. By the same token, he declines further and further in his social position, namely from senator's nephew to elevator boy to low technical worker at the outskirts of the Theater of Oklahoma. After having disappeared from Europe, Karl undergoes a second gradual disappearance in America. Complying with the system's disciplinary requirements and finding a place in it does not entail securing a stable and prosperous subjectivity, but losing it.

Karl's training and gradual disappearance coincide because assuming one's position in the mechanism and fulfilling one's task in accordance with the requirements of rhythmic presence and absence cannot be done without the actor's self-effacement. His or her existence becomes impossible to separate from the commands and expectations that condition it from moment to moment. Yet there is, paradoxically, also no outside position to the mechanism where an unconditioned subjectivity could be staked out. Karl only ever becomes 'someone' (a millionaire's nephew, an elevator boy, a technical worker) *inside* some mechanism, albeit temporarily: in his subsequent states as an outcast, Karl is even more indeterminate. When Karl falls out of the system, the chapter ends, as he falls out of the cohesion of a narrative, only to be reinserted in a different place and time in the beginning of the next chapter. To become a moving image, i.e. to suspend the dichotomy of surface versus depth, is also to suspend the question of the autonomous subject. The machine hall poses a dilemma to the subject striving for individuation: fascination with either the images or the machine makes the subject forget itself; going to work in the machine hall makes it disappear. To insist on a stable subjectivity is to disrupt the mechanism and fall out of it; to play by the rule of rhythmic presence and absence is to meld into the mechanism and have a subjectivity that is inseparable from it. No matter how Karl interacts with moving images, and no matter which lessons he draws for his practical conduct, there is no safe locus to which an autonomous subjectivity could retreat.

Precisely this harrowing dilemma of the subject's precarious and ambiguous position was at the heart of many cinema critics' proto-theoretical positions around 1910. As Heller repeatedly stresses in his study on cinema's impact on the literary intelligentsia, film emerged as an object of theorisation when social structural changes consigned the idea of the representability of the individual to the realm of fiction (1985: 3, 247). As such, a heterogeneous and often polemical debate erupted that grappled with the subject's existential and representational dilemma in various ways. Critics saw film both as a freeing of the gaze by opening visual realms never seen before (see Baeumler 1992; Polgar 1992) and the gaze's domination by bombarding it with images (see Klemperer 1992; Serner 1992). They identified it as a tool for public education (see Roland 1992) and a moral corrupter (see Tucholsky 1992). They debated its role as a means for proletarian mass mobilisation (see Förster 1992; Grempe 1992) and a promoter of apathy and laziness (see Heimann 1978; Pfemfert1992). These disparate stances could emerge because, regardless of one's engagement with the cinema, and no matter what its effects would turn out to be, the subject, as previously understood, was irretrievably disappearing.

The paradoxical situation of the subject comes to the fore in the unfinished, fragmentary structure of the novel: if it is the task of a subject to find its place in a disciplinary mechanism that renders the subject inseparable from it, then the subject's story must end in a non-ending, i.e. in a grey area in which the subject has faded from view. Whether or not the subject has successfully achieved its task (and whether the ending is thus hopeful or catastrophic) cannot be meaningfully asked, as the subject has slipped into a space in which this question is undecidable. To ponder the problems raised by cinema is to ponder this paradox. The problematics of domination, the disorientation of the gaze and the subject in a world that has become a gigantic machine hall, and the cinema as both source and symptom of those ambiguities, come to the fore in Kafka's remarks to Brod and Janouch, and are worked out in *The Man Who Disappeared*. In light of these considerations, Kafka's novel fragment is much more than a filmic novel in the aesthetic sense. It can be read as an invested attempt to make headway in understanding 'the cinematograph, the machine hall and the geishas not just for us, but also for the world'. One response would be that the modern subject of Kafka's time comes to a clearer understanding of itself by recognising itself as disappearing.

NOTES

1. The curious placement of 'zusammen' is even more striking in the German original. It says: 'Das einzige was ich aber überzeugend daraus erkenne, ist, daß wir noch lange und oft den Kinema, die Maschinenhalle und die Geishas zusammen uns ansehen müssen, ehe wir die Sache nicht nur für uns, sondern auch für die Welt verstehen werden' (1999: 87). 'Zusammen' appears between the enumeration 'den Kinema, die Maschinenhalle und die Geishas' and the reflexive 'uns' referring back to the subject 'wir'. It is thus completely ambiguous as to whether 'zusammen' refers to the subject or the object of the sentence. This ambiguity is lost in the available English translation (cf. 1977: 44).
2. Heller refers to the 1924 works of Otto Stindt (*Das Lichtspiel als Kunstform*), Otto Foulon (*Die Kunst des Lichtspiels*) and Béla Balázs (*Der sichtbare Mensch*), and the 1926 works Rudolf Kurtz (*Expressionismus und Film*) and Rudolf Harms (*Philosophie des Films*). As late as 1923, Hugo Zehder proclaimed: 'Film has the great advantage of still being a problem. […] Naturally, film is in the process of becoming something. Tomorrow!' (1923: 9; my translation). Slightly more fledgling attempts at theorizing film came from creators of film such as E. A. Dupont (*Wie ein Film geschrieben wird und wie man ihn verwertet*; 1919) and Urban Gad (*Der Film. Seine Mittel – seine Ziele*; 1921).
3. Long before the last chapter, Karl finds himself in acting school for the Theater of Oklahoma.
4. In her essay focusing on photography in Kafka's *The Man Who Disappeared*, Carolin Duttlinger makes a similar observation: 'The uncle's criticism of Karl's visual indulgence is thus symptomatic of a more general disciplinary agenda: the viewer's transformation into a productive and docile member of capitalist society' (2006: 431).
5. The first time photographs are mentioned, the text does speak of 'photographs' (1996: 67). Whether or not this is an uncorrected slip of the pen by Kafka, Karl's subsequent engagement is with a single photo, and its singularity is crucial for the absurd unfolding of the episode. Throughout the rest of the novel, the photo is mentioned in the singular.
6. Figure obtained from a personal count in the German original.

BIBLIOGRAPHY

Alt, Peter-André (2009a) *Kafka und der Film. Über kinematographisches Erzählen*. Munich: Verlag C. H. Beck.

____ (2009b) 'Kino und Stereoskop. Zu den medialen Bedingungen von Bewegungsästhetik und Wahrnehmungspsychologie im narrativen Verfahren Kafkas', *Literatur intermedial: Paradigmenbildung zwischen 1918 und 1968*, eds. Wolf Gerhard Schmidt and Thorsten Valk. Berlin: Walter de Gruyter, 11–47.

Baeumler, Alfred A. (1992 [1912]) 'Die Wirkungen der Lichtspielbühne: Versuch einer Apologie des Kinematographentheaters', in Jörg Schweinitz (ed.) *Prolog vor dem Film. Nachdenken über ein neues Medium 1909–1914*. Leipzig: Reclam, 186–95.

Brabandt, Anne (2009) *Franz Kafka und der Stummfilm. Eine intermediale Studie*. Munich: Verlag Martin Heidebauer.

Brod, Max (1992 [1909]) 'Kinematographentheater', in Jörg Schweinitz (ed.) *Prolog vor dem Film. Nachdenken über ein neues Medium 1909–1914*. Leipzig: Reclam, 15–18.

Dupont, André-Ewald (1919) *Wie ein Film geschrieben wird und wie man ihn verwertet*. Berlin: R. Kühn.

Duttlinger, Carolin (2006) 'Visions of the New World: Photography in Kafka's Der Verschollene', *German Life and Letters*, 59, 3, 423–45.

Förster, Franz (1992 [1913]) 'Das Kinoproblem und die Arbeiter', in Jörg Schweinitz (ed.) *Prolog vor dem Film. Nachdenken über ein neues Medium 1909–1914*. Leipzig: Reclam, 131–8.

Gad, Urban (1921) *Der Film: Seine Mittel, seine Ziele*. Berlin: Schuster & Loeffler.

Grempe, P. Max (1992 [1912/13]) 'Gegen die Frauenverblödung im Kino', in Jörg Schweinitz (ed.) *Prolog vor dem Film. Nachdenken über ein neues Medium 1909–1914*. Leipzig: Reclam, 120–7.

Hart, Julius (1992 [1913]) 'Schaulust und Kunst', in Jörg Schweinitz (ed.) *Prolog vor dem Film. Nachdenken über ein neues Medium 1909–1914*. Leipzig: Reclam, 253–59.

Heimann, Moritz (1978 [1913]) 'Der Kinematographen-Unfug', in Anton Kaes (ed.) *Kino-Debatte: Texte zum Verhältnis von Literatur und Film 1909–1929*. Tübingen: Niemeyer Verlag, 77–81.

Heller, Heinz-B. (1985) *Literarische Intelligenz und Film: Zu Veränderungen der ästhetischen Praxis unter dem Eindruck des Films 1910–1930 in Deutschland*. Tübingen: Max Niemeyer Verlag.

Jahn, Wolfgang (1962) 'Kafka und die Anfänge des Kinos', *Jahrbuch der deutschen Schillergesellschaft*, 6. 353–68.

____ (1965) *Kafkas Roman 'Der Verschollene' ('Amerika')*. Stuttgart: J. B. Metzlersche Verlagsbuchhandlung.

Janouch, Gustav (1971) *Conversations with Kafka*, trans. Goronwy Rees, second edition. New York: New Directions.

Kaes, Anton (ed.) (1978) *Kino-Debatte: Texte zum Verhältnis von Literatur und Film 1909–1929*. Tübingen: Niemeyer Verlag.

Kafka, Franz (1977) *Letters to Friends, Family, and Editors*, trans. Richard and Clara Winston. New York: Schocken Books.

____ (1996) *The Man Who Disappeared (Amerika)*, trans. Michael Hofmann. London: Penguin.

_____ (1999) *Franz Kafka Kritische Ausgabe: Briefe 1900–1912 Bd.1*, ed. Hans-Gerd Koch. Frankfurt a.M.: Fischer Taschenbuch Verlag.

Klemperer, Victor (1992 [1911/12]) 'Das Lichtspiel', in Jörg Schweinitz (ed.) *Prolog vor dem Film. Nachdenken über ein neues Medium 1909–1914*. Leipzig: Reclam, 170–82.

Lange, Konrad (1992 [1913/14]) 'Die Zukunft des Kinos', in Jörg Schweinitz (ed.) *Prolog vor dem Film. Nachdenken über ein neues Medium 1909–1914*. Leipzig: Reclam, 109–20.

Mack, Max, ed. (1916) *Die zappelnde Leinwand. Ein Filmbuch*. Berlin: Eysler.

Pfemfert, Franz (1992 [1911]) 'Kino als Erzieher', in Jörg Schweinitz (ed.) *Prolog vor dem Film. Nachdenken über ein neues Medium 1909–1914*. Leipzig: Reclam, 165–9.

Pinthus, Kurt (ed.) (1913/14) *Das Kinobuch: Kinodramen*. Leipzig: Kurt Wolff.

Polgar, Alfred (1992 [1911/12]) 'Das Drama im Kinematographen', in Jörg Schweinitz (ed.) *Prolog vor dem Film. Nachdenken über ein neues Medium 1909–1914*. Leipzig: Reclam, 159–64.

Roland (1992 [1912/13]) 'Gegen die Frauenverblödung im Kino', in Jörg Schweinitz (ed.) *Prolog vor dem Film. Nachdenken über ein neues Medium 1909–1914*. Leipzig: Reclam, 127–31.

Schweinitz, Jörg (ed.) (1992) *Prolog vor dem Film. Nachdenken über ein neues Medium 1909–1914*. Leipzig: Reclam.

Serner, Walter (1992 [1913]) 'Kino und Schaulust', in Jörg Schweinitz (ed.) *Prolog vor dem Film. Nachdenken über ein neues Medium 1909–1914*. Leipzig: Reclam, 208–14.

Tucholsky, Kurt (1992 [1913]) 'Erotische Films', in Jörg Schweinitz (ed.) *Prolog vor dem Film. Nachdenken über ein neues Medium 1909–1914*. Leipzig: Reclam, 51–4.

von Molo, Walter (1992 [1912]) 'Im Kino', in Jörg Schweinitz (ed.) *Prolog vor dem Film. Nachdenken über ein neues Medium 1909–1914*. Leipzig: Reclam, 28–39.

Zehder, Hugo (1923) 'Einleitung', *Der Film von Morgen*, ed. Hugo Zehder. Berlin: Rudolf Kaemmerer Verlag.

Zischler, Hanns (2003) *Kafka Goes to the Movies*. trans. Susan H. Gillespie. Chicago: University of Chicago Press.

NOISES OFF: CINEMATIC SOUND IN KAFKA'S 'THE BURROW'

KATA GELLEN

What sort of a noise is the noise in Franz Kafka's burrow? 'Der Bau' ('The Burrow', 1931) is a late, unfinished story about a creature that devotes its energies and thoughts to the protection and preservation of its underground home. At a certain point, about halfway through what exists of the literary fragment, it begins to hear a persistent yet unidentifiable sound: hissing, scratching, scuttling, scraping. The rest of the story can be described as an anxious, even paranoid attempt to understand and explain this noise, to read a sign whose signifier consists of a series of related but non-identical acoustic effects. In this essay, I attempt to name and analyse this sound through concepts from film theory, specifically theories of sound in cinema. The noise in the burrow is both acousmatic (a sound whose source is not seen) and non-diegetic (a sound that is external to the fiction represented). To designate the noise in the burrow in these terms is to recognise an inherent contradiction: the source of the noise cannot be discovered because it is located beyond the realm in which its acoustic effects are perceived. From the perspective of the narrating burrower – which is the only perspective available in this first-person narrative – it is a sound without a source. This phenomenon is impossible in the real world; but in fiction, it is a reality.

Kafka's strange sound object enables an exploration of the borders of fiction from within a work of fiction. It offers, in the context of a first-person literary narrative, an encounter with a noise whose source can only lie in a realm beyond that of the fictional character's world. The sound is an 'interference' from the outside – not just outside the burrow, but outside the burrower's world – which implies the possibility of a character's reckoning with its own fictional status in the context of a story that has no other obvious meta-fictional traits.

In the final section of this essay, I introduce another example of a fictional consciousness that discovers its reality is in fact the product of authorial machinations: Peter Weir's *The Truman Show* (1998). In that film, unlike in Kafka's story, the main character comes to recognise fully that he has been trapped in a fiction and finds a way out of it 'into the real'. *The Truman Show* portrays this unsettling self-discovery directly, while in Kafka's story it is not at all clear that the burrower has any inkling that the noise it hears is uncaused and thus a sign of its createdness. Still, the comparison is fruitful, for it suggests that in both film and literature sound can serve as a means through which to explore the boundary between fiction and reality.

I. ACOUSMATIC LISTENING

To hear and depict sound in itself, without reference to a cause: this is what the French composer and sound theorist Pierre Schaeffer sought to achieve for musical listening. He unearthed the ancient story of the Acousmatics, disciples of Pythagoras who listened to his teachings from behind a curtain, so as to be able to concentrate entirely on the voice of their master, and offered the following definition: 'Acousmatic, adjective: is said of a noise that one hears without seeing what causes it' (2004: 77). Schaeffer focused on the positive consequences of acousmatic listening: if one can listen to sounds without being distracted by how they are produced or transmitted, one can presumably hear more distinctly, clearly and accurately. That is, one can attend to the character of sound itself. This kind of 'pure listening', free from the influence of the other senses, allows a listener to isolate sound for the purpose of reflection and study. It creates what Schaeffer called 'sonorous objects', sounds described only 'through an analysis of the content of our [auditory] perceptions' (2004: 78).

It is clear that acousmatic sound was useful for training the musical ear and for bringing a degree of directness and objectivity to descriptions of acoustic phenomena.[1] And it was natural that Schaeffer, born in 1910 and trained as a radio engineer and announcer, became interested in the possibilities of separating sound from its source. The radio, phonograph and telephone were among the earliest technologies to record or transmit sounds and deliver them to another time or place. It had always been possible to hear a sound without seeing its source, but this was due to physical constraints (for example, the walls of a house separating a listener from the chirping of a bird in a tree outside). Technologies of acoustic reproduction and transmission changed the fundamental nature of sound, hearing and the cognitive process of reckoning with sounds whose sources were absent. Suddenly there could be a sound whose cause was not simply blocked from view, but was truly not there. A voice recorded and played back on a phonograph was therefore acousmatic in a stronger sense than the bird chirping outside. No matter how hard one looked, the source of the sound could not be found, since the singer belonged to another time and place.[2]

The phenomenon of producing synthetic sound, which began with near simultaneous experiments with inscription in the United States, the Soviet Union and Germany in the 1920s, offered an even more radical experience of acousmatic sound. Synthetic sound represented the first acoustic experience that was not *of* something, 'a sonic event whose origin was no longer a sounding instrument or human voice, but a graphic trace' (Levin 2003: 34). These sounds seemed to come from nowhere; they had no discernible physical origin. Synthetic sounds do not follow the expected sequence of events whereby sounds are made, possibly heard, recorded and played back. Instead, their inscription is primary, a first cause, so that when they are played they are in fact being heard for the first time, rather than being 'played back'. Rainer Maria Rilke's *Ur-Geräusch* ('Primal Noise', 1919) poses the question of what sound would be generated by a phonograph needle tracing the coronal suture of a human skull. This thought experiment, which received a great deal of attention from the early media theorist Friedrich Kittler, encourages us to imagine the possible consequences of playing sounds that had never been recorded, 'the decoding of a track that no one had ever encoded' (Kittler 1990: 316). As such, the text exemplifies the modernist fascination with uncoupling acoustic effects from causes. Moving beyond the particular problem of sound and source, Kittler saw a parallel to other modern thinkers such as Georg Simmel and Sigmund Freud, who all proposed methods that 'can track traces without a subject. A writing without the writer, then, records the impossible reality at the basis of all media: white noise, primal sound' (ibid.). Kafka, I will show, is deeply engaged with this thought/sound experiment. As I will discuss later, 'The Burrow' presents an example of primal sound – one that is audible without being traceable, and technological without being linked to any apparatus. It is a literary manifestation of a sound without a source.[3]

In the 1980s, the French filmmaker and theorist Michel Chion seized upon Schaeffer's definition of the acousmatic and built a theory of cinematic experience around the notion of disembodied sounds, the *acousmêtre*. He argued that the power of sound film to withhold visually what it presents acoustically is its most distinctive and provocative feature. Other media present acousmatic sound, but only film can play with the concealment and revelation of sound sources, which makes acousmatic sound a central agent of narrative propulsion. Sounds that 'wander the surface of the screen, awaiting a place to attach to' (Chion 1999: 4) are ghostly and unsettling. They awaken the viewer-listener's natural impulse to localise and identify the source of sounds. For Chion, the thrill of cinematic experience derives from the fact that we do not know if, when, and how the source of sounds will be made visually manifest (a process he calls 'de-acousmatisation').

If the *acousmêtre* in film could prove so unsettling, actual encounters with disembodied voices and unidentifiable noises in the early days of sound reproduction technologies were even more so. Voices that seemed to come from nowhere were thought to derive from the ether, a realm associated with the dead and undead.[4] Other sounds, even if they did not seem ghostly, eerie or netherworldly, could still pose the threat of unknowability. Once the phonograph, telephone and radio could sever sound from its source – all of which, it must be noted, was happening well before the advent of synchronised film sound – the process of de-acousmatisation was no longer guaranteed. A sound could remain unlocatable, unidentifiable and invisible for an indefinite length of time. This is the scenario that 'The Burrow' presents. It is an expression not only of the fear induced by a sound whose cause cannot be discovered; it is haunted by the even more disturbing idea that if noise in modernity can be said to derive from an unidentified *elsewhere*, is it not also possible that it comes from an unknowable *nowhere*?

II. THE NOISE IN THE BURROW

Kafka's 'The Burrow', written in 1923, is an unfinished, slightly rambling narrative, told by a burrowing creature that builds a subterranean home for itself, guided by a wish for solitude and safety. About midway through what exists of the literary fragment, the creature begins to hear a noise. Its attempt to identify the sound occupies its reflections and determines its actions, which include the gradual destruction of its home in an effort to discover the source of the sound. The narrative thwarts every attempt at de-acousmatisation: the burrowing narrator never comes close to discovering what is causing the sound, and every attempt it makes to name and describe its purported cause fails. The process Chion describes, whereby the film viewer-listener latches on to an acousmatic sound and tries to follow it, trace its path and pin down its origin, simply cannot take place in Kafka's story. 'The Burrow' is thus a companion text to the more famous 'Josefine, die Sängerin oder das Volk der Mäuse' ('Josefine, the Singer or the Mouse People', 1924). In these stories about elusive creatures and sounds there is always something that cannot be pinned down: Josefine is all body and no (articulable) sound,[5] whereas the noise in the burrow is all sound and no identifiable body.

As J. M. Coetzee remarks in his insightful essay on the problem of time in 'The Burrow', 'it would be naive to think that the whistling is a warning and that "the enemy" is some beast whom the reader does not get to see' (1981: 575). In other words, the noise in the burrow is not the sound *of* something. Though the desire to de-acousmatise is the driving force of the whole narrative, it is clear that such a revelation could never happen, even if Kafka had finished the story. First of all, nothing can be said about the location of the noise, since 'it is not even constant, the way such noises are as a rule; there are long pauses' (Kafka 2007b: 177). The disturbance seems to come and go, and these variations make it difficult to analyse. And yet, at times the problem also seems to invert itself, only to grow more insoluble in the process:

> It is really nothing, sometimes I think that no one except me heard it; I hear it now, of course, more and more distinctly with an ear grown more acute by practice, although in reality it is exactly the same noise everywhere, something I can prove to myself by the comparative method. (2007b: 178)

Here the issue is no longer that the noise keeps changing, but that it is non-variable and omnipresent. This is in direct contradiction to the previous description of the noise as constantly changing, though it actually poses a similar obstacle to de-acousmatisation. Whether the noise keeps changing in unpredictable ways or remains precisely the same noise everywhere, it is impossible for the burrower to gauge its distance from it or position with respect to it. It would need to perceive steady and measurable changes in tone or volume to orient itself in relation to the sound. Thus, the burrower complains, 'it is exactly this steady equivalence at all spots that bothers me most' (ibid.). As Mladen Dolar notes, 'there are no clues or too many clues, which amount to the same, and the even distribution of clues makes them useless' (2011: 116). Whether the noise in the burrow is too invariable to be pinned down or not variable enough to offer orientation, the consequence is clear: it has not been and indeed cannot be de-acousmatised.[6]

The non-localisability of the noise in the burrow is the first of several clues that the noise in the burrow is a sound without a source. The variety of designations that the noise accrues is a further indication of this status. The act of naming the noise, a linguistic process, could be seen as a way around the problem of localising it, which is an audio-visual matter. If the cause of the sound cannot be discovered and confirmed by visual means, it might at least be asserted and posited by linguistic ones – or so the burrowing narrator might think. For Chion, who has spent much of his career theorising the relationship between sound and image, the process of de-acousmatisation is fundamentally visual.[7] He contends that film presents the most interesting acousmatic sounds because it is always engaged in the 'play with showing, partially showing, and not showing' (1999: 21). Radio, for example, can present an acousmatic sound, but its source will never be revealed visually.

I want to challenge the idea, suggested by Chion and adopted explicitly or implicitly by other theorists, that de-acousmatisation is an exclusively visual process. There are other ways to 'know' sound, even to reveal and discover sound sources, than to see them with the eyes. Once acousmatic sound is wrested from the exclusive domain of cinema, these alternatives become clear. One can *name* sounds, which is the primary means available in literature. Thus, de-acousmatisation can be a linguistic process.

Throughout 'The Burrow', the narrator introduces a broad range of words to describe the noise in the burrow, from the most direct designations of the sound itself (hissing, whistling, noise) to the most concretised and personified – or, more accurately, animalised – names for the creaturely agent presumed responsible for the noise (opponent, enemy, persecutor, assailant, etc). At the first end of this spectrum the noise is treated as a Schaefferian 'sonorous object', according to which the sound alone is described and nothing about its source or effects is assumed or extrapolated. The onomatopoetic quality of a word like *Zischen* ('hissing') exemplifies this kind of name: nothing can be designated beyond the qualities of the sound perceived. At the opposite end of this nomenclatural spectrum, the names assigned are the result of speculation, imagination and personification: sources and origins are assumed, embodied and animated. These designations represent the full metonymic progression from noise as sensory impression to noise as living creature. The problem with the latter kind of name is that there is no evidence of a creature responsible for the noise; it involves assumptions and guesses that do not conform to the burrower's perceptions. The problem with the former type of name is that it can seem incomplete, though in fact it is not: the source is absent not because it is not known, but because it does not exist. This is an impossibility in the real world, but it is the 'reality' of the fictional world Kafka presents. The question, then, is whether to interpret the story according to the rules of fiction or reality. The rules of fiction would compel us to accept what is given in the text and forbid us to impose outside standards onto the fictional world, whereas the rules of reality would force us to accept that there can be no sounds without sources, and thus where no sources are presented, they must be assumed.

Coetzee flatly rejects readings that assume there must be a creature behind the noise, and I concur with him. Dolar's reading of 'The Burrow' performs the temptation of accepting this assumption, though whether he fully affirms it is unclear. After identifying 'an enigma pertaining to causality' at the heart of the story, he suggests that 'the impossibility of pinning down the cause to a locus and of unravelling its source, of discerning the indiscernible, offers a crack where fantasy comes in' (2011: 115, 120). One must *imagine* a sound source, given that the story so persistently defies our attempts to find one. In my reading, uncaused sound can exist as a fictional phenomenon, whereas for Dolar 'the dislocation of natural causality' sparks 'fantasy', which 'unifies the absent cause of sounds into a single beastly creature' (2011: 121). On the one hand, Dolar's 'beast' gives form and flesh to the source of the sound, which is in its essence uncaused; it lends coherence and plausibility to something that is incoherent and impossible, at least outside of fictional worlds. On the other, it gives form and flesh only in name, not in spirit, for Dolar's 'beast' is really just a way to designate the nonsensicality of an uncaused noise:

> The impossibility of finding a univocal location of the sound in reality opens up a crack where fantasy comes flooding in [...]. By virtue of its dis-location, the sound has the structural propensity of leading to the assumption of the beast. Only the beast can straighten out its crooked causality and provide it with being, location, oneness, stability, duration, meaning – all those things that one was incapable of achieving. With the mere supposition of the beast, by a single stroke, it all makes sense, if beastly sense. It displays the beastly part of making sense – the part where the sense fills in the crack, underpinned by fantasy. (2011: 133)

For Dolar, 'fantasy' posits the 'beast' because this is the only way to produce a reading that makes sense, to normalise and rationalise a situation that is otherwise impossible.

I think it is in fact possible to grasp the seemingly impossible situation that 'The Burrow' presents – the unreal but imaginable situation of an uncaused sound, an autonomous sound object – without conceptualising its cause as a 'beast'. In this, my reading diverges from Dolar's, and the reason for this rests on the means through which de-acousmatisation can occur. If the identification of sound sources must happen through visual processes then perhaps one really does need to imagine the 'beast' – one needs to be able to *see something*, if only in the mind. But since 'The Burrow' opens up the possibility that there are other modes of de-acousmatisation, literature and literary thinking are free to articulate possibilities closed off to film and visual thinking. Simply to accept the burrower's inferences about the noise – that where there is sound, there is something causing it – is to normalise a situation that is actually presented, in the text, as abnormal. It is to impose the standards of our world onto another, one we have little reason to think resembles ours so closely. After all, the story gives no indication that the noise is a symptom, effect or consequence of something else. It provides no justification for confirming the established pattern of experience or interpretation, that if there is a sound, it must have an outside source, since a sound cannot cause itself. The plain but unlikely fact about Kafka's 'The Burrow' is that the disturbance in the burrow is noise itself, akin to Schaeffer's 'pure sonorous object' or Rilke's and Kittler's 'primal noise'.

Such an audible but acoustic object is fictional in two senses. First, it is unreal: there is no such thing as a sound without a cause (synthetic sound, too, is caused by the machines and programmers that create it, even if it has no referent). Second, it can only 'exist' in art forms that are capable of producing fictional worlds, such as film and literature. These art forms can, in acts of playful manipulation, undo the necessary link between a natural sign and the thing it signifies: they can present smoke without fire, colour without object and sound without a source. One cannot encounter an uncaused sound in the real world, because such a sound cannot exist. There is no scenario in which one could 'hear' the noise in the burrow. It could not be present to our perceptual faculties, since heard sounds always have causes. However one can imagine and represent such a sound, given the right tools. Fiction can transcend the humanly possible, as Kafka's burrower reveals. If we identify a cause, no matter how ghostly or beastly, we elide this truth about the noise in the burrow.

There is one further possibility that every interpretation of the noise in the burrow must entertain: that it is merely imagined or caused by the burrower itself in some other way; it comes from within, which is why it is always there and yet remains unlocatable.[8] While it is true that Kafka's fictions take place at the border of dream, fantasy or hallucination, they remain *at* this border, never definitively transgressing it. This is the condition of much that is peculiar and uncanny in Kafka: that the characters and events described are real, and not merely imagined, dreamed or metaphorical. After all, strange dreams are far less strange than strange realities. In addition to attributing the inexplicable in Kafka to dreams, certain psychological and physical conditions can also be called upon to normalise and rationalise the inexplicable. In the case of seemingly uncaused sounds, one could argue that certain psychological disturbances cause auditory hallucinations (such as the phenomenon of hearing voices), as do certain physical conditions (Kafka himself suffered from tinnitus). And yet, to apply these explanations to the noise in the burrow is to eliminate the presence of the incommensurable, which is the hallmark of Kafka's writing. Perhaps we do better to stay within Kafka's world, so to speak – to try to grasp the strangeness that results from the fictional conditions of Kafka's works, rather than to appeal to external rationalisations. These rationalisations flatten Kafka's worlds; they do a disservice, even if they make his fictions more palatable. As Dolar notes, 'there is a moment of phantasmagoria when the sound wavers, if ever so minimally, between its reality and unreality' (2011: 116). Even if there are grounds for thinking that the noise is imagined, this wavering prevents us from settling on this reading, just as the non-localisability of the sound prevents us from isolating its source. We can be certain neither that the noise is audible in the burrow, nor that it is not. This is the text's only guarantee: an infinite capacity to destabilise listeners and readers.[9] It would be a mistake to content ourselves with the version of reality that conforms with our lived experience, simply because the reality of Kafka's fictions is too strange and off-putting.

III: SOUNDS FROM BEYOND

There exists a moment of revealing self-doubt in Coetzee's essay on the paradoxical temporality of 'The Burrow'. For him, the central problem of time lies in the iterativity of the first (pre-noise) part of the narrative, which seems to be followed by the event of the onset of noise. And yet it is not in fact this simple: the noise returns continually, and there are clues that this return is familiar, even expected.

> The shift from *ich* to *man* is maintained for much of the rest of the paragraph, in conformity with the new hypothetical mode of the narrative. It seems impossible to square this mode with a non-iterative understanding of the narrative unless one grants to the narrator the effective position of a fictional creator, someone toying with sequences which may or may not be inserted into the narrative. While this possibility cannot be dismissed absolutely, there is nothing else in the text to support the notion that the operations of writing are being so radically unmasked. On the other hand, if one understands the narrative as iterative, then the hypothetical sequence fits in as one which may or may not occur in a given iteration. (Coetzee 1981: 564)

Coetzee hints tentatively at a reading that he is ultimately unwilling to advance, because he does not believe there is enough textual evidence to support it: that the burrowing narrator is not fully 'in' or 'of' the story, but rather has some consciousness of itself as a literary creator. I would not pull away from this reading as quickly as Coetzee does. Kafka's burrowing narrator *does* transcend the limits of its fictional world. This does not necessarily make it a 'fictional creator', but it implies that it is a fictional character with an extraordinary power to access a world beyond the one in which it exists, the world of its creator. Though nothing suggests that the creature is in a position of control or mastery, it nevertheless possesses a consciousness that transcends the limits of the fictional text, 'The Burrow' that houses the burrow which is its home.

Contrary to Coetzee, I think there *is* something else in the text that suggests that 'the operations of writing are being so radically unmasked': the fact that Kafka's burrowing narrator hears a sound from another world – a 'non-diegetic' sound, to invoke the language of film studies. In cinema, non-diegetic sounds come from a space outside the narrative and are inaudible within the narrative; they belong to a world unknown within the filmic diegesis, and are added by the director or sound editor for the benefit of the viewer-listener. The noise in the burrow, I argue, may be thought of as acousmatic on the one hand, and non-diegetic on the other. For if the burrower hears a sound with an unknown source, that sound is acousmatic, whereas if the sound comes from another world, it is non-diegetic. And yet, there is no possible intersection between these kinds of sounds: an acousmatic sound must have a source, even if it is never discovered, and non-diegetic sound can never be heard by characters within the fiction, if the borders of the fiction are to remain intact. Kafka not only imagines this impossible intersection, he presents its literary manifestation: the noise in the burrow is a non-diegetic acousmatic sound. This means that the burrower, in listening, transcends the boundaries of its created world. It hears acoustic intimations from beyond.

Coetzee articulates the paradox of time in 'The Burrow' through the complex technical language of literary theory, which leads him to suggest the possibility of a meta-fictional reading. The paradox of sound, which can be expressed in the language of film sound theory, enables me to propose a related reading. As stated previously, the noise in the burrow is the literary manifestation of an acousmatic sound whose source cannot be discovered. As such, the noise in Kafka's work is audible in the burrow – which is to say, within the fictional diegesis or 'story world' of the text – though not subject to de-acousmatisation. It is part of the burrower's world, even if it cannot locate its source. In fact, Kafka's literary *acousmêtre* exemplifies Chion's point about the power of acousmatic sound to produce narrative suspense. The central motivating puzzle of 'The Burrow' consists of how and when the burrower will find out what is making the noise. And yet the noise in the burrow does not have a source. It is not simply that the cause of the sound is elsewhere – which would make it an instance of the 'diegetic off-screen' in literature – but that it is actually *nowhere*. This fact seems to align the noise in the burrow less with acousmatic sound and more with non-diegetic film sound, such as voice-over and mood music. Such cinematic sounds can be understood as 'uncaused' from a perspective within the diegesis, where they are actually also unheard; they simply do not exist for the characters within the fiction.

The problem of sound in 'The Burrow' is that a noise that must be considered *uncaused* is in fact audible to the burrower. It is both non-diegetic and acousmatic, which is a contradiction.[10] This is a practical problem for the burrower: it destroys its home in pursuit of something that does not exist. But it is not an ontological problem: since the creature does not realise that the noise is non-diegetic, it can unwittingly take comfort in the false belief that the source of the noise is discoverable. It is, however, an ontological problem for the reader, who cannot share the first-person narrator's position of privileged ignorance. The burrower might not realise that it is hearing something that cannot actually be audible to it, but the viewer-listener *does* understand this paradox and must find a way to explain it.[11]

We can shed some light on the problem of audible sounds without sources by comparing their manifestation in film and literature. Film is never first-person in a strict sense, despite some radical and largely unsuccessful experiments with extreme subjectivity.[12] Thus, non-diegetic sounds are not only possible in film, but a frequent and natural occurrence. A movie usually contains a multiplicity of perspectives, and presents various forces that organise and influence the presentation of sight and sound: different characters, locations, camera angles and so on. This is why it is so difficult to speak of a 'narrator' in film.[13] Indeed, it is perhaps the very essence of film that the camera does not align permanently or perfectly with one character's vision or audition, let alone consciousness. This kind of radical mono-perspectivism is possible in literature, indeed it is quite common; it describes the situation in an exclusively first-person narrative, of which 'The Burrow' is a prime example. Everything in the story issues from the burrower's consciousness: thoughts, feelings, desires and perceptions. The story is told in its voice, and there can be no distance from it – no outside perspective, no broader narrative frame, nothing 'above' or 'beyond' or 'outside' the narrator's monologue. Consequently, it would seem impossible to speak of non-diegetic sound in an exclusively first-person narrative.

And yet, the burrower hears an uncaused sound: it truly hears it and it is truly uncaused, since it is neither a figment of its imagination nor an auditory hallucination. This is not perceived as a problem by the burrower, since it does not realise it is hearing a sound from another world, one that comes from 'outside' its fictional reality, so to speak. But it is a problem for the reader who recognises this paradoxical truth. For the reader *cannot* really account for the fact that the burrower hears an uncaused sound. The reader *cannot* really explain the fact that the burrower seems to perceive something that derives from a world or dimension that is supposed to be completely inaccessible to it – that of its creator.[14] Whether this creator is an implied author or Franz Kafka himself is less important than the fact that this supposedly impermeable boundary of fiction has been transgressed: a non-diegetic sound is audible within the diegesis. While there is no indication that the burrower itself understands what has been done to it – perhaps it could not endure such blinding insight into its own createdness – the implications for reading are still staggering. One begins to suspect, as Coetzee himself suggests, that the story's fundamental aim is to expose the bare bones of writing.

The phenomenon I am beginning to articulate – and can only scratch its surface here – is what I would tentatively call the problem of 'species transcendence' in Kafka. This is when an animal or group of animals begins to grasp how circumscribed its perspective on the world really is; it is not just that there is so much they cannot perceive and understand, but that these limits cause them to misunderstand and misinterpret their world. Species transcendence names the moment that a creature perceives something from 'beyond', whether or not it realises it has done so and whether or not it can rationalise the impression (correctly or incorrectly). The clearest example of this in Kafka's oeuvre is presented in 'Forschungen eines Hundes' ('Investigations of a Dog', 1931), wherein the narrating dog names various mysteries about *die Hundeschaft* ('dogdom') which inspire questions for research: Where does their nourishment come from? And why do some dogs, the *Lufthunde* ('air-dogs'), practice a kind of levitation? That story, unlike 'The Burrow', is a farce. Thus, in 'Investigations of a Dog', all the mysteries of dogdom can eventually be resolved by the reader, a member of the human race who eventually figures out that humans are responsible for producing all the seemingly uncaused and inexplicable effects experienced by the dogs. The outside perspective unavailable to the narrating dog is available to us. The dogs, we realise, can see and eat the food left out for them, but not the humans responsible for putting it there; they perceive their fellow lapdogs as 'floating' because they are blind to the laps upon which they sit. This means, in turn, that topics that they consider to be worthy of intensive study are mundane and obvious from the human perspective.

One can thus speak in this story of a kind of 'species consciousness' with certain limits; membership in a species means only being able to perceive and understand a set of facts about the world one inhabits, and formulating puzzles and research topics around those facts beyond one's grasp. Of course an allegorical reading is tempting and largely justified: the dogs symbolise the hubris of humans, who pose research questions that sound penetrating and deserving of a lifetime of study, but in response to which members of another species, smarter and more perceptive than humanity, could effortlessly give simple and banal answers. More important for my present purposes, however, is the fact that 'Investigations of a Dog' presents the idea of a species with partial access to a realm beyond, a *jenseits*. This access is so minimal, however, that it causes more confusion than insight. This has comic effects, since the narrating dog comes up with far-fetched and overly complicated explanations for simple phenomena. It does not and cannot know that there are basic and straightforward solutions to all the problems it voices and investigates, but that it is sensorily and cognitively incapable of grasping them.

The idea of 'species consciousness' is also relevant to 'The Burrow' since it introduces the idea of minor or partial 'interferences' from another realm that raise countless questions and incite the interpretive drive, but remain fundamentally resistant to explanation and rationalisation. The mysterious phenomena that the narrating dog perceives are akin to the mysterious noise in the burrow: these sensations derive from a realm beyond; they are perceived in 'this' world even though they were produced in 'another'. There is no way that these first-person narrators could grasp the strangeness, indeed the paradoxical nature of what they are perceiving – phenomena whose effects are perceptible in their world but whose causes reside in another – and yet the reader must try to do precisely this. It is not so much that the burrower is forced to confront its own fictional status, as that the reader is forced to entertain the radical possibility of this confrontation. This possibility, to speak with Coetzee, is what 'unmasks' 'the operations of writing'.

IV. THE ENCOUNTER WITH THE LIMITS OF FICTION: *THE TRUMAN SHOW*

Though it is possible to speculate about how Kafka might have continued and potentially even finished 'The Burrow', it is difficult to imagine the burrower coming to full consciousness of the fact that it is hearing a sound from another world. There would be no easy way for it to deal with the fact that the noise it thought was acousmatic was in fact non-diegetic, for the very concept of 'non-diegetic' requires it to take a position outside of the first-person narrative. Thus, any recognition of this possibility would presumably be met with disbelief. The creature could not possibly recognise that it was hearing a non-diegetic sound, since non-diegetic sounds are by definition inaudible within the diegesis – and, anyway, the burrower is living its life, not a fictional tale. In other words, from its perspective – and again, there is no other – the diegesis *is* its world; there is no outside to it, no 'creator' or 'author' or 'director'. The burrower could not possibly be expected to grasp the fact that it is a fictional character in a world created and maintained by an outside agent. And yet at some point the actuality and persistence of the perception might lead it to do precisely this – to question the only reality it had ever known. It might insist that it *had* to believe its ears and that it *had* to deny that the sound's cause was in its own world. Rather than accept the thoroughly unreal scenario of a sound without a source, it might be willing to entertain the slightly less implausible notion that its world was a fictional construct. Would it then confront its creator? Would it finally leave its burrow, in search of the edge of fiction? Would it grasp its status as a fictional character and try to find a way out of it, to a true reality?

Peter Weir's film, *The Truman Show*, plays with this scenario of a character's emergence from fiction into reality. Truman Burbank lives on an enormous television studio set where everyone else is an actor; he is the star of a proto-reality show who thinks he is just living his life, whereas everything he does is dictated by the show's producer, Christof, and orchestrated by the show's staff in order to provide maximum entertainment to the viewing audience. Truman is monitored 24-hours-a-day to ensure that the illusion remains seamless. In one of the first scenes of the film a lamp falls from what appears to be the sky, but is clearly (to us) a spotlight from the set of the show. To rationalise this interference from the outside world, Truman is played a story on the radio about an airplane malfunction that caused pieces of metallic debris to fall from the sky. Shortly thereafter he hears a voice on the radio that sounds suspiciously like it is narrating his own life. These sounds have been picked up from behind the scenes and broadcast in error, and they too must be explained away so as to quell any suspicions that might arise in Truman. In other instances too, 'interferences' from the outside world impinge upon Truman's world and must be rationalised in order to maintain the illusion that the fiction of the show represents the true limits of reality. At the end of the film, when Truman's suspicions – that the world he inhabits has been artificially constructed and that there is a true reality beyond the fictional one he has always inhabited – solidify, he climbs in a boat and sails to the end of the set of 'The Truman Show', where he bumps into a painted azure cardboard sky: here the sky really is the limit. Christoph, speaking directly to his creation, tries to persuade Truman to stay where he can be protected, but Truman leaves: he chooses a potentially dangerous reality over a safe fiction. The last we see of him is when he opens the door to step into the real world, a realm he has never experienced even though it is the source or cause of everything he has ever known. The film leaves us, and Truman, at this edge, which raises as many questions as it answers: has Truman walked off the set of Christoph's show or Weir's film? We cannot know to which external reality he gains entrance, an uncertainty that resonates profoundly with the situation in Kafka's 'The Burrow' and 'Investigations of a Dog'.

In some sense, *The Truman Show* realises the experiment that Kafka's 'The Burrow' introduces – the possibility of exposing the constructedness of fiction and the narrative operations responsible for it, all *within* a work of narrative fiction. While Truman is confused about various experiences and impressions throughout his life, the film viewer can understand all of them as external manipulations. *We* can see the puppeteer and all the strings; only Truman does not. The story ends with Truman's enlightenment and his breaking free from his creator – for Truman is not in fact a fictional character, he was just forced to live as one for about thirty years. He can now finally experience reality, rather than the fiction that was constructed for him and to which he was made to conform, whose walls were only occasionally and accidentally breached. Those instances in which the real world impinged on Truman's fictional world are akin to the moments in 'The Burrow' when a non-diegetic sound becomes audible within the fictional diegesis, or the moments in 'Investigations of a Dog' when a human effect is visible to the dogs, while the human cause remains hidden. These impressions are impossible from the perspective of the person or creature who inhabits the diegesis and knows no other world, but thoroughly comprehensible when viewed from a wider perspective, from a point outside the constructed fiction. *The Truman Show* is constantly giving us both perspectives, Truman's and Christoph's, which dissolves the paradoxes that emerge from the first-person narration of 'The Burrow'. Kafka's speciality, which owes a great deal to the privilege of his medium, is to ensure that the paradox is never dissolved; this is as brilliant as it is frustrating. The non-diegetic does not exist in and for first-person narratives. There is, in the end, no such thing as the non-diegetic acousmatic sound that is the noise in Kafka's burrow. And yet this designation is the closest we can come to naming it, to knowing it, and to de-acousmatising it.

NOTES

1. Another word for 'pure listening' is 'reduced listening'. Film theorist Michel Chion differentiates this from both 'causal listening' (which is focused on identifying sound sources) and 'semantic listening' (which is focused on discovering meaning in sound). 'Reduced listening' is the only model of listening that 'focuses on the traits of the sound itself, independent of its cause and its meaning' (1994: 29). Schaeffer assumed there was a privileged relationship between acousmatic listening and reduced listening – that is, that when one was not distracted by the optical presence of the sound source, one could focus on its purely acoustic qualities. Chion notes, however, that the opposite is the case: not seeing the source is a distraction; it makes it impossible to focus on the sounds themselves, because the listener becomes so intent on identifying its source. This is how acousmatic sound creates narrative suspense (1994: 32).
2. Historian of sound Jonathan Sterne rejects the separation of sound and source as the foundational idea for discussing sound reproduction technologies. This idea assumes the primacy of face-to-face communication and bodily presence, as well as

the coherence and timelessness of such notions as 'the body' and 'sensation' (2003: 19–21). This is a valid critique for someone who, wanting to write a history of sound recording, is reluctant to accept the premise that all recorded sound is degraded and disrupted. He begins instead from the idea of 'transduction': all recorded sound involves the transformation of sound into something else – electricity, grooves on a record, zeros and ones – and its retransformation back into sound (2003: 22). Transducers give Sterne a neutral and objective starting point from which to begin his historical study. This does not change the fact that countless modernist works of art represent the separation of sound and source, making it a central idea in and for modernist artworks. See, for example, Lutz Koepnick's article (2006), which compares the separation of sound from its source in two exemplary works of modernism, Rilke's novel *Die Aufzeichnungen des Malte Laurids Brigge* (*The Notebooks of Malte Laurids Brigge*, 1910) and Fritz Lang's *M* (1931). In their introduction to the volume *Sound Matters*, Nora Alter and Lutz Koepnick also refer to 'the dissociation of the visual and the sonic that structures modernity' (2004: 8). They argue that 'sonic modernism embraced the acoustical in order to construct subjects and communities that could supercede experiences of cellularization and isolation' (2004: 9).

3 In his analysis of this idea, Brian Kane focuses on the phenomenological underpinnings of acousmatic theories (2014: 15–41). He also devotes a section of his book to a reading of 'The Burrow', which converges with mine at several points (2014: 134–61). Kane presents Kafka as a '"counter-theorist" to Schaeffer,' who thinks one can actually arrive at an autonomous sound object through acousmatic listening (2014: 138). Kafka's burrowing animal shows that 'the sound object is never quite autonomous; that this nearly-but-not-quite autonomous auditory effect necessarily underdetermines attributions of source and cause'; this is the 'tension inherent in acousmatic sound' (2014: 148).

4 For example, in his description of his childhood encounter with the telephone, Walter Benjamin associates the telephonic voice with the voice of the dead and speaking von drüben (from beyond) (1991: 391). Early on, it was believed that the phonograph liberated the voices of the dead, so that they could speak from beyond the grave (Sterne 2003: 288–90).

5 I argue elsewhere that Josefine the singer's whistling/singing is distinctive not on an acoustic level, but on a corporeal and gestural one: the story only seems to be about her singing, but it is in fact about the architecture of her body as she assumes the singing pose. For a brief version of this argument, see Gellen 2010. A longer version appears in my book-length manuscript tentatively titled *Kafka and Noise: The Discovery of Cinematic Sound in Literary Modernism*.

6 In my reading, noise is Kafka's exemplary figure for disturbance. As Vivian Liska puts it, there are numerous 'unsettling beings', or figures of disruption, in Kafka's oeuvre. They produce struggles that cannot be resolved, since they are not simple enemies

or antagonists; they are instead associated with distortion, uncertainty, restlessness, endless deferral and the impossibility of closure (2009: 35–6). Along similar lines, Hansjörg Bay argues for a 'poetics of the intruder' in Kafka's works (2006: 64).

7 In Dolar's reading, too, the process of de-acousmatisation is also figured in predominantly visual terms: locating the sound in space is a matter of the gaze (2011: 116–17, 131).

8 Both Kane (2014: 159–61) and Dolar (2011: 116, 133–4) make reference to this possibility.

9 The burrower begins to hear the sound at the moment it wakes up from a long sleep, much like Gregor Samsa of 'Die Verwandlung' ('The Metamorphosis') and Josef K. of *Der Process* (*The Trial*) awaken at the start of their respective narratives. There is something precarious and productive about this in-between state – 'awakening is the riskiest moment', writes Kafka – which Dolar seizes upon; he thus wants to 'dwell on the particular edge that is crucial for Kafka: the blurred line between sleep and wakefulness, the edge of awakening' (2011: 127, 125). There are further comparable 'edges' in Kafka – between fiction and reality, between the metaphorical and the literal – which could be the object of fruitful reflection.

10 This contradiction becomes clear on the definitional level when one considers that another word for acousmatic is 'diegetic off-screen': it is part of the story world, but the source of the sound is not shown (Buhler et al. 2010: 72). Clearly something cannot be diegetic off-screen and non-diegetic at the same time.

11 This tension is also what leads Brian Kane to choose Kafka as a 'theorist' of acousmatic sound who falls neither on the side of positing an independent and autonomous sound object ('reduced listening') nor on the side of a listening that is forever in search of sources and causes. In Kafka's story, the 'strange auditory "effect" is neither directly related to its source or cause, nor is it an object in its own right' (2014: 149).

12 The most illustrative example of this is Robert Montgomery's *Lady in the Lake* (1947), in which everything is filmed from the perspective of the detective Philipp Marlowe. But there are subtle cracks in this conceit – do we really hear everything as he does? – and more overt ones: there are periodic 'breaks' from the subjective camera, scenes in which Marlowe is being filmed and talking directly to the camera, which raises the question, by whom? In other words, who is doing the seeing when he is being seen? Even within the long sequences of subjective camera, the fact of editing points to the presence of an outside force that is shaping and moulding the presentation of Marlowe's perspective. First-person literary fiction does away with these outside perspectives, though even there the presence of an 'implied author' can complicate the status of a first-person narrator.

13 As David Bordwell writes, 'in watching films, we are seldom aware of being told something by an entity resembling a human being. [...] To give every film a narrator

or implied author is to indulge in an anthropomorphic fiction' (1985: 264). Bordwell therefore proposes that we speak of narration in film, rather than of a narrator. He defines narration as 'the organization of a set of cues for the construction of a story. This presupposes a perceiver, but not any sender, of a message' (ibid.).

14 The cinematic equivalent to this would be a film that introduced explicitly extra-diegetic mood music for the benefit of the viewer/listener, which suddenly became audible to the characters in the movie and influenced their experiences, feelings, thoughts and actions. Another example, essentially realised in Marc Forster's romantic comedy *Stranger Than Fiction* (2006), would be a film that used voiceover, a fundamentally non-diegetic acoustic technique in film, but made it audible to the characters in the film. This makes no sense: the figure of the narrator belongs to fiction, not reality. Forster's movie presents this scenario and plays brilliantly with its non-sensicality: the protagonist Harold Crick begins to hear a mysterious voice, which, it turns out, is the voice of an author narrating his life. Does this make his life a fiction or does it make the narrator, also a 'real' person in the film's diegesis, a fiction? This scenario – namely non-diegetic sound that becomes diegetic – is another instance of an acoustic phenomenon that straddles fiction and reality, thus existing both inside and outside the 'story world'.

BIBLIOGRAPHY

Alter, Nora M. and Lutz Koepnick (2004) 'Introduction: Sound Matters', in Nora M. Alter and Lutz Koepnick (eds) *Sound Matters: Essays on the Acoustics of Modern German Culture*. New York: Berghahn, 1–29.

Bay, Hansjörg (2006) 'Kafkas Tinnitus', Odradeks Lachen. in Hansjörg Bay and Christof Hamann (eds) *Fremdheit bei Kafka*. Freiburg: Rombach, 41–68.

Benjamin, Walter (1991) 'Berliner Kindheit um 1900', *Gesammelte Schriften*, eds. Rolf Tiedemann and Hermann Schweppenhäuser. Frankfurt: Suhrkamp, 7, 1, 385–433.

Bordwell, David (1985) *Narration in the Fiction Film*. Madison, WS: University of Wisconsin Press.

Buhler, James, David Neumeyer and Rob Deemer (2010) *Hearing the Movies: Music and Sound in Film History*. Oxford: Oxford University Press.

Chion, Michel (1994) *Audio-Vision. Sound on Screen*, ed. and trans. Claudia Gorbman. New York: Columbia University Press.

_____ (1999) *The Voice in Cinema*, ed. and trans. Claudia Gorbman. New York: Columbia University Press.

Coetzee, J. M. (1981) 'Time, Tense and Aspect in Kafka's "The Burrow"', *MLN*, 96, 3, 556–79.

Dolar, Mladen (2011) 'The Burrow of Sound', *Differences*, 22, 2/3, 112–39.

Gellen, Kata (2010) 'Hearing Spaces: Architecture and Acoustic Experience in Modernist German Literature', *Modernism/Modernity*, 17, 4, 799–818.

Kafka, Franz (1971 [1931]) 'Investigations of a Dog', *The Complete Stories*, ed. Nahum N. Glatzer. New York: Schocken Books, 310–346.

_____ (2002 [1931]) 'Der Bau', *Nachgelassene Schriften und Fragmente* II, ed. Jost Schillemeit. Frankfurt: Fischer, 576–632.

_____ (2007a [1924]) 'Josefine, the Singer or the Mouse People', *Kafka's Selected Stories*, ed. and trans. Stanley Corngold. New York: W. W. Norton, 94–108.

_____ (2007b [1931]) 'The Burrow', *Kafka's Selected Stories*, ed. and trans. Stanley Corngold. New York: W. W. Norton, 162–89.

_____ (2009 [1925]) *The Trial*, trans. Mike Mitchell. Oxford: Oxford University Press.

_____ (2013) *The Metamorphosis*, ed. and trans. Stanley Corngold. New York: Modern Library.

Kane, Brian (2014) *Sound Unseen: Acousmatic Sound in Theory and Practice*. Oxford: Oxford University Press.

Kittler, Friedrich (1990) *Discourse Networks 1800/1900*, trans. Michael Metteer. Stanford, CA: Stanford University Press.

Koepnick, Lutz (2006) 'Rilke's Rumblings and Lang's Bang', *Monatshefte*, 98, 2, 199–214.

Levin, Thomas Y. (2003) '"Tones from out of Nowhere": Rudolph Pfenninger and the Archaeology of Synthetic Sound', *Grey Room*, 12, 32–79.

Liska, Vivian (2009) *When Kafka Says We: Uncommon Communities in German-Jewish Literature*. Bloomington, IN: Indiana University Press.

Rilke, Rainer Maria (1986) 'Primal Sound', *Rodin and Other Prose Pieces*, trans. G. Craig Houston. London: Quartet Books, 127–32.

_____ (2009 [1910]) *The Notebooks of Malte Laurids Brigge*, ed. and trans. Michael Hulse. London: Penguin.

Schaeffer, Pierre (2004) 'Acousmatics', in Christoph Cox and Daniel Warner *Audio Culture: Readings in Modern Music*. New York: Continuum, 76–81.

Sterne, Jonathan (2003) *The Audible Past: Cultural Origins of Sound Reproduction*. Durham, NC: Duke University Press.

GESTURE, WARDROBE, BACKDROP AND PROP IN FRANZ KAFKA'S *THE MAN WHO DISAPPEARED* AND PETER WEIR'S *THE TRUMAN SHOW*

IDIT ALPHANDARY

Franz Kafka's *Der Verschollene* (*The Man Who Disappeared*; *Amerika*, 1946 [1927])[1] and Peter Weir's *The Truman Show* (1998) are stories about 'foundlings'. In the former, Karl Rossmann's family disclaims him; in the latter Truman is an orphan. In Kafka's novel, the parents of sixteen-year-old Karl send him from Prague to America following a scandalous affair with the family's housemaid. Concerned with the shame born by the affair, which left the housemaid pregnant, Karl's parents force him to emigrate by ship to New York's harbour. In America, Karl is alone and wants to find a job and make friends. As a new immigrant he is subject to abuse by his American uncle, his employers and his peers. All this changes when he finds a job as a technical worker for the Nature Theater of Oklahoma. This job marks a huge transition for Karl and, as I will show, allows him, finally, to become American. Along with the new job, Karl acquires a new name. He consciously acts his part and is glad to find that he is accepted in America. But in order to reach this state of unproblematic acceptance as a revolutionised person – one who is not subject to the old, European signifiers of identity but is capable of communicating according to American ideas – Karl must learn about intersubjective connections in America. His initial troubles as an immigrant teach him to be attentive to the environment and to be amicable with his fellow Americans, both women and men. Some of these new acquaintances do not extend friendship to Karl but he respects them and submits to their demands and in the process learns much about his new country and about the limits of friendship.

In Weir's film, 29-year-old Truman Burbank is shown adopted at birth by a TV production company. Unknowingly, he is the star of a television show that broadcasts his every movement to viewers 24 hours a day. He eventually discovers his real situation, breaks free from his captors and the film ends with the suggestion he will go on to lead a private life away from the show. It is suggested that his success depends on his becoming attentive to his fellow men and women, thus exposing their deceitful character, while retaining his own candid nature.

My central contention is that similar, basic American values are at stake in Kafka's *The Man Who Disappeared* and Weir's *The Truman Show* and only the complicated presentation of gesture, wardrobe, backdrop and prop (GWBP) enables the author and the director to access these values that appear either as desirable or as corrupt. Karl and Truman are the protagonists who realise that GWBP succumbs to intricate binds that they must unfasten before becoming experienced actors who play themselves in the political theatre of intersubjective interaction in the American public sphere. To substantiate this reading of the role of GWBP in Kafka and Weir, I proceed as follows. Firstly, I present Stanley Cavell's (1989) articulation of American values as the ability to become self-reliant by communicating with others. This means that one should not clutch at people and things and should not obscure oneself. Yet one is born from an experience of foreignness and death that one learns to share with others. I will then show that Cavell's use of gesture and prop brings to mind the fact that Walter Benjamin assigns use to gesture and prop in Kafka's entire oeuvre. Kafka trusts in independent, dynamic agents and his portrayal of Karl's integration in America includes a new birth that stems from death and an exemplar ability to communicate pain and hope.[2] From this, in conclusion, I deduce that Kafka supports the implementation of certain philosophical values that are constitutional of American ethics and aesthetics.

Before I begin to closely study these works I would like to introduce the American self-representation or the American ideology that lurks behind both. Kafka and Weir elaborate, comment on, question, critique and embrace an American ideology that worships self-understanding and self-reliance. Their protagonists wrestle with an American *zeitgeist* that sometimes proves to be decent and genuine and sometimes proves to be deceitful and enslaving. These protagonists succeed in becoming American because they learn how to escape from circumstances that are foreboding misfortune and enhance people, places and ideas that carry hope for a future in which they will achieve self-reliance and self-fulfilment. The protagonists remain innocent because they do not enslave others even if every now and then they use treacherous means to escape from the grip of the authorities. They do not allow norms to ensnare them. Both stories notably conclude with a similar gesture: climbing a 'stairway to heaven', to use the words of Led Zeppelin. This climb precipitates, for both characters, their ability to participate in everyday life in America. For example, Karl sees his friend Fanny dressed as an angel. She allows him to look behind the scenes and see the backdrop, which is a ladder that holds her up in the sky: 'And she parted her draperies so that the pedestal and a little ladder leading up to it became visible' (Kafka 1946: 277). In the last sequence of *The Truman Show*, Truman walks up a set of stairs, reaches for a doorknob and opens the door to heaven, leaving behind the backdrop, a gigantic makeshift TV studio that has been controlling his life. The heaven that Truman accesses is consubstantial to reality but the transition from being a captive of the show to breaking free from the gigantic studio is symbolised using the image of a door in the sky or an ability to traverse heaven in order to return to reality as a revolutionised person. Truman, like Karl, is revolutionised in the process of becoming an integral member of social life in America. I intend to show in an elaborate form that these gestures and props signify that after a long period of enslavement by domineering powers, by the end of the novel and film the protagonists are integrated in America.

It makes sense that theatre and show business loom large in these works and that both characters are focused on perfecting the art of acting and observing. Acting, for Karl and Truman, is the alternative to being subjected to an oppressive environment. Acting and observing are means of fulfilling the 'American dream'. The minimal requirement of the 'American dream' is that self-fulfilment will come true when one seeks and finds opportunity that leads one to immersion in the social, economic and cultural American life-line. Karl's insistence to learn English is a way to make good the 'American dream'. Truman's insistence to reunite with his lost love is a way to make good the 'American dream'. In each one of these examples opportunity is denied to the protagonists but they refuse to remain enslaved by circumstances and they dare, devise new breakthroughs and insist on their right to be self-fulfilled.

Karl and Truman become American when they devise ways to obtain self-reliance. This means that they cease to be the recipients of other peoples' words and actions and are able, instead, to lead lives based on their private judgements and actions. Both learn that they have to play themselves on this stage of the American theatre because the interaction between people is always performative in the public sphere. People speak and act in order to advance private and common goals.[3] Even critics of Kafka's novel that suggest that Karl remains a disenfranchised exile in America point to the conjunction between alienation and performativity 'that is both provocative and insubordinate' (Rokem 2009: 122).[4] Karl and Truman play themselves when they choose how much to say and when to keep silent. They act either openly or discretely when they do not want others to have too much information about them. On the one hand they never impose their judgements and actions on others. On the other, they devise new ways to fulfil their wishes when their plans are thwarted. Both signify the true American spirit of freedom and happiness while the rest of the actors in the theatre of America corrupt American values and aesthetics.

I. 'WHEN WE SEEK TO DENY THE STANDOFFISHNESS OF OBJECTS BY CLUTCHING AT THEM'

In what follows I would like to engage Cavell's philosophy of the everyday to suggest that Karl and Truman succeed in breaking free of complicated circumstances and establishing themselves in America because both devote themselves to studying the machinations that control their lives, and it is this close study of their own situation in the various social and economic contexts that leads each one to his discovery. More than simply manipulating objects, these characters learn how to detect the ulterior motives behind people's behaviours. Karl and Truman are able to see through manipulation and can diffuse it without resorting to manipulation in the process. They are accepted as Americans because they live a fulfilling private life in the midst of an everyday reality that clutches at them. In both works, to be accepted as American means that one is able to seek and seize opportunity not at the expense of others but in collaboration with employers, friends and loved ones. Karl comprehends the American language; cultural intelligence enables him to communicate, understand and cater to the requirements of his fellow men and women and yet achieve private goals. At the same time, to become American is to become self-reliant. This means that both Karl and Truman must agree to leave behind their dependence on old character traits and be revolutionised, to accept and create new ideals that they choose to follow.

Karl Rossmann/Horse Man and Truman/True-Man are genuine but they learn to master the utilisation of the power of GWBP. The reason that they are more sophisticated than their fellow men and women is that they survive trial, peril, displacement and are reborn from the experience of death. Karl undergoes a traumatic experience when he is severed from the existence that he knows and is thrust to the unknown. He is forced to leave Europe and fight for his survival in America, and Truman undergoes a traumatic experience when his entire system of belief and self-understanding collapses. He gradually realises that his whole life has been a television show, not a reality. The experience of death accompanies radical hardship or failure to achieve their desires despite the fact that they work and practice devotion within the human and professional contexts that they belong to. In all these situations Karl and Truman retain a childish fascination with the world and nurture their connections with others. Both are passive, attentive to others and passionate, oriented toward successfully handling tasks in the world. They accept others and study them at the same time. They neither impose their desires on others nor decline to attain the knowledge they seek about GWBP.

The Man Who Disappeared and *The Truman Show* offer, respectively, a literary and cinematic representation of what it is to be an American. Karl must be American in the early twentieth century while Truman has to be American at the end of the twentieth century. Despite the years that separate the two, in order to belong to America both have to survive through the use of GWBP. In his lecture entitled 'Finding as Founding', Stanley Cavell suggests that in order to speak philosophically about America one has to inherit the language of Ralph Waldo Emerson, particularly of his essay entitled, 'Experience'. In this work, Emerson struggles to accept the terms of a new world that does not submit to grasping. As the essay progresses Emerson realises that America is unapproachable. It becomes an imperative in Cavell's study of Emerson so that to exist in America is to enable people and things to remain unapproachable or free, not reduced to rational explanations. Cavell describes the 'handsome' relation to things and to other people as already specified in Emerson's 'Experience'. The following passage from Cavell's work is important because it speaks against suffocating *gestures*:

> 'I take this evanescence and lubricity of all objects, which lets them slip through our fingers then when we clutch hardest, to be the most unhandsome part of our condition.' Look first at the connection between the hand in unhandsome and the impotently clutching fingers. What is unhandsome is I think … what happens when we seek to deny the standoffishness of objects by clutching at them; which is to say, when we conceive thinking, say the application of concepts in judgments, as grasping something, say synthesizing. (1989: 86)

Thinking requires gesture because it intervenes in everyday actions. 'Handsome' conditions involve an opening to the world that reveals itself to us. Emerson writes: 'I am ready to die out of nature and be born again into this new yet unapproachable America I have found in the West' (quoted in Cavell 1989: 90). This means that one accepts one's existence as birth preceded by death and hence as a form of being part of a world in which one learns to suffer losses. Once we accept this we realise that we are 'foundlings' (1989: 91).

The very concept of experience suggests trial, peril, birth and death, learning a language, voyaging and approaching (self-)understanding. These experiences are commensurate with reflections and gestures that bring about transformation. They turn a private being into an actor in the public sphere and transform real people into theatrical agents who belong to a world of GWBP. The desirable reflections and gestures are those that enable the self to be insightful and active without clutching at knowledge and at the others. According to Emerson, even a private experience such as mourning the death of one's son becomes meaningful when one is able to re-turn toward society and engage the other in a conversation that does not hang on to the pain.

Emerson's 'Experience' is written in response to his son's death. Philosophy, literature and film make it possible for humanity to transcend death and suffering by making sense of both, and, by extension, life itself. This capacity to start over even as one is impoverished by loss is signified by Emerson's very deliberate choice of words: 'transcendence, transformation, aversion, the response to an infinite object, the drawing of a new circle' (Cavell 1989: 107). For Emerson, power is a form of passivity and passion: 'All I know is reception' (quoted in Cavell 1989: 108). Indirection emerges from the willingness not to grasp at things and instead undergo transformation. Emerson suggests that we find ourselves, 'In a series of which we do not know the extremes' (quoted in Cavell 1989: 115). One must not give in to either the tyranny of the majority or to seclusion from the world. One must not conform to pre-existing conceptions about accepted forms of living but rather revolutionise existence. This means that thinking never reaches an end, for every new step that one takes requires further thinking. Cavell does not insist that everything is language. Like Emerson, he points out that speaking a language already posits us in the midst of great 'intelligence' (quoted in Cavell 1989: 117). There are modes of communication other than language in the world, including GWBP. Cavell ends his article the way he opened it with a gesture: 'I clap my hands in infantine joy, thus risking infantilization, leaping free of enforced speech, so succeeding it' (1989: 118). Philosophy is successful specifically when thinking is grounded in everyday forms of theatricality and/or engagement with others. Cavell's approach to gesture is prefigured in Walter Benjamin's reading of Kafka's work.

II. BENJAMIN'S HYMN TO KAFKA'S STUDY OF GESTURE AND BACKDROP

In their final gestures, Karl rides a train that will lead him westward in America and Truman meets his beloved somewhere in the real world.⁵ These final gestures are significant because, like Scheherazade's tales, they leave all options open. In an essay on Kafka's work, Benjamin refers to the paradigmatic storyteller of the *Arabian Nights*. Like Scheherazade, the protagonists of *The Man Who Disappeared* and *The Truman Show* live on pain of death. Each time hope seems to give way they devise a new gesture of hope through the open ending, which suggests the ever-evolving trajectories of their lives. Each chapter of the novel or episode of the film introduces new circumstances to their lives and they have to survive within this constellation. *The Truman Show* ends when Truman leaves the studio but his life-story continues away from the limelight. Karl and Truman have to be sophisticated enough to introduce their own voice into the stories that imprison them. Thus each ends up as the proper storyteller of his respective life story. Karl's and Truman's stories are made of life. They fulfil their wishes only because they know how to subject technical knowhow to their need for intersubjective communication and outsmart the dictates of business and technology. Yet they are easygoing in their interaction with the objects and with other people. They come across as attentive to their surroundings.

Benjamin's essay, 'Franz Kafka: On the Tenth Anniversary of His Death' (1934), begins with the story of Potemkin, who is sequestered in his room and suffering from depression. The clerk Shuvalkin goes to him with state papers to sign. Potemkin performs the correct gesture but he does not use his own name. Instead, he signs the papers using the name Shuvalkin. Thus the value of the signature is in gesture but essentially the papers remain in need of Potemkin's signature. Benjamin suggests that this paradoxical folk tale precedes Kafka's storytelling. It presents one of the obsolete bureaucrats whose powers are grounded in mythical laws and are thus all but extinct. The obsolete bureaucrats are similar to the domineering fathers who try to overpower their sons by imposing the archaic law of the father on them. Yet these legal servants/fathers do not render consequential the relationship of the state and the citizen/the father and the son. Like parasites they feed on the citizen/son. They may rise from decay and use their power to deal a death sentence to the citizen/son. This perverse world order is embodied in GWBP.

I am interested in the potentially revolutionary impact of seemingly insignificant aspects of theatre. The table is a central prop in Benjamin's essay because Kafka's students use it to study, scribes write on it and legal or financial assistants use it for their documents. Yet desks can be the symbol of both positive and negative power. The desks that the old bureaucrats/fathers use to pass judgement are signifiers of clutching power. When Kafka mobilises the figure of the table he mobilises an entire world-order so as to appropriate the symbol and make it useful to assistants that propel action. Hence the table signifies positive, liberating power. Thus the passage that Benjamin cites from Georg Lukács describes the fabrication of a table in order to examine the historical relation of the past to the present:

> Lukács once said that in order to make a decent table nowadays, a man must have the architectural genius of a Michelangelo. If Lukács thinks in terms of historical ages, Kafka thinks in terms of cosmic epochs. The man who whitewashes has epochs to move, even in his most insignificant gesture. On many occasions, and often for strange reasons, Kafka's figures clap their hands. Once the casual remark is made that these hands are 'really steam hammers'. (1999: 795)

Clapping hands is a gesture crucial in the works of both Cavell and Benjamin, where it is symbolic of a positive form of power.[6] Clapping hands is a hopeful gesture that moves epochs because it overturns the compulsive reign of the old at the same time that it welcomes the young to the protagonists' world. As for the infantilising suggestion expressed by the gesture, clapping hands signifies curiosity in the world despite the fact that the bureaucrats and the fathers object to seeking the new and would like to envelop the citizen/son with the old ways of their own worlds. In Cavell's study, philosophical wisdom neither eliminates the ability to clap hands nor causes this gesture to be shameful. In Benjamin, clapping hands is a gesture of those who have escaped from their proper family circle and hence from the tyrannical bureaucrats and fathers: 'It is for them and their kind, the unfinished and the hapless, that there is hope' (1999: 799). These are the marks of Karl and Truman – they are foundlings, 'unfinished' and 'hapless'. Affirmation of the world is a sign of power that is registered in the form of passivity or passion.

Benjamin points to the roles of GWBP in Kafka's *The Man Who Disappeared*, because specifically this novel forces Karl to understand his own congenitally European gestures as a hindrance. He must learn to understand the American gesture and prop, and still more critically, he has to learn how to *use* American gestures and props. Such acculturation includes what Cavell views as a necessary acceptance of the evanescence of objects and concepts (1989: 86). It includes remaining a child and knowing how to signify hope with clapping one's hands.

Benjamin is most interested in the very last chapter of the novel because it is rife with GWBP, music, childishness and hope. This last chapter features a more mature Karl. He successfully escaped from all of the imposing employers and friends he had. He is no longer in touch with his dictatorial uncle. Karl is at a material and conceptual crossroads and this is a sign of hope. He could make a choice that will lead him to a hopeful new chapter in the story of his becoming an American. At this point he sees a sign that offers employment to everyone and hence also addresses him. The employer is the Nature Theater of Oklahoma, Karl's last refuge, but this does not preclude the possibility that it is Karl's salvation. Benjamin points to the sign that invites everyone to Clayton to join the Nature Theater of Oklahoma. It begins with the words, 'Today, from 6A.M. until midnight, at Clayton Racetrack, the Oklahoma Theater will be hiring members for its company. The great Theater of Oklahoma calls you!' (quoted in Benjamin 1999: 800). Karl reads this post. He imagines that happiness awaits him in there. He is transparent, and lacks character, ego, individuality, all that constitutes the subject of the Enlightenment. His 'purity of feeling' (Benjamin 1999: 801) is a sign of openness and wisdom. Benjamin associates ancient Chinese wisdom with lack of character, the voluntary decline of individuality and with attentiveness. Such purity enhances sensitivity to gestural behaviour and is expressed in deed. About the Nature Theater of Oklahoma, Benjamin argues that 'One of the most significant functions of this theater is to dissolve events into their gestural components' (ibid.). All of Kafka's creation is immersed in gesture but this accumulation becomes meaningful in the Nature Theater of Oklahoma. The gestures address heaven because 'the gestures of Kafka's figures are too powerful for our accustomed surroundings and break out into wider areas' (ibid.).

Benjamin senses that Kafka, through the gestures of his writings, points to the limits of language when it is faced with the depth of personal and cultural significance that resides in the singular gesture, which is pregnant with meaning. 'Each gesture is an event – one might say a drama – in itself' (1999: 802). Gesture is the ultimate expression of the protagonist's state of mind. Gesture is something between the singular, radically individual on the one hand, and the general and codified on the other. It is also something between voluntary and unconscious – this is what makes it so appealing: it opens up a third alternative. Gesture signifies the desire of a protagonist and the way s/he would like to be understood by others, the way s/he understands others. For example, the workers at Uncle Jacob's warehouses gaze at the floor. This gesture simultaneously signifies discontent and submission. In another example the opponents engage in cat-calling during an American election of judges. The gesture makes explicit the dominance of desire in American democracy. At the same time gesture is so intimately related to worldliness and it discloses mental and even biological marks of identity. Thus Brunelda's gestures are those of a star although she is no longer a singer: she is fat, divorced and poor. Her elitist gestures enable her to enslave Delamarche and Robinson, who worship her every gesture. 'The stage on which the drama of gesture takes place is the World Theater, which opens up toward heaven' (ibid.). But this heaven is only a backdrop and it continues to exist only when the protagonist is persistent, when s/he keeps playing roles that make her/him loved and accepted:

> Like El Greco, Kafka tears open the sky behind every gesture; but as with El Greco – who was the patron saint of the Expressionists – the gesture remains the decisive thing, the center of the event. [...] But it is always Kafka; he divests human gesture of its traditional supports, and then has a subject for reflection without end. (Ibid.)

Because Kafka always studies 'how life and work are organized in human society' (1999: 803), Benjamin believes the author's world is masked and in this sense it is theatrical so that human beings are acting in it from the very beginning. This does not mean that the world is a theatre but it does mean that one has to play oneself according to conventions, or in opposition to them. One has to know if one's playacting is conforming or revolutionary, successful or self-defeating. Hence the Nature Theater of Oklahoma hires everyone. These job applicants do not have to be artists or have dramatic talents. '[A]ll that is expected from the applicants is the ability to play themselves. [...] For all of them this place is the last refuge, which does not preclude it from being their salvation' (1999: 804). Benjamin goes on to say that Kafka sought a relation between gesture and the freedom to express one's belonging to the social bond between people. Salvation is what the Ape in 'A Report to an Academy' calls 'a way out' (ibid.); it is not a mystical premium on existence. The one whose life is salvaged does not become a moral or social example of righteousness. Salvation means that one devises a way to persist and act one's role or revolutionise oneself as does the ape when he begins to speak, plays himself although he no longer remembers his prehistory as an ape. The backdrop of the angels in the Nature Theater of Oklahoma is like a 'country church fair' (1999: 805) or like 'a children's festival' (ibid.). Backdrop goes hand in hand with the gesture of clapping hands and it is amenable to music – the music of the trumpeters. This is Karl's 'way out', the image of hope that Karl is immersed in by the end of the novel.[7]

Benjamin contends that in the stories that Kafka left us 'narrative art regains the significance it had in the mouth of Scheherazade: its ability to postpone the future' (1999: 807). The peripatetic Karl Rossmann composes episodes in a never-ending life-story just like Scheherazade's oral instalments compose an infinite literary oeuvre. Kafka is attentive in a world that yields meaning only through the use of gestures and props. Attentiveness is Karl's most capacious relation with the world. Attentiveness is a form of learning in the world it is also 'what Melebranche called "the natural prayer of the soul"' (1999: 812). Karl asks a student when he sleeps and the student replies that he will sleep when he finishes his studies. For Benjamin this is reminiscent of children who do not want to go to bed; children and students are too curious about the world and everything that is happening in it concerns them:

> The crowning achievement of asceticism is study [...]. Perhaps these studies amounted to nothing. But they are very close to that nothing which alone makes it possible for a something to be useful [...]. This is the resolute, fanatical mien which students have when they study; it is the strangest mien imaginable. The scribes, the students, are out of breath; they fairly race along [...]. It may be easier to understand this if one thinks of the actors in the Nature Theater. Actors have to catch their cues in a flash, and they resemble those assiduous students in other ways as well [...]. They study this role and only a bad actor would forget a word or a gesture from it. For the members of the Oklahoma troupe, however, the role is their earlier life; hence the 'nature' in this Nature Theater. Its actors have been redeemed. (1999: 813–14)

A new gesture comes to the fore: the mien of a student concentrating on his study materials. It is connected to the gesture of clapping hands because it embodies curiosity, the same sensation that prevents children from sleeping at night. The mien that expresses attentiveness to the world is natural and those who practice it belong to the Nature Theater because they are not afraid to play themselves. In this role one is redeemed.

Salvation might emerge from a situation that for Karl (and by extension Kafka) is the last resort. The encounter with the student precedes the episode of the Nature Theater of Oklahoma and it is Karl's last resort for he is already lost in America. Karl's (and by extension Kafka's) alienation propels studying and attentiveness. '[Study is] where he [Kafka] may encounter fragments of his own existence – fragments that are still within the context of the role. He might catch hold of the lost *gestus* [...]. He might understand himself, but what an enormous effort would be required! It is a tempest that blows from forgetting, and study is a cavalry attack against it' (Benjamin 1999: 814). The purest connection between singularity and the theatre of the world is revealed in gesture. Gesture is opaque to both the actor and the company around him. To study the personal mythology and rationale that give birth to one's gestures amounts to a revolution. Emerson calls this revolution 'conversion'; for Kafka this is metamorphosis. One has to go back to the past in order to be able to know oneself in the future. One has to find hope for the future in an altered self-understanding that resides in the past. If one could see oneself differently, then one would be like the beggar in the tale that Benjamin tells. The beggar is sitting alone on the bench listening to worldly men around him express their extravagant wishes for the future.

When the company asks the beggar what is his wish for the future the beggar replies that he wishes he were a king fleeing in his shirt from a cavalry attack and succeeding to retrieve his seat on the bench. The men do not understand what good this would do to him. He is already a beggar. The beggar explains that it would give him a shirt on his back. The truth is that this parable captures the meaning of a tempestuous life that includes rupture, metamorphosis and salvation. To be thus transformed is consubstantial to surviving the turmoil that life presents. Survival means that one forgets in order to continue living and remembers in order to be transformed. This is what Karl Rossmann is adept at doing. Scheherazade does this in order to stay alive. 'Reversal is the direction of study which transforms existence into script' (Benjamin 1999: 815). The student is capable of studying or of reading life the way one reads a script because his power is grounded in attentiveness, not in the utilitarian pursuit of a future goal. Hence Benjamin concludes, 'The law which is studied but no longer practiced is the way to justice. The gate to justice is study' (ibid.). The mien of the student signifies studies and this gesture embodies promise as do the gestures of prayer and clapping hands. Studying is the gate to justice, attentiveness is an attitude consubstantial to approaching the world, clapping hands surpasses the meaning of words, and yet it embodies a passionate relation to the world. Specific gestures signify that one undertakes deeds, brings about salvation.

III. THE STUDENT AND HIS DESKS OR 'LEARN TO UNDERSTAND YOUR POSITION'

It is important to stress that proof of the fact that Karl is naturalised in America inheres in narrative progression of events such as that he leaves his uncle, drops his job as an elevator boy at the Occidental Hotel and escapes the grip of the bullies, Delamarche and Robinson. Only then, after having freed himself of these crippling forces in his life, does he land a job at the Nature Theater of Oklahoma. Karl is accepted as one of the actors/technicians by the Nature Theater, where his job is to play himself: he needs to be passive and passionate as the assistant of American engineers. His passivity allows him to be attentive to his employers while his passion enables him to be an efficient assistant. Hence he masters and produces the technical work required by the Nature Theater of Oklahoma, which is a symbol of America. This is the job that Karl dreamed of having when he was a student in Europe. He causes everyone he meets to love him, be these his uncle, Mr. Pollunder or the manageress and Therese in the Hotel Occidental or Fanny and 'the manager of this company' (Kafka 1946: 281) on the race track at the Nature Theater of Oklahoma, who says to Karl, 'and I bid you welcome' (ibid.). Although both Karl and Truman make themselves known to others they understand that their peers are manipulative and oppressive. Rossmann follows his Uncle Jacob's every instruction yet he is expelled for good when he goes to a dinner party without his uncle's consent. How does Rossmann on his way to becoming a self-reliant American retain the goodness of his nature and wrestle to subvert the others' needs to dominate him?

Karl studies the GWBP that his fellow women and men use because these are valuable in two diametrically opposed ways. Karl, on the one hand, learns how to play himself. He uses GWBP to make himself known to his fellow men and women. His peers, on the other hand, use GWBP to obscure who they are and what their intentions are in order to benefit at Karl's expense. He uses GWBP to reveal himself to others. At the same time he casts doubt on these same means because GWBP may also be used to obscure real intentions and to dishonestly assert control over free agents. Karl achieves mastery of the use of GWBP in the theatre of American life each time that he is passive and passionate in his inter-subjective interaction with others. His passivity helps him to be open to others and thus get to know them better; his passion helps him to introduce private insights and actions to the world and hence regain his freedom in it.

I suggest that the most persistent prop that keeps appearing in Kafka's *The Man Who Disappeared* is a desk or a table, since Karl is a student and studying involves desks and tables.[8] Karl is a student of life in America and his studying involves attentiveness to GWBP, which enables him to encounter different supervisors in different professions and acquire new gestures. He becomes naturalised in America when he ceases to cling to gestures and props that tie him to his family in Europe. He remembers his parents and clearly the old gestures leave their traces in the new ones that he acquires, but Karl does not cling to what is lost to him. Although his candid traits are still his most significant signs of identification he becomes an American 'foundling', in Cavell's language, when he is on a train going westward, lost in America with no passport, no family photos, but with a job as an actor at the Nature Theater of Oklahoma where his name is changed from Karl to 'Negro'. Many scholars interpret this ending as ominous but it might be hopeful too.[9] The first person that Karl encounters in the Nature Theater of Oklahoma is Fanny, an old European friend. She is the one who touches the heavens with her trumpet. This suggests that Karl does not necessarily forget his old European GWBP but rather that he knows not to cling to it. When these old gestures, props and people show up in his life he is always happy to unite with revelations of his old self.

Backdrop announces that Karl is in America because the Statue of Liberty appears and with it the New York skyline as the ship that Karl is on draws closer to the shores of America. When Karl is asked to state his name he shows his passport, too, but this gesture that presumes that he has an identity is immediately overturned. Karl has to contend with the fact that 'It is Senator Edward Jacob who has just declared himself to be your uncle. You have now a brilliant career in front of you, against all your previous expectations, I dare say. Try to realize this, as far as you can in the first shock of the moment, and pull yourself together!' (Kafka 1946: 24). Uncle Jacob commands Karl to undergo transformation using American diction: 'learn to understand your position' (1946: 35). The discussion of desks will continue. Each time that this prop appears it signals a tension. On one hand, the desk signifies that Karl is intent on learning how to behave in order to profit from the new circumstances that he encounters. Studying involves gesture and prop in a most intimate sense because Karl has to undergo radical changes. On the other, the desks that belong to those who surround Karl signify that these power-holders want him to learn how to be obedient. They dismiss his intimate desire. The desk is the prop that engenders the conflict between studying oneself and learning to cooperate with social demands.

Uncle Jacob is a father figure but he is also an American multi-millionaire with a huge business for the mobilisation of goods between manufacturers. He controls and operates sophisticated communication technology such as the telephone and the telegraph. His power brings to mind the power of the American President. This mediation between Karl and his uncle creates alienation. The table in Karl's room is the prop that registers all this new information absorbed by Karl. Yet the same table enables Karl to fondly remember his own father and the European culture to which he belongs. Karl is learning in order to understand himself in this new context and to please his uncle:

> [A]n American writing-desk of superior construction, such as his father had coveted for years [...]. For example, it had a hundred compartments of different sizes, in which the President of the Union himself could have found a fitting place for each of his state documents; there was also a regulator at one side and by turning a handle you could produce the most complicated combinations and permutations of the compartments to please yourself and suit your requirements. Thin panels sank slowly and formed the bottom of a new series or the top of existing drawers promoted from below; even after one turn of the handle the disposition of the whole was quite changed and the transformation took place slowly or at delirious speed according to the rate at which you wound the thing round. It was a very modern invention. (1946: 41)

This backdrop shows that Karl is not at ease in his uncle's house because it stresses Karl's belonging to an old world in which writing-desks that exude power do not exist. The desk is alienating. Karl feels that if one uses such a sophisticated desk one has to excel in one's studies. Karl has always been a persistent yet poor student. Despite all, every morning he begins his English studies at 7:00am, 'already over his exercise books at the desk' (1946: 44). Benjamin would have suggested that Karl's studies mobilise innovation in a way that resists the coerciveness of the decayed moral order which he left behind him. The desk that Karl uses recalls the feebleness of his father who could not afford to buy such a desk; the powerfulness of his uncle who owns a desk that could cater to the needs of the American President; and the omnipotence of the American President, the most important American elected official who probably owns a similar desk. Karl dissociates himself from all these past, present and prospective father figures in order to do something very basic: he learns the English language in the hope that he might become integrated into an unapproachable America. Studying a new language forces Karl to undergo transformation. He must express and understand himself in a new language – has to play a role, exist in terms that are not his own.

Gesture and the lack of affectionate gestures register the fact that Uncle Jacob is only interested in work. At his warehouses, workers glanced at paperwork 'which fluttered with the wind of progress' (ibid.). Karl also interprets the gestures that he captures and he is able to associate American bureaucracy with progress. Does he capture the irony in the description of desk-work as that which ushers in progress? He is able to see that his own gestures and his own relation to bureaucracy must be transformed. Karl's ability to be attentive to these gestures means that he is already considering the meaning of progress in this new culture. Yet he will have an opportunity to let the wind of progress pass him by when he will leave his job at the Hotel Occidental because his judges will become unjust. The ironic attitude toward the wind of progress is related to what Benjamin refers to when he mentions that Kafka is mobilising 'cosmic epochs' (1999: 795).

On the way to Mr. Pollunder's country house the narrative becomes surreal, distances become impossible to traverse, Karl loses consciousness, and time is irreparably prolonged or wasted. Karl's sleep in Mr. Pollunder's car is the gesture that shows that from here on Karl will be rejected and will have to make do on his own in America. Karl is thrown into the vastness of eternal time and space. Either he will be absorbed in progress and belong among the Americans who clutch at things, or he will passively and passionately study the world that he belongs to, undergo transformation and reach salvation. His sleep is like a coma from which he will emerge to a completely new reality. This rebirth stems from death because it is too abject and the question is how he could learn to establish his own human existence in such inhuman conditions of isolation. In order to become American, Karl is not obliged to forget his origins. He will refer to his parents through his voyages. He does not have to repress his natural gestures. Yet he must undergo transformation. This means that he will acquire new gestures, make use of a different wardrobe, function naturally in an unknown backdrop and learn to operate strange props. At the very end of the novel Karl will meet an old European friend, Fanny, and a new American friend. Both of these acquaintances will work with him in the Nature Theater of Oklahoma where he effectively will be playing himself. Being himself means that he is able to reconcile between the old and the new and thus retain his attentiveness. This is a hopeful gesture implemented in a transformed world.

Karl imagines that when he will sit with his uncle again at the breakfast table they will speak informally: 'perhaps as a result of such informal breakfasting, as was almost inevitable, they would meet oftener than simply once a day and so of course be able to speak more frankly to each other … perhaps this unlucky visit would become the turning-point in his relations with his uncle' (Kafka 1946: 64). This wishful thinking indicates that Karl is already using a trait that will help him in his voyages in America, he trusts in candid interpersonal relationships, not just in triumphant business relations. But Mr. Green and Mr. Pollunder are not amicable people. They sit at the table smoking and conspiring like two criminals: 'one might quite easily have suspected that some criminal plan was being discussed here and no legitimate business' (1946: 66). These gestures bring to the fore the American culture of masculinity. Karl's femininity comes to the fore when Clara overpowers him suggesting that he learn 'jiu-jitsu' (1946: 69). But a table re-enters the narrative to show that Karl is a student who prefers to get to know the other in the light of reflection. He 'stood again by his table in the light of the candle' (1946: 72). This table signifies loss, loneliness and thoughtfulness. It brings to mind the table at which a solitary scholar of the Talmud sits while reading his book by the light of a single candle.

Karl's journey continues and again the text becomes surreal. Backdrop is meticulously described so that the corridors sluggishly stretch and arch, floors pile up on each other inside the house (1946: 82).[10] Karl understands that he is not a guest in this house but a prisoner and that he will never see his room again. At this point his uncle's note arrives sending him away to become his own American man. 'Against my wishes you decided this evening to leave me; stick, then, to that decision all your life. Only then will it be a manly decision' (1946: 94–5). The note is consubstantial to a verdict handed down by a mighty father. It condemns the son to hard labour. But Karl's reaction is supple: 'So he chose a chance direction and set out on his way' (1946: 98). Holding a prop, his box, like Charlie Chaplin, Karl becomes the tramp and this gesture embodies his courage to brave his own future life experiences.[11]

Robinson and Delamarche are homeless and what explains this fact to Karl is wardrobe: 'they did not look very trustworthy, chiefly because without any understandable reason they were sleeping in their clothes; one of them actually had his boots on' (1946: 99). Karl feels lonely, as if he were the outlawed rogue and a different prop, a photo, and a new gesture signify this sensation. In the photo his mother's hand is 'near enough to kiss' (1946: 104). In *Kafka Goes to the Movies*, Hanns Zischler studies the genealogy of Kafka's *The Man Who Disappeared*. He elaborates the scene where Karl studies his parents' photo and concludes: 'When Kafka has a photograph before him, he can explore and feel his way across it and enter into an almost osmotic relationship with the person whose image is represented' (2003: 59).[12] The rogues steal his money and his photo but Karl is open to new experiences. He is offered and accepts his first real job as a lift-boy at the Hotel Occidental.[13]

The work at the hotel is menial and the excess of gestures coupled with minimal verbal communication with the guests point to the fact that Karl is beginning at the very bottom of society. The most important prop in this chapter is an elevator. Karl learns to haul on a cable that passes inside the elevator in order to increase the speed when he is alone in it. He works 'with strong, rhythmical heaves like a sailor' (1946: 147).[14] The backdrop in this chapter are the dormitories in which the boys sleep. The place is enveloped in a 'general haze' (1946: 149) because the lift-boys smoke when they are off-duty in their beds. Karl is hopeful in relation to his future although the prospects offered by his current job are bleak.[15] When Karl decides to help Robinson, although he is acting in direct contradiction to the workers' manual, it becomes clear that Karl's character is more relevant to Whitman's and Emerson's vision of America than to capitalistic norms that flourish on the East Coast in the early twentieth century.

A table appears briefly because the Head Waiter, Karl's judge, 'laid the lists on the table' (1946: 173). When Karl is dismissed at the end of his trial an inner monologue relates his thoughts. A fair trial is based on communication and he did not receive justice: '"It's impossible to defend oneself where there is no good will," Karl told himself, and he made no further answer to the Head Waiter' (1946: 188). Silent reflection shows that Karl is learning the technology of human relations in America. Submission to power is terrible for both Kafka and Benjamin yet Karl submits to benign power. He merely undertakes the gesture that Uncle Jacob prescribes: 'learn to understand your position' (1946: 35). These judges who indict him are different from the European judges – figures of decay – typical of stories such as 'Vor dem Gesetz' ('Before the Law', 1915). These judges belong to what Benjamin calls the 'assistants'. The Head Waiter is literally an assistant to the manager and he works in the hotel's food services. 'After all, the Head Waiter himself had begun as a lift-boy' (1946: 158). He hardly has time to conduct Karl's trial. The Head Porter is a co-worker who tries to improve his position in the hotel. These peculiar 'assistants' are the young, dynamic employees and bureaucrats that serve American capitalism and democracy. If they cannot be positive figures for either Kafka or Benjamin it is not because they manipulate negative power, for they have no power, but because they clutch at objects and people rather than acknowledge that passivity and passion enhance the ability to revolutionise the world and be transformed in it. Hence the next episode in which Karl is involved depicts American democracy.

Gestures and props are used to give material existence to American democracy. Democracy encompasses a celebrity, the masses, the other candidates, the law enforcement and the pundits that can both participate in and reflect on the hope that presides in America. Each one of these issues merits a full discussion but Kafka evades content, he uses gesture to hint at the shape that cultural criticism takes in America. The gestures are American, the props, the wardrobe and the backdrop cannot be mistaken as European. Hence the meaning of the events presides in detecting the relevance of gesture and prop to the theme at hand, not in textual interpretations.[16]

Karl does not want the job at Brunelda's that Delamarche offers him yet he has no choice and thus he tries to run away before Karl walks into the apartment. The description of his attempted escape from the policeman seems to be directly taken from *City Lights* (1931). The passage accurately records feverish gestures but in addition it shows how helpless the police are when up against a hoodlum like Delamarche and an innocent tramp like Karl. This helplessness of the police belongs to the ethos of American silent films and this tradition continues in *The Truman Show* where the 'outlaw' is an honest protagonist who is found in opposition to the law because of structural reasons, rather than because he is guilty.

> Karl … turned about and with a few great bounds for a start set off at full speed […]. 'Stop him!' the policeman shouted … and kept pointing his baton at him […]. [The policeman] began to blow really deafening blasts on his whistle […]. Karl had to think first and attend to his running only in the intervals between weighing possibilities and making decisions … he was just putting on a faster spurt so as to pass the first cross-street in a flash … when an arm darting out from a little doorway seized him and he was drawn into a dark entry, while a voice said: 'Don't move!' It was Delamarche, quite out of breath […]. The two policemen were really running past, their feet ringing in the empty street like the striking of steel against stone. (1946: 218–20)

The escape from the police is successful but Karl does not safely escape the job at Brunelda's apartment. The image and function of Brunelda is grounded in nothing other than GWBP. When Robinson saw her for the first time she was still a singer. Gesture registers how lovely she was: 'I [Robinson] couldn't help touching her back, but quite lightly, you know, just a touch' (1946: 235). Karl becomes Brunelda's slave yet the housework he is required to do only has meaning because he is in touch with props, 'so you could make an inventory straightaway of all our stuff' (1946: 244).

In the early morning hours this episode's table appears. This table is very simple because it belongs to a student and I suggest that this simplicity signals that now Karl is less of an alien in America. The meeting with the student introduces hope to Karl's life because studying is its own reward. Studying introduces freedom of thought to the life of the least free servant of the capitalist market. The student always does something interesting when he is reading even if he never finds a very interesting job. The table is bare and useful and the gestures signify reading. But other necessary props also appear, such as books, an electric lamp and, finally, black coffee:

> The scraping of table-legs on the next balcony made Karl aware that someone was sitting there reading. It was a young man with a little pointed beard, which he kept continually twisting as he read, his lips moving rapidly at the same time. He was facing Karl, sitting at a little table covered with books; he had taken the electric lamp from the parapet and shored it between two big volumes, so that he sat in a flood of garish light. (1946: 262)

I indicated that for Benjamin, Kafka himself is always studying and thus creating a tempest that carries him into the past and the future simultaneously. This is a tempest that might enable the student to understand himself. Benjamin relates this particular student with the assistants probably because Joseph Mendel does not believe that he might become a practicing physician despite the fact that he studies medicine. Yet Karl's need to study may be related to his genuine interest in the other, '"Are you studying?" asked Karl. [...] "My name is Joseph Mendel and I am a student."' (1946: 263, 265). This question and the reply suggest that frank characters have a place in America. Studies bring 'consistency' (1946: 267) to the lives of Americans. Backdrop signifies that Karl appreciates the efforts of this saintly student: '[Karl] glanced once more at the student, who now sat quite motionless in his ring of light, surrounded by the vast darkness' (1946: 269). Backdrop is used to investigate the wishful thinking that Karl engages in and the most important prop is still a desk, 'and in the future [Karl] might sit at his own desk as a regular clerk' (1946: 270).

When Karl reads the placard of the Theater of Oklahoma he is a changed person. It is not that 'today only and never again' (1946: 272) signifies a specific date but that each person embarks on the need and capability to be committed to a public life – a life that prefers contacts with others rather than narcissistically nursing the wounds that such encounters inevitably cause. Clayton promises that if Karl insists on playing a role in the theatre of life then his role will belong to the public sphere, he will express himself and act together with other people and practice, in the words of Hannah Arendt, 'sharing of words and deeds' (1958: 198). 'Up, and to Clayton!' (1946: 272) implies that Karl's new life will be established on gesture and the kind of theatricality that participation in the politics of everyday living requires. Karl senses that he is welcome because he trusts in a basic democratic attitude typical of America: 'Everyone is welcome' (1946: 273). In *Song of Myself* (1855), Walt Whitman expresses the same democratic notion when he asserts, 'I am large … I contain multitudes' (1992: 87). Karl knows from the student that if one is willing to both study and work then one can bring some consistency to one's life in America.

The encounter with the trumpeters is consubstantial to theatre at its best. GWBP appears in the description of 'hundreds of women dressed as angels in white robes with great wings on their shoulders were blowing on the trumpets that glittered like gold' (1946: 274). The women are mounted on high platforms, 'which could not however be seen, since they were completely hidden by the long flowing draperies of the robes … the women looked gigantic' (ibid.). They seem omnipotent despite the fact that they are human: 'And all these women were blowing their trumpets' (ibid.). The gesture they perform seems to be breaking open the sky by both pointing the trumpet at it and by aiming the sound of the blows straight to the heavens. In addition, a young couple with a baby in a 'perambulator' (ibid.) appears. This prop surely suggests that the Theater of Oklahoma favours everyone's pursuits of happiness. When Karl insists that his name is 'Negro' (1946: 286) he undertakes the ultimate theatrical gesture and presents himself as an original American labourer: he does not seek benefits but a job. Although Karl does not have papers he is engaged: 'but the clerk made a definitive gesture with his hand, said: "Engaged," and at once entered the decision in his book' (ibid.). Karl's new name appears on the electronic board and his profession is fastened to his arm: 'When Karl lifted his arm to see what was written on the band, there, right enough, were the words "technical worker"' (1946: 291). On the train with a new name and a new job Karl may safely disappear in America.[17]

IV. A TRUE MAN'S REFRAIN: 'IF I DON'T SEE YOU AGAIN…'

Weir's Truman also becomes active as the plot progresses and he leaves behind the two actresses who play his wife and mother as well as the actor who plays his best friend and walks away from the backdrop, which is the office building where he was employed. Most important, Truman has the courage to leave behind the director, who had raised him and directed his life and made him the organising principle of the show itself. By leaving, Truman ceases to be one of the production's props and moves on to find a new love and a new life. Truman is a good enough performer to leave the television production in *The Truman Show* in order to act a productive role in his unscripted private life. In Weir's film too, the actor acts in such a way that everyone loves his playacting; that is, everyone loves Truman, or pretends to love him. Truman relates his every feeling to his friend Marlon, yet Marlon uses this information to perfect the surveillance of Truman's every move. How does the candid Truman benefit from his intersubjective encounters with those who are trying to benefit at his expense?

Truman explores the GWBP that is extent in his surroundings. Thus, on the one hand Truman learns how to play himself. He constantly repeats typical gestures, makes use of wardrobe to reveal who he is, takes backdrop into consideration when he undertakes action and studies the use of prop. His peers, on the other hand, use GWBP to disguise their actions, concealing their true selves and thus manipulating the naive protagonist, whose attentiveness to those around him leads him to understand how GWBP can either reveal or obscure the true actions and intentions of the person, and in this way he rises above the situation. Truman, too, uses GWBP to reveal himself to others. At the same time he suspects these same means because GWBP may also be used to obscure real intentions and to dishonestly assert control over his freedom as an agent. Truman invariably uses candid gestures even when he needs to explore his spontaneity in hiding.

The Truman Show documents the everyday life of protagonist Truman Burbank. He is twenty-nine years old and lives in Seahaven, an island city in Florida. He is married to Meryl, a nurse at the local hospital, and works as a salesman for a life insurance company. His best friend is Marlon, who stocks vending machines with candy bars and other snacks. Truman's mother lives not far from him; his father apparently drowned in a sailing accident when Truman was a young boy. Truman's traumatic memories include the fact that he witnessed his father's death and he believes that he is to blame for the fact that the boat veered so deep into the sea. Later on he is traumatised by the sudden disappearance of Laura/Sylvia, a woman he had a crush on. She tried to tell him that his life was not real and that he was on TV but her father rushed her away from the beach where they met, telling Truman that she was schizophrenic. Truman hates his job. As a child he wanted to be a discoverer of continents. He still dreams of leaving Seahaven and going to remote places such as Fiji, or even Chicago. His relationship with his wife is tense and unhappy. She wants a child although she knows that the marriage and work are very frustrating to him. Truman's mother is demanding – whenever she is ill he has to take care of her – but she is willing to speak to him about his father whenever he needs reassurance.

What Truman does not know is that he lives inside an immense TV studio, a manmade dome that covers an entire town in Burbank, California. The environment inside the dome is controlled so that the weather, the time of day, the people, the seascape, the landscape and the entire existence of Seahaven is made of GWBP. Halogen lights cover the surface of the dome and they create sunshine during the day and moonlight and the appearance of stars at night. The sea is a tank with salt liquid controlled by turbines so that it can be still or tempestuous. The rain falls when the crew uses effects. All the people are hired actors who have a contract with the Omnicam Corporation. 'Everything on the show is for sale – from the actors' wardrobe, food products, to the very homes they live in' (Niccol 2012: 108). Christof, the director of this TV show, controls its everyday broadcasting using some five thousand cameras planted everywhere in Seahaven and inside Truman's home. Truman is on camera and he is seen from multiple angles twenty-four hours a day, seven days a week. Truman does not know that he is the only one who does not have a contract with the production company, the only one who is a True-Man because his gestures are not scripted. Truman plays himself. Adopted by Christof at birth, Truman is the property of the production company. When Christof is pressured by one of the viewers who argues that Truman is the company's prisoner he asserts:

> The only difference between Truman and ourselves is that his life is more thoroughly documented. He is confronted with the same obstacles and influences that confront us all. He plays his allotted roles as we all do [...]. If his was more than just a vague ambition [to flee Seahaven], if he were absolutely determined to discover the truth, there's no way we could prevent him. (Niccol 2012: 80)

The studio's objective is that the show will continue for as long as Truman is alive. Yet the GWBP that sequesters Truman inside this huge studio also betrays the fact that these are the building blocks of a manmade, fictional world dependent on technological innovation and control panels. In order to realise his freedom, Truman has to first discover the machination of GWBP. Only when he learns to subdue these powers can he use them to advance his plan of escape from Seahaven. From Truman's point of view the film is about studying the world that surrounds him and about studying the role that he plays in this world. His goal is to effect change in his life and hence be able to break free from the powers that keep him imprisoned in an artificial world. The elements that define Truman's world are not unlike the signposts that Karl Rossmann studies in order to become American, even while he remains himself and plays himself in the Nature Theater of Oklahoma. Truman studies the same signposts and discovers how they are being used to mislead and control him. Truman is able to restore the positive and transformative attribute of GWBP and counter the effects of a controlled reality by playing himself, being spontaneous, genuine and energetic. In so doing, Truman succeeds in unmasking an oppressive manipulation from above.

From the viewers' perspective this is a film about the power that basic American values carry. If Truman can discover the truth about his incarceration and escape from captivity then every American can likewise fulfil their wishes provided that they are willing to closely study the uses of GWBP and use their knowledge to play themselves candidly.

In *Amusing Ourselves to Death*, Neil Postman explains the difference between technology and medium. 'A technology ... is merely a machine. A medium is the social and intellectual environment a machine creates' (1985: 84). Truman can transform the machine that imprisons him by using the very same tools of GWBP in order to enhance his attentiveness and passion in the world. In this sense he is an American hero.

The props that Truman studies range from TV technology and image-making apparatuses such as mirrors and stills, to lighting, sound, makeup, broadcasting, wardrobe, scripted speech and acting. Yet he has to study the financial manipulations of a media mogul and a culture of franchise merchandising. In the beginning of the film Truman studies his own face in the mirror as if trying to discover something that may be invisible to him. Unbeknownst to him, the mirror hides the fact that it is an image-making device. He begins talking to himself pretending that he is a world famous explorer participating in a TV interview. The mirror is the prop that reflects how genuine and loveable Truman is. At the end of the film, when Truman knows that he is constantly under surveillance, he looks into the mirror differently. His gaze discloses the fact that he knows that this is a two-way mirror. The technicians on the other side of this two-way mirror are spooked: 'Is he looking at us?' (Niccol 2012: 80). Truman does not want to expose himself yet, so he embarks on his regular routine and takes on the imaginary TV interview. The first object that introduces prop and lighting to Truman's consciousness is a 'large spherical glass object [that] falls from the sky and lands with a deafening crash on the street, several yards from his car' (2012: 3). Truman thoroughly studies the object. He begins to study his surroundings, including the sky from which the object came. He is able to read the label on the fixture 'SIRIUS (9 Canis Major)' and he loads the halogen projector into his trunk. Thus begins his need to study his environment in order to break free from a life that is suffocating him.

When Truman comes across acting as a central device in his world the actor who mostly affects him is related to his childhood memories. Truman sees a homeless person and thinks he recognises his father, as if his real father did not die. This gesture implies that Truman is questioning the people that belong in his life. He could accept a new person in his life because he trusts his memory and this homeless person resembles his father. It might be that what he knows about his own childhood is false – maybe his father did not die. Truman discovers the use of stills and make-up in the glossy magazines that he buys. Secretly, Truman tears pages from these magazines with women's facial features and tries to create an identikit of a specific face. In his trunk at home he keeps the paper-cutouts with different shapes of nose, cheeks, mouth, ears, hair and eyes. These features belong to Sylvia, who is the owner of the red cardigan that he keeps in the same trunk. She was the woman that Truman had a crush on. Sylvia forces Truman to be spontaneous for the first time when she encourages him to leave with her immediately and flee to the beach. They kiss and that makes Truman trust Sylvia. She tells him that his life is fake. Truman learns from Sylvia to act spontaneously. The 'spontaneous gesture', to use the words of D. W. Winnicott (1984: 145), helps him to expose the fact that he lives in an artificial reality. It is thanks to Sylvia that Truman begins to have doubts about the integrity of his environment and he decides to hide the calls he makes to the operator in search of Sylvia's phone number in Fiji. Secrecy thus enhances Truman's attentiveness to his surroundings for he correctly suspects that he is being followed. Acts of surveillance, including the composition of a complicated jigsaw puzzle that would help him locate Sylvia, force Truman to improve his technical proficiency. He becomes more alienated in the world, he turns sceptical of the actors, backdrop and props that furnish his life in order to find the kind of knowledge and information that might be considered reliable because it advances his desires.

Truman learns about role acting when he senses that people around him act against his genuine need to explore the world in which he lives. The actors and the production crew are not passive in response to the laborious studies of his world that Truman practices. His wife Meryl dismisses him when he says that he wants to leave Seahaven: 'This'll pass. Everybody thinks like this now and then.' Marlon encourages Truman's mediocrity and assures him that Seahaven is the best place on Earth and that Truman just needs a son. Marlon lies to Truman when he tells him that the light he found 'dropped off from an airliner'. When Truman imagines that the homeless man he sees is his father, actors block his movement. A woman and a man cut him, a troupe of runners hits him and these actors lift the homeless man off the ground and push him into a bus. Cars block

Truman's way as he runs after the bus. His mother argues that it is inconceivable that his father is not dead.

Truman is helpless when the others thwart his investigations into his environment. He is an open person who tends to trust the people around him and to accept them just the way they are. It would be easy for Truman to assume that the people around him are honest, for any other feelings toward them would cast him as paranoid. Yet Truman undertakes to study the mechanism of others' relations to him. Is it true that others do not make themselves known to him as he makes himself transparent to them? Truman's experiments mean that he ceases to view gesture as a semi-unconscious reaction to him and begins to see gesture as a planned behaviour intended to sabotage his ability to know the world and better conduct himself in it. He learns that when his own gestures are spontaneous they catch his fellow women and men off guard. Then he can learn more about the coercive management of the technological and the human environment around him. He bolts into an office building that is not his own. He realises that the elevator is just a prop. People in there are having refreshments. A guard tells him that they are remodelling. Truman remarks of others' reactions towards him: 'It's when I'm unpredictable. They can't stand that' (Niccol 2012: 45). A spontaneous gesture is the sign of humanity and authenticity because it is always singular and meaningful. The meaningful gesture emerges from somewhere between consciousness and the unconscious, the self and the intersubjective relation to the other, and hence it expands one's possibility of action in the world. This gesture uses props without clutching at them. But in Truman's reality the gestures and the props that belong to the others are designed for surveillance and clutch at him. They prevent him from fully exploring his potential as a human being. Truman approaches the world and reaches out to it when he uncovers the fraudulent gestures and the clutching objects in his surroundings.

Truman's explorations enhance his non-conformity and he trusts his intuitions. His mother shows him a photo album with pictures of remote places that they took him to visit as a child, including Mount Rushmore. He senses that this is a montage and says, 'It [the mountain] looks so small' (2012: 76). He continues to study the album and, using a magnifying glass, he examines a photo of his wedding. He notices that Meryl's fingers are crossed in a photo of the couple kissing. Suspicious of their relationship he rushes into Meryl's hospital to see her in the operating room functioning as a professional nurse. The actors use gestures and props such as a scalpel but the patient on the operating table jumps up in horror when it looks like the person acting the surgeon is about to cut into her knee. Again a guard has to escort Truman out of the makeshift backdrop.

Truman forces Meryl to observe the movement of cars on the street together with him. He can anticipate which cars will come from behind the curve and he is never mistaken. This means that the environment is controlled. The props appear on a loop. He spontaneously decides to take Meryl and simply drive out of Seahaven. His discoveries make him more oriented toward the future and the postponement of death. He realises that for as long as he is willing to break the bounds of his known reality then he is interested in the forward motion that more storytelling and more experimentation is opening up.

At a roadblock a policeman tells Truman that no traffic is allowed, since there is a leak at the power plant. Truman has to believe this and says, 'thank you' only to hear the officer's improbable retort, 'You're welcome, Truman' (2012: 63). He understands that this is backdrop again and the policeman is an actor. Truman becomes violent with Meryl because he knows enough to demand the truth from her. She pretends to calm him down suggesting that he drink some cocoa which the show is being paid to advertise, and Truman understands that she is part of the conspiracy against him. He grabs Meryl, who cries out 'Do something!' (2012: 65). For the first time Truman has proof of the fact that he is under surveillance. He is demanding to know, 'Who are you talking to?!' (ibid.).

From here on Truman investigates the reality that surrounds him in complete secrecy. On one hand he becomes a scripted actor when he is acting Truman's role in public; on the other he is secretly finding a way to act not in front of the camera. Truman learns to outsmart the camera, act under cover. Here gesture is all. The viewers see the gestures that are disclosed to the camera and these are the gestures that Truman stages. He knows how to stage himself sleeping when he is not in his bed. The genuine gestures no longer appear on camera so no one knows them. This enables Truman to have a private life and renders him a normal human being – not merely the star of 'The Truman Show'.

The only one who believes that Truman will find out that he is living a simulated life as a TV star is Sylvia. She challenges Christof when he is on TV taking calls from the viewers, by arguing that Truman will find a way out of Seahaven. Christof states that he likes his prison cell, but Sylvia objects, 'No, you're wrong! He'll prove you wrong!' (2012: 80). Truman is capable of true love because he is a true-man and Sylvia is a true lover and hence she trusts in her lover's powers that will bring them together at some point. Sylvia represents a large number of other TV viewers who would like Truman to break free and they want Christof's makeshift world of GWBP to be eliminated so that the open-ended reality can be established and Truman's spontaneous gestures can allow freedom to proliferate in the world. Hypocritically Christof points out to his viewers that the programme is rife with truth-talk: 'While the world he inhabits is counterfeit, there's nothing fake about Truman himself. It's not always Shakespeare but it's genuine' (2012: 75). Christof is the one who misses the point when he thinks that the show is about Truman. In fact the show has turned to be about

Truman's struggle to triumph against a media mogul. Truman knows that the world he inhabits is counterfeit. He has to triumph in this world and approach a real world by being himself at the same time that he satisfies the needs of those who control the make-believe world he is incarcerated in. If Truman can break free from TV, then at least one American has enough power to do what all Americans are scared to do, stop living vicariously through someone else's script. In this sense Peter Weir's film is the story of an American hero, not a victim: Truman is a true none-conformist, he has the stamina to always be himself. When Truman escapes from his house unnoticed, the programme is off the air and a sign indicates to the viewers, 'Technical fault. [...] Please stand by' (2012: 92).

Truman anticipated this reaction to his disappearance and takes to the sea. Since he undertakes to study his own terms of existence in a false reality, he has to brave his fear of the sea. When Christof resumes transmission he operates the weather programme on the computers and creates a storm complete with high waves, clouds, darkness and driving rains. Truman understands that all this is backdrop and props and he yells, 'Come on, is that the best you can do? You're gonna have to kill me!' (2012: 153). When Truman's boat is capsized he is tied to the vessel in the middle of a stormy sea with his life under threat. This gesture is very specific: he becomes Ahab – or Gregory Peck in John Huston's *Moby Dick* (1956) – who will either fulfil his desire or die. Christof gives in and on the calm surface of the water Truman sails on. The bow of Truman's boat hits a wall. He walks on deck to check out what happened and discovers that a spherical bubble envelops him. What he thought was the sky over his head is nothing but backdrop painted in blue. Violently he tries to break the backdrop. He walks on the rim of the water until he reaches a staircase. It ends next to a doorknob marked 'exit' and Truman opens the door. This gesture signifies that Truman is a free man. He explored and understood the world that incarcerated him for so many years. He also broke free of the hold that the trauma of his father's death had on him. When he is ready to leave Christof speaks to him over the many loudspeakers in the cyclorama saying that he is the creator of a TV show that many viewers watch because it gives them hope. Christof tries to dissuade him saying that the real world is as dishonest as the one that he inhabits – people always play a role, no one is honest and authentic. Truman replies with a gesture: he bows and utters his refrain, 'If I don't see you again – good afternoon, good evening, and good night', and leaves the show through the door in the sky. He is not embittered. Just like Kafka's 'Negro' who is travelling on the train into the vast country in search of a new life, Truman, too, is a private man and he can start his real life in America. Both Weir's Truman Burbank and Kafka's Karl Rossmann give back to GWBP the usefulness that belongs to it. Both protagonists remain attentive to the world around them. They do this through studying – rather than clutching onto – the very objects and people that try to clutch onto them.

NOTES

1   In the English translations, Kafka's novel is commonly referred to as both *Amerika* and *The Man Who Disappeared*.
2   I will show that Karl finds a home in America even though this approach is debatable for various other critics propose different interpretations. I thank the editors of this anthology, Shai Biderman and Ido Lewit, who suggest that I refer to Kafka's diary entry from 30 September 1915: 'Rossmann and K., the innocent and the guilty, both executed without distinction in the end. The innocent one with a gentler hand, more pushed aside then struck down' (1949: 132). In contrast to this intension stand Max Brod's memories of the period in which Kafka wrote and read to his friends passages from the novel he was working on. In the 'Afterword' to the English translation of the novel there is a citation from Brod who mentions that he knows from Kafka that Kafka meant the novel to end 'on a note of reconciliation' (1946: 298). Klaus Mann's text is translated for the 'Preface' of the English edition of the novel. He both cites Brod and adds in his own words that Kafka liked Americans because they are healthy and optimistic. He continues to suggest that Karl's arrival at the Nature Theater of Oklahoma is optimistic because it might enable him to pick up his professional life as a technical worker, 'his security and freedom, and perhaps even his homeland and parents' (1946: xvi). In the preface to his 2008 translation of the novel, Mark Harman also suggests to read the novel's ending as ambiguous, based on notes by both Kafka and Brod (Kafka 2008: xxiv–xxv). Further along I cite from Freddie Rokem but it is worthwhile mentioning that although Rokem thinks that the theatre of Oklahoma suggests death this death is allegorical. He states: 'It [the Theater of Oklahoma] is the core of life' (2009: 125). He suggests that Karl's journey in America will end in a return to origins and cites the fact that Karl meets Fanny whom he knows from Europe as support of his claim. Rokem agrees that Kafka's text is 'a story of survival' (2009: 127). Rokem insists that if the completion of such a journey is possible the reason is that the subject undergoes radical 'transformation' (ibid.). Later I will refer to this radical transformation and name it a revolution. I will show that both Karl and Truman are integrated in America as revolutionised agents. It is important to mention that both Mann and Rokem suggest that Karl reaches the Nature Theater of Oklahoma after many years and by then he is certainly not a youth who has recently left Europe.
3   It is taken for granted that American democracy is born from performative action of citizens in search of making themselves heard and acquiring influence on the

authorities that inevitably silence 'the people'. The trust in performative action is seminal to the American ideology; see, for example, Perkins 1946: 166; Al-Sayyid 2000: 51; Ottaway and Carothers 2000: 293–4.

4 Rokem further suggests that the American performances that Kafka elaborates particularly at the end of the novel devoted to the Nature Theater of Oklahoma express 'a wish for integration and redemption in a world governed by forces that are much more powerful than the individual. The wish is a gesture through which the wishing in itself, regardless of its fulfilment, or even the possibility that it will ever be fulfilled, is performative' (2009: 123–4).

5 The significance of gesture is such that even if the film does not show Truman reuniting with his beloved then the fact that Sylvia who is watching TV leaves home at the same time that Truman leaves the studio means that she undertakes the responsibility to find Truman and unite with him. After all, propelled by his love to Sylvia, Truman found a way to escape from the makeshift cyclorama and enter into reality.

6 This suggests that Cavell is an heir to continental philosophy, not just to Emerson and Thoreau and that Benjamin inherits Emerson, not just continental philosophy and Jewish mysticism.

7 See note 2 above.

8 Karl is also associated with music. He has a piano at his uncle's house. Clara asks him to play the piano in the country house, and he is immersed in music at the Nature Theater of Oklahoma. This is relevant to Benjamin's contention that Kafka associates music with the ability of unformed creatures to undergo change. Hence these creatures have hope; see Benjamin 1999: 799.

9 See, for example, Henry Sussman's discussion of the novel's political relevance to slavery and to the death camps. Sussman speaks about 'the novel's railroad station of thinking' (2007: 195) to show that it is possible that Rossmann and the other emigrants will be as good as dead when they are lost and enslaved somewhere in America's mid-west. Further down I suggest that Sussman's train of thought begins with Adorno; see note 17 below.

10 For Benjamin this would be a moment where the prehistoric swamp life appears in order to recapture Karl.

11 In Parker Tyler's article 'Kafka's and Chaplin's *Amerika*', he suggests that 'in one sense it seems obvious that Karl is nothing but Kafka's "Charlie"' (1950: 302). Chaplin was an immigrant who arrived to America from the UK in 1910 and some four years later Kafka finished writing his novel. In those years Chaplin was touring America as an actor in the vaudeville theatre. The reason that Karl and Chaplin are similar is that both of them are young immigrants who journey in America 'trying to start a new life and trying to rise to a level beyond any available to him in his native land' (1950: 301). Chaplin excelled and became more famous than Senator Edward Jacob, Karl's uncle. Yet it is Chaplin's tramp who embodies the trials that Karl undergoes.

The tramp is undesirable, destined to fail in his economical pursuits of success. He is always suspect in the eyes of the law. He carries an umbrella and a bundle and fences with his umbrella to signify that sheer force is required to get by in America. Karl undergoes very similar experiences. He is always treated as an alien, finds it very difficult to hold on to a profitable job that he likes, and when he comes into America he owns a bundle in the form of a rundown suitcase and he sees a statue of liberty that holds a sword in hand, not a torch. But Tyler acknowledges that 'There is no deep symbolism about these casual parallels' (1950: 302). It is still interesting to see that the sensibilities of these two different artists are such that one is illuminating the other. In order to exemplify these similar sensibilities Tyler cites the fact that uncle Jacob repudiates Karl at the same time that in *City Lights* a drunk millionaire befriends Charlie but repudiates him when he is sober again. He cites more similarities when the issue of love is at stake. In Chaplin's *The Kid* the tramp dreams that he is transported to heaven on the wings of a girl-angel. Generally the tramp is alienated not loved. Karl is not loved by Carla and later on he meets mother figures that he could not fall in love with. Tyler also suggests that the tramp usually flees from trouble but Karl faces the world and in his encounters in the world one feels 'the steadiness of a direct, open, frontal gaze' (1950: 311). The mixture of fantasy and reality extant in Kafka's and Chaplin's America enables one to access innocence and guilt, job and joblessness, and nature and machine. Such a fantasy is difficult to separate from reality and in it the youth is making its way in the world.

12 In Lacan's language a photo might serve as a mirror in which the observer finds his ego ideal or his ideal ego. Karl will have to find his ideal ego or his ego ideal in the specular relationship with real, not fantasised others. Yet Karl also finds the reflection that he identifies with in an old photo from Europe that the manageress has in her room at the hotel Occidental. He sees a young soldier who is both subject to commanders and retains his arrogance, '…who was standing erect with a thatch of wild black hair and a look of superimposed but arrogant amusement.' (1946: 138) This gesture is similar to the gesture that Karl tries to acquire for it include complacency and independence.

13 In 'Kafka's Amerika', Martin Greenberg suggests that 'The Road to Rameses' is the chapter that announces that *The Man Who Disappeared* is a picaresque novel that develops on the open road. Robinson and Delamarche are rogues but Karl is the opposite of a rogue. 'His very innocence, however, makes him a social outsider like the rogue, for the world in which he finds himself violently rejects innocence. He is a kind of upside-down *picaro*' (1966: 75, emphasis in original). This approach is very different from the one that Cavell discloses. Yet it might be that Kafka is writing in the footsteps of Emerson and Walt Whitman whom he read and loved.

14 Carl Steiner argues that Kafka depicts America as the land of industrialised, impersonal, dehumanising conditions. 'The thirty elevators in the hotel provide its hub

as they are constantly whizzing the guests up and down [...]. The mechanical and physical mobility which these elevators display stands in an inverse ratio to the social mobility of its harried and rather hapless operators' (1977: 460).

15 Michael Burwell also senses that a Marxist critique is in place in relation to these jobs that Kafka depicts in his novel. 'It is interesting that the above working conditions and their effect on the workers have produced precisely those two states against which Karl Marx inveighed so heavily: *Entmenschlichung* (e.g., man being turned into a machine) and *Entfremdung* (emphasized here by the loss of meaningful communication)' (1979: 198). Richard Ruland is another critic who stresses the episode of the Hotel Occidental as related to the importance of technology in American society. 'Once again Kafka comes painfully close to delineating America's machine culture' (1961: 38).

16 I will not closely study the scene of campaigning for elections, as Henry Sussman thoroughly examines the scene in Ideals of the Wanderer (2007: 185–6). Sussman analyzes gesture and prop to reach the conclusion that American democracy is impervious to descent and in this sense it is enslaving. I take issue with this argument. I suggest that Kafka uses gesture and props to argue that in America judges are not nominated but elected, they can be seen in the open air among the general public, not just in attics or stale basements and dusty archives. Gesture and props are used in order to certify that descent is represented in this democratic process: 'However, all the enemies of the present candidate united in a general cat-calling, and even many of the gramophones were set going again' (1946: 251).

17 Sussman suggests that this final scene is very pessimistic and compares the race track to the Paris Vélodrome where Jews were rounded up to be sent on trains to death camps (2007: 193). I think that this corresponds to Theodor Adorno's 'Notes on Kafka'. Adorno suggests that Kafka's world is similar to the world of the Third Reich. He suggests that in Kafka the judge and the people are not very different from each other. 'In *The Castle* the officials wear a special uniform, as the SS did – one which any pariah can make himself if need be [...]. Acts of unbridled violence are performed by figures in subordinate positions, types such as non-commissioned officers, prisoners-of-war and concierges [...]. The unemployed – in *The Castle* – and emigrants – in *Amerika* – are dressed and preserved like fossils of the process of *déclassement*' (1981: 259–60; emphasis in original).

BIBLIOGRAPHY

Adorno, Theodor (1981 [1953]) 'Notes on Kafka,' *Prisms*, trans. Samuel and Shierry Weber. Cambridge, MA: MIT Press, 243–71.

Al-Sayyid, Mustapha Kamel (2000) 'A Clash of Values: U.S. Civil Society Aid and Islam in Egypt', in Marina Ottawaway and Thomas Carothers (eds) *Funding Virtue: Civil Society Aid and Democracy Promotion*. Washinton, D. C.: Carnegie Endowment for International Peace, 49–73.

Arendt, Hannah (1958) *The Human Condition*. Chicago: University of Chicago Press.

Benjamin, Walter (1999 [1934]) 'Franz Kafka: On the Tenth Anniversary of His Death', *Selected Writings, Volume 2, 1927–1934*, eds Michael W. Jennings, Howard Eiland and Gary Smith, trans. Rodney Livingstone. Cambridge, MA: The Belknap Press of Harvard University Press, 792–818.

Burwell, Michael L. (1979) 'Kafka's *America* as a Novel of Social Criticism', *German Studies Review*, 2, 2, 193–209.

Cavell, Stanley (1989) 'Finding as Founding', *This New Yet Unapproachable America*. Chicago: University of Chicago Press, 77–118.

Greenberg, Martin (1966) 'Kafka's America', *Salmagundi*, 1, 3, 74–84.

Kafka, Franz (1946 [1927]) *Amerika*, trans. Edwin Muir. New York: New Directions Books.

____ (1949) *The Diaries of Franz Kafka: 1914–1923*, ed. Max Brod, trans. Martin Greenberg with the cooperation of Hannah Arendt. New York: Schocken.

____ (1971 [1915]) 'Before the Law', *The Complete Stories*, ed. Nahum N. Glatzer. New York: Schocken, 3–4.

____ (2008 [1927]) *Amerika: The Missing Person*, trans. and preface by Mark Harman. New York: Schocken.

____ (2009 [1925]) *The Trial*, trans. Mike Mitchell. Oxford: Oxford University Press.

Lacan, Jacques (1977) 'The Mirror Stage as Formative of the Function of the I', *Écrits, 1–7*. New York: W. W. Norton.

Niccol, Andrew (2012) *The Truman Show: The Shooting Script*. New York: HarperCollins.

Ottaway, Marina and Carothers, Thomas (2000) 'Toward Civil Society Realism', in Marina Ottawaway and Thomas Carothers (eds) *Funding Virtue: Civil Society Aid and Democracy Promotion*. Washington, D. C.: Carnegie Endowment for International Peace, 293–310.

Perkins, Frances (1946) *The Roosevelt I Knew*. New York: The Viking Press.

Postman, Neil (1985) *Amusing Ourselves to Death: Public Discourse in the Age of Show Business*. New York: Penguin.

Rokem, Freddie (2009) 'Theaters in America: Brecht and Kafka', in Silvija Jestrovic and Yana Meerzon (eds) *Performance, Exile and 'America'*. New York: Palgrave Macmillan, 119–33.

Ruland, Richard E. (1961) 'A View from Back Home: Kafka's Amerika', *American Quarterly*, 13, 1, 33–42.

Steiner, Carl (1977) 'How American is *Amerika*?', *Journal of Modern Literature*, 6, 3, 455–65.

Sussman, Henry (2007) *Idylls of the Wanderer: Outside in Literature and Theory*. New

York: Fordham University Press.

Tyler, Parker (1950) 'Kafka's and Chaplin's *Amerika*', *The Sewanee Review*, 58, 2, 299–311.

Whitman, Walt (1992 [1855]) 'Song of Myself', *Leaves of Grass*, New York: The Library of America, 27–88.

Winnicott, D. W. (1984 [1960]) 'Ego Distortions in Terms of True and False Self', *The Maturational Processes and the Facilitating Environment*. London: Karnac Books, 140–52.

Zischler, Hanns (2003) *Kafka Goes to the Movies*, trans. Susan H. Gillespie. Chicago: University of Chicago Press.

THE POSSIBILITY OF THE CINEMATIC IN 'THE METAMORPHOSIS' AND 'THE BURROW'

KEVIN W. SWEENEY

Franz Kafka wrote 'Die Verwandlung' ('The Metamorphosis', 1915) and 'Der Bau' ('The Burrow', 1931) during the period from the middle of the 1910s to the middle of the 1920s, a decade which saw the introduction, wide distribution and public acceptance of feature-length narrative films. Since Kafka wrote at the time of this new art form's emergence, can one gain insight into his narrative aesthetic by examining how both works might be adapted to the screen? Certainly, literature and film are quite different media: Kafka's works are presented solely with words; whereas film narratives, which can use words, primarily use filmed pictorial images to present their stories. Yet, even with this difference, addressing how Kafka's two works might be adapted to the screen illuminates an aspect of Kafka's aesthetic, especially his use of an indeterminately formed protagonist. In particular, there are interesting similarities in Kafka's and narrative film's use of point of view. In addition, considering how one might adapt 'The Metamorphosis' and 'The Burrow' as narrative films illustrates how Kafka uses a character's point of view to introduce narrative space.

During the decade in which Kafka wrote the two stories, several different narrative film styles developed. One of the major cinematic styles emphasised filming a scene in such a way that the objects in the image were seen to be set in what film audiences would recognise as a natural unified space. This emphasis on providing a natural spatial context for the objects or action in a scene was referred to by Siegfried Kracauer (1960: 27–40) as a component of the 'realist' cinematic tradition.[1] Films in this realist style could present narratives about imaginary situations or characters; however, they needed to show them in a spatial setting that the camera recorded or that would be accepted by film audiences as being natural and familiar. Thus, there could be magical beings in a magical narrative world, but the space in that narrative could not be magical but had to be presented as natural in the sense of not regularly allowing violations to the narrative's unified three-dimensional spatial environment.[2]

During this same decade, one can see a change or evolution in thinking about spatial realism within the German Expressionist film aesthetic. A prominent example of an Expressionist film with an international following was Robert Wiene's *Das Cabinet des Dr. Caligari* (*The Cabinet of Dr. Caligari*, 1920). Although there were segments in it where space was filmed so as to appear as a natural spatial setting, what was innovative in the film was the graphic creation of space by having stylised spatial representations drawn onto the film's *mise-en-scène*, thereby challenging the appearance of a natural space. This was undertaken in a modernist spirit which urged that pictorial illusion should be challenged. Although several other films employed this graphic creation of space, by the time of F. W. Murnau's *Nosferatu, eine Symphonie des Grauens* (*Nosferatu, a Symphony of Horror*, 1922), the German Expressionist film aesthetic had undergone a transformation. Now space was created by using the camera so as to make it appear as a natural spatial setting. Stylised effects or distortions consistent with the Expressionist aesthetic were created by camera angles or the use of lighting and shadow (see Bordwell and Thompson 1994: 108–15).[3]

For example, Paul Wegener's *Der Golem, wie er in die Welt kam* (*The Golem, How He Came into the World*, 1920) presented the town's architecture in a stylised Expressionist way, but the space in which the characters acted was a natural one. *The Golem* narrates the Jewish tale of the fabulous creature of Prague, but shows this robot-like creature as an integrated being, having a determinate physical body, set in a spatial context that film audiences would have recognised as familiar. He/it occupies space in the same way as the other characters in the film. Given the Golem's physical determinacy, one imagines that there were few obstacles to shooting the film in a natural spatial style. However, given the indeterminacy of both of Kafka's protagonists in 'The Metamorphosis' and 'The Burrow', could those characters also be easily filmed in a spatial 'realist' style? Or would the very indeterminacy of their physical form present impediments to their being characters in films that conform to a natural spatial style?[4]

I. THE INDETERMINACY OF THE CREATURES IN 'THE METAMORPHOSIS' AND 'THE BURROW'

Initially, it might seem that there would be major obstacles prohibiting both of Kafka's works from being shot in a natural-spatial stylistic way. In 'The

Metamorphosis' Kafka identifies Gregor Samsa not as a particular kind of insect but as a 'monstrous vermin'.[5] Gregor is described as having both human and insect body parts that resist an organic unification. He has insect-like legs and a large carapace back; however, he has other features that insects do not have: a jaw, nostrils, eyes that tear, and he breathes – insects have a different form of respiration. These latter human characteristics seem to be part of Gregor's pre-transformed body; however, they do not seem to be recognised as Gregor's body parts by his family, the office manager or the cleaning woman, who refers to Gregor as a dung beetle. Her labelling Gregor in this way has never settled the question among commentators about the kind of insect Gregor is. Gregor's sister, Grete, finally refers to him as a monster. Thus, Kafka's description of Gregor as physically indeterminate renders him a different kind of character from the Golem. This difference creates problems for how 'The Metamorphosis' might be adapted to the screen.

The protagonist of 'The Burrow' seems to share a similar indeterminate physical form to Gregor's; however, there is the difference that the denizen of the burrow, unlike Gregor, existed in its present form prior to the beginning of the narrative. Still, this continuity of form does not lessen its physically ambiguous nature. Just as commentators have speculated about what kind of insect Gregor is, so they have tried to identify the kind of animal that inhabits the warren of tunnels and spaces in 'The Burrow'. Stanley Corngold has described some of the possible animal kinds this creature might be, as a 'badger, vole, or mole' (2007: ix). However, the burrow's inhabitant maintains a physically indeterminate nature regardless of any specific animal identification. He/it is described as having specific body parts (e.g. head, thigh, legs, teeth and claws) which can be taken to refer literally to non-human body parts.

Nevertheless, on occasion one may interpret some of the creature's features, such as its claws, metaphorically. For example, the creature's clawing may be interpreted as in saying of a ruthless businessman that he *clawed* his way to the top. However, my point is not to claim that this creature has human as well as a burrowing animal's parts, only that a general ambiguity exists about its form. Indeed, the creature's sometime colloquial narration (e.g. using expressions like 'small fry') contributes to this ambiguity by raising the possibility that the references to the specific body parts might at times be used metaphorically.

In addition to the physical indeterminacy of both Gregor and the creature in the burrow, the two also share a mental indeterminacy. Gregor is psychologically split by possessing both a private psychological interiority with a seemingly rational consciousness, and at the same time exhibiting insect-like behaviour. Yet it is difficult to think of Gregor as being able to maintain a rational consciousness that is entirely distinct from and unaffected by being attached to an alien body. The authority of his consciousness, grounded in his verbal thinking and functioning memory, is undermined by his not always knowing why he behaves as he does. For example, does Gregor choose to hide under the couch because he does not want the sight of his body to frighten his family? Or is his hiding an instinctive insect-like act just like the snapping of his jaws at the spilling coffee? The reader is never given clear evidence about the exact nature of Gregor's behaviour, which would lead the reader to trust Gregor's thoughts about the motivation for his actions. In fact, even Gregor comes to doubt his initial beliefs about some of his behaviours. For example, at first Gregor thinks that he is offering intelligible reassuring words to his family on the other side of his locked bedroom door; however, he soon suspects that his utterances are nothing but unintelligible chirpings.

Gregor's psychological indeterminacy is matched in certain respects by the psychological indeterminacy of the protagonist in 'The Burrow'. Both creatures have a rational consciousness that conflicts with their being identified with an animal. Insects and burrowing animals do not have a consciousness that can be used to express verbally a range of thoughts and feelings. In describing his burrow and worries about his safety, the narrator inhabitant of this underground maze presents his thoughts in rich linguistic detail. He is concerned to explore verbally the subtleties and nuances of his life underground and his fears for his future. Wanting to investigate the subtle psychological aspects of his being, he seeks to state his ideas about his existential condition as accurately as possible. Rather than just an animal who behaves only by instinct, he shows himself to be a rational agent who wants to understand his world. For example, he rationally plans and conducts an experiment to determine the specific source of the hissing sound that he insists he hears.

Yet his behaviour at times conflicts with his rational sensitivities. For example, he gorges himself on the raw carrion that he has piled up in his central hall, what he refers to as his 'castle court': 'diving ever more deeply into the smells, until I can't stand it any longer and on a given night, storm into the castle court and wreak havoc among the provisions, gorging myself to the point of total torpor on the greatest delicacies I have' (2007: 167). Such an incident suggests that he is not above engaging in mindless behaviour. On another occasion he awakens from slumber to discover that there is 'still hanging from my teeth a rat' (2007: 166). Such brutish behaviour clashes with the verbal insights he offers that otherwise give the impression of his being a discerning individual sensitive to subtle aspects of his environment.

II. OBSTACLES TO A REALIST CINEMATIC ADAPTATION OF 'THE METAMORPHOSIS' AND 'THE BURROW'

Given the indeterminacy of Gregor's physical form and character, it would seem difficult to present Gregor in a film that is shot in a way that positions him in a natural spatial environment. Kafka was aware of this problem of pictorially presenting the transformed Gregor as an organically unified being. Kafka's publisher had proposed including a picture of a hideous giant insect in the book in order to identify the work as being a horror story and boost sales. Kafka pleaded with his publisher not to show any picture of the creature.

Hartmut Binder has investigated Kafka's response to his publisher's proposal, and he relates that 'Kafka had learned that the illustrator Ottomar Starke had been commissioned to draw a title-page illustration. For this reason on 25 October 1915, he wrote to his publisher:

> It struck me that Starke, as an illustrator, might want to draw the insect itself. Not that, please not that! I do not want to restrict him, but only to make this plea out of my deepest knowledge of the story. The insect cannot be depicted. It cannot even be shown from a distance. Perhaps there is no such intention and my plea can be dismissed with a smile – so much the better. But I would be very grateful if you would pass along my request and make it more emphatic. If I were to offer suggestions for an illustration, I would choose such scenes as the following: the parents and the head clerk in front of the locked door, or even better, the parents and the sister in the lighted room, with the door open upon the adjoining room that lies in darkness. (1996: 185)[6]

Kafka's plea was intended to preserve the ambiguity of Gregor's physical form and appearance. Nevertheless, in pleading with his publisher not to use such a picture, Kafka suggested two alternatives. These suggestions are important for our purposes in that they reveal what Kafka might have found acceptable for how 'The Metamorphosis' could be adapted to the screen.

In both suggestions Kafka urges that the family not have any direct perceptual contact with Gregor. However, Kafka's suggestions show characters doing something: in their directed look or point of view gaze, they are connecting or trying to connect two narrative spaces: the living room and Gregor's bedroom. The connection between point of view and narrative space is an important aspect of Kafka's narrative style in 'The Metamorphosis'. The only spaces that are articulated in the novella are spaces that are the object of some character's point of view. The reader knows that the Samsas' apartment also contains a kitchen and the parents' bedroom, but little information is given about these rooms because they are not objects of a character's point of view.

In support of the idea that in 'The Metamorphosis' visual point of view articulates narrative space, consider where in the apartment Grete's bedroom is. One knows that early in the narrative Grete in her bedroom communicates across Gregor's bedroom with her parents in the living room. Because Gregor's bedroom has four walls, one knows that one wall contains a window looking out on the street and another has the door to the living room, but on which of the other two walls is Grete's bedroom? One does not know because there is no visual connection of Grete's bedroom with the living room. One is therefore unable to reconstruct the apartment because the point of view is restricted to only a few of the rooms.

It might seem that Kafka's suggestions, which emphasise the family's perspective and only represent Gregor as an absence, undermine or even diminish Gregor's importance as the protagonist. However, the point of view relationship of the family to Gregor's bedroom should not be understood just as a representation of Gregor as an absence. The room has significance beyond being a separate space in which the creature resides. It is first described as a 'regular human room' (1996: 3). None of the other rooms in the apartment is described this way. Describing the room as 'human' identifies it with Gregor. Since the bedroom contains mementos of Gregor's past and his ties to his family, it becomes a space that is a psychological stand-in for Gregor, and its deteriorating condition over the course of the narrative parallels the decline in Gregor's life.

Fearing that Gregor might be ill, his parents call to him in his locked bedroom. Unable to respond intelligibly, Gregor resembles a stroke victim who is still conscious but no longer physically able to communicate. Initially, not only is he consciously 'locked' inside his body, but he is locked inside his bedroom, an enclosure that also prevents him from communicating with his family. When the family sends for both a doctor and a locksmith, Gregor feels 'integrated into human society once again and hoped for marvelous, amazing feats from both the doctor and the locksmith, without really distinguishing sharply between them' (1996: 11). Gregor's not distinguishing between what he hopes the doctor or the locksmith might be able to accomplish emphasises the identification between Gregor's body and his bedroom.

Gregor's relation to his bedroom has a parallel in the protagonist of 'The Burrow's' relation to his underground labyrinth. Both the bedroom and the labyrinth are identified with the protagonists of their respective stories. Both protagonists are responsible for their private spaces. Gregor's room has objects from his past that he has kept there, and 'The Burrow' begins with the protagonist claiming that he has successfully created his underground hideout. This burrow is the sole preserve of its narrator inhabitant. Although he considers the idea of another being sharing it with him, this idea is never confirmed. The 'small fry' that race around in the maze's tunnels are only snacks for him.

Even when he is outside gazing at the moss-covered entrance to his subterranean home, he looks on it as someone might who reflects on their body that through effort has been restored to health. There is a sense of pride in the achievement but also a vigilant concern that one must always work to maintain or improve one's condition. As a consequence, the protagonist's point of view about the condition of his burrow and the threats to it from outside constitutes a reflection on himself. The creature sees that 'the vulnerability of the burrow has made me vulnerable, the injuries it suffers pain me as if they were my own' (2007: 186). He recognises that an invasion of his burrow would be a threat to his continued existence. In addition, the burrow serves as an extension of his consciousness, particularly his hearing. He notes that 'the best thing about my burrow is its silence' (2007: 164). He is anxious about any intruding sound, and worries about the source of what he describes as a 'hardly audible hissing' (2007: 177). On another occasion, he says that it is 'more like squeaking' (2007: 178), and later claims that it 'is actually a rushing sound' (2007: 185). Since he never discovers the source of this indistinct sound, it is unclear whether it is real or delusional.

III. OVERCOMING THE OBSTACLES TO FILMING KAFKA'S TWO STORIES

In addressing how Kafka's two stories might be adapted to the screen, two restrictions should be adhered to that are based on Kafka's own reservation and suggestions about picturing the narrative of 'The Metamorphosis'. First, since Kafka pleaded with his editor not to show a picture of the transformed Gregor, a film adaptation should avoid showing Gregor's physical appearance. That restriction should also apply to 'The Burrow' since that story's protagonist is also physically indeterminate. Second, following Kafka's suggestions, a film adaptation should emphasise shots from a character's point of view without in the case of the protagonist presenting a reverse shot showing that character's physical appearance. It should also track characters' movement through narrative space.

These two points reveal why film rather than theatre is the appropriate visual medium for adapting Kafka's two stories. The conventional theatrical setting has the audience sitting at a fixed point from the action on the stage. There is usually no variation in that physical distance, and as a result giving the audience a sense of moving into or through narrative space can only be accomplished in a limited way through lighting. There is also no way for theatre audiences to adopt a character's point of view. With the physical indeterminacy of both of Kafka's protagonists, theatre is handicapped in having these characters function as protagonists since a theatre audience cannot adopt a character's point of view.

With these issues in mind, consider the relationship of the protagonist of 'The Burrow' to narrative space. He is the only character in a position to relate the narrative. As the creator of the burrow, he has a slightly different relation to narrative space than do the characters in 'The Metamorphosis'. One reason is that he describes the maze, pointing out that there is a central castle court with tunnels that run off of it, and indicates that the maze has been constructed with some structural ambiguity in order to confuse any invader. However, even with his verbal description of the burrow, the creature also creates narrative space by his point of view as he moves from one part of the maze to the other. There is also his stationary perspective as he hides outside watching the entrance to his burrow, but his main perspective is mobile. In any cinematic adaptation of 'The Burrow', his point of view must be the central focus for telling the tale of the creation of the labyrinth, the creature's life in the maze and his fears that his stronghold might be breached. Yet because of the creature's physical ambiguity, clear shots of his appearance, especially his face, would be problematic. Nevertheless, his visual point of view, coupled with an aural sensitivity to his environment, directs his movement through the maze. Tracking this movement so as to emphasise his point of view would be a key way to adapt 'The Burrow' to the screen.

In 'The Metamorphosis', there is a related coupling of point of view and directed motion, although point of view motion is not quite as extensive as in 'The Burrow'. Gregor leaves his bedroom three times during the course of the narrative. On each occasion, one could track his movement and point of view as he enters the living room and as he turns his head to retreat to his bedroom. However, other characters in the narrative also have a point of view and their movements could also be tracked. Another opportunity to track motion is to have a parallel tracking shot of the trolley that the parents and Grete take at the story's conclusion.

While the protagonist of 'The Burrow' does not have to hide while he is in the maze, in 'The Metamorphosis' Gregor faces a different situation. If one follows Kafka's plea, Gregor's identification with his bedroom could be cinematically used to present at least some of the unfolding relationship between Gregor and his family. While in his bedroom, Gregor usually conceals himself from Grete. His presence is usually revealed by the results of his new insect-like behaviour, such as his new food preferences and the marks of his crawling on the walls and ceiling. In addition, as suggested by Kafka, Gregor's bedroom is dark; at least it is in the early morning hours when Gregor awakens transformed. The darkened or visually indistinct interior of Gregor's bedroom, as contrasted with the lighted living room, could be used cinematically to hide the creature, at least from the film audience. In a film, Grete could be shown directing her gaze towards where Gregor is in the darkened room; however, the object of her point of view could be obscured in the film image.

Two additional topics need to be discussed. First, as other commentators have pointed out there is another metamorphosis besides Gregor's that occurs in the story (Straus 1996; Reynaga 2010: 70; Swinford 2010: 228). This is Grete's transformation from child to young woman. Her metamorphosis should not be dismissed as a minor incident. In fact, its importance is structurally foregrounded by the opposing symmetry between the trajectory of Gregor's psychological metamorphosis and Grete's transformation. The opening and closing sentences of 'The Metamorphosis' note two physical changes: first Gregor's and finally Grete's. They frame two opposing psychological transformations. Gregor's station as breadwinner and assertive family member is gradually eclipsed with the introduction of his alien insect-like behaviour. His decline is also emphasised by his increasing inability to recognise the motivations for his actions. Grete is introduced as a child, but she starts to assume a more mature position in the family when she takes responsibility for feeding Gregor and cleaning his room. She is certainly accepted as an adult family member when she counsels her parents that they have to get rid of the 'monster' in Gregor's bedroom. The novella's closing sentence when Grete gets up and stretches her shapely body confirms her physical and psychological transformation into an adult.

An important difference between Gregor's metamorphosis and Grete's transformation should not be overlooked. As Kafka has created him, Gregor lacks an organically unified appearance; however, Grete's transformation never violates her organic integrity. There is no indeterminacy about her body, only the natural transformation that occurs in the few months of the story. Although she is not a witness to Gregor's epiphanal appearance to the office manager and her parents, as the narrative unfolds she becomes more and more visible in family life. During the momentous family table discussion that she initiates about getting rid of the monster, she shows herself to be dominant, subsequently enabling her to assume an increasingly authoritative role in the exposition of the narrative. In later scenes, her point of view provides a central focus for the unfolding of events. In adapting 'The Metamorphosis' to the screen, one needs to recognise that Grete's initial lack of presence, followed by her central role in later scenes, can serve as the basis for a pictorial exposition of the later unfolding of the narrative.

Second, before sketching what a cinematic exposition of both narratives would look like, one needs to consider another variable in their adaptation to the screen. In that early period of film history that saw the introduction of feature-length films, at the time Kafka wrote both stories, narrative film was mute. Silent films were screened with an added musical accompaniment, but the audience could not hear the characters speak. In considering whether the two stories could be adapted to the screen, one would have to recognise that there would be disadvantages to adapting both works to a silent medium.

For instance, interspersed title cards to represent verbal interactions or provide extra-diegetic commentary tend to break up the presentation of the scene. Showing dialogue in script, or even transcribing sounds onto title cards, makes it more likely that some of the crucial ambiguity of the sounds or the tonal nuance of speech in Kafka's works would be lost. With a talking picture, the narrative flow of a scene is not interrupted. The full impact of characters' conversation would be heard and felt. More important, a talking film could use voice-over narration that would allow viewers to hear Gregor's unspoken thoughts as well as the burrower's on-going verbal commentary. In addition to allowing the audience to hear the characters speak and to hear the sounds of the narrative world, a talking picture would let them hear the absence of sound. By having the added aural dimension of silence, a talking picture can play with whether or not characters are hearing something or if there is no sound to be heard. The ability to project silence into the filmed narrative world would be an important technique for showing Gregor's new relationship with his family. Family members talk at Gregor, but there is no conversation with him. After his first attempts to communicate with his family, he falls silent. An important aspect of a cinematic adaptation would be the ability to convey Gregor's silence, while at the same time giving the audience access to the verbal expression of his private thoughts through voice-over narration.

In 'The Burrow', letting the audience hear the 'rustle of silence' (2007: 180) in the underground maze as well as the silence of the outside world that envelops the creature as he watches the entrance would bring out an important aspect of the narrative. Conveying whether the creature actually hears something that is causing the hissing sounds, or whether those sounds are imaginary would depend on the medium's ability to distinguish silence from sound. At the same time, voice-over narration of the creature's verbal thoughts could be employed in a way that would not have to show the creature mouthing the words or emotionally supplementing these thoughts with gestures.

IV. A SKETCH OF A CINEMATIC ADAPTATION OF 'THE METAMORPHOSIS'

'The Metamorphosis' is structurally divided into three main sections and a concluding epilogue. Each present different concerns for bringing the novella to the screen. The following sketch is divided into four parts which correspond to the novella's structural parts. Of course, the sketch is not a script or a storyboard; it only makes general observations about how to adapt the novella cinematically, while adhering to Kafka's concern that the transformed Gregor not be shown.

Part I. The film opens with a shot of Gregor's darkened bedroom; the camera pans from the window, which shows some early morning light, to the bed and then to the locked door. A voice-over narrator using Kafka's words relates Gregor's transformation. A change in tone establishes that the voice-over is now Gregor thinking about his new situation and what he should do about it. The creature is not shown, but in the obscure image of the darkened room one could see movement under the bedclothes. One would then hear the concerned parents calling to Gregor. Voice-over narration would give Gregor's intelligible replies.

After a cut, the camera shows the parents in the lighted living room, by then joined by the office manager. The parents and the office manager speaking to Gregor are shown reacting to what are now Gregor's unintelligible sounds. At this point, the parents send Grete to summon a doctor. In a point of view (POV) tracking shot, the camera shows her perspective as she runs out of the living room and halfway down the stairs. She stops, turns, and in a POV looks up the stairs. She hears but does not see the parents' and the office manager's startled reaction to the sight of Gregor in the open doorway. The office manager then rushes past her down the stairs and she takes off to find the doctor. Returning to the living room just as the bedroom door is slammed shut, Grete looks at and hears the parents tell about the creature's appearance and retreat back into the bedroom.

Part II. A shot of the dim bedroom shows movement under the couch indicating Gregor's location. Gregor's voice-over tells about his new taste in food (an insert of the left-over food is shown) and his new pastime of crawling on the walls and ceiling. In a tracking POV, Grete enters his bedroom. There are shots of Grete talking at Gregor who is hiding, and on another occasion she opens the window. The audience hears more of Gregor's voice-over thoughts.

In the next scene, there is another tracking POV of Grete going into Gregor's bedroom with her mother and moving furniture. Gregor hears his mother's reservations about moving the furniture, and in voice-over resolves to stop them. In a very fast pan, Grete sees 'the gigantic brown blotch' (1996: 26) on the wall. Following the direction of Grete's gaze the mother reacts and collapses. Grete is shown shouting at Gregor and helping her mother out of the bedroom, out of the living room, and into an off-screen space. The father arrives and starts throwing apples towards the open door to Gregor's bedroom. The mother rushes back in and begs for Gregor's life.

Part III. The scene opens with a shot of the open door into Gregor's darkened room. Gregor hears his sister and mother in the living room urging his father to go to bed. The next scene shows the cleaning woman addressing the couch under which Gregor is hiding and calling him a dung beetle. A third scene shows the three boarders listening to Grete play the violin. The boarders point in horror at Gregor's open bedroom door, but the father moves to block their view. Loud chirpings can be heard from the bedroom. Registering their disgust, the boarders give notice that they will leave tomorrow. They retreat into their room. Slamming the bedroom door shut and locking Gregor inside, Grete begins arguing that they have to get rid of the monster because it is not Gregor. There is a shot of Gregor's darkened bedroom. In voice-over, the narrator recounts Gregor's demise, beginning with the sentence, 'He thought back on his family' (1996: 39). The voice-over is occasionally interrupted by feeble chirpings. The next day the cleaning woman opens Gregor's bedroom door and pointing towards the couch announces that the dung beetle is dead. The boarders try to look into the bedroom, but the father again blocks their view and tells them to leave immediately.

Epilogue. In voice-over, the narrator informs the viewers that the parents and Grete are going to take the day off. They are shown getting on a trolley car which proceeds out into the country. A parallel tracking shot follows the trolley. In a relaxed and cheerful mood, all three are shown expressing their relief at being free from the burden of the monster in Gregor's bedroom. Father and mother now exchange glances. In voice-over the narrator delivers the final sentences of the story while Grete gets up and stretches.[7]

V. A SKETCH OF A CINEMATIC ADAPTATION OF 'THE BURROW'

As in 'The Metamorphosis', the protagonist in 'The Burrow' has an indeterminate physical form that makes problematic showing a clear image of him. Unlike 'The Metamorphosis', however, 'The Burrow' has no independent narrator who could comment in voice-over on the creature's situation. The voice-over commentary used in the film adaptation would be the creature's own internal verbal thoughts.

Also, unlike 'The Metamorphosis', 'The Burrow' has no clear textual divisions that structurally separate the story into several parts. Moreover, the story is unfinished, and it is unclear how much more narrative was intended to complete it. Nevertheless, there seem to be three thematic parts to the extant narrative: description of the underground burrow; the creature's activities in the burrow and his watching its entrance from outside; and a third part in which he expresses his concern that an enemy is digging towards him and is the source of the hissing sound. Admittedly, this division imposes an artificial structure on the narrative, but in light of the story's unfinished ending, it provides some cohesive continuity.

Part I. There is an opening establishing shot of a mossy area which turns out to be the entrance to the burrow. A tracking POV shows motion towards the burrow's entrance. A second shot shows the 'trap door' (2007: 169) which covers the entrance being closed from the inside. There follows another POV tracking shot with the creature's voice-over moving from the entrance into the interior. It is dark, and only occasional air holes provide some illumination, except for the castle court which has more illumination than the tunnels. The darkened interior allows there to be obscure images of the creature being tracked moving around without having to show him fully illuminated. The creature's voice-over describes the burrow's construction and layout according to his 'master plan' (2007: 166). There will be occasional insert point-of-view shots of the 'small fry' scampering away into the tunnels.

Part II. A series of tracking shots shows the creature's activities. They are accompanied by his voice-over commentary. He talks about making necessary repairs. He also talks about the carrion provisions that he has amassed in the castle court. Several shots show a heap of small animals in the dimly lit central chamber. In addition, he discusses his hunting and occasional gorging on animals killed. He also comments on his deep slumbers in the silence of his labyrinth.

In the second part's final scene the creature, hidden behind a bush outside his burrow, discusses whether he would allow another individual of a similar species to inhabit his burrow with him. He rejects that thought and makes the point that he feels at one with his creation. Any compromise of its integrity is registered as painful.

Part III. In the interior, a series of tracking shots, some of which are POV, show the creature expressing feelings of vulnerability. He worries that with his advancing years there might be a powerful predator that would dig its way into his inner sanctum. He claims to hear a hissing sound and wonders if that might be an approaching enemy. He wanders around the burrow trying to find the source of that sound. There is no independent confirmation that the sound actually exists. He notices that the sound seems to change, but can never pinpoint an actual source. He speculates about the possible invader. The film ends with his defiant assertion that if he cannot buy off this invader with some of his provisions, the two will 'show each other our claws and teeth in a mutual frenzy' (2007: 189).[8]

CONCLUSION

Both 'The Metamorphosis' and 'The Burrow' present a challenge to screen adaptation: how to show an indeterminately formed protagonist? Kafka opposed any pictorial image of the transformed Gregor, and presumably he also would have rejected showing a picture of the protagonist of 'The Burrow'. The problem is compounded by both protagonists exhibiting verbally active mental processes that seem to suggest a unified rational agent, even though at times their brutish behaviour stands opposed to their rationality. If filmed in keeping with Kafka's wishes, cinematic adaptations of both works would have to find some other way to represent the protagonists than by showing them as physically unified beings. Any solution is made more difficult by Kafka's placing the two narratives in spatially unified settings that seem to call for showing a protagonist's physical appearance.

Fortunately, film has the resources to solve some of these problems. A key to adapting these works to film would be to rely upon the protagonist's point of view without showing a reverse shot revealing his appearance. These point-of-view shots could be combined with tracking shots of the characters moving through space. In fact, one of the aspects of Kafka's narrative aesthetic that emerges in considering how to adapt these two works to film is how characters' point of view and movement through space develops the presentation of narrative space. Of course, there are subtleties to Kafka's use of language, connotations from comic to tragic that are not easily translated into images. However, the problems faced in bringing Kafka's works to the screen and the choices a director would make in successfully resolving them reveal a great deal about Kafka's narrative aesthetic and show the finely crafted nature of his narratives. For that reason there is great benefit to be had in considering how both these works could be adapted to a film medium.[9]

NOTES

1   In *Theory of Film*, Kracauer not only speaks of film's special ability to record physical reality in ways that can show objects in a natural space, but also stresses its power to reveal reality. Kracauer's thinking about how film can reveal reality underwent some development from his early days as a journalist in the 1920s to his later thoughts when he published *Theory of Film*. In his earlier thinking, Kracauer held the view that films which conformed to an aesthetic that presented a narrative in a natural space were not as successful in revealing reality to people as works in modernist avant-garde styles. For further discussion on the transition that Kracauer's thinking underwent, see Hansen 1991.

2. Perhaps no term in film theory or criticism has been used in more different senses than 'realistic'. Different national cinemas in different eras (e.g. French 'New Wave' or Italian Neo-realism) had strong views on what a realistic narrative was and was not. There is also an ontological debate about whether the film image is basically realistic: André Bazin claimed it was, and Sergei Eisenstein claimed that it was not, and that only the clash of images in montage was able to give one a sense of reality. My use of the term 'realistic' is confined to the natural appearance of a spatial context. I grant that there is an historical aspect to this stylistic feature. Some later film styles could record in an otherwise realistic way but also manipulate film space. Akira Kurosawa's use of telephoto lenses, for example, tended to collapse the appearance of distant objects into a shallow space. Orson Welles and some later Hollywood directors used wide-angle lenses that extended or elongated the appearance of space. For further discussion of a film viewer's recognition of a natural space and objects in it, see Carroll 1996: 78–84.
3. Even though he used this later Expressionist aesthetic in *Nosferatu*, Murnau still introduced a scene in the film that violated it. The carriage ride that takes Hutter to the vampire's castle is shown using a negative film image rather than the positive film images used in the rest of the film. The speeded-up action of the carriage ride also challenges recognising the scene as having a natural space.
4. Hanns Zischler (2002) has investigated Kafka's writings about the movies he went to see; however, he makes no mention of Kafka's having seen either *The Golem* or *Nosferatu*.
5. Stanley Corngold translates Kafka's original expression, *ungeheuren Ungeziefer*, as 'monstrous vermin.' For discussion of his translation of Kafka's original, see Corngold 2007: 86–9.
6. Binder quotes from Kafka 1977: 114–15.
7. For a cinematic adaptation of 'The Metamorphosis' that does not show Gregor's transformed body, uses POV tracking shots, but does not use independent voice-over narration, see Jan Němec's 'Die Verwandlung' (1975).
8. For an alternative film adaptation, see Danielle Parsons's *The Burrow* (2009), in which the burrow's creator is a gopher.
9. I would like to thank my editors, Shai Biderman and Ido Lewit for very helpful advice about this essay.

BIBLIOGRAPHY

Binder, Hartmut (1996) '*The Metamorphosis*: The Long Journey into Print', in Franz Kafka, *The Metamorphosis*, ed. and trans. Stanley Corngold, New York: W. W. Norton, 172–94.

Bordwell, David and Kristin Thompson (1994) *Film History: An Introduction*. New York: McGraw-Hill.

Carroll, Noël (1996) *Theorizing the Moving Image*. New York: Cambridge University Press.

Corngold, Stanley (2007) 'Preface', *Kafka's Selected Stories*, ed. and trans. Stanley Corngold. New York: Norton, vii–xi.

Hansen, Miriam (1991) 'Decentric Perspectives: Kracauer's Early Writings on Film and Mass Culture', *New German Critique*, 54, 47–76.

Kafka, Franz (1977) *Letters to Friends, Family, and Editors*, trans. Richard and Clara Winston. New York: Schocken.

____ (1988) *The Complete Stories*, ed. Nahum Glazer. New York: Schocken.

____ (2007 [1931]) 'The Burrow', *Kafka's Selected Stories*, ed. and trans. Stanley Corngold. New York: W. W. Norton, 162–89.

____ (1996 [1915]) *The Metamorphosis*, trans. & ed. Stanley Corngold. New York: W. W. Norton.

Kracauer, Siegfried (1960) *Theory of Film: The Redemption of Physical Reality*. New York: Oxford University Press.

Reynaga, Tahia T. (2010) 'Agents of the Forgotten: Animals as the Vehicles of Shame in Kafka', in Marc Lucht and Donna Yarri (eds) *Kafka's Creatures: Animals, Hybrids and Other Fantastic Beings*. Lanham, MD: Lexington Books, 67–80.

Straus, Nina P. (1996) 'Transforming Franz Kafka's *Metamorphosis*', in Franz Kafka, *The Metamorphosis*, trans. & ed. Stanley Corngold. New York: W. W. Norton, 126–40.

Swinford, Dean (2010) 'The Portrait of an Armor-Plated Sign: Reimagining Samsa's Exoskeleton', in Marc Lucht and Donna Yarri (eds) *Kafka's Creatures: Animals, Hybrids and Other Fantastic Beings*. Lanham, MD: Lexington Books, 211–36.

Zischler, Hanns (2002) *Kafka Goes to the Movies*, trans. Susan. H. Gillespie. Chicago: University of Chicago Press.

PART TWO

THE KAFKAESQUE CINEMA

'THE ESSENTIAL IS SUFFICIENT': THE KAFKA ADAPTATIONS OF ORSON WELLES, STRAUB-HUILLET AND MICHAEL HANEKE

MARTIN BRADY AND HELEN HUGHES[1]

In a diary entry of 6 December 1921 Kafka notes that 'metaphors are one of the many things which make me despair of writing' (2002h: 875). As part of the preparations for their adaptation of Kafka's novel *Der Verschollene* (*The Man Who Disappeared*, 1927),[2] entitled *Klassenverhältnisse* (*Class Relations*, 1983), Jean-Marie Straub and Danièle Huillet pasted this note into their shooting script as an admonition. However, whilst visualisation and adaptation may result in what Allen Hoey, referring to Kafka's struggles with metaphor, terms a 'slippage of signification' (1988: 27), they can also, as many 'Kafkaesque' adaptations amply demonstrate, produce images which are visually arresting and memorable. Perhaps the most famous is Orson Welles's 1962 adaptation of *Der Proceß* (*The Trial*, 1925) with its menacing architecture and myriad typists. In short, the problem of picturing confronts any visual artist who turns to Kafka for source material or inspiration; as Sander L. Gilman has put it, 'Kafka's world was a visual world even though (or exactly because) it was one that could not be represented' (2005: 144). In what follows we will examine picturing and representation in the Kafka adaptations of Welles and Straub-Huillet together with Michael Haneke's 1997 adaptation of Kafka's unfinished third novel, *Das Schloss* (*The Castle*, 1926).

Whilst the opposition of word and image is inescapable in all literary adaptation, it is particularly acute in the case of an author who systematically problematises this very relationship in his writing. As Kafka wrote in a letter to Felice Bauer, 'images are beautiful, we cannot do without images, but they are also a source of much anguish' (1967: 164). Few filmmakers who have turned to

Kafka for material to adapt or to stage – and there are many of them[3] – seem to have confronted this issue explicitly. One thing that can be said about the majority of Kafka films is that they are conspicuously, often spectacularly, illustrative, supplying visual substitutes for what is described in the text. In so doing they not only unwittingly endorse Bertolt Brecht's remark that in Kafka's texts it is 'the images' that 'are good' (see Benjamin 1966: 122), but at the same time they also ignore Kafka's own reservations about illustration.

As Günther Nicolin neatly put it in the catalogue to an exhibition in Bonn of prints, drawings and paintings based on Kafka's stories and novels: 'It is easy to illustrate Kafka's text in the traditional way, i.e. to draw each image of that wonderfully clear prose – Kafka himself feared as much – but nothing is gained by this, rather, attention is wrenched away from Kafka's diction' (1974: 5).

I. ORSON WELLES, *THE TRIAL*

The dilemma facing the illustrator confronted with images that lose their impact in transit corresponds to a paradox in Kafka's writing. On the one hand there is the strongly visual use of language – metaphor, analogy, a meticulous naturalism in the description of architectural space and landscape, for example – and on the other the restricted viewpoint of the protagonists. Together these make for the disconcerting world-view generally labelled 'Kafkaesque'. For a cameraman, for example, they present a conundrum. Yet, despite all these pitfalls and admonitions, the straightforward appeal of the image has been strong enough for visual artists to disregard Kafka's qualms, making their illustrations, paintings, films and videos controversial documents of that abiding interplay of text and image and the problem that is literary adaptation.

Mention has already been made of Orson Welles's canonical film *The Trial*. It is probably the most famous of all Kafka screen adaptations, and was described by Welles himself as 'the most autobiographical movie that I've ever made, the only one that's really close to me' (Bogdanovich and Welles 1992: 283). It also remains controversial for two main reasons: first, it takes considerable liberties with the text, in particular with the parable 'Before the Law'; second, the personality of Welles tends to overshadow Kafka's novel. With the director taking on the role of the Advocate and providing the voice which introduces and closes the film, *The Trial* exhibits an unsettling yet striking symbiosis of author, character and filmmaker. James Naremore has described Welles as 'something of a patrician, a man who has always been more interested in the psychology of the oppressors than in the anxieties of the oppressed' (1989: 199). Gertrud Koch characterises Welles as a showman creating a show trial whilst drawing on all the trends in interpretation that were fashionable in the 1960s: 'a little religion, a little of the nightmare, cultural critique of mass society, and at the end the atomic threat as an existential condition' (1984: 173).

Welles's staging of the arrest towards the beginning of the film is where Kafka's text and the director's interpretation mesh most easily and it is in the legal scenes punctuating the film that Welles follows the original text most closely. It is perhaps hardly surprising in the wake of McCarthyism, and at the height of the Cold War, that concepts such as civil liberty, accusation and defence and emotions of guilt, helplessness and confusion are eminently transferrable from the context of a Czech citizen born before World War I to the immediate concerns of an American citizen two decades after World War II. Welles achieves a fine balance of paranoia and surreal humour in juggling the awkwardness of a private space invaded with the corruption of the men arresting Josef K., and the protagonist's own confused feelings of guilt and outrage. Crucial to the success of this scene is the near-hysterical performance of Anthony Perkins in the role of Josef K.

Kafka's novel is repeatedly given specific historical and geographical connotations in Welles's film. The director's post-war sensibility draws out in particular the notion that the individual victim may and indeed should stand up for all victims. Diverse issues such as post-war collective guilt, the desolation of the modern metropolis and its dehumanising architecture, computer technology and the status of modern art are introduced as substitutes for Kafka's observations on Austro-Hungarian Prague. The painter Titorelli provides a neat, if incidental, example of Welles's method of actualisation and re-contextualisation. Whereas Kafka's Titorelli sells K. three heath landscapes, Welles's sells 'action paintings' of 'wild nature'.

The social environment is transformed in Welles's film by the use of an estate of concrete slab blocks in Yugoslavia as equivalents for the tenement blocks described by Kafka, suggesting the Stalinist atmosphere of the Cold War in which individuals are isolated by their environment rather than thrown together. In summary, Welles's approach could be seen as the triumph of what we understand as the 'Kafkaesque' over Kafka himself, the description 'almost completely uniform buildings, high and grey' (Kafka 2002c: 53) being expanded into a vision of lives dwarfed within massive building projects and town planning. Kafka's vision of the modern bureaucratised society as organic, labyrinthine, a complex of individual networks, is metamorphosed into the grids and plans of post-war modernism. As Jeffrey Adams puts it in an essay on the film's 'noirish' quality:

> By projecting the expressionist look of film noir onto *The Trial*, and by emphasizing the sense of disorientation, paranoia, and alienation that the noir

worldview shares with Kafka's unique rendering of German Expressionism, Welles was able to create the cinematic equivalent of that strange blend of nightmare absurdity and theatrical farce that now goes by the name of Kafkaesque. (2002: 141)

At the beginning of the film, towards the end of the 'Before the Law' episode,[4] Welles declares, as the directorial 'voice of God', that the story has 'the logic of a dream, of a nightmare', and the final line of the film, 'My name is Orson Welles', signals the triumph of Welles over Kafka at the end of a sequence which returns to the theme which obsessed the director from *Citizen Kane* (1941) to *F for Fake* (1973) – the relationship between truth and fiction, and the substantiality of illusion, in particular cinematic illusion. For Adams, 'Welles is at least as interested in playing with noir aesthetics as in recreating a classic of world literature for the screen' (2002: 144). If Kafka's text has been read as a critique of bureaucratised structures, language and processes of interpretation, the final minutes of *The Trial*, a compendium of cinematic quotations and encyclopaedia of filmic devices (incorporating deep focus, wide panoramas, shadows, silhouettes and projections, jump cuts, handheld camera and freeze-framing), amount to a Wellesian mini-essay on the power, both positive and negative, of cinematic illusion. The fireworks of this dénouement, however, and the assertion of the director's own presence amount to an affirmation of creative energy over the demise of the protagonist. Ultimately Welles's picturing of *The Trial* paralyzes Kafka's text and subjugates it to the monocular vision of cinema.

II. ROBERT BRESSON AND AUTEURIST ADAPTATION

In identifying the inimitable qualities of Straub-Huillet's and Haneke's Kafka films, commentators have tended to ignore the fact that they actually have a good deal in common: they are the same length, both fragmentary in their structure, often minimal in their *mise-en-scène*, both eschew non-diegetic music, avoid such cinematic conventions as establishing shots, and could both be categorised as auteurist 'slow cinema'. To some extent these similarities may be explained by a shared admiration for the 'transcendental style' associated with Robert Bresson and Carl Theodor Dreyer in which, in the words of the latter, 'the essential is sufficient' (Delahaye 1966: 11). Specifically, Bresson's famous *Notes on the Cinematographer* can be read as a primer for the austerity of both Straub-Huillet and Haneke's adaptations:

[Fragmentation] is indispensable if one does not want to fall into REPRE-

SENTATION. See beings and things in their separate parts. Render them independent in order to give them a new dependence. [...]
The real is not dramatic. Drama will be born of a certain march of non-dramatic elements. [...]
Expression through compression. To put into an image what a writer would spin out over ten pages. [...]
One does not create by adding, but by taking away. (1996: 84–7)

Moreover, Straub-Huillet and Haneke have claimed – and here too they differ fundamentally from Welles – that in adapting Kafka they function as *metteurs-en-scène*, either presenting a reading they believe has been insufficiently recognised (Straub-Huillet's materialist rendering of *The Man Who Disappeared*) or to introduce a new audience to the text (Haneke's 1997 'anti-televisual' version of *The Castle*). Seen this way it also becomes apparent that both films are explicitly, if very differently, political in their intention.

III. STRAUB-HUILLET, *CLASS RELATIONS*

With *Class Relations* Straub and Huillet explicitly reject Welles's illustrative, Kafkaesque method in favour of one based on documentation:

> Film is, after all, not an instrument for illustration or description. Writers' descriptions are best left to the writers.
> There are a number of reasons for this. There had already been a Kafka film before ours, *The Trial* of Orson Welles. He tried to show what Kafka described. For example ... a room where forty girls sit and type. In our film there is just *one* lift. We wanted to do the opposite of what Orson Welles did; we didn't want to show in any way what Kafka described. (1983: 272)

It is consistent with Straub-Huillet's historical-materialist approach that they should read Kafka as a realist:

> He could not be less metaphysical and unrealistic. On the contrary, every relationship in his text is thoroughly realistic, everyday even. [...] The incredible thing about Kafka is that he was the first (and to date probably the only) writer of our so-called industrial society. (Schütte 1984: 39)

Seen in this context the film's provocative title not only implies a socio-political dissection of its source material but also highlights an absence in the text: whilst there are manifest social *differences* in *The Man Who Disappeared* there are, in fact, no significant *relations* or *relationships* bridging them.[5] According to Straub and Huillet, stripping a text to its bare bones – 'what we are looking for is simply a spine, a skeleton' (Schütte 1984: 54) – is the only way of ensuring that a literary adaptation does not slip into the illustrative or reiterative mode. Unsurprisingly, given their reputation as the most intellectually uncompromising of literary adaptors, *Class Relations* is entirely consistent with the materialist, Brechtian method of exploring literary source material developed in their previous films: critical dissections of Böll, Bach, Bruckner, Corneille, Brecht, Schönberg, Mallarmé, Fortini, Pavese and Duras:

> You don't actually 'film' a book, you enter into a dialogue with it, you want to make a film out of a book because the book relates to your own experiences, your own questions, your own outbursts of hatred or your own declarations of love. The first thing I always do is to start copying things out. (Straub quoted in Schütte 1984: 46)

Elsewhere in the same interview Straub remarks:

> We didn't want to make a 'historical film', we had had it up to here with costumes and we wanted to put Kafka's 'Amerika' text to the test, simply test it, 1920 and now, because in capitalist societies history does unfortunately repeat itself, perhaps not exactly, but there is a continuity. (1984: 45)

In *Class Relations* Kafka's text is treated as a document of a particular time and place; the decision to shoot the film in contemporary Hamburg, for example, derives not only from the obvious fact that Kafka never visited America, but also recognises that in the novel Karl Rossmann carries the baggage of the old world around with him.

Straub-Huillet's approach to translating Kafka for the screen – producing a metatext, an 'interlinear version' as Walter Benjamin uses the term – takes as its starting point Kafka's alleged definition of capitalism as a 'system of dependencies' (ibid.) and embraces the novel's fragmentary form.[6] The aim is to open up the text to scrutiny, to suspend and stall it through a method akin to that of materialist historiography as defined by Benjamin:

> A constructive principle lies at the heart … of materialist historiography. Thinking does not consist exclusively of the movement of thoughts but also in bringing them to a halt. Where thinking stops in a constellation packed with tensions, it deals it a shock through which it crystallizes out as a monad.

The historical materialist only approaches a historical object where he encounters it as a monad. (1977: 260)

The aesthetic principles underpinning Straub-Huillet's reading of *The Man Who Disappeared* are the cinematic equivalents of 'bringing to a halt' and 'shock': on the structural level epic fragmentation, and stasis alternating with abrupt montage; on the photographic level unconventional framing and extreme perspectives; on the performative level non-naturalistic acting and delivery; on the linguistic level a breakdown of the prose into non-semantic 'quotations'. The result is in fact nothing more mysterious than a form of linguistic estrangement. Just as the narrative of *The Man Who Disappeared* changes direction unexpectedly – the abandoning of the Stoker, for example – so the caesuras in the dialogue of Straub-Huillet's film suggest a linguistic bifurcation. The halting pace allows the viewer to become aware of the construction of meaning and leaves sufficient space for an anticipated meaning to be fleetingly registered before being contradicted. A given statement could simply branch off in another direction at each artificial pause. Those who speak without pausing – Uncle Jakob for example – are simply those whose position of absolute power extends to, or rests on, language. Uniquely amongst filmmakers, Straub-Huillet have invented a vocal equivalent for the celebrated polysemy of Kafka's prose:

> Straub: This has first and foremost to do with contents, nothing else. And then these contents become rhythms...
> Huillet: Contents, where one attempts not to establish a *single* content; to leave it open to the viewer and listener so that he can decide for himself how to deal with what is spoken... (Schütte 1984: 54)

The result of this process when applied to Kafka's novel is a kind of cinematic *Lehrstück* (Learning Play) in the Brechtian sense and a thoroughgoing demystification of the text. The dissection shows the text 'in proper perspective'. Moreover, the atomisation of narrative and language, coupled with the startling beauty of the film's black and white photography, open up *The Man Who Disappeared* to a lucid, thoroughly non-'Kafkaesque', even optimistic reading. As Straub rather laconically puts it:

> Perhaps Karl is heading at the end to somewhere where a utopia exists which we will only have reached in 300 or 3,000 years; but it could also be that he is heading somewhere entirely different – into oblivion, away with him. [...] But I do believe that he *is* a rebel – just as he is. That is how he is in the film. But that was always the strength of Kafka's story. (1984: 42, 58)

IV. MICHAEL HANEKE, *THE CASTLE*

Michael Haneke's *Das Schloss* (*The Castle*, 1997), was commissioned by Austrian television, but also received a cinema release: it was premiered at the Berlin Film Festival just three months before *Funny Games* (1997) was first screened at Cannes. Both films star Ulrich Mühe and Susanne Lothar in the leading roles. Several writers, both on Kafka and on Haneke, have examined the dialogue between filmmaker and writer, suggesting either an influence of Kafka on Haneke or that an analysis of Haneke's film adaptation is a means to understand his cinematic language.[7] Just as in *Funny Games* Haneke turned the consumer-driven family home – with its fitted kitchen, well-appointed sitting room and uncanny television, a stock site of the contemporary horror film – into a potent allegory for the atonement of bourgeois sins, so Kafka had transformed the gothic image of the castle – an established literary trope of the late nineteenth century and by 1920 a genre film staple – into a weird mix of medieval and modern administrative communications that could stand in as a critique of perverse inefficiency or a parody of corporate bureaucracy.

Kafka is thought to have begun writing *The Castle* while convalescing in the Riesengebirge during January and February 1922, just two months after he made the observation on metaphor quoted at the outset of this essay. Diary entries provide ample evidence for a transformation of his own physical and mental condition into the story of K., a new arrival who convinces the inhabitants of a small village, and the authorities of the castle that owns it, that he has been summoned as a land surveyor (2002b: 61–4). Kafka's struggles with language and metaphorisation suggest that *The Castle* can be understood as a depiction of the process of succumbing to metaphor. Tellingly, however, Haneke opens this film with an image which seems to suggest, almost programmatically, that his film will not, in the manner of Welles's film, offer eye-catching visual equivalents for the metaphorical meanings suggested by Kafka's novel.

Haneke never visualises the castle directly, despite Kafka's extensive descriptions of it from K.'s point of view in the novel, first from a panoramic distance and then from a closer, less favourable, perspective (2002a: 17). Instead, at the beginning of the film, Haneke places what appears to be a torn print of a hillside village on the door to the inn with a yellowing timetable where the castle might have been. Wanting to claim the film as another contribution to the canon of auteurist 'film adaptations as literary interpretations', rather than allowing it the status of a pragmatic *mise-en-scène* for television, Willy Riemer has argued that this infidelity to the text, along with other decisions such as the addition of an anachronistic radio and a shift of emphasis from the castle to the village, amount to a diffraction of Kafka's text through the apparatus of cinema which puts the film on 'equal terms' with its literary source (2011: 132).

Alexander Schlicker also claims a privileged status for Haneke's adaptation by interpreting it as a mapping of the novel onto Haneke's own concerns about contemporary society, particularly the 'glaciation' of emotions which the director repeatedly claimed was the overarching theme of his preceding Austrian trilogy (*Der Siebente Kontinent* [*The Seventh Continent*, 1989]; *Benny's Video*, 1992; *71 Fragmente einer Chronologie des Zufalls* [*71 Fragments of a Chronology of Chance*, 1994]). Schlicker argues that this text was specifically chosen by Haneke for the impenetrability of its central character as well as the incorporation of technologies of communication – including telephone and radio – in ways which suggest an interrogation of the effects of mediation on social behaviour (2013: 18). Like Riemer, Schlicker proposes ways in which the adaptation of Kafka's text to film reveals Haneke's inimitable approach to cinema. He discusses the point-of-view shot in particular, comparing the economy of the gaze in Kafka's work with that in Haneke's film. The alignment of the camera either with the gaze of the protagonist, in extensive and largely silent shot/reverse-shot sequences, or with a depersonalised, 'authorial' point of view is interpreted as patriarchal, characteristic of Haneke's critical exploration of the mediatisation of the gaze (2013: 13).

There is, however, a problem facing these assessments of Haneke's television adaptation as an auteurist film in which the filmmaker's vision supplants, in the manner of Welles, that of the author. Each decision – the inclusion of the epigrammatic print of the village, the use of deep focus and medium shots, frequent and recurring tracking shots, the brief insertions of black film between scenes – can be traced directly back either to the text, including its status as a fragment, or to the genres and strategies of silent cinema which, as other essays in this volume demonstrate, in all probability had a decisive influence on the shape and rhythm of Kafka's prose. The surprising conclusion to be drawn from this is that Haneke's film is in fact, belying the current orthodoxy on literary adaptation, robustly faithful to the text.

Taking the aforementioned print as an example, it is an image in the style of an early map, setting out the boundaries of a village and the lands around a castle. The village that is depicted, with its compact rows of larger and smaller buildings, a church on one side and a larger mansion on another, is strikingly similar to the description of the Castle in the text. By incorporating this image into the film, Haneke can be seen to follow the example of Kafka in mapping quite straightforwardly, yet also uncannily, one image or place onto another: the snow-bound village *becomes* the Castle. There is also a subtle detail here that is easily overlooked: towards the end of the film the print reappears on the door with the torn-off fragment inexplicably re-instated, perhaps alluding to the presence of the Castle within the novel which Haneke, as part of his strategy of restrained visualisation, has otherwise excluded.

The Castle deploys selected scenes from the novel to engage a television audience with a canonical text; it is clear from Haneke's comments that he understands his task as one of text mediation, rather than as an opportunity to enter into a collaborative, inter-subjective dialogue with the author, as Welles had claimed for *The Trial*, or revealing its 'true meaning', as Straub-Huillet's political reading implies:

> I would draw a definite line between *The Castle* and *The Piano Teacher*, because *The Castle* was made for television, and I'm very clear about the distinction between a TV version and a movie. Films for TV have to be much closer to the book, mainly because the objective with a TV movie that translates literature is to get the audience, after seeing this version, to pick up the book and read it themselves. My attitude is that TV can never really be any form of art, because it serves audience expectations. I would not have dared to turn *The Castle* into a movie for the big screen; on TV, it's OK, because it has different objectives. But with *The Piano Teacher*, if you compare the structure of the novel to the structure of the film, it's really quite different, and I feel I've been dealing very freely with the novel and the way it was written. (Quoted in Foundas 2001)

In keeping with his modest ambition for *The Castle* – a modesty his apologists seem reluctant to acknowledge – Haneke introduces the film as 'an adaptation of a prose fragment' and ends it abruptly, mid-sentence with an intertitle explaining that this is where the novel breaks off. Within this explanatory frame the story of K.'s arrival in the village and his struggle to form relationships is played out through a sequence of precise *mises-en-scène* locating the story within crowded but sparsely furnished interior spaces connected by an almost exclusively nocturnal outside space rendered hostile by snow and wind. Haneke constructs the film as a series of discrete fragmentary scenes by inserting the aforementioned black film between passages of dialogue and the inclusion of long tracking shots of K. moving arduously from one space to another. The scenes chosen focus on encounters with Frieda, the school master, the superintendent and the insomniac official, and are shot predominantly from the point of view of K. Where K. is identifiable as the one who sees, his point of view is clearly articulated. Scenes in the text which do not identify the point of view are shot from a variety of Bressonian angles which allow unexpected appearances within the frame and a focus on essential detail (hands engaging in acts of physical exchange and feet trudging through deep snow, for example). Voiceover narration is frequently phased in over spoken dialogue to indicate where a character's articulation is overlaid with K.'s or the narrator's interpretation of the reason for speaking rather than the spoken words themselves.

Of course, as already indicated, Haneke's authorial 'modesty' and fidelity to the text are far from guileless. In the light of his much-cited dislike of television his aesthetic restraint acquires a political, media-critical dimension, especially when viewed with the violent and hectoring small-screen imagery of *Benny's Video* in mind. Haneke's *The Castle* proposes a Bressonian, anti-televisual television which rigorously avers that the small screen should be nourished and sustained by literature rather than devour it.

Haneke's K., like Kafka's K., manages on arrival in the village to transform himself from a suspicious stranger into a no less suspect land surveyor. His identity remains unstable in the film not because Haneke interprets or deciphers it as such, but because he takes pains to make his images as clear and as concrete as those in Kafka's prose: each image and text fragment in his adaptation focuses on the bare essentials, often leaving images – as in the novel – on the borderline between visualisation and symbol. In the film and the text, K. engages with the village and its inhabitants from the outset in full awareness of the fact that he is dealing with a distorting, myth-making mirror-image or likeness of the Castle he wishes to storm, with the villagers transformed into clients of the Castle, the tanner transformed into a herald, the local laddish comedians into K.'s assistants, the barmaid into the receptionist, the inn into the waiting room, the school room into the bedroom, the bedroom into the office and the long snowy spaces between them all into exhausting white corridors. The strength of the film lies in its acceptance of the virtuosity of the literary source and its promotion of its capacity to transform the everyday material world into scenes of human misunderstanding and metaphysical reinterpretation.

V. KAFKA AND 'TRUE IMAGES'

In the transfer from page to screen, literary adaptations engage in a process of translation, substitution and interpretation, and the material thus displaced essentially stands in a symbolic relationship to the original text. As the examples discussed in this essay amply demonstrate, Kafka's prose is not, of course, in any way intrinsically unsuited to translation to the screen. Theodor W. Adorno went so far as to argue that his novels represent 'the last, disappearing texts connecting literature to silent cinema (which not by chance disappeared at almost exactly the same time as Kafka's death)' (Adorno and Benjamin 1994: 95). The farcical Keystone Kops-style policemen in Straub-Huillet's film may indeed be an acknowledgement of this cinematic echo in Kafka's prose. The problem, as we have seen, is to find a cinematic method of translation which is productive rather than illustrative or derivative.

In Kafka's short story 'Beschreibung eines Kampfes' ('Description of a Struggle', 1912) the narrator describes the problem metaphor poses for the relationship between language and things as 'a seasickness on *terra firma*': having forgotten the 'true names for things' people pour arbitrary ones over them (2002f: 89). The slippages resulting from arbitrary nomination are not, however, incurable. After all, the narrator in 'Description of a Struggle' acknowledges that 'true names of things' do in fact exist. Similarly there are also instances of 'true images' to be found in Kafka's writing. In *The Man Who Disappeared*, for example, the protagonist finds solace in a photographic image of his mother:

> How could one possibly gain from a picture so completely the incontrovertible conviction that here was revealed a hidden emotion of the person depicted. […] The picture slipped from his hands, he then laid his face on the picture, its coolness felt good on his cheek and with a pleasant sensation he fell asleep. (2002d: 135, 136)

The comfort Karl gains from the picture is based on its stillness, which allows contemplation, and its candour. It is these two qualities, which, in very different ways, are the guiding principles of Straub and Huillet's, and Haneke's methods of Kafka adaptation. Straub-Huillet's first principle, as we have seen, is 'copying out', a pre-translational exercise; the subsequent process of translation to film entails observing the minutiae of rhythm and pause in Kafka's prose. *Class Relations* is unique amongst Kafka films in that it not only maintains a critical distance between Kafka's text and the filmmakers' images, but also achieves what Kafka himself termed the 'stillness of reality' (2002h: 937). The dialectical relationship between words and pictures that results opens up space for a complexity of meaning commensurate with that of Kafka's prose.

Haneke, for his part, attempts something seemingly impossible: to translate the images of Kafka's novel into readable visual equivalents without reducing them to the status of clear-cut, unambiguous metaphorical cyphers in the manner of Orson Welles. Whilst inevitably offering the audience his reading of the text, he skilfully manages to avoid transforming it into a palimpsest over-written with his own auteurist script.

Film is, by and large, consolidatory in its synthesis of images, words and sounds. When confronted with a form of language use that emphasises the discrete and the separate, as in the case of Kafka, a filmmaker is forced either into monocularity or into using film in a radically different way. In either case the reader-turned-viewer is obliged to observe how metaphors work differently from images, and how experiences brought together in words are not the same as events bracketed together in time. In a striking remark on the *Kaiserpanorama*, Kafka himself conceived of a cinema which would do away with that incessant movement which drains cinema of the 'stillness of reality', supplanting it with a three-dimensional plasticity and depth of field: 'Why is there no such union of cinema and the stereoscope?' (2002h: 937).

VI. JEAN-MARIE STRAUB, *JACKALS AND ARABS*

Although, as Hanns Zischler rightly suggests in *Kafka Goes to the Movies*, this proposed union 'cannot exist – unless the film were to come to a halt and turn into a frozen tableau vivant' Kafka is able to 'think cinema as something different' (2003: 27, 28).

Dudley Andrew has identified a particular kind of auteurist adaptation that is characterised by intersection and disjuncture rather than illustration. His examples include films of Bresson (*Mouchette*, 1967) and Straub-Huillet (*Othon*, 1970; *Chronik der Anna Magdalena Bach* [*Chronicle of Anna Magdalena Bach*], 1968):

> All such works fear or refuse to adapt. Instead they present the otherness and distinctiveness of the original text, initiating a dialectical interplay between the aesthetic forms of one period and the cinematic forms of our own period. In direct contrast to the manner in which scholars have treated the mode of 'borrowing,' such intersecting insists that the analyst attend to the specificity of the original within the specificity of cinema. An original is allowed its life, its own life, in the cinema. The consequences of this method, despite its apparent forthrightness, are neither innocent nor simple. The disjunct experience such intersecting promotes is consonant with the aesthetics of modernism in all the arts. This mode refutes the commonplace that adaptations support only a conservative film aesthetics. (2000: 31)

The films of Straub-Huillet and Haneke discussed here are consistent with Andrew's concept of a disjunctive, modernist intersection of different media within adaptation, in opposition to the less frictional, overtly illustrative mode as represented, for example, by Welles's *The Trial*. In a similar vein Robert Stam describes adaptation in his essay 'Beyond Fidelity' as 'a form of criticism or "reading"', one which exploits cinema's 'synthetic multiplicity of signifiers' and its potential for 'disunity and disjunction' (2000: 58, 62, 60). Straub, as we have seen, has claimed that the process of adaptation begins with 'copying things out', which relates it not only to the broader practice of 'recycling, remarking and every other form of retelling in the age of mechanical reproduction' but also what Naremore terms a 'general theory of repetition' (2000: 15).

In 2011, five years after the death of Danièle Huillet, Straub returned to an earlier joint project to adapt Kafka's short story 'Schakale und Araber' ('Jackals and Arabs', 1917).[8] Originally published by Martin Buber in the journal *Der Jude*, this story of a European traveller entreated by the leader of a pack of desert jackals to take revenge on their age-old enemy, the Arabs, has been read allegorically in many different, frequently irreconcilable ways: the jackals, for example, have variously been construed as the native Czech population in Bohemia, the assimilated Jews of the Western Diaspora and as Zionist settlers in Palestine; the traveller has been read as the European Powers (Britain in particular) pursuing imperial interest in Middle East, as the Messiah and as Kafka himself.[9]

In *Jackals and Arabs*, Straub pares back the staging of the text much more radically than in the case of *Class Relations*. The film, one of only a handful of Straub-Huillet productions to bear the title of its source text, consists of a mere sixteen shots preceded and followed by credits. It opens with the seventh fragment from part four of György Kurtág's 'Kafka-Fragments' for soprano and violin, with the text 'Again, again, exiled far away, exiled far away. Mountains, desert, a vast country to be wandered through' (Kafka 2002g: 514) presented black on white as intertitles, thereby drawing attention to film as a mixed or, in André Bazin's terminology, 'impure' medium, one which unites – or, in Straub-Huillet's case, also demonstratively separates – its 'inherited media' (Stam 2000: 61) of literature, photography, music and theatre.

Straub presents Kafka's text as a recitation to camera, in the director's own Parisian flat, with three actors: his regular collaborator Barbara Ulrich as the Jackal, the Professor of Italian literature Giorgio Passerone as the Arab and Straub himself (under the anagrammatic pseudonym Jubarite Semarin) as the unseen, off-camera narrator, whose utterances are generally accompanied by black inserts. The polyvalence of Kafka's animal story is achieved through the eschewal of any kind of visualisation of the text save for one single object, the scissors with which the traveller is invited to kill the Arabs. However, it employs the resources of cinema – medium-shots alternating with close-ups, emotionally-charged delivery, high-contrast (natural) lighting, the alternation of on and off-screen space and the aforementioned blackouts – to underscore the murderous violence of the conflict and the disturbing sense of the uncanny it provokes: in other words it realises the Kafkaesque without illustration. Straub's film not only uses Kafka's text to reflect on past and present conflict, without pinning it down to a single interpretation, it also thinks cinema as something different.

NOTES

1. This essay develops and expands ideas expounded in the essay 'Kafka adapted to film' by the same authors (Brady and Hughes 2002). The authors would like to thank Claire Taylor and Cambridge University Press for permission to use this material. All translations from the German in this essay are by the present authors.
2. The novel's title has been variously translated as *Amerika* (Willa and Edwin Muir), *Amerika: The Man Who Disappeared* (Michael Hofmann), *The Man Who Disappeared (America)* (Ritchie Robertson), *Amerika: The Missing Person* (Mark Harman).
3. The authors compiled a list of forty screen adaptations of Kafka's works in 2000.
4. Welles opens the film with the 'Before the Law' parable, which returns later towards the film's end.
5. In interview Straub referred to the title as 'very rash and a bit brutal' whilst Huillet termed it 'merely a suggestion' (Schütte 1984: 56).
6. Straub's quotation appears in the discussions with Kafka published by Gustav Janouch (1968: 205). The authenticity of these discussions is now widely disputed. They do, however, contain some pithy remarks on cinema which have gained common currency within Film Studies, although in his book *Kafka Goes to the Movies* Hanns Zischler chooses to ignore them (2003: 5).
7. See Sauermann 2008; Schlicker 2013.
8. The 2012 Independencia Distribution press pack for the collection of films which included *Jackals and Arabs* (entitled *L'Inconsolable*) dates the project to 1987 when Huillet's version of Kafka's story was submitted for publication in a special edition of *Cahiers du Cinéma* edited by Wim Wenders (1987).
9. See, for example, Rubinstein 1967; Shumsky 2009; Hanssen 2012.

BIBLIOGRAPHY

Adams, Jeffrey (2002) '*The Trial*: Film Noir and the Kafkaesque', *College Literature*, 29, 3, 140–57.

Adorno, Theodor W. and Walter Benjamin (1994) *Briefwechsel 1928–1940*, ed. Henri Lonitz. Frankfurt am Main: Suhrkamp.

Andrew, Dudley (2000) 'Adaptation', in James Naremore (ed.) *Film Adaptation*. New Brunswick, NJ: Rutgers University Press, 28–37.

Benjamin, Walter (1966) *Versuche über Brecht*. Frankfurt am Main: Suhrkamp.

____ (1977) 'Über den Begriff der Geschichte', in *Illuminationen*. Frankfurt am Main: Suhrkamp, 251–61.

Bogdanovich, Peter and Orson Welles (1992) *Orson Welles Talks*. New York: HarperCollins.

Brady, Martin and Helen Hughes (2002) 'Kafka adapted to film', *The Cambridge Companion to Kafka*, ed. Julian Preece. Cambridge: Cambridge University Press, 226–41.

Bresson, Robert (1996) *Notes on the Cinematographer*. London: Quartet Books.

Delahaye, Michel (1966) 'Between Heaven and Hell: Interview with Carl Dreyer', *Cahiers du Cinéma in English*, 1, 4, 7–17.

Foundas, Scott (2001) 'Interview: Michael Haneke: The Bearded Prophet of *Code Inconnu* and *The Piano Teacher*'. *Indiewire*; available at: http://www.indiewire.com/article/interview_michael_haneke_the_bearded_prophet_of_code_inconnu_and_the_piano (accessed 28 December 2014).

Gilman, Sander L. (2005) *Franz Kafka*. London: Reaktion.

Hanssen, Jens (2012) 'Kafka and Arabs', *Critical Inquiry*, 39, 1, 167–97.

Hoey, Allen (1988) 'The Name on the Coin: Metaphor, Metonymy, and Money', *Diacritics*, 18, 2, 26–37.

Janouch, Gustav (1968) *Gespräche mit Kafka: Erinnerungen und Aufzeichnungen*. Frankfurt am Main: Fischer Verlag.

Kafka, Franz (1967) *Briefe an Felice und andere Korrespondenz aus der Verlo-bungszeit*, eds Erich Heller and Jürgen Born. Frankfurt am Main: Fischer Verlag.

____ (2002a [1926]) *Das Schloß*, ed. Malcolm Pasley. Frankfurt am Main: Fischer Verlag.

____ (2002b [1926]) *Das Schloß: Apparatband*, ed. Malcolm Pasley. Frankfurt am Main: Fischer Verlag.

____ (2002c [1925]) *Der Proceß*, ed. Malcolm Pasley. Frankfurt am Main: Fischer Verlag.

____ (2002d [1927]) *Der Verschollene*, ed. J. Schillemeit. Frankfurt am Main: Fischer Verlag.

____ (2002e) *Drucke zu Lebzeiten*, eds W. Kittler, H-G Koch, G. Neumann. Frankfurt am Main: Fischer Verlag.

____ (2002f) *Nachgelassene Schriften und Fragmente I*, ed. Malcolm Pasley. Frankfurt am Main: Fischer Verlag.

____ (2002g) *Nachgelassene Schriften und Fragmente II*, ed. J. Schillemeit. Frankfurt am Main: Fischer Verlag.

____ (2002h) *Tagebücher*, eds Hans-Gerd Koch, Michael Müller and Malcolm Pasley. Frankfurt am Main: Fischer Verlag.

Koch, Gertrud (1984) '"Nur von Sichtbarem lässt sich erzählen": Zu einigen Kafka-Verfilmungen', in Wolfram Schütte (ed.) *Klassenverhältnisse: Von Danièle Huillet und Jean-Marie Straub nach dem Amerika-Roman 'Der Verschollene' von Franz Kafka*. Frankfurt am Main: Fischer, 171–8.

Naremore, James (1989) *The Magic World of Orson Welles*. Dallas, TX: Southern Methodist University Press.

_____ (2000) 'Introduction: Film and the Reign of Adaptation', in James Naremore (ed.) *Film Adaptation*. New Brunswick, NJ: Rutgers University Press, 1–16.

Nicolin, Günther (1974) *Kunst zu Kafka: Ausstellung zum 50. Todestag*. Bonn: bücherstube am theater.

Riemer, Willy (2011) 'Tracing K.: Michael Haneke's Film Adaptation of Kafka's *Das Schloß*', in Benjamin McCann and Davod Sorfa (eds) *The Cinema of Michael Haneke: Europe Utopia*. London and New York: Wallflower Press, 129–38.

Rubinstein, William C. (1967) 'Kafka's "Jackals and Arabs"', *Monatshefte*, 1, 59, 13–18.

Sauermann, Eberhard (2008) 'Kafkas Roman Das Schloss in den Verfilmungen von Noelte/Schell und Haneke', in S. Neuhaus (ed.) *Literatur im Film: Beispiele einer Medienbeziehung*. Würzburg: Konigshausen & Neumann, 215–38.

Schlicker, Alexander (2013) 'Ein (Fernseh) Auteur und seine Blickregime: Zu Formen impliziter Filmtheorie und Autorkonstruktion in Hanekes Verfilmung von Kafkas Romanfragment *Das Schloß*; available at: http://www.medienobservationen.lmu.de/kontrovers.htm (accessed 28 December 2014).

Schütte, Wolfram (1984) 'Gespräch mit Danièle Huillet und Jean-Marie Straub', in Wolfram Schütte (ed.) *Klassenverhältnisse: Von Danièle Huillet und Jean-Marie Straub nach dem Amerika-Roman 'Der Verschollene' von Franz Kafka*. Frankfurt am Main: Fischer, 37–58.

Shumsky, Dimitry (2009) 'Czechs, Germans, Arabs, Jews: Franz Kafka's "Jackals and Arabs" Between Bohemia and Palestine', *AJS Review*, 33, 1, 71–100.

Stam, Robert (2000) 'Beyond Fidelity: The Dialogics of Adaptation', in James Naremore (ed.) *Film Adaptation*. New Brunswick, NJ: Rutgers University Press, 54–76.

Straub, Jean-Marie and Danièle Huillet (1983), 'Wie will ich lustig lachen, wenn alles durcheinandergeht: Danièle Huillet und Jean-Marie Straub sprechen über ihren Film *Klassenverhältnisse*', *Filmkritik*, 19, 5, 269–78.

Wenders, Wim (1987) Cahiers du Cinéma 400; available at: http://www.independencia-societe.com/wp-content/uploads/2012/02/DP-INCONSOLABLE_HQP.pdf (accessed 14 June 2015).

Zischler, Hanns (2003) *Kafka Goes to the Movies*, trans. Susan H. Gillespie. Chicago: University of Chicago Press.

K, THE TRAMP AND THE CINEMATIC VISION: THE KAFKAESQUE CHAPLIN

SHAI BIDERMAN

In his memoirs, *Conversations with Kafka* (1971), Gustav Janouch recalls Franz Kafka's impression of Charlie Chaplin. A mutual acquaintance has sent Kafka a bundle of stills from Chaplin's short comedies, along with an invitation to go to the movies to see the recent work of the filmmaker. According to Janouch, Kafka politely refused the invitation, but had most interesting reflections to share regarding the cinematic master and his profession:

> That's a very energetic, work-obsessed man. There burns in his eyes *the flame of despair at the unchangeable condition of the oppressed*, yet he does not capitulate to it. Like every genuine comedian, *he has the bite of a beast of prey, and he uses it to attack the world*. He does it in *his own unique way*. Despite the white face and the black eyebrows, he's not a sentimental Pierrot, nor is he some snarling critic. *Chaplin is a technician*. He's *the man of a machine world*, in which most of his fellow men no longer command the requisite emotional and mental equipment to make the life allotted to them really their own. They do not have the imagination. As a dental technician makes false teeth, so he manufactures *aids to the imagination. That's what his films are. That's what films in general are.* (1971: 158–9; emphasis added)

One can understand these reflections in two complimentary ways. First, they can be seen as a subtle description and as a fair analysis of Chaplin's cinematic performance at the time (late 1910s–early 1920s). Recall that the Chaplin of those days was still a contract player in the Mack Sennett comedies. His masterpieces – *The Kid* (1921), *The Gold Rush* (1925), *The Circus* (1928), *City Lights* (1931), *Modern Times* (1936) and *The Great Dictator* (1940) – had not yet been released, and, most importantly, his iconic tour de force figure, 'the tramp' (also known as 'the little man'), had not yet reached its full cinematic potential. However, it is this exact potential which makes the case for Kafka's foresight and, accordingly, for a second understanding of the text. Here, Kafka joins commentators, contemporaries and successors alike, who acknowledge Chaplin's ingenuity, his unique role as the speechless voice of a generation, and his mastery of a craft that is still in its infancy (cinema). One of these commentators is Max Brod who, in the preface to Kafka's first novel, *Der Verschollene* (*Amerika*, 1927), acknowledges that some of Kafka's grotesque and comical scenes remind him of Chaplin films (Brod 1946: ix; see also Rahv 1939: 65–6; Alt 2009: 8). Another such commentator is Walter Benjamin who repeatedly pairs Chaplin with Kafka, while claiming, 'Chaplin holds a genuine key to the interpretation of Kafka' (quoted in Leslie 2007: 119; Hansen 2008: 373). Following these interpretations of Kafka's reflections, one is liable to assume that there is more to them than a mere cultural admiration of Chaplin's cinema, an admiration that was rather common among Kafka's contemporaries, especially among Russian intellectuals, as pointed out by several scholars (see Cavanagh 1995: 286–92; Decherney 2012: 70).[1] With a glimpse of premonition, and with Benjamin's words in the background, we can read Kafka's reflections on Chaplin as an admiration of a different kind (and magnitude). Kafka, in fact, *identifies his cinematic counterpart*. When he depicts Chaplin as 'a technician' of his craft (cinematic comedy), attacking the world through his craft – his 'flame of despair' which echoes the 'unchangeable condition of the oppressed' in 'a machine world' – one can almost hear the sound of introspection and self-justification lurking in the background.

Admittedly, this reading might be taken as somewhat overly enthusiastic. However, and despite conventional wisdom which seemingly sets Chaplin and Kafka apart (the former acknowledged as an anguishing martyr and the latter adored through his clownish antics) (see Prince 1986: 36), I wish to pursue Benjamin's idea that it is Chaplin whose cinema can aptly be seen as a modification (or interpretation) of the Kafkaesque. The idea of Kafkaesque cinema – namely, the idea that the world of the moving image can uniquely and exclusively employ, explore and embrace the experience of the Kafkaesque philosophy and worldview – will therefore be exhibited in the superbly orchestrated world of Charlie Chaplin.

I. A GENUINE KEY TO THE INTERPRETATION OF KAFKA: CHAPLIN AND THE KAFKAESQUE

The question pervading Chaplin's connection with Kafka is at the forefront of a contemporary debate. Triggered by Benjamin's observation, this question has been made prominent through the scholarly insights of many. While taking under consideration the various aspects of the Kafkaesque and, similarly, Chaplin's greatest masterpieces, the advocates of Benjamin's observation have based the affinity between Kafka and Chaplin on either form or content. In terms of form, a common conception of Kafka and Chaplin relations perceives their respective styles as embedding sharp and sardonic dark humour. In terms of content, most commentators acknowledge a similar criticism of late modernism, as well as similar pictures of alienation, reification and the Jewish pariah, in the respective works of the two masters. As these points differ in content and origin, they are nevertheless united in their utmost support of Benjamin's words. All ways lead, it seems, to the realisation that Chaplin is, indeed, a Kafkaesque cinematographer.

Several commentators have detected affinities between Kafka's and Chaplin's humour sensitivities. While such an analogy might seem at first dubious – Kafka is not particularly noted for his humour, and is largely read as the 'prophet of the absurd' (see Glicksberg 1975) and the 'poet of shame and guilt' (see Friedlander 2013), while Chaplin constitutes the epitome of comedy – it is in fact evident that both masters blended existential angst with dark comedy. Wes Gehring sees both artists as 'dark comedy prophets sending out a warning about the precarious plight of modern men and women' (2014: 121). Similarly, as noted by Astrid Klocke (2008), both Kafka and Chaplin serve as the point of departure to Edgar Hilsenrath's dark-comic novel *Der Nazi und der Friseur* (*The Nazi and the Barber*, 1971). Ben La Farge goes as far as to claim that Kafka's 'Die Verwandlung' ('The Metamorphosis', 1915) is 'the greatest black comedy in the Western tradition' (2011: 294). What makes this story a black comedy, according to La Farge, is 'the implacable logic by which the story slowly unravels toward a bitter ending that completes the disaster implied by the nightmarish beginning' (2011: 295). Similarly, Jean Collignon detects a thin line of comic interlude in Kafka's narratives, especially in the manner by which they unfold, which suggests that the protagonists of these narratives are not exclusively tragic, but also, at least mildly, a literary manifestation of comical irony. Such is the case with Josef K. (who is arrested and executed), K. (who is never officially admitted to the castle), Karl Rossmann (who is treated with suspicion and distrust), and Gregor Samsa (who is unexpectedly metamorphosed to a vermin). Despite these awful (and dreadfully unavoidable) destinies (which await the protagonists from the outset), they all 'preserve their sense of humor and we are expected to smile with them' (Collignon 1955: 54).

What stems from these examples, according to Collignon, is the need 'not only to define Kafka's humor, but primarily to become aware of it and to approach it' (1955: 53). However, once becoming aware of its significance, a definition is in order. Such definition, according to Collignon, makes the comparison of Kafka's humour with Chaplin's even more plausible. Kafka's humour, as explicated in his protagonists, is 'the humor of a man both oppressed and depressed who smiles not in order to forget but to assert his independence, and makes plain his determination not to be overwhelmed by hardships' (1955: 53–4). However, this assertion of independence is a sham, as it cherishes the protagonists' innermost conviction that, 'try as they may, they are fighting a losing battle' (1955: 55). They will be defeated, and they know it, as there is no hope for rescue or salvation – but they will 'keep smiling at the whole procedure', as it is an inextricable part of the whole bargain (1955: 53). Chaplin's humour, on the contrary, 'lurks not only a comforting sense of his intrinsic superiority over a silly and ruthless system of control, but also *the hope*, apparently childish though finally vindicated, that he will manage to find the weak point in the system' (1955: 55; emphasis added).

The discussion of style and form preludes the pairing of Kafka and Chaplin despite their mutual content and philosophical attitude. Here, the central motif in the many readings of Chaplin's Kafkaesque oeuvre focuses on the human condition in the technological age. The cinematic figure that many see as a preeminent manifestation of self-alienation, immiseration and the overpowering nature of modern technology is, not surprisingly, Chaplin's tramp. The tramp, in a unique manner, imbricates the condition of being expelled and disinherited (see Hansen 2008: 373–4). As befits his nameless wandering entity and the precarious way by which he handles himself and his surroundings, he is always homeless and poor. He does not have a home, and, in any case, he cannot afford one. Whenever he finds a habitat, it is always short lived. Such is the case with the ramshackle hut in *Modern Times* and the similarly wretched attic in *The Kid* (see Gilman 1993: 483; Payne 1997: 34). Whenever he faces the might and machining force of machines, he yields to their overwhelming power. Such is the case with the iconic assembly line in *Modern Times*, for which the tramp is but 'a mere means of production' (Fracchia 2008: 44). Such is also the case with the feeding machine, tested at the outset of the same film, which turn the tramp 'into the production process itself' (ibid.). The impoverished tramp thus embodies the detachment and utter defeat of humankind, and the hopeless resentment against the loss of humanity.

The alienated tramp is also the centrepiece of Parker Tyler's innovative work, 'Kafka's and Chaplin's "Amerika"' (1950). Here, Tyler argues that Kafka's portrayal of America (and the American experience) in his novel, is akin with Chaplin's portrayal of America. Complimentarily, Tyler notices the cinematic qualities of the novel. Following Phillip Rahv, who describes the formal outline of the novel in a somewhat Hollywoodish style as 'a tale of the wanderings of a sixteen-year-old boy in the mechanized cities of America' (1939: 65–6), Tyler claims that specific passages in the novel are 'positively cinematic' (1950: 304). One such passage describes a panoramic impression of New York, and resembles, according to Tyler, the visual impression of Chaplin's portrayal of the metropolis in *Modern Times* or in *City Lights*. The passage reads as follows:

> When the car, emerging out of the dark, dully echoing narrow lanes, crossed out of these great thoroughfares which were as wide as squares, there opened out on both sides an endless perspective of pavements filled with a moving mass of people, slowly shuffling forward, whose singing was more homogeneous than that of any single human voice. (1946: 49)

While quoting this passage, Tyler notes that 'this might be an actual excerpt from a synopsis meant to indicate montage effects of audio-visual nature: superimposed marchers with vocal chorus and music' (1950: 304–5). A Chaplinesque read of this quasi-cinematic moment in *Amerika* is definitely worthy of consideration.

This said, the gist of Tyler's argument run the other way. For Tyler, Kafka's *Amerika* is 'reciprocally telescoped by Chaplin' (1950: 305). Here, Tyler argues that Karl Rossmann, the protagonist of Kafka's *Amerika* and the first of K.'s incarnations, can be best illuminated by Chaplin's iconic figure, the tramp. The pretext to this comparison is the deep-rooted sensibilities both artists share regarding the immigrant standpoint. This standpoint is manifested in Rossmann's view of America – an America which strangely merges the Statue of Liberty as the iconic image of 'the land of opportunities' with the provincial and uninspiring ethos of the Nature Theater of Oklahoma – and is echoed in the tramp's wandering demeanour, which is a reflection of Chaplin's own experiences as an English immigrant in the United States (1950: 300).

The most obvious reason for this comparison, which cannot pass as insignificant, is the resemblance between the plot of *Amerika* and the plots, the mannerisms and the general atmosphere of various Chaplin comedies. According to Tyler, both Rossmann and the tramp are heroes of 'the identical international myth', namely, 'the great adventure of the young foreigner coming head-on to the United States to start a new life and hoping to rise to a level beyond any available to [them] in [their] native land' (1950: 301). However, their efforts are predetermined, and ultimately fail. As both the tramp and Rossmann are misfits, immigrants who are unable to climb the socio-political ladder of success, they are unable to extricate themselves from the suspicion of crime and from the unshakable notion of being 'undesirable' (ibid.).

A demonstration of this picture – the undesirability of immigration and the shortcomings of social integration – appears in a Chaplin short which bears a most indicative title, *The Immigrant* (1917). The casual symmetries between the tramp (in *The Immigrant*) and Rossmann, while probably accidental, are nevertheless quite revealing. For instance, as the tramp's most recognised artefact is his cane, so is Rossmann's uncle's, who first appears holding a 'bamboo cane'. The tramp uses his cane as a weapon, demonstrating remarkable, yet often cunning, swordsmanship skills. Rossmann, in turn, imagines the Statue of Liberty's torch as a sword. Upon arriving to the new world, the tramp finds himself in a restaurant, and loses his money through a hole in his pocket. Upon meeting Delamarche and Robinson, Rossmann finds himself in a restaurant, his money is misplaced, and he has to dig for it.

Moving from *The Immigrant* to Chaplin's other masterpieces, we can see how these parallels run even deeper. This, per Tyler, indicate 'an essential brotherhood between Karl and Charlie' (1950: 306). Such is the case, for instance, with Rossmann's nightmarish vision that resembles certain sequences in *Modern Times*. Such is also the case with Rossmann's encounter with Pollunder's daughter, who almost knocks him backward out a window, in a manner that echoes the physical antics of the tramp. Finally, in *City Lights*, the relationship the tramp has with his surrounding echoes a similar attitude exhibited by Rossmann. In the film, the protagonist obtains good jobs (thus perpetuating the hope for social acceptance and, plot-wise, remedy for the blind flower girl), then has run-ins with the law (which seems to be 'especially allergic to an immigrant' [1950: 304]), loses the job, and is deemed outcast (and poor) again. The mirror image of this predicament is the character of the maniac millionaire, who befriends the tramp while drunk, only to renounce him when sober. This hopeless relationship – which, per Chaplin, epitomises the state of an immigrant in the modern society – is exhibited in the bipolar relationship Rossmann has with his uncle (1950: 302–3).

Finally, Kafka's and Chaplin's outcasts-connection is best exemplified in Hannah Arendt's essay 'The Jew as Pariah: A Hidden Tradition' (1944), where she constructs, by presenting four types of Jewish Pariah – Heinrich Heine, Bernard Lazar, Charlie Chaplin and Franz Kafka – an 'outline of a "hidden tradition" of cultural exclusion' (Momigliano 1987: 231). Arendt reveals that 'between these four types there is a significant connection – a link which in fact unites all genuine concepts and sound ideas when once they achieve historical actuality' (2007: 277).

II. 'THAT'S WHAT HIS FILMS ARE. THAT'S WHAT FILMS IN GENERAL ARE'

Though sustainable, the inextricable connections between Kafka and Chaplin, in both form and content, are subservient to a larger affinity between the two. Here, the focus shifts from the particular expressions of the two artists to the medium by which they express themselves. For Kafka, it is the language and the written word that serve as medium for his craft. For Chaplin, surely enough, it is the world of moving images which shapes his artistic posture. As can be extricated form the postscript of Kafka's articulation of Chaplin's craft, the essential nature of the cinematic medium is an intrinsic key in understanding Chaplin's ingenuity. If Chaplin's films are, as Kafka suggests, indicative to 'what films in general are' (Janouch 1971: 159), and if Benjamin is right in his claim that Chaplin holds a genuine key to the interpretation of Kafka, then one is liable to agree that the Chaplin's mastery over his medium offers a unique insight into the Chaplin phenomena.

A similar claim can be made regarding Kafka's mastery of his own medium. When we focus our attention on the philosophical branch of Kafka criticism, it seems that we find ourselves in the midst of an endless exegesis and interpretation to which Kafka's works are mercilessly subjected. Despite this multitude, it seems that Kafka's text easily defeats any of its specific readings, as if 'every sentence says "interpret me", but none will allow it' (Adorno 1981: 246). This inexplicable (and unavoidable) defeat is indicative to Kafka's relations with his medium, which, in his case, is language and the verbal means of expression. The medium, according to Kafka, is not only the means by which he creates scenes and narrative events. It is, primarily, an intrinsic way to instantiate a failure, which is, by nature, a linguistic one. Noting this, Shlomo Biderman claims that for Kafka 'language is anything but linear' (2008: 189). In its circularity, Biderman continues, 'a character [or an anonymous narrator] will set out to say whatever he has to say, only to immediately retract, then to uphold what he had said to begin with, only to have reservations about his very retraction' (ibid.).[2] What stems out from this depiction is that Kafka's style of writing is indicative to his control over the linguistic medium, and, as such, is an archetypal condition of the Kafkaesque. This control, however, emerges in a language that is at its core paradoxical, or at least ambivalent. Challenging both structure and reference, Kafka's language exhibits a self-defeating notion of reality, a notion that is, at all times, both sustainable and incoherent. As Biderman concludes, Kafka's sentences demonstrate 'a dialectics lacking an upward movement', as they 'writhe around each other, or else turn and twist around imperceptible axes' (ibid.).

If Kafka's language is imperceptible and self-defeating, Chaplin's image, by analogy, is interposing and incongruent. As Michel Chion (1989) notes, the fundamental feature of the figure of the tramp is the disturbing notion that he is always in the way. Echoing Chion, Slavoj Žižek suggests that the tramp 'is always interposed between a gaze and its "proper" object, fixating upon himself a gaze destined for another, ideal point or object – a stain which disturbs "direct" communication between the gaze and its "proper" object, leading the straight gaze astray, changing it into a kind of squint' (1992: 5). According to Žižek, this is a fundamental motif for Chaplin. The tramp, by its very cinematic nature, 'accidently occupies a place which is not his own, which is not destined for him' (ibid.): he is mistaken for a rich man in *City Lights*, he unexpectedly finds himself on a circus stage (and later on a rope at the top of the circus tent) in *The Circus*, and so on. The tramp is, to coin Žižek, a 'stain in the picture' (ibid.), appearing for the sake of appearance, defining himself cinematically as an image that requires the attention of a misdirected gaze.

An example to this affect is Chaplin's *City Lights*. In this film, Chaplin presents us with the story of the little tramp, as he falls in love with a blind flower girl who mistakes him for a rich benefactor. Her blindness prevents her, of course, from seeing reality for what it is. The tramp, determined not to disappoint the girl, goes out of his way to support her, and provide her the means for the operation that will restore her eyesight. Though succeeding in this task, the tramp deteriorates to extreme poverty. The girl, now rehabilitated, works in a successful flower shop, daydreaming about her mysterious benefactor, and wonders if she will ever see him again. She does meet him, in the final moments of the film, and recognises him by feeling his hands. 'You?' she asks, as the climactic moment unfolds. The tramp nods, shyly yet full of emotions, and the film ends with the famous close-up on his kind eyes.

In the very first scene of *City Lights*, a crowd is gathered in an inauguration ceremony of a monument, titled 'peace and prosperity'. After the dignitaries make their speech, the monument is unveiled. To the great surprise of the applauding crowd, the little tramp is really unveiled, sleeping in the lap of one of the statues. The tramp awakes, and while realising that he is an unexpected focus of attention tries to descend from the monument. However, comically enough, he falls on the drawn sword of another statue. Greeting the crowd with a wave of his hat he tries to make a break, only to be stopped by the national anthem which is suddenly played. As the distress of the dignitaries and law enforcement grows, the tramp tries to leave the monument. As he descends, the drawn sword of the statue confronts him. In a blink of the moment, the tramp draws his cane, and looks as if he is engaged in a duel with the statue. This gesture is immediately replaced by a more defensive one, then with an apologetic one, and then, finally, with the tramp leaving the scene.

This scene provides a nice illustration to Žižek's 'stain in the picture'. The tramp assumes a role which is not his to have, and, once again, becomes 'an object of a gaze aimed at something or someone else' (ibid). This scene, cinematically comprised from a sequence of shots and ingenious editing, presents a visual image which constructs a narrative. If we were to narrate this scene 'linguistically', we would probably say: 'the tramp is unveiled sleeping on the monument, and then descends in a comical manner'. But this would be *missing the point of this cinematic presentation altogether*. If we want to give a more accurate portrayal, we would point out the physical attributes of the nameless tramp, and the fact that everything happens on a monument titled 'peace and prosperity'. The accumulation of these facts – achieved 'purely' by cinematic means, without a word being said – creates a certain experience of a man's struggle against the conformity of empty statements and surpassing values. The unveiling of the monument soon becomes an illusion – it is the little tramp that is unveiled, nameless and asleep, thrown into the visible world (which, as we already know, will challenge its own visibility throughout the film's plot), forcing our gaze to fixate on his coming to be. His many gestures and reactions, constructed visually as a sequential narrative, becomes an on-going counterargument to the overwhelming (yet, somewhat pathetic, or megalomaniac) force of 'peace and prosperity' (a force which, by a wave of a cane for a fraction of a second, is exhausted and depleted). As an embodiment of an aversion against the tyranny of novel ideals, the tramp exposes the duplicity and (probably) immorality of these governing ideals, and mocks the law-enforcers and dignitaries of society, by comically locating them in the feet of the monument. The point of view of the camera, the various gestures and motions, the unique embodiment of the 'tramp mentality' – all exist in the aesthetic domain of the cinematic image, and are effective as a philosophical argument against conformity strictly in this visual capacity.

This refusal of language and the prioritisation of the image are indicative to Chaplin's mastery of the cinematic medium. Notice that in 1931 talking movies were already a common practice, yet Chaplin made *City Lights* as a silent movie, wilfully deciding to ignore the possibility of sound (with the exception of the mandatory background music). This remarkable directorial decision results in a film that presents us with a pure image, which is not 'corrupted' by the parallel existence of voiceover or dialogues. Since the silence of this film – that is, the absence of any linguistic component therein – results not from any sort of impossibility, but rather is a result of intentional decision, we must take notice.

This becomes all the more important in another wonderful scene from *City Lights*. Later in the film, the tramp visits the blind flower girl at her residence. He reads her the paper, where a news article reports that 'Vienna doctor has cure for blindness'. At this point, the spectators are often happy and relieved, that they miss the subtitle of this article, which surprisingly states: 'free operation for the poor'. Why is that so utterly surprising? Because the main premise of the entire film, as stemmed from the film's plotline thus far, gave us the impression that a cure, if it at all to be found, is costly, and hence beyond the reach of the poor girl, and definitely beyond the reach of the tramp (despite being misidentified as a rich man).

What we saw here – what Chaplin *made us see* here – can be depicted as the turning point of the narrative plot: a cure is found, and the emotional blind girl learns that her rich benefactor – who, as we know, is actually a poor, yet warm hearted, tramp – will finance her recovery. However, the subtitle which states: 'free operation for the poor' is almost meant not to be seen. It is hidden in smaller print, inside an article which we, as film spectators, are not meant to read. As we engage with a visual experience, we are expected to miss this bit of news, which, if comprehended, undermines the entire narrative thus far! For if the operation is free for the poor, and the blind girl definitely qualifies as poor, why do we need the tramp altogether?

Chaplin's point here is that *not only do we need the tramp – we cannot do without him.* His presence – his visual and phenomenological presence – is what the film is all about, what the film does and what the experience of watching the film should ultimately mean. The knowledge which undermines the narrative does exactly that: it abolishes the priority and coherency of the narrative, and instead urges us to focus our attention on the visual, aesthetic, imagistic and cinematic domains. Notice the double-layered strategy which Chaplin uses here: he *shows* us the *words* ('free operation for the poor'), for just enough time for them not to be read. The words themselves undermine the logic of the narrative; however, by showing them (and not showing them at the same time) Chaplin manages to beautifully play on the blurry margins of the medium. Employing these strategies, Chaplin achieves an inventively unique Kafkaesque quality, which, if anything, indulges Benjamin's dictum with a new (and wonderfully rich) meaning.

NOTES

1. Such is the case with the Russian poet, Anna Akhmatova, whose poem reflects an admiring conversation with Chaplin and Kafka. Such is also the case with Russian formalist Viktor Shklovsky, who devoted an entire collection of essays to Chaplin; Russian writer Yuri Tynianov, who coined the term 'Chaplinism' in his observations on Russian cultural history; and Russian poet and essayist Osip Mandelstam, who devoted a poem to Chaplin and City Lights.
2. An acute example to such sentences appears in the last section of 'Der Kriesel' ('The Top', 1936): 'Once the smallest detail was understood, then everything was understood, which was why he busied himself only with the spinning top. And whenever preparations were being made for the spinning of the top, he hoped that this time it would succeed: as soon as the top began to spin and he was running breathlessly after it, the hope would turn to certainty, but when he held the silly piece of wood in his

hand, he felt nauseated. The screaming of the children, which hitherto he had not heard, and which now suddenly pierced his ears, chased him away, and he tottered like a top under a clumsy whip' (1971: 444).

BIBLIOGRAPHY

Adorno, Theodor W. (1981 [1953]) 'Notes on Kafka', *Prisms*, trans. Shierry Weber Nicholsen and Samuel Weber. Cambridge: MIT Press, 243–71.

Alt, Peter-André (2009) *Kafka und der Film. Über kinematographisches Erzählen*. Munich: Verlag C. H. Beck.

Arendt, Hannah (2007 [1944]) 'The Jew as Pariah: A Hidden Tradition', in Jerome Kohne and Ron. H. Feldman (eds) *The Jewish Writings*. New York: Schocken, 275–98.

Benjamin, Walter (1991 [1997]) *Gesammelte Schriften Volume II*, eds. Rolf Tiedemann and Hermann Schweppenhauser. Frankfurt am Main: Suhrkamp.

Biderman, Shlomo (2008) *Crossing Horizons: World, Self, and Language in Indian and Western Thought*. New York: Columbia University Press.

Brod, Max (1946 [1927]) 'Preface', Franz Kafka, *Amerika*, trans. Edwin Muir. New York: New Directions, iii–x.

Cavanagh, Clare (1995) *Osip Mandelstam and the Modernist Creation of Trad-ition*. Princeton, NJ: Princeton University Press.

Chion, Michel (1989) *Les lumières de la ville: Charles Chaplin*. Paris: Nathan.

Collignon, Jean (1955) 'Kafka's Humor', *Yale French Studies*, 16, 53–62.

Decherney, Peter (2012) *Hollywood's Copyright Wars: From Edison to the Internet*. New York: Columbia University Press.

Fracchia, Joseph (2008) 'The Capitalist Labour-Process and the Body in Pain: The Corporeal Depths of Marx's Concept of Immiseration', *Historical Materialism*, 16, 35–66.

Friedlander, Saul (2013) *Franz Kafka: The Poet of Shame and Guilt*. New Haven, CT: Yale University Press.

Gehring, Wes D. (2014) *Chaplin's War Trilogy: An Evolving Lens in Three Dark Comedies, 1918–1947*. Jefferson, NC: McFarland.

Gilman, Sander L. (1993) 'Franz Kafka-a.k.a. Franz Kf; Akfak Znarf; Kranz Fafka-K.K. Raaanz-Na! Farfkakz?-And No End', *Monatshefte*, 85, 4, 478–86.

Glicksberg, Charles Irving (1975) *The Literature of Nihilism*. Lewiburg, PA: Bucknell University Press.

Hansen, Miriam Bratu (2004) 'Room-For-Play: Benjamin's Gamble with Cinema: The Martin Walsh Memorial Lecture 2003', *Canadian Journal of Film Studies*, 13, 1, 2–27.

____ (2008) 'Benjamin's Aura', *Critical Inquiry*, 34, 2, 336–75.

Hilsenrath, Edgar (2013 [1971]) *The Nazi and the Barber*, trans. Andrew White. Barber Press.

Janouch, Gustav (1971) *Conversations with Kafka*, trans. Goronwy Rees, second edition. New York: New Directions.

Kafka, Franz (1946 [1927]) *Amerika*, trans. Edwin Muir. New York: New Directions.

⎯⎯⎯ (1971) *The Complete Stories*, ed. Nahum N. Glatzer. New York: Schocken.

Klocke, Astrid (2008) 'Subverting Satire: Edgar Hilsenrath's Novel *Der Nazi und der Friseur* and Charlie Chaplin's Film *The Great Dictator*', *Holocaust and Genocide Studies*, 22, 3, 497–513.

La Farge, Ben (2011) 'Comic Anxiety and Kafka's Black Comedy', *Philosophy and Literature*, 35, 2, 282–302.

Leslie, Esther (2007) *Walter Benjamin*. London: Reaktion.

Momigliano, Arnaldo (1987) *On Pagans, Jews, and Christians*. Middletown CT: Wesleyan University Press.

Payne, Kenneth (1997) 'Franz Kafka's America', *Symposium: A Quarterly Journal in Modern Literatures*, 51, 1, 30–42.

Prince, Gerald (1986) 'Re-Membering Modiano, or Something Happened', *SubStance*, 15, 1, 49, 35–43.

Rahv, Phillip (1939) 'Franz Kafka: The Hero as Lonely Man', *The Kenyon Review*, 1, 1, 60–74.

Tyler, Parker (1950) 'Kafka's and Chaplin's "Amerika"', *The Sewanee Review*, 58, 2, 299–311.

Žižek, Slavoj (1992) *Enjoy Your Symptom!: Jacques Lacan in Hollywood and Out*. New York: Routledge.

'THE MEDIUM IS THE MESSAGE': CRONENBERG 'OUTKAFKAS' KAFKA

IRIS BRUCE[1]

Echoes of Franz Kafka's writings appear in many of David Cronenberg's films, even though these are not specifically based on Kafka but on stories or novels by other writers, such as George Langelaan's 'The Fly' (1957) or William Burroughs' *Naked Lunch* (1959). Kafka's human-sized beetle/vermin, Gregor Samsa, is prominent already in *The Fly* (1986), and Cronenberg himself compares the two protagonists in his introduction to a recent re-translation of Kafka's 'Die Verwandlung' ('The Metamorphosis', 1915), entitled 'The Beetle and the Fly' (1996). The Kafka beetle's second appearance is in Cronenberg's *Naked Lunch* (1991), where his continuous presence as a real character emerging in various transformations or disguises turns the vermin/extermination metaphor into a *leitmotif*. It matters little that *The Fly* or *Naked Lunch* are not about Kafka, that the first is a remake of Kurt Neumann's *The Fly* (1958), via Langelaan's story, and the latter is based on a Burroughs novel. In fact, Cronenberg himself remarks that knowing the source text often limits his films' multiple layers of meaning: 'So someone who walks in cold off the street, and maybe doesn't even know my work or Burroughs', would get the purest screening of the film' (quoted in Baldassare 1992).

At the same time, Cronenberg naturally highlights his source:

> Burroughs' life is a very fascinating subject for me, especially since, in a way, the theme of the film, one of the main subjects, is the writing process, the creative process and how it relates to life. This is really a meditation on Burroughs, the rosean imagery of the Burroughs' sort of universe rather than a direct translation of the book. (Ibid.)

Kafka's influence on Burroughs is also well-known (see Meyer 1990), and even if Cronenberg was exposed to Kafka largely through Burroughs' writings, Kafka has nonetheless become a constitutive part of Cronenberg's postmodern vision. I will examine the two artists' different representations of (early and late) twentieth-century societies, moving from Kafkaesque dreams and nightmares to Cronenbergian possible worlds of scientific and technological advancements, which project future possibilities for mankind, as well as realities of indescribable horror. Does Kafka share some of the anxieties, fears, hopes, aspirations and longings of Cronenberg's protagonists (scientists, artists, entrepreneurs, media gurus, the psychologically vulnerable), all of whom struggle with (post) modernity and its discontents? Both artists depict this struggle by examining relations between metamorphosis, (sexual) violence, power and technology, yet Cronenberg's ongoing metamorphoses in *Videodrome* (1983), *The Fly* and *Naked Lunch* 'outkafka' Kafka by far.

I. THE BEETLE AND THE FLY

When told that 'the polluted air that we breathe [in *The Fly*] has much in common with that in the room of the hero of Kafka's *Metamorphosis*' (Grünberg 2000: 82), Cronenberg replies that Kafka's understanding of Otherness is very different from his own:

> You talk about Kafka. You say of course he was the other because he was German-speaking. He was Czechoslovakian and he was a Jew, so he was the other twice removed. So on and so on. I don't feel that about myself *per se*. I don't think that's what I'm expressing, at least not on a level I feel very strongly. Consciously anyway. I think the other is a seductive possibility. A dangerous one perhaps and a scary one, but something you could become. You've seen the example of someone else being that. That means it's a possibility for you. (Grünberg 2000: 93)

Yet perhaps Kafka was not quite the loner and outsider that he is frequently taken to be. In a diary entry from 1911, after spending some time with two well-known contemporary artists, Kurt Tucholsky (1890–1935), a political satirist very comfortable with metamorphoses since he himself wrote under five pseudonyms, and Kurt Szafranski (1890–1964), illustrator of one of Tucholsky's novels and publishing director in Berlin, Kafka notes: 'Reminds me that I too have a pronounced talent for metamorphosing myself, which no one notices. How often I must have imitated Max [Brod]. Yesterday evening, on the way home, if I had observed myself from the outside I should have taken myself for Tucholsky. The alien being must be in me, then' (1948: 71). What is clear is that both Kafka and Cronenberg have a fascination with metamorphoses, which manifest themselves in divergent forms. But Cronenberg's distancing himself from Kafka is also correct: though they share a modernist vision and their metaphors, symbols and themes frequently overlap, nonetheless, the fact that these artists are virtually a century apart and work in a different (print/visual) medium does inform their art as well as determine the readers'/audiences' perceptions of their works.

Thus, metamorphosis is largely a metaphor of mental instability and dislocation for Kafka, but often a new, exciting experience in Cronenberg. Kafka insists on absolute ambiguity when it comes to Gregor's metamorphosis. For instance, the Eucharist is alluded to in Kafka's title, '(Ver)wandlung', except, as a modernist writer, Kafka is denying any religious significance through the negative prefix 'Ver', which turns the religious 'Wandlung' into a distortion of the original transsubstantiation. Gregor Samsa's new identity also remains uncertain throughout the entire narrative. Not only is Gregor not a 'beetle' (*Käfer*) in the original German but a 'monstrous vermin' (Kafka 1996a: 3; *ungeheures Ungeziefer*), an inherently contradictory, oxymoronic phrase which carries multiple meanings (incredible, outrageous, huge, monstrous vermin), but the double negative 'un' makes it impossible for any reader to identify him as a particular species and thus renders his metamorphosis metaphorical: 'Gregor's opaque body is thus to maintain him in a solitude without speech or intelligible gesture, in the solitude of an indecipherable sign' (Corngold 1996: 89). Indeed, Kafka expressly asked his publisher Kurt Wolff (in 1915) that the insect not be depicted:

> Dear Sir, You recently wrote that Ottomar Starke is going to do an illustration for the title page of The Metamorphosis. Now I have had a slight … probably wholly unnecessary shock. It occurred to me that Starke … might want, let us say, to draw the insect itself. Not that, please, not that! I don't want to restrict his authority but only to make this request from my own naturally better knowledge of the story. The insect itself cannot be drawn. It cannot even be shown at a distance. (1996b: 70)

However, this does not prevent Kafka from representing Gregor's initial reaction to his metamorphosis with a great deal of humour. There is a visual, theatrical dimension when we see Gregor exploring his new body, with his many legs wiggling in all directions; he imagines, wishes that what happened to him could happen to the office manager as well, and cannot help smiling. There is humour when the vermin opens the door and first appears in public: his family's fearful response and their exaggerated gestures when they first see him are funny; and he enjoys the power he has gained all of a sudden when he even manages to chase away the office manager, who is threatening the entire family. All of this is presented with slapstick humour. The humour stops at the end of Part I when Gregor is mistreated by his father. His wounding continues throughout the entire story (physically and psychologically); but the most severe physical abuse occurs when the father bombards him with apples at the end of Part II, one of which lodges in his back and becomes a great (symbolic) wound: 'Gregor's serious wound, from which he suffered for over a month – the apple remained embedded in his flesh as a visible souvenir since no one dared to remove it' (1996a: 31–2). This wound, which is never treated, rots and infects his body, marking the beginning of his physical deterioration and contributing to Gregor's death in the end (1996a: 7–15, 29; see also Bruce 1996: 114–16).

Unlike Kafka, who always plays with linguistic ambiguities in his prose, Cronenberg, in his horror film *The Fly* from the beginning makes visible the grossness of the insect that Kafka did not spell out and did not want to be depicted: the film's very success lies in its combination of horror, fantasy and science fiction. Cronenberg agrees that 'metaphor is … the bedrock … of all literature' and that 'pure ideas are invisible', yet 'you can't do [it] on the screen in the same way. I have *to make the word be flesh*, and then photograph the flesh because I can't photograph the word' (Grünberg 2000: 91, 92). Thus, unlike Kafka, who keeps minimising the shock effect of Gregor's metamorphosis into a horrible vermin by increasingly bringing out the humanity inside him, Cronenberg wants the viewer to experience visually the physical and psychological effects of the metamorphosis on his protagonist and cannot spare the audience the sight of Seth's physical deterioration. Here we have an illustration of Marshall McLuhan's famous slogan, 'the medium is the message'. To be sure, media manipulates content and thereby the audience's response, but so can prose. Nonetheless, it is telling that despite their different art forms and techniques Kafka and Cronenberg also communicate a similar message. Walter Benjamin adds an important dimension to this discussion when he remarks that modern film 'is the art form that is in keeping with the increased threat to his life which modern man has to face. Man's need to expose himself to shock effects is his adjustment to the dangers threatening him' (1968: 250). Benjamin recognises that modern film 'corresponds to profound changes in the apperceptive apparatus' but relates these changes to a personal level even, to the alienating experience of individuals in 'big-city traffic' (1968: 250). Without this content – the threat of modernity, the anxieties of alienated modern man – modern film would not resonate with the audience. Content and form are thus inextricably linked. Benjamin's comments therefore apply to Kafka's (visual, metaphorical) prose as well, for outside of the protagonists shocking individual metamorphoses, there are many other threatening transformations – of contemporary social, political, racial, sexual, psychological, biological norms and prejudices – that the reader/viewer of both Kafka and Cronenberg needs to face, confront and adjust to.

Kafka's sensitivity to power relations – domination, subjugation, humiliation – pervades his entire oeuvre, and it is as true for him as for Cronenberg that 'the drive to transform is intimately related to issues of control and claims of and for agency' (Wilson 2011: 4). Without identifying specific issues, and still insisting on the vermin's indecipherable signifier ('vermin is born of the void' [Kafka 1954: 113]), Kafka nonetheless relates Gregor's fate to the negativity of his age:

> I have vigorously absorbed the negative element of the age in which I live, an age that is, of course, very close to me, which I have no right ever to fight against, but as it were a right to represent [...]. I have not been guided into life by the hand of Christianity ... and have not caught the hem of the Jewish prayer-mantle – now flying away from us – as the Zionists have. I am an end or a beginning. (1954: 114)

The specific 'issues of control and claims of and for agency' are the socio-political, economic and biological, essentialist, genetic discourses and prejudices of Kafka's age (see Gilman 1991, 1995): capitalism, 'scientific' racism and sexism, though only Gregor's sister Grete is directly affected by the latter.

Cronenberg points out the rather different social and economic situation of the two protagonists. Seth Brundle is a successful late-twentieth-century scientist, 'a star in the firmament of science, and it was a bold and reckless experiment in transmitting matter through space' (2014: 14), while the early-twentieth-century salesman Gregor Samsa is exploited on the job as well as by his own family. The economic situation of the Samsa family has been difficult, and Gregor only 'seems' well adjusted before his metamorphosis. He managed to cope after the bankruptcy of his father's business when he became the sole supporter of the family until the fateful morning of his metamorphosis. But he really is not adjusted at all, has no time for himself, hardly any friends and no love relationship (1996a: 31–2). The cause for his metamorphosis is seen as largely work-related: Gregor's mother believes that overwork made him sick, and Gregor himself immediately identifies his 'grueling job' (1996a: 3, 8) as responsible for his present condition. Gregor vividly describes domination and humiliation at the workplace: his boss at work is hard of hearing and makes his employee literally crawl to him (1996a: 4); and it is also a bit extreme to send the office manager to his home only a few hours after Gregor did not show up for work. The thought of having a little revenge on the manager or his boss naturally crosses his mind (1996a: 4, 8). Indeed, Kafka's social critique of capitalist society has been the subject of many critical commentaries on 'The Metamorphosis' (see, for example, Hughes 1981).

Gregor also states how easy it is for a travelling salesman to become the victim of 'prejudice … gossip, contingencies, and unfounded accusations' (1996a: 13). All of a sudden, though, a very specific prejudice is catching up with Gregor when he changes into vermin. Kafka mostly alludes to contemporary racial discourses and never establishes a clear link between the vermin metaphor and anti-Semitic discourses; nonetheless, contemporaneous genetically-based racial discourses are also responsible for Gregor's metamorphosis. Gregor experiences a regressive, backwards metamorphosis, a return to an essentialist original state. His increasing filthiness, when he 'drag[s] around with him on his back and along his sides fluff and hairs and scraps of food' (1996a: 35), intimates that there is no escaping from his genes: in the end he literally becomes the stereotypical expression 'dirty Jew' (see Gilman 1995: 195–6).

At this point, Kafka's and Cronenberg's protagonists are worlds apart. Cronenberg stresses that Brundle's metamorphosis is a 'rebirth … and transformation' which means that 'so much of what was there before is still there, and that's a fascinating thing to me, because we are constantly regenerating ourselves. Reinventing ourselves' (Grünberg 2000: 90). Clearly, Kafka's time period makes it impossible for Gregor to regenerate or reinvent himself, for the very reason that 'so much of what was there before is still there' (i.e. racism). Moreover, the very fact that Cronenberg can say of his Brundlefly's metamorphosis that it 'got interesting when it began to deal with the concept of genetic fusion' (Grünberg 2000: 84) again shows the great gap between the two artists. Cronenberg's ambitious scientist Seth Brundle consciously strives to overcome the boundaries of biological determinism by transporting himself into other spatial dimensions through teleportation, and succeeds. Kafka's lowly Gregor, involuntarily, also overcomes the boundaries of biological determinism by changing into vermin, yet ironically his particular metamorphosis reduces him to his supposed racial genotype by bringing out a genetic make-up, which was invisible before. While Cronenberg's protagonist's metamorphosis may have (r)evolutionary consequences for science, Gregor's is a death sentence.

The Fly represents Cronenberg's meditation on the dangers of modern science and technology in late-twentieth-century society and reveals the disastrous consequences that can result from human error. The film depicts a postmodern 'metamorphosis in its cybernetic transformation through media and computing devices […]. By the time David Cronenberg directs his 1986 remake of the 1950s versions, the personal-computerization of the teleporter adds to the text a posthuman narrator that drives the updated metamorph – the Brundlefly – to the edge of posthuman viability' (Clarke 2008: 10). Yet Seth Brundle's scientific experiment has gotten out of hand because of 'human' error, for Seth, in a fit of jealousy and alcoholic delusion, abandons his rational, scientific faculties when he decides to test the experiment on himself, enters the transporter, does not notice the presence of a housefly, their molecules merge, leading to the creation of the Brundlefly.

Like Kafka, Cronenberg presents us with a humorous side to the metamorphosis, when Brundlefly begins to explore his new life, and even remains humorously detached when Seth's body is changing, ageing and undergoing various stages of bodily disintegration, as when his ear falls off. What is thoroughly Kafkaesque in these scenes is the combination of humour and horror in Cronenberg's exploration of deeply rooted anxieties, which include the fear of losing control over one's body, of succumbing to irrational animalistic impulses, of being entirely at their mercy, which we see in Gregor as well. But Cronenberg also introduces a new and unforeseen element, reversing Gregor Samsa's situation, when he highlights that Seth, while deep in the throes of his transformation into a hideous fly/human hybrid, warns his lover with the remark: 'I'm an insect who dreamt he was a man and loved it. But now the dream is over, and the insect is awake.' Unlike Gregor, Seth has always been curious to embrace his new life even at the cost of losing his 'human' identity. As a scientist, Brundlefly is eager to analyse and study his own 'evolution' (he places his human body parts which fall off into 'the Brundle Museum of Natural History' to preserve this evidence for posterity). Gregor, however, will never accept his vermin status, has no desire to explore and understand his vermin consciousness, and instead keeps searching for his human signified. In contrast, once the 'insect is awake', Seth willingly opens himself up to the violent, amoral instinctual side of existence, lurking under the thin layer of civilisation. Seth realises that he has inadvertently been 'reborn' as *a new being* on the evolutionary scale. The genetic fusion has now given him human and insect consciousness with different degrees of awareness. He is indeed unique, one of a kind, and keeping a record monitoring his changes may be very valuable scientific evidence for the future evolution of mankind.

For this reason, Cronenberg's protagonist needs to uphold the constant tension between determinism, liminality and freedom, between the fixing of meaning vs. the flow of signification. This is also extremely important for Gregor, for the fluidity of signification is absolutely necessary for him to stay alive: it is a death sentence for him to be reduced to the vermin signifier. Cronenberg's Brundlefly, on the other hand, needs this freedom to enter ever-new levels of existence, of consciousness, of perception, reaching out for what no human has ever experienced before. Brundlefly's continuing new insights during his ongoing metamorphoses also provide further interpretive layers to the film, as when Seth Brundle states: 'Have you ever heard of insect politics? Neither have I. Insects ... don't have politics. They're very brutal. No ... compassion. No ... compromise. We can't trust the insect. I'd like to become the first insect politician.' The existence of creatures like Brundlefly, products of genetic experiments whose psychological and physical changes are irreversible, will obviously have political consequences for mankind. What is involved in these 'insect politics'? A new master/slave morality? Surely this means 'to begin to imagine a new order of consciousness; one that, for Brundle, does away with compassion and compromise' (Wilson 2011: 3).

However, this type of amoral postmodern consciousness is not new to Kafka at all; not surprisingly, he already in his own time foresaw modernity ushering in a similar new consciousness that also manifested itself in and through a 'new body'. Kafka's 'The Metamorphosis' ends with the liberated body of Grete, as we see her 'stretch[ing] her young body' (1996: 42), asserting her sexuality (ironically her moment of freedom is fleeting since she will soon be married off and her newly gained independence will be suppressed again in a new patriarchal household). Another example is the equally Nietzschean ending of Kafka's story 'Ein Hungerkünstler' ('A Hunger Artist', 1922) where the artist after his death is replaced by 'a young panther', 'whose noble body ... seemed to carry its freedom around with it; it seemed to lodge somewhere in the jaws; and the joy of life sprang from its maw in such a blaze of fire that it was not easy for the spectators to withstand it' (2007: 94). Through the metaphor of the young panther Kafka envisions the explosion of a body within the confines of a cage, bursting with power and sexuality. Thus, for Kafka an amoral animalistic 'humanity' is indeed ready and about to surface with the next generation, without any need for fusion of human and non-human genes at the genetic level. Both Kafka and Cronenberg, then, highlight the audience's attraction to a ruthless, instinctual humanity underneath the civilised surface of modernity.

II. *VIDEODROME* AND *A COUNTRY DOCTOR*: SEXUAL FANTASIES

Kafka's 'Ein Landarzt' ('A Country Doctor', 1917) is a surreal short story about a doctor who has been called to a patient in the middle of the night. The doctor cannot heal the patient, and the plot follows the protagonist's associative dream logic during which temporal and spatial distance collapse, reality and fantasy merge, until we reach the nightmarish end, which condemns the doctor to an endless wandering, like the Eternal Jew, 'Naked, exposed to the frost of this unhappiest of ages' (2007: 65). In contrast, Cronenberg's *Videodrome*, filmed in 1981 – when videotapes were new and digital media and computers were embryonic – 'announced the arrival of *homo technologicus,* that being who fuses the organic with the mechanical, in an apocalyptic atmosphere' and a plot which moves forward through hallucinations and 'fantasy logic' (Grünberg 2000: 64). Despite the different individual themes, Kafka's larger focus is on science and modernity, while Cronenberg's is on technology in postmodernity. Most strikingly, at the centre of both Kafka's and Cronenberg's narratives there is a remarkable 'great wound' that opens unexpectedly in the two protagonists' abdomens.

From the beginning, Kafka's country doctor is 'completely at a loss': he has been called to a patient but has no way of getting there because his horse has just died. Upset, he kicks the empty pigsty and out come two 'thickly steaming' horses, 'powerful animals' who 'crammed [the low doorway] full to bursting' (2007: 60). Along with them comes a groom, a brutal, animalistic human being; an alter-ego of the doctor (see Gray et al. 2005: 175) , he proceeds to assault the doctor's maid Rosa, the only one who has a (symbolic) name (see Goldstein 1966: 215–16), and leaves 'red marks of two rows of teeth' (ibid.) on her cheek. As the doctor is placed in a carriage, which 'sweeps him along like a piece of wood in a current' and arrives in no time at the patient's home, the last he hears is 'the door of his house bursting and splintering under the groom's assault' (2007: 61). As in a film, space and time collapse as the location suddenly shifts and the doctor enters a surreal, nightmarish virtual reality. The entire scene is filled with Freudian, sexual imagery, which bursts into the life of this man of science out of the 'unclean' pigsty.

Ironically, religious symbolism accompanies the doctor's encounter with patient and family. Kafka's allusion to the nativity myth, the 'Christ in the manger imagery' is obvious but represented in a humorously ironic fashion. The horses, 'lowering their well-formed heads like camels' (2007: 61), are not from the Czech countryside: they now push open the window from the outside and stick their heads in to look at the patient, the sick boy, who is surrounded by his family. At first the doctor is convinced that 'the boy is healthy', when all of a sudden he discovers 'yes, the boy is sick' upon seeing his 'open wound', like Jesus's, on 'his right side, near the hip' (2007: 62, 63). At this point the shape and colour of the wound causes a (con)fusion of the boy's physical and the doctor's own, psychological, 'wound': 'Poor boy, no one can help you. I have discovered your great wound; this blossom in your side will destroy you' (2007: 63). The word 'blossom' conjures up his love for his maid Rosa whose sexual attractiveness he only noticed when the groom wanted her, and this after years of living in the same house with her ('you never know what things you have in your own house!' [2007: 60]). The boy's wound now tellingly metamorphoses into a vagina with rose-red, 'Rosa', phallic worms 'writhing up toward the light' (2007: 63), representing the doctor's repressed sexuality.

Jesus imagery is also used with the country doctor himself: after the country folk undress him, he stands 'with [his] head bowed', another visual gesture, reminiscent of Jesus hanging on the cross, before they 'take [him] by the head and feet and carry [him] into the bed' laying him right next to the patient, 'beside the wound' (2007: 64). The doctor's undressing all the while has been accompanied by a choir of school children with their teacher, singing a song which makes clear that the health of the entire community depends on the doctor saving the boy: 'Undress him, then he'll cure us, / And if he doesn't cure us, kill him! / It's only a doctor, it's only a doctor' (ibid.). But this doctor knows he is no 'saviour'; he is 'only a doctor'. He understands the nature of the wound as a symbol of the ailment of modernity: a reminder that the country folk 'have lost their old faith; the pastor sits at home, plucking his vestments into shreds, one after the other; but the doctor is supposed to accomplish everything with his tender, surgical hand ... if you use me up for holy purposes, I will put up with that, too; what more can I ask for, an old country doctor, robbed of my maid!' (ibid.).

The doctor is a man of science who embodies modernity: being medium and message at the same time, he cannot heal what he *represents*. Similarly, the patient's wound, representing the illness of modernity, cannot be cured by the very science which causes it. Besides, the doctor is an atheist. The patient knows this and wants to 'scratch [his] eyes out' (ibid.). This kind of journey is bound to fail with horses that come from the 'pigsty' and the doctor noting 'blasphemously' how 'one horse neighs loudly at the ceiling' (2007: 62) instead of to heaven. As a matter of fact, the doctor cannot breathe in the ignorant environment ('the narrow confines of the old man's thoughts would make me sick' [2007: 62]) of this less than holy family, which is so irrational and superstitious that the doctor must eventually run for his life because they will kill him if he does not heal the patient.

'That's the way it is,' the doctor thinks, reflecting on the role of medical science in view of the psychological ailments of modernity; 'writing prescriptions is easy but all other communications with people are difficult' (2007: 63, 64). In a case like this he is impotent as a physician, and – to make matters worse – the sudden metamorphosis of the boy's wound into a vagina-like wound containing phallic worms reveals his sexual impotence to him as well. Ironically, it is now far too late even to save himself: no one can be saved, and his practice and Rosa are 'lost'. The only one who will survive is the raging groom who is assaulting Rosa. In Kafka's surreal, Freudian, commentary on modernity and its discontents, it is not the civilised man of reason and science who is fit to survive, but the instinctual, brutal, sexual, amoral individual who will triumph. As in many Kafka texts, this insight comes too late: 'Betrayed! Betrayed! ... It can never again be made good' (2007: 65). As far as the humane or moral advancement of mankind in the post-Enlightenment period is concerned, there is no visible progress in either Kafka or Cronenberg.

Thus, Cronenberg's representation of science/technology in *Videodrome* only initially reveals possibilities for human advancement: as in *The Fly*, technology can physically alter bodies, as well as change the way humans experience and perceive the world. During one of protagonist Max Renn's hallucinations in *Videodrome* a deep wound opens unexpectedly in the protagonist's abdomen, another 'imagined abdominal vagina' (Cronenberg 1997: 97). Max instinctively places his entire hand into the stomach slit to verify that the wound is really there. Cronenberg and Grünberg discuss this wound in relation to the famous Caravaggio painting, *The Incredulity of Saint Thomas* (1601–2), in which Thomas verifies that Jesus is alive again by placing his finger into the stabbing wound on his right side. Since Max is verifying the truth through his body, by reaching into his wound, Cronenberg is asked if he 'meant to say cinema becomes flesh' (Grünberg 2000: 72). His reply is that this 'would be the ultimate trans-substantiation. The Eucharist. The blood and body of humans made cinema' (ibid.). Cronenberg elaborates further, not on the level of content but theoretical speaking, that in cinema it is 'still a representation of flesh', never the 'real flesh', always an 'image' or a 'reflection of the flesh' (ibid.).

While Kafka, like Joyce, often plays with religious symbolism through linguistic puns or by transforming it humorously or ironically, as seen in his '(Ver)wandlung', or in 'A Country Doctor' where Jesus's wound quickly metamorphoses into a wound crawling with phallic worms, Cronenberg proceeds to redefine the concept of trans-substantiation for his own film medium. (Re)moving 'faith' to an entirely personal level of perception, he argues that 'we are able to make that translation ourselves. It's a force of will to be able to believe that wine is blood and that cinema is the human body' (ibid.). Reducing religious faith to 'a force of will' Cronenberg places it on the same level as any subjective experience of reality, truth or metamorphosis, no matter whether these experiences are drug induced or created through other kinds of hallucinations. Thus, Renn's abdominal wound stays with him throughout the entire movie. In fact, Cronenberg invents an entire hallucinatory plot with subplots around the wound and the 'new flesh,' moving – as Kafka often does – from one metaphor to another.

Exploring or deconstructing several layers of interpretation (also like Kafka), Cronenberg's first subplot 'posit[s] the possibility that a man exposed to violent imagery would begin to hallucinate. I wanted to see what it would be like, in fact, if what the censors were saying would happen, did happen. What would it feel like? What would it lead to?' (1997: 94). Thirty-four-year-old protagonist

Max Renn runs a small cable TV station, 'Civic TV' (based on Toronto's still existing City TV, co-founded by Moses Znaimer, which, in the 1970s and early 1980s, broadcast softcore pornography, the so-called 'baby-blue films' [Criterion Collection 2004]). Max cannot compete with bigger networks and is trying to drum up publicity by pirating free videos and showing them on his TV station. This is when he comes across the show 'Videodrome', which offers nothing but torture and murder. Max manages to get his hands on it and has no compunction about airing it on TV, rationalising 'better to live out your fantasies at home than in real life'. But soon after he has been exposed to the video, Max begins to hallucinate, and it later turns out that watching 'Videodrome' causes a malignant brain tumour. It also comes to light that the media guru Professor Brian O'Blivion (modelled on Canadian professor and philosopher of communication theory, Marshall McLuhan) had himself been working on these scientific experiments. As Prof. O'Blivion explains in a video before he dies, his tumour is not really a tumour but a new part or extension of his brain: ironically he also becomes the first victim of his 'philosophy'. Cronenberg aptly comments that it is no longer our environment that affects changes (as was the case with Gregor Samsa); rather, it is our mind and our technology that achieve this now (on the Criterion Collection DVD's special features, 2004). Max's physical and mental state is not unlike Seth's metamorphosis in *The Fly*: also by choice, though the situation is different, he is changing into a new species and becomes a human who can absorb objects or merge with technology. Cronenberg imagines a most original metamorphosis, transforming a yet inert TV set into an interactive one, turning it into a living, breathing being with veins and muscles. In an unforgettable scene, we see Max's body (in another metamorphosis induced by hallucinations) dissolve and join with the image of his lover Nicki on the screen, which moves and bulges out: he touches her lips and makes love to Nicki entering the TV set.

While Max is 'hallucinating his way through many transformations' (ibid.), the plot thickens with the addition of a political subplot, which develops out of 'the suggestion that the technology involved in *Videodrome* is specifically designed to create violence in a person; we know that by the use of electrodes in certain areas of the brain you can trigger off a violent, fearful response, without regard to other stimulants' (Cronenberg 1997: 94). Originating in the phenomenon of 'strange religious and self-help groups from the 1966s and 1970s' (ibid.), Cronenberg imagines a research group project or institute for Prof. O'Blivion, the Cathode Ray Mission, and the kinds of people it might attract. Prof. O'Blivion is oblivious to the fact that soon he is infiltrated by a right-wing group with a religious agenda, under the leadership of Dr. Barry Convex who has a very different 'vision' for the future of mankind (ironically he is the head of the Spectacular Optical Corporation). This group appropriates O'Blivion's research, directs his own technological insights against him, kills him, and 'sees' O'Blivion's TV as the perfect tool for manipulating and brainwashing the public. Their inhumane vision for a future society results in the creation of the 'Videodrome' tape: their weapon to power.

Fortunately, the 'Videodrome' seed, as it later turns out, is embryonic at this stage since it was not yet intended as a broadcast video for the world after all. In a Kafkaesque fashion, Cronenberg merges Kafka's ending of 'Vor dem Gesetz' ['Before the Law'] ('this entrance was intended only for you' [2007: 69]) with a twisted, postmodern version of Kafka's 'Eine kaiserliche Botschaft' ('An Imperial Message', 1931). Kafka's imperial messenger embodies a message intended for the world (a Christ-like, pre-McLuhan, literal enactment of 'the medium is the message'). The messenger was 'programmed' by a biblical emperor figure who entrusted him with this urgent message just before his death. Though the 'divine word' (Logos), carried within the messenger, has become 'new flesh' now, this messenger is only human: in Kafka's modernist, alienated universe, any hope for mankind is thwarted, because the message never arrives despite the messenger's super-human efforts. In Cronenberg, however, the message arrives: Max receives the 'Videodrome' message because it was all along meant specifically for him. Cronenberg hereby satirises his fictional Marshall McLuhan's scientific mission in manifold ways: by highlighting the religious foundation (Catholicism) of his slogan 'the medium is the message' through his Cathode Ray Mission, by giving him the name Professor O'Blivion for not 'seeing' the evil, destructive, right-wing forces infiltrating his mission, by making him the first victim of his scientific experiments which result in the 'Videodrome' invention, and lastly by turning the 'Videodrome' medium into a message of destruction for the world. The right-wing religious, fundamentalist group hates Max because he represents the freedom of postmodernity: they believe that his softcore porn TV station is 'rotting us away from the inside': 'North America is getting soft ... the rest is getting tough ... we have to be pure and direct and strong to survive them.' Convex and company, in fact, intentionally exposed Max to the video so that they could manipulate him for their ideological cause.

In Cronenberg's own words we are dealing here with 'a political group led by Dr. Convex, which plans to take over North America and do it through video brainwashing and managing to convince all of us that we are getting into dangerous times and need to get tougher and it's happening through TV' (Criterion DVD). Cronenberg highlights the significance of Max's friend Masha, a softcore pornographer, who alerts him to the dangerous ideology of this group and warns him: 'They have something that you don't have, Max; they have a philosophy.' Adding that 'more people get murdered in the name of various religious or philosophical concepts than do out of sheer animalistic anger and viciousness and even out of sheer sexuality in the form of rape and pillage and so on,' Cronenberg stresses how much more popular a murderous and perverse movement will be if it has a 'philosophy' behind it (ibid.). It is important that Dr. Convex's distorted vision is modelled on the American TV evangelist James Bakker, host of a popular Christian TV show (1974–89). Here we have 'a man of the cloth drawing in the right people in order to eliminate them' (ibid.).

Even though Kafka's superstitious country folk have distorted visions and are out to kill the doctor, there seems to be little that Kafka's modern malaise (nothing or no one to believe in) can have in common with Cronenberg's dangerous, right-wing fundamentalist political movement. Kafka's country folk have not found a new 'philosophy' yet, but religious superstition or fundamentalist fanaticism, combined with racism, have always existed across the ages. It is a question of degree, the extent of imminent or inflicted violence, which separates Kafka and Cronenberg here. The colour 'red' (Rosa) in Kafka can be linked with Nicki's red dress in Cronenberg: 'red' symbolises sexual arousal and violence, sado-masochistic practices, and Videodrome's sexual torture scenes. Moreover, the torture machine in Kafka's 'In der Strafkolonie' ('In the Penal Colony', 1914–1919), which draws blood while inscribing the victims' transgressions deep into their bodies, can be said to have an equivalent in Cronenberg's 'red clay wall', which evokes a Nazi torture chamber with body imprints engraved in the wall, an entire 'sculpture of pain and agony' (Criterion DVD). In turn, fundamentalist movements (evangelical or otherwise) in their most recent contemporary forms after 9/11 draw heavily on technology for brainwashing, indoctrination and terror in their conspiracy against the modern world. It has been said that 'although the film was made in 1983 in the waning years of the cold war, *Videodrome* is surprisingly in tune with the traumas of the post-9/11 audience' (Arroyo 2006: iv). To be sure, in Cronenberg generally 'it's your body that is the monster', yet he also acknowledges:

> In a strange way *Videodrome* did anticipate quite a few things that a lot of people have thought of this film as prophetic. I myself have never been interested in being a prophet of any kind, and I've never even been interested in inventing science fiction that would anticipate technological developments … but when your antennae are out there waving in the breeze and you allow them to develop because you consider yourself an artist, you will understandably pick up some signals from somewhere in the *Videodrome* way that other people don't pick up and I think it's inevitable perhaps that you anticipate things that other people have not. (Criterion DVD)

As for Max's wound, it also resembles a vagina, but Cronenberg 'outkafkas'

Kafka by turning the wound into an incubator where objects like a gun and the Videodrome tape become alive and turn into flesh. When Barry Convex and his followers insert the tape into Max's body, the Videodrome message takes over his mind and they can control him completely. Gregor Samsa's metamorphosis has been called 'a metamorphosis of the metaphor' (Corngold 1996: 82) because he literally becomes vermin. Similarly, by embedding or incorporating the tape into Max's body, Max undergoes a metamorphosis of McLuhan's slogan since his body has now literally become medium and message at the same time. Unlike Gregor's metamorphosis (which invites more interpretations than Gregor has legs), Max's metamorphosis reduces his mutated body to only one meaning, one message: the fleshy Videodrome tape, the new organ inside him, is ordering him to kill. The incubating gun was just waiting for the Videodrome tape to be inserted and waiting for the moment to be pulled out; the metal immediately penetrates Max's hand, fusing object and body, and like a killing machine Max goes on a killing spree and murders his colleagues. In this regard, it would be amazing to think of the torture machine in Kafka's 'In the Penal Colony' coming alive and having a life of its own. What if this new 'liberal' era in Kafka's story would not reject the torture machine but saw it as the beginning of a new relationship between humans and technology? What kind of horrendous penal colony could be created if this torture machine became flesh and would not merely drop its victims into the pit but merge with them? Kafka does not go there. His torture machine self-destructs in the end. Logically speaking, it has to break down when the officer himself, who embodies the message of the old commandant, places himself under the very medium which executes the message. At the same time, it seems as if the machine all of a sudden has a mind of its own, everything malfunctions; 'this was plain murder', revealing to the officer once and for all that his and its time is over by not granting him 'the promised deliverance' (2007: 57, 58).

In the end, Cronenberg does not go all the way either: his last subplot also involves ironic reversals. After pushing his protagonist to the limit, making him kill his friends and almost Brian O'Blivion's daughter Bianca, she eventually fights back and beats him with her father's same weapons: the TV becomes alive, a weapon emerges, reaches out of the TV set and shoots back at Max. Bianca then re-programmes Max and turns him around to fight for the 'good' cause of her father, by using the same manipulation techniques against the right-wing fundamentalists. Ironically, the same tools can be used in the service of opposing ideologies for the good or the bad of mankind. In order to crush the religious-fundamentalist conspiracy, Max now uses his wound as an incubator for weapons with which to fight the terrorists. Thus, he kills his former friend Harlan who turned out be the enemy: when Harlan reaches into his wound to place another fleshy tape into it, the wound closes and will not let go of his arm. When Harlan finally manages to pull it out, his hand is gone and instead a World War I hand-grenade is fused to his arm, killing Harlan. Max then proceeds to kill Barry Convex in public, at the Spectacular Optical trade show, with his flesh gun: Convex's entire body breaks open, spilling out his animated, squirming cancerous flesh, which rises to the surface like the phallic worms in Kafka's wound in his tale, 'A Country Doctor'.

After his mission is accomplished, Max retreats to an abandoned vessel in the Toronto harbour: isolated and alone, his last hallucination is of his lover Nicki on a TV screen, followed by his own suicide depicted on the screen, upon which the TV explodes, its human/animal guts bursting out. The TV message is clear: in order to rid himself of his own cancerous flesh, and in the name of the 'new flesh' (whatever this may mean, for there is no religious afterlife), he must kill himself. Since the Videodrome message was only meant for him instead of the entire world, Max is thereby able to save the world. Yet, as with Kafka, there is a final irony for we know that Max's suicide is not entirely a matter of free will, since the medium dictates the message: thus, it is intimated that Max is merely imitating the dictates of technology when he shoots himself. In the end, Max self-destructs like the officer and his torture machine in Kafka's 'In the Penal Colony'. Quite fittingly, the last sentence of the following interpretation of Renn's suicide or sacrifice for mankind eerily evokes the inscriptions of Kafka's torture machine in that story, which were engraved into the bodies of the accused before their inhuman and senseless murder: 'Unable to bear the physical transformation he has undergone, Renn shoots himself. In this last gesture, Renn's death is played out as an act of both sacrifice and emancipation, yet its deliberate ambiguity suggests that there is also nothing beyond carnality, the absolute truth and enlightenment written only in the mortality of the flesh' (Quinlivan 2012: 113).

III. KAFKA AND *NAKED LUNCH*

Naked Lunch is Cronenberg's most sophisticated and innovative transformation of the metamorphosis metaphor within a postmodern framework, where 'Otherness' is not a racial or social issue but a gender issue which extends even to 'bugwriters', i.e. male and female insect or – more specifically – cockroach typewriters. The Kafka references suggest that Kafka's work functions as a point of departure into the postmodern worlds of Interzone (here an imaginary place for Beatnik hippie counterculture involving drugs, writing, sexuality and corruption) and Annexia where different laws apply. The *leitmotif* of the movie is 'Exterminate all rational thought', echoing Joseph Conrad's *Heart of Darkness* (1899) – compare Kurtz's famous line, 'Exterminate all the brutes' and his final words, 'The horror! The horror!' Kurtz's experience in the Congo's heart of darkness is matched by Cronenberg's protagonist Bill Lee's journey to Interzone, a journey into irrationality, madness, 'down the tubes of hell' where there is 'no light at the end of the tunnel', 'looking for the bottom of humanity, the core' (Cronenberg, on the Criterion Collection DVD's special features, 2003). The events in the film are loosely based on Burroughs' own stay in Tangiers where he composed his autobiographical novel, *Naked Lunch*.

A major theme is extermination: the protagonist, Bill Lee, is an 'exterminator', a pest-control man by profession. As Janet Maslin points out, 'the film begins with smallish bugs. Then it moves on to ever more huge, horrible, and intelligent ones. Bill works in New York City as an exterminator and sees even that as a metaphor. "Exterminate all rational thought – that is the conclusion I have come to," he says' (2013: n.p.). Bill's wife, Joan, is one among many who is addicted to insecticide or bug powder and the first and only one who ever mentions Kafka directly. Shooting up the bug powder she remarks, 'it's a very literary high, a Kafka high. You feel like a bug.' Her comment feels like a mundane joke, a casual self-deprecating reference. Yet Kafka takes on a new twist when Gregor Samsa actually appears 'in flesh', in an official position, after Bill is arrested by two men (like Joseph K. in *Der Process* [*The Trial*, 1925]) and taken to the Interzone authorities who control the insect powder addiction business. Ironically, Joan's Kafka joke is really no joke any more when none other than Gregor Samsa, the representative of Interzone, pronounces her non-human, bug-like, and designates her as the first human to be exterminated: 'But who says she's really a woman? In fact, who says she's human at all?' According to him, Joan was an agent of Interzone Inc. and 'an elite corps centipede'. Gregor (he is nameless in the film) becomes Lee's 'case officer' and Lee his 'agent'.

Cronenberg's insect/beetle/cockroach is an innovative fusion of Kafka and Burroughs: he is a talking beetle who speaks through a hole in his back, which in 'The Metamorphosis' was caused by the wound created by the apple which his father threw at Gregor. Here, however, Cronenberg has transformed Gregor's wound into a Burroughesque anus: the bug talks through his asshole. Looking for a way to preserve this obscene metaphor of having an asshole talk (Burroughs 2009: 110) without having the censors descend on him, Cronenberg made Kafka's Gregor Samsa accomplish the task (Criterion DVD). The contrast between Kafka's Gregor who is so vulnerable that he hurts himself when he opens the door of his room (Kafka 1996a: 11) and Cronenberg's cold, vulgar and inhuman Interzone agent could not be greater. In addition, Cronenberg invents a wide range of insect substances and drug paraphernalia that move his plot along, such as drugs made from average insects, the 'black meat' of the giant Brazilian centipede or the 'Mugwump jism'; human insect breath that kills bugs; insect typewriters which dispense fluid and produce orgasmic writing. Kafka's beetle is also joined by other real and fabulous creatures, such as the afore-mentioned Mugwumps (alien junkies from Burroughs' novel *Naked Lunch* [Criterion DVD]), which become flesh in Cronenberg, or authentic giant African millipedes, venomous and a foot long. Cronenberg's universe clearly 'outkafkas' Kafka by bringing to the screen an absolutely original futuristic Kafkaesque world.

The title, *Naked Lunch*, suggests that nourishment is at least as important a metaphor for Cronenberg as it is for Kafka. Gregor Samsa, at one point, when he has almost forgotten that he is still human, hears his sister playing the violin and feels 'as if the way to the unknown nourishment he so longed for were coming to light' (1996a: 36). Similarly, Kafka's unger artist explains, 'I have to starve, I can't help it … because I could not find the food I liked' (2007: 94). Neither Gregor nor the hunger artist ever find the nourishment they are searching for. Cronenberg's Interzone has the answer: there is nourishment everywhere for everyone no matter who enters: it exists in the form of drugs, sexuality or through live typewriters who can even type on their own when they sense the writers' thoughts or ooze different kinds of fluid – to inspire the writers, or to express likes or dislikes of what they write.

Yet *Naked Lunch* is also a critical meditation on addiction, which 'is a metaphor for all the evils of escapism and all excursions into escapism' (Criterion DVD): addiction in Interzone is reached through drugs, sexuality and writing, all of which can overlap at any time. Almost the entire action of the film takes place in Interzone, where Bill is sent after he has killed Joan. However, in 'reality' Bill never leaves his New York apartment, though it transforms into an Interzone apartment. Cronenberg stresses that Interzone is a state of mind rather than a real exotic place like Tangiers in Morocco, where Borroughs lived after he killed his own wife. Interzone thus represents a mental space, an amoral world outside of the laws of civilisation, where no moral judgement is ever passed. Here, the protagonist becomes increasingly isolated and removed from the world and centred around himself. Bill's journey becomes a 'spiral of destruction' (ibid.), as we become witness to the deconstruction of his multiple identities the more he gets addicted to insect powder and insect nourishment, writing and heteroerotic, as well as homoerotic, sexual activity. Indeed, most humans in Interzone turn into postmodern human parasites, and are addicted to bug-powder and insect typewriters.

'Otherness' in Interzone is not a racial or social issue but decidedly a gender question, which is not deconstructed and presented critically. Bill, for one, is very ambiguous about his gender identities, which he can live out and explore here. Though homoeroticism is the preferable choice and overtly so, there is a great deal of phobia and anxiety associated with it, as was typical of Burroughs' time in the 1950s when it was impossible for artists like him or Allen Ginsberg to openly acknowledge and embrace their sexual orientation (ibid.). Bill meets an artist couple, the Frosts, who are sexually ambiguous in public – privately he seeks out boys, and she makes love to Bill but also has a relationship with her housekeeper, Fadela, who later turns out to be really Dr. Benway (who holds absolute power in Interzone) in disguise. Some sexual preferences are 'covers', like the masks that individuals wear to hide their identities.

The representation of women is extremely troubling in *Naked Lunch*: they are eliminated (at one point a female insect typewriter is brutally crushed by a male typewriter). We know already that Bill was ordered to 'exterminate' his wife before entering Interzone; we now find out that his entrance into the next stage, 'Annexia', requires the murder of his second wife, Joan. At this point the women turn out to be identical (they are also killed in the same fashion), which reveals the movie's underlying circular structure. This circularity, where endings and beginnings are arbitrary, though characteristic of postmodernism, also reveals the emptiness when *différance* becomes no more than a system of infinite circularity. Seeking ecstasy in this vicious circle, the individuals in Interzone participate in unlimited mutual destruction – thus, they also become victims of their own libidinal desires: eros and thanatos.

Writing is very important in this situation of existential emptiness, and not only because Bill Lee [i.e. Burroughs] is trying desperately to write his novel 'Naked Lunch', in order to create a true narrative about the murder of his wife. The agony of writing and the virtual impossibility to express oneself truthfully is something Kafka addresses in his diaries over and over again. Gregor Samsa therefore naturally appears in connection with writing. It is telling that writing is literally performed on live typewriters which have the shape of Samsa-like insects, for writing is indeed parasitical (not only in Cronenberg) because it feeds on itself. The bugwriters in *Naked Lunch* experience writing erotically and secrete fluids – a further example where medium and message exist together – which the artists who have regressed to the level of infants literally feed on in return. In addition, typing is depicted as an addictive, tactile-erotic activity. According to Janet Maslin,

> Mr. Cronenberg's hideously clever contribution in the latter realm is the insect-cum-typewriter that supposedly assists Bill in his efforts but clearly has a mind of its own. Both the writing bug and the Mugwump, a man-size and rather *soigné* strain of monster, are capable of registering their approval by oozing viscous, intoxicating substances from various parts of their anatomies. (2013: n.p.)

Here Cronenberg moves beyond the narcissistic self-referential type of writing, and evokes any writer's very real struggle: it shows in any artist's torment over how to express him/herself, as well as in the loathing of or intoxication with one's own work. Moreover, once the work is finished it will have a life of its own: at this stage it can reject or misrepresent the writer, and therefore the bugwriter may well ooze a toxic fluid when it senses the artist's work will turn against its creator.

This kind of organic, orgasmic and self-referential function of writing can be said to have an analogy in the many sadistic and masochistic hetero- and homosexual relationships in Interzone where individuals feed on themselves and each other through their creativity/writing and (homo-)sexuality. The link between writing and sexuality is present in Kafka as well who famously likened the writing of 'Das Urteil' ('The Judgment', 1912) to giving birth, 'covered with filth and slime' (1948: 278), and stated that the ending had made him think of 'a strong ejaculation' (Brod 1947: 129). Gregor's metamorphosis embodies masochistic self-destruction, but he also indulges in incestuous, sexual fantasies with his sister: he 'would raise himself up to her shoulder and kiss her on the neck, which, ever since she started going out to work, she kept bare, without a ribbon or collar' (1996a: 36). Unlike Gregor, Joseph K. in *The Trial* acts out his sexual fantasies: '"I'm coming," K. said, rushed out, seized her, kissed her on the mouth, then all over her face, like a thirsty animal lapping greedily at a spring it has found at last. Then he kissed her on the neck, right at her throat, and left his lips there for a long time' (1998a: 33).[2] Corngold rightly points out that 'the sexuality of writing is anaclitic on feeding as well' (2007: 83). As seen earlier, Gregor's sexual fantasies are caused by his sister playing the violin, which arouses his sexuality and makes him feel 'as if the way to the unknown nourishment he so longed for were coming to light' (2007: 61).[3]

Moreover, sexual paranoia and the fear of women are represented humorously in the 'bird' metaphor which Kafka employs for a flock of young women in *The Trial*, thirteen years and under, 'a mixture of childishness and depravity', who flutter around the painter Titorelli. These girls push themselves on him, insist on entering his apartment, manage to sneak in when he is absent, he finds them under his bed at night. They are a pest that he cannot get rid of and continually needs to chase them away (the joke is obvious for a German speaker because the verb 'vögeln' means sexual intercourse [see Kafka 1998a: 141–3]). On a more serious note, Karl Rossman in *Der Verschollene* (*The Boy who Sank out of Sight* or *Amerika*, 1927) is punished for fathering a child after being seduced by an older maidservant for whom he had 'no feelings' (1946: 26–7). In turn, Frieda's rape of K. in *Das Schloss* (*The Castle*, 1926), which continues for hours in 'the small puddles of beer and other rubbish with which the floor was covered', leaves K. with the feeling that 'he was lost or had wandered farther into foreign lands than any human being before him', suffocating 'from the foreignness but where the meaningless enticements were such that one had no alternative but to go on and get even more lost' (1998b: 41).

Kafka's writings are also 'saturated with homoerotic images' (Corngold 2007: 86). The word *Schmarotzer* [parasite] 'has a code meaning ... in the gay argot of Prague German at the fin de siecle. It means "gay"' (ibid.) and indeed a recent 2014 performance of *The Metamorphosis* made the gay reading quite explicit (see Farr 2007). Homoeroticism is depicted humorously at the end of 'The Metamorphosis' in order to satirise the three (religiously observant and meticulous) lodgers: these 'serious gentlemen' with 'long beards' who are 'obsessed with neatness', insist on having their food and environment pure and clean, 'especially in the kitchen' (1996a: 33). Kafka thereby exposes their own 'uncleanliness' according to religious law, and ridicules them, 'hopping right after [their leader]' (1996a: 41) as they are dismissed from the Samsa home. Moreover, apart from the voyeuristic male punishment fantasies in *The Trial*, when Franz and Willem are beaten and tortured in a 'junk room' for days on end (1998a: 80–7), 'In the Penal Colony' is 'sex-besotted – and at the level of the letter' (Corngold 2007: 83). The torture machine punctuates, pierces and penetrates the bodies of men who are stretched out on a vibrating 'bed' in the presence of a large audience, turning their punishment into a voyeuristic spectacle.[4] The universe of Kafka's 'In the Penal Colony' more than any other work equals Cronenberg's sado-masochistic amoral Interzone world in *Naked Lunch*. Kafka's formerly strict and unforgiving justice system of the penal colony has now been weakened through the influence of women, with female emancipation signifying the emerging liberal age where enlightenment or understanding is not produced through torture. However, despite the recent change in political leadership, symbolised by the new commandant who represents this new way of thinking (he is said to listen too much to women [2007: 47, 50]), there is no real change on the horizon.

The visitor, a 'great researcher from the West', who represents the enlightened, humanist thought of the modern world, could indeed speak up and help the modern forces to end this brutal procedure: since he had been invited as a legal expert, his 'judgment' was likely 'desired' and 'the inhumanity of the execution' was 'beyond all doubt'; but he refuses to interfere with internal state affairs, because he came 'with the sole purpose of observing' (2007: 46, 50). The final irony is that the researcher does not merely remain a passive observer: when the soldier and the formerly condemned man run after him and want to jump into his boat, instead of helping them he threatens and prevents them from escaping to the West, though both of them are products of the new age, as is suggested by their fixation with the ladies' handkerchiefs (2007: 55–6, 59). The enlightened Western researcher thus becomes an accomplice, not unlike Joseph K. in the flogging scene of *The Trial*. Fearing that Franz's scream, 'scarcely human, as if it came from some tortured instrument', will draw attention to K.'s presence in the room, K. brutally pushes Franz away from him, 'hard enough that the witless ['unconscious' in the original German] man fell to the floor and clawed convulsively about with his hands' (1998: 84, 86). Sado-masochism, voyeuristic sexual punishment fantasies, political opportunism and the weakness, cowardice, shallowness and emptiness of so-called enlightened Western societies characterise Kafka and Cronenberg's (post)modern worlds.

Very few of Kafka's characters are able to break out of societal structures and pressures, let alone 'come out' of the closet and assert their personal longings and (sexual) desires. One of Cronenberg's main themes in *Naked Lunch* is to psychologically explore Burroughs' fears of acknowledging homoeroticism as well as his desire for escape and rebellion, thereby exposing Burroughs' generation's sexual ambiguity, their fear of homoeroticism, and their self-destructive longings. Cronenberg's characters do embrace and live out their fantasies. Yet Kafka is never predominantly concerned with sexuality: though he addresses fear of women, as well as incestuous, heterosexual and homoerotic longings, there are many other non-gender-related interpretive (psychoanalytic, racial, political, cultural-historical) angles. The 'gay code' as well, 'while striking, is one of the many cultural allegories' (Corngold 2007: 86) that Kafka inscribes in his texts. Kafka's characters spend most of their lives in a web of shame and accusations, often caused by a higher authority that is never identified and can never be reached. Ironically, in *The Trial*, Justice is represented as an allegorical figure (in a Titorelli painting) who is blindfolded and represents 'justice and the goddess of Victory in one'. 'That's a poor combination, said K. smiling', insisting that Justice must be stable; however, this Justice figure turns out to be ever shifting: a few moments later she has already metamorphosed into 'the goddess of the Hunt' (1998: 145, 146).

Ultimately, gender is not the all-determining factor in Cronenberg either. Celebrating or embracing sexuality does not lead to sexual freedom for either sex because, as in Kafka, ultimately power relations are more important than gender (which is part of power politics). Unlike Kafka, Cronenberg does not even intimate the possible existence of an absent higher (God-ordained) authority. His authority figures are similar to Kafka's lowly, ugly, impotent, petty, lazy authorities, but his films send a stronger political message. Seth Brundle's statement, 'I'm an insect who dreamt he was a man and loved it. But now the dream is over, and the insect is awake,' along with his 'insect politics' without mercy or compassion, do become reality in *Naked Lunch*. There is real premeditated cruelty, murder and exploitation in Interzone of all who are psychologically vulnerable. Individuals literally turn into giant centipedes and eat each other alive.

Hans's drug factory in Interzone, which brings in a fortune, looks like a slaughterhouse with all the poor Mugwumps in chains in every corner, barely alive, being milked for money.

Moreover, Cronenberg's final recognition scene reveals where the real centre of power in Interzone lies. Two humans in particular turn out to be true insect types: one is Dr. Benway the spider, 'Big Brother', who has spread his spider web of power all over Interzone. He manipulates every mind; he is 'the ultimate ringmaster of the perverse', the charming doctor who is always so ready to help unfortunate addicts, though he has never even received his own medical degree (Criterion DVD). Nonetheless, he has managed to reduce everyone in Interzone to an infantile state of total dependency. Dr. Benway is not alone; significantly he exists in duplicate because he can be equally pleasant and cruel in male and female form (as the female Fadela and as himself), and in a final triumphant metamorphosis he rises up and reveals himself in his disguise. The other insect type is Ives Cloquet, the Swiss dandy, wealthy, attractive, smooth, intimidating and frightening, a 'sinister sexual predator' who 'devours [Bill]'s little friend Kiki' after he metamorphoses into a gigantic centipede (Grünberg 2000: 124). This kind of 'naked lunch' exposes a deep societal reality under the civilised veneer: the exploitation of *any* Other is not only amoral, without love, hate or passion, but ultimately no more than an exercise of brutal power. This insight, literally and symbolically, represents the end of Bill's journey to the core of humanity, Conrad's 'heart of darkness'. Stripping society and human nature to the very bone, Kafka and Cronenberg share Conrad's bleak philosophical position.

It is a miracle that Bill Lee is able to leave Interzone and escape from Benway's clutches. Crossing the threshold of the next stage, Annexia, suggests a return to the umbilical cord, which allows us to see the whole journey as one back to an origin, after this odyssey: home. He is the only character in the three Cronenberg films who survives. But the return home leaves us with only more postmodern circularity, self-referentiality, open-endedness and a continual deferral of meaning, particularly since we never see Annexia, which supposedly stands for the return to Bill's real old life. There is no resolution or closure since we are left in complete ambiguity as to whether the disappearance of the protagonist in Annexia amounts to final self-destruction or whether his return home should be seen as an act of self-liberation. The very name, Annexia, though, suggests that there will be as little freedom as in Interzone. No matter what political system or alternative realities, the human desire for power, control and domination at all levels of society is not likely to change.

In all three films Cronenberg has drawn on Kafka to present both the liberating and frightening aspects of (post)modern art by crossing and overcoming social, political and moral boundaries. *The Fly* takes 'The Metamorphosis' into the world of late-twentieth-century science, confronting the audience with the reality of genetic experiments and exploring the consequences. In turn, *Videodrome* changes Gregor's wound in 'The Metamorphosis', as well as the wound in 'A Country Doctor,' into a sci-fi wound which serves the power of the media to manipulate Max Renn into fighting for their right-wing evangelical cause; yet, the very same wound is also used to incubate weapons to fight the media's manipulation, indoctrination and terrorism. *Naked Lunch* transforms Kafka's vermin metaphor into postmodern human parasites that feed on themselves and each other through their creativity/writing, sexuality and endless mutual destruction.

Unlike Kafka, Cronenberg pushes his protagonists to the limit and beyond. His 'readings' of the unsettling and threatening possibilities in Kafka's metamorphoses and especially of his insect metaphor are highly original and even include a humorous dimension. When one considers how many postwar readers of Kafka have missed the humour and playfulness in his work, Cronenberg's insightful appropriation and transformation of Kafka is a rare exception. He shares Kafka's ironic vision of modernity, his sensitivity to power, his ironic detachment and dark comedy, which is evident even in gruesome scenes. To be sure, Cronenberg 'outkafkas' Kafka by pushing him into postmodernity. But does he leave him behind? Yes and no. Gregor Samsa, Joseph K., the victims in the Old Penal Colony, and many others do not survive, nor will the country doctor; similarly, Brundlefly needs to die, Max Renn races towards his own suicide, sacrificing himself for mankind, and it is doubtful if Bill Lee will find a new start in life. Like Kafka, Cronenberg may question the legacy of humanism as naïve; but ultimately he, too, offers no alternative.

NOTES

1   Four short paragraphs on Cronenberg's *The Fly* and *Naked Lunch* from a previous publication have been revised, integrated and developed into a new argument for this present essay; see Bruce 2002: 243–4.

2   Similarly, the groom, the country doctor's alter-ego, acts out his fantasies as well: 'But she had hardly reached [the groom] than the servant wraps his arms around her and slams his face into hers. She screams and comes fleeing to me: imprinted on the maid's cheek are the red marks of two rows of teeth. "You beast," I shout furiously, "do you want a whipping?"' (2007: 61).

3   Outside of the Hunger Artist who never finds his nourishment, there is also the vulture, drinking/eating the blood of the narrator/victim: '[the vulture] took wing, leaned far back to gain impetus, and then, like a javelin thrower, thrust its beak

through my mouth, deep into me. Falling back, I was relieved to feel him drowning irretrievably in my blood, which was filling every depth, flooding every shore' (1971: 443).

4   Many thanks to John Stout at McMaster University, Canada, for suggesting I include 'In the Penal Colony'.

BIBLIOGRAPHY

Arroyo, David (2006) *Videodrome, Trauma, and Terrorism: An Examination of Organizational and Emotional Dynamics* (MA thesis); available at: http://diginole.lib.fsu.edu/cgi/viewcontent.cgi?article=4181&context=etd (accessed 13 July 2015).

Baldassare, Angela (1992) 'Cronenberg's Naked Lunch: A Journey Beyond Reality', *Eye Magazine*; available at: http://www.davidcronenberg.de/eyelunch.html (accessed 24 June 2015).

Benjamin, Walter (1968) 'The Work of Art in the Age of Mechanical Production', *Illuminations*, ed. Hannah Arendt, trans. Harry Zohn. New York: Schocken, 217–51.

Bruce, Iris (2002) 'Kafka and Popular Culture', *The Cambridge Companion to Kafka*, ed. Julian Preece. Cambridge: Cambridge University Press, 242–6.

Burroughs, William S. (2009 [1959]) *Naked Lunch*. New York: Grove Press.

Bruce, Iris (1996) 'Elements of Jewish Folklore in Kafka's Metamorphosis', *The Metamorphosis*, Franz Kafka, ed. and trans. Stanley Corngold. New York: W. W. Norton, 107–25.

Brod, Max (1947) *Franz Kafka: A Biography*, trans. G. Humphreys Roberts. New York: Schocken.

Clarke, Bruce (2008) *Posthuman Metamorphosis: Narrative and Systems*. New York: Fordham University Press.

Conrad, Joseph (2005 [1899]) *Heart of Darkness*, ed. Paul B. Armstrong. New York: W. W. Norton.

Corngold, Stanley (1996) 'Kafka's Metamorphosis: Metamorphosis of the Metaphor', *The Metamorphosis*, Franz Kafka, ed. and trans. Stanley Corngold. New York: W. W. Norton, 79–106.

_____ (2007) 'Kafka & Sex', *Daedalus*, 136, 2, 79–87.

Cronenberg, David (1997 [1992]) *Cronenberg on Cronenberg*, ed. Chris Rodley. London: Faber & Faber.

_____ (2014 [1996]) 'Introduction: The Beetle and the Fly', *The Metamorphosis*. New York: W. W. Norton, 9–17.

Farr, David (2007) *Metamorphosis* by Franz Kafka, David Farr, and Gisli örn Gardarsson (Adapter). London, UK: Oberon Books. Toronto performance by British playwright and director David Farr with the Icelandic theatre company Vesturport. Royal Alexandra Theatre, Toronto, Canada (January 28–March 9 2014).

Gilman, Sander (1991) *The Jew's Body*. New York and London: Routledge.

____ (1995) *Franz Kafka, The Jewish Patient*. New York and London: Routledge.

Goldstein, Bluma (1966) 'A Study of the Wound in Stories by Franz Kafka', *Germanic Review*, 41, 202–17.

Gray, Richard T., Ruth V. Gross, Rolf J. Goebel and Clayton Koelb (2005) *A Franz Kafka Encyclopedia*. Westport, CT: Greenwood Press.

Grünberg, Serge (2000) *David Cronenberg – Interviews with Serge Grünberg*. London: Plexus.

Hughes, Kenneth (1981) *Franz Kafka: An Anthology of Marxist Criticism*. Hanover, NE: University Press of New England.

Kafka, Franz (1946 [1927]) *Amerika*, trans. Willa and Edwin Muir. New York: Schocken.

____ (1948) *The Diaries of Franz Kafka 1910 – 1913*, ed. Max Brod, trans. Joseph Kresh. New York: Schocken.

____ (1954) *Wedding Preparations in the Country and Other Posthumous Prose Writings*. London: Secker & Warburg.

____ (1971) *The Complete Stories*. ed. Nahum N. Glatzer. New York: Schocken.

____ (1996a [1915]) *The Metamorphosis*. ed. and trans. Stanley Corngold. New York: W. W. Norton, 1–42.

____ (1996b) 'Background and Context: Letters and Diaries', *The Metamorphosis*, ed. and trans. Stanley Corngold. New York: W. W. Norton, 61–73.

____ (1998a [1925]) *The Trial*, trans. Breon Mitchell. New York: Schocken.

____ (1998b [1926]) *The Castle*, trans. Mark Harman. New York: Schocken.

____ (2007) *Kafka's Selected Stories*, ed. and trans. Stanley Corngold. New York: W. W. Norton.

Langelaan, George (2005 [1957]) 'The Fly', *Adaptations: From Short Story to Big Screen: 35 Great Stories That Have Inspired Great Films*, ed. Stephanie Harrison. New York: Three Rivers Press, 176–203.

Maslin, Janet (2013) '*Naked Lunch*: Drifting In and Out of a Kafkaesque Reality', *The Criterion Collection*, 9 April 2013 (originally appeared in *New York Times*, 27 December 1991); available at: http://www.criterion.com/current/posts/305-naked-lunch-drifting-in-and-out-of-a-kafkaesque-reality (accessed 1 July 2015).

Meyer, Adam (1990) '"One of the Great Early Counselors": The Influence of Franz Kafka on William S. Burroughs', *Comparative Literature Studies*, 27, 3, 211–29.

Quinlivan, Davina (2012) *The Place of Breath in Cinema*. Edinburgh: Edinburgh University Press.

Wilson, Scott (2011) *The Politics of Insects: David Cronenberg's Cinema of Con-frontation*. New York: Continuum.

THE ABSURDITY OF HUMAN EXISTENCE: 'THE METAMORPHOSIS' AND *THE FLY*

WILLIAM J. DEVLIN & ANGEL M. COOPER

In Kafka's novella, 'Die Verwandlung' ('The Metamorphosis', 1915), Gregor Samsa awakens to find that he is a monstrous vermin. With the physical transformation having already taken place, Kafka invites the reader to follow Gregor's inner metamorphosis as he struggles with the challenge of losing his humanity to vermin-like instincts. Along the way, we find that Gregor loses this battle, as he transitions from clear consciousness, self-awareness and human concerns to an immersion into his bug-like body with less and less rational or conscious awareness.[1] At the same time, we find that Gregor also loses his social identity, as his family is forced to adjust to Gregor's bizarre condition. Though he initially desires to continue his role as provider for his family, Gregor instead becomes a burden to the family framework. Furthermore, as we suggest in this essay, it could be said that with the continued loss of both his humanity and his emotional and social connections to his family, Gregor succumbs to the meaninglessness of his existence and dies.

David Cronenberg creates a film inspired by 'The Metamorphosis' with his *The Fly* (1986) (and further writes the introduction to Susan Bernofsky's translation of 'The Metamorphosis').[2] Cronenberg tells the story of Seth Brundle, a quirky and eccentric scientist who creates telepods, or teleportation devices. While being documented by Veronica Quaife, a journalist for *Particle* magazine, Brundle discovers how to teleport animate objects. However, using himself in a human trial, he accidentally fuses with a housefly at the molecular genetic level. Unlike 'The Metamorphosis', however, Cronenberg invites the audience to follow Brundle's external metamorphosis as he gradually develops physical qualities of a housefly. Even though we witness the transformation from the objective perspective, Cronenberg captures the Kafkaesque loss of Brundle's humanity in the face of his bizarre condition. Deprived of his ability for clear mental reflection, his emotional stability and his social relationship with Quaife, Brundle loses his humanity. Like Gregor, he succumbs to the meaninglessness of his existence and asks Quaife to kill him.

In this chapter, we argue that both Kafka and Cronenberg present us with existential depictions of Albert Camus' notion of the Absurd. Camus maintains that the human condition is Absurd insofar as two conditions necessarily hold: (i) human beings live their lives searching for meaning in the world; and (ii) the world, itself, is devoid of any meaning whatsoever. Both 'The Metamorphosis' and *The Fly* demonstrate the absurdity of human existence by telling the tale of a human being in the bizarre setting of becoming a vermin. Furthermore, following Camus' analysis of the Absurd, both Gregor and Brundle must struggle with how to react to this condition of human existence. However, neither character follows Camus' advice to live with passion, revolt and freedom, thereby becoming the Absurd hero. Instead, both characters fall prey to Camus' other option – namely, suicide – as they lose their humanity and give up on life, resulting in their deaths.[3] Ultimately, we argue that both Kafka and Cronenberg's use of the bizarre setting of a physical metamorphosis into a vermin help amplify Camus' idea of the human condition, thereby forcing us, the audience, to reflect upon the absurdity of our own existence. Furthermore, we argue that because of the nature of these two media – the novella and the film – each work is able to depict the confrontations with the Absurd in its own unique way. On the one hand, Kafka provides the reader with Gregor's internal dialogue, primarily focusing on his mental struggle with the Absurd through his thoughts and feelings. On the other, Cronenberg provides the audience with Brundle's external transformation, primarily focusing on his physical struggle with the Absurd through his bodily changes and actions. Together these two works give us a deeper sense of the confusion, horror and feeling of exile that arises from the confrontation with the Camusian Absurd, thereby enhancing the audience's (reader and filmviewer) experience and understanding of the Absurd.

I. CAMUS AND THE ABSURD

Echoing the philosophy of the Ancient Greeks, Camus focuses his philosophical attention on the question of *eudaimonia*. But unlike his philosophical predecessors, Camus' assessment of human existence is darker and more sceptical. In his essay, *Le Mythe de Sisyphe* (*The Myth of Sisyphus*, 1942), Camus suggests that the human condition is essentially characterised by the Absurd. Paradoxical in nature, the Absurd is understood as the conjunction of two necessary conditions.

On the one hand, there is what we can call *the human-condition*: all human beings seek out a meaning or purpose or *telos* in their lives. Again similar to the ancient Greeks, Camus acknowledges that we are driven by a sense of wonder in life and so we question, what is the meaning of life? We are drawn to this question and cannot help but seek a reasonable answer so that we can make sense of our existence. For Camus, 'the meaning of life is the most urgent of questions' (1991a: 4) as it literally becomes a matter of life or death. But, on the other, there is what we can call *the world-condition*: the world is such that it does not reveal to us any such meaning or purpose. Instead, 'this world in itself is not reasonable, that is all that can be said' (1991a: 21). As such, though we seek meaning and purpose in our lives and in the world, the world is ultimately devoid of it. Herein lies the essential outcome of the Absurd: human beings live their lives by seeking that which does not exist.

It is important to note that, according to Camus, the Absurd is not simply an attribute of the human being; nor is it simply a property of the world: 'the Absurd is not in man (if such a metaphor could have a meaning) nor in the world, but in their presence together'; it is the combination of both the human and world conditions and is considered to be 'what links them' (1991a: 30). In this respect, the Absurd is 'the confrontation of this irrational [world] and the wild longing for clarity whose call echoes in the human heart. The Absurd depends as much on man as on the world. For the moment it is all that links them together' (1991a: 21).

Camus explains that one cannot circumvent the challenge of the Absurd by eliminating one of its conditions: 'To destroy one of its terms is to destroy the whole. There can be no absurd outside the human mind. Thus, like everything else, the absurd ends with death. But there can be no absurd outside this world either' (1991a: 30–1). One cannot cease to seek meaning in the world. Similarly, the world cannot suddenly reveal a meaning or purpose. Instead, the human being recognises that there is 'a confrontation and an unceasing struggle' (1991a: 31) with the Absurd. In *L'Homme révolté* (*The Rebel*, 1951), Camus suggests that the Absurd is 'an experience that must be lived through, a point of departure, the equivalent, in existence, of Descartes's methodical doubt' (1991b: 8). Camus admits that this lived experience is challenging, as it entails that the human being suffer through the feelings of exile: 'in a universe suddenly divested of illusions and lights, man feels an alien, stranger'; the human being is 'divorced' from his life and world, exiled from his home and without any real 'hope of a promised land' (1991b: 6).

Camus suggests that there are at least three different responses to the Absurd. The first response offers a solution to the problem by implicitly treating the necessary conditions of the Absurd as horns of a dilemma: either the human being stops seeking meaning in the world (i.e. eliminating the human condition) or there actually *is* meaning in the world (i.e. eliminating the world condition). With this dilemma in mind, one responds by accepting that the world really is meaningless and without purpose. Since this is the case, it follows that the human being must stop seeking a meaning or purpose in life. The only way to achieve this goal, however, is suicide. For Camus, the question of suicide is the 'one truly serious philosophical problem', the most 'urgent' and 'fundamental question of philosophy' (1991a: 3). Furthermore, a common response to the Absurd is to a make confession – 'It is confessing that life is too much for you or that you do not understand it' (1991a: 5). In other words, suicide is the act which focuses on the first horn of the dilemma of the Absurd by eliminating the human drive for meaning and purpose. Further, by admitting that either (a) it is too challenging to live in the world and not seek meaning or (b) it is too challenging to comprehend what it means to live in a meaningless world, suicide secures the elimination of the human condition by removing the human being entirely from the equation. Since the Absurd is the combination of both the human and the world conditions, suicide not only destroys the human being, it also destroys the Absurd.

Like suicide, the second response to the Absurd also offers its solution by implicitly treating the necessary conditions of the Absurd as horns of a dilemma. While suicide focuses on the first horn of the dilemma, responding to the Absurd by eliminating the human condition, the second option focuses on the second horn by attempting to eliminate the meaningless world, i.e. the world condition. Such a world is sublimated through hope, 'hope of another life one must deserve', an idea 'will transcend' the world and 'give it a meaning' (1991a: 8). The feeling of exile, associated with the exhaustion of living a meaningless life and the confusion about a meaningless world, may help motivate the response of suicide. However, Camus suggests that hope is another common response: 'In a man's attachment to life there is something stronger than all the ills in the world. The body's judgment is as good as the mind's, and the body shrinks from annihilation' (1991a: 8). Human beings quickly 'get into the habit of living', a habit developed prior to the 'habit of thinking' so that, even in the face of the Absurd, we shy away from both suicide and accepting that life is meaningless. Having grown accustomed to living, we would rather choose to continue living and, with hope and faith, hold steadfast to the belief that the world ultimately provides us with meaning and purpose. By doing so, one is able to escape the Absurd by destroying it – not by destroying the human being, but by destroying the world.

Ultimately, Camus rejects both responses. On the one hand, he recognises that suicide is a means to escape the Absurd, but one that rests on faulty logic.

He acknowledges that 'One kills oneself because life is not worth living' is a truism, but is 'unfruitful' as a reason for suicide as it remains unclear as a *justification* for suicide (1991a: 8). That is, Camus opens up room for exploring alternatives that may exist between moving from the premise that the world has no meaning to the conclusion that one should commit suicide. Thus, he remains sceptical of eliminating the human condition. On the other hand, Camus suggests that hope is, itself, an act of suicide – particularly a 'philosophical suicide' (1991a: 28–51) as it is a means to escape the Absurd through a 'typical act of eluding, the fatal evasion' (1991a: 8). It is a 'diversion' and 'trickery' insofar as one practices self-delusion by believing in a world that does not exist. Targeting the existentialists, Camus argues that, 'through an odd reasoning, starting out from the absurd over the ruins of reason, in a closed universe limited to the human, they deify what crushes them and find reason to hope in what impoverishes them' (1991a: 32). Similar to the response of suicide, that of hope makes a logical error of moving from the meaninglessness of the world to the deification of the Absurd. The Absurd's properties of paradox and irrationality then become qualities of God. God, in turn, restores meaning to the world, thereby making life worth living. Thus, as with suicide, Camus is sceptical of eliminating the world condition through subterfuge and misguided logic.

Following 'absurd reasoning', Camus suggests another reason for rejecting both suicide and hope: namely, both commit a false dilemma. More specifically, both responses assume that there are only two responses to the Absurd – either eliminate the human quest for meaning or eliminate the meaningless world. Given this dilemma, each response chooses one horn and follows through to eliminate one of the necessary conditions and with it, the Absurd itself. Together, each response reveals alternative methods for escaping the paradox. But Camus suggests that, by only recognising two choices, each response misses a third option. Rather than escape the Absurd, the third option entails living with the Absurd. Here, the individual accepts both of the necessary conditions that constitute the paradox, and lives through the experience of the Absurd as a confrontation and unceasing struggle. To do so, Camus explains that one lives with *revolt*, *freedom* and *passion*. Analogous to one who is condemned to death, the human being is filled with revolt insofar as he rebels against the meaninglessness of the world (1991a: 54–5); he has an Absurd freedom insofar as he lives independently for the moment and unbound to any future (1991a: 56–60); he lives with passion insofar as he has the 'most living', or the greatest depth in the moments of life he experiences (1991a: 60–4).

Camus uses Sisyphus as the paradigm of the 'Absurd hero' to flesh out this option (1991a: 119–23). First, Sisyphus faces the Absurd through his condemnation by the gods to eternally push a boulder to the top of a mountain, only to find it roll back down to the bottom. His consistent act of pushing the boulder marks the human condition of seeking meaning and purpose (in this case, the successful completion of keeping the boulder on top of the mountain). Meanwhile, the fact that the boulder will eternally roll back down demonstrates the world condition. The boulder will never remain at the top, so Sisyphus is struggling for something unattainable. His world will not provide the meaning he desires in that it is not possible for him to reach his goal. Second, Camus argues that Sisyphus confronts the Absurd. But rather than escape it by suicide or hope that meaning will be restored, he accepts it by living with revolt, freedom and passion. In turn, Sisyphus's ceaseless struggle gives him a 'silent joy' as it is *his* struggle and the rock 'is his thing'. Following Sisyphus's plight up and down the mountain, Camus concludes that 'one must imagine Sisyphus happy' (1991a: 123).

II. GREGOR SAMSA AND THE INTERNALISATION OF THE ABSURD

Philosophically, 'The Metamorphosis' is a foray into the Camusian Absurd. Kafka presents a narrative that depicts a physical manifestation of the Absurd through the character of Gregor Samsa and his interactions with the world around him. Gregor is a human being who has morphed into a monstrous vermin, but who continues to try and live a traditional human life. Following Camus' analysis of the human predicament, Gregor desires meaning in a world that is meaningless. However, the world around him is not able to provide the meaning he craves.[5] Gregor remains in the human environment, living in his apartment with his human family. As a vermin, this environment can no longer give Gregor meaning because a vermin cannot achieve the goals and purposes of a human being. Gregor experiences a literal divorce between his desire for a human life and the reality of his insect existence. Therefore, in the Camusian sense, Gregor must experience, and struggle with, the Absurd.

Kafka offers us insight into this experience and struggle by writing in the third-person limited point of view of Gregor. In this respect, while Gregor does not directly tell the story of his metamorphosis and struggle with the Absurd, we, the readers, still get his voice from the narrator. As such, we are privy to the internal workings of Gregor's mind. We have direct access to his personal thoughts and feelings about the situation he is in, his mental responses to the world around him, and his emotional predilections in his bug-like state.[6] Here, Kafka presents the internalisation of the struggle with the Absurd, and invites the reader to experience Gregor's internal struggle. Not only do we see Gregor's actions as he struggles to accept a life devoid of the meaning he craves, but we also experience the mental anguish he feels due to his Absurd condition. It is mostly through Gregor's internal voice that we observe him follow Camus' three responses to the Absurd condition. Gregor undergoes each of Camus' responses to the Absurd, and although he has a brief moment of Absurd heroism – namely, through accepting his condition with the passion of listening to his sister play the violin – he ultimately fails to become the Absurd hero, instead choosing the first response to the Absurd, physical suicide.

Prior to his metamorphosis, Gregor is a normal, everyday man who seeks meaning and purpose in his existence. For Gregor, such meaning is centred on being the provider for his family and working as a travelling salesman. He describes himself as working hard, never missing work due to sickness and quickly moving up in his career because of his excellent work ethic. His mother explains, 'that boy has nothing on his mind but the business' (1986: 10). Though Gregor does not love his work, he recognises it gives his life purpose and stability. He spends much of his time working and thinking about his job, as he explains that 'travelling is a hardship, but without it I couldn't live' (1986: 16).[7] Furthermore, Gregor's hard work at his job is done for the sake of his family. Gregor's family is important to him, and one of his most defining characteristics is the care he has for them. Here, we see Gregor's human-condition of the Absurd. The meaning and purpose in his life is found in providing for his family. He dotes on supporting his family, explaining that after his family's business disaster 'his sole concern had been to do everything in his power to make the family forget as quickly as possible the business disaster' (1986: 27). Not only is it important to Gregor that his family is financially stable, but also that they are free from worrying about their future stability. Thus, his relationship with his family and his role as their provider give his life meaning.

To achieve this meaning, Gregor relies upon his capacity for reasoning and problem-solving, valuing the ability for calm rational deliberation. At first, he rationally determines what he should do in his odd situation. He thinks about whether he should get out of bed or try and go to sleep 'forgetting all this nonsense' (1986: 3). He attempts to reason with his family and his manager in order to deal with his metamorphosis. And he is systematic in his thoughts and arguments. When attempting to persuade the manager into allowing him to go to work as a vermin, he explains each point as to why that manager should allow him to work: i) he needs his job and he is willing to work; ii) he has great past accomplishments, which suggests he will work all the harder; and iii) he appeals to the manager's unique perspective and understanding of the trials of the travelling salesmen (1986: 16). Moreover, he mentions that his family does not understand his work and finances, so it's important to him to be the rational one, who can think things through calmly. Thus, Gregor identifies himself as the provider of his family and the rational head of the household.

However, when Gregor wakes at the start of the story, we find that the goals and purposes he previously had are unattainable due to the fact that he is now a vermin. In the Camusian sense, Gregor's insect body serves as a metaphor for the world-condition of the Absurd. Despite all of Gregor's goals and plans to achieve a meaningful life, the world itself will provide no such meaning. He can no longer maintain his human identity, fulfil his plans, and hold onto connections to the world. First, as a vermin, he cannot work as a travelling salesman. When his boss arrives at his apartment, one look at Gregor's new form sends him running for the door. Gregor can barely communicate with others as a vermin, let alone go to work. Second, he loses his relationship with his family. Once they discover that Gregor is a vermin, they are disgusted by him. Neither his mother nor his father will even enter his room. His father treats him with hostility, chasing him with a cane and throwing things at him. Even his sister, Grete, who is initially sympathetic to Gregor's vermin-state, eventually finds him to be a burden and stops caring for him. Third, although he retains his capacity for reason in Part I of the novella, his rationality eventually diminishes. His vermin-like instincts take over, and he often acts before thinking. When trying to reason with the manager and his family, he instinctively snaps at the spilled coffee (1986: 18). When his father is hissing at him, the narrator explains that the sound made 'Gregor lose his head completely' (1986: 19). As the story continues Gregor thinks less and relies more heavily on his vermin instincts, using his antenna, hiding under the couch and crawling on the ceiling.

Gregor thus embarks upon his experience of the Absurd. His world becomes devoid of the meaning it once had since he is incapable of attaining his goals or pursuing his purposes. With the loss of his goals, he also loses his identity. He is no longer the provider for his family, the travelling salesmen or the calm voice of reason. More importantly, he cannot be those things. As Camus explains, it is one's relationship to the world that makes for the Absurd. Gregor's desire for human meaning in a world where he is a vermin is doomed to failure. Kafka thus provides an existential depiction of the human being experiencing the Absurd by creating the strange circumstances of the human being becoming a vermin. Through the metaphor of the metamorphosis, and Kafka's internalisation of the struggle to carry out a meaningful life under such conditions, the reader more easily understands Camus' idea that the world is meaningless and without purpose. We see how senseless Gregor is as he strives to initially carry on like nothing has changed. And, following Camus, we can more easily see how Gregor, the paradigm of the common man, has three options for how to respond to the Absurd.

Gregor explores all three of Camus' responses. Gregor's first response to the Absurd is philosophical suicide: although he can no longer secure the meaning he craves in his new existence as a vermin, he has hope that his search for meaning will somehow bear fruit. In other words, by eliminating the world-condition, Gregor attempts to follow the same purposes he had as a human being, essentially, ignoring his vermin-state. He holds out hope that his life will return to normal and he will find meaning from the world, thereby escaping the Absurd.

We can see Gregor cling to hope in various ways. He attempts to retain his identity as a travelling salesman by trying to get out of bed and go to work. Though it is inconceivable that he can continue to work as a vermin, he tries, nonetheless. He rolls about on his bed, tipping himself onto the floor, thinking about how long it will take him to pay off his family's debt and about getting dressed. Anxious about being late, he focuses on a human problem rather than a vermin one: he needs to hurry or he will be late. This is a problem for the travelling salesman. However, his real problem is that he is a vermin and cannot go to work at all, but he ignores that problem at this stage. The narrator explains Gregor's reasoning, stating:

> He saw clearly that in bed he would never think things through to a rational conclusion. He remembered how even in the past he had often felt some kind of slight pain, possibly caused by lying in an uncomfortable position, which, when he got up, turned out to be purely imaginary, and he was eager to see how today's fantasy would gradually fade away. That the change in his voice was nothing more than the first sign of a bad cold, an occupational ailment of the traveling salesman, he had no doubt. (1986: 6)

Rationalising that his vermin-state is a temporary sickness, Gregor continues focusing on the mundane human problems and thinks of himself as a travelling salesman, rather than acknowledge the problems of being a vermin. He hopes that like phantom pains he has felt in the past, being a vermin will turn out to be a fantasy. Furthermore, we see his attempt to maintain his capacity for calm rationality. Even in his vermin-state, he strives to rely upon reason to solve his problems, believing that if he could just think rationally, all would be well again. As mentioned previously, Gregor tries to reason with his manager. He stands upright – as a human would stand – at his bedroom door and gives a long speech to his boss so as to explain that he will work out the problem of his vermin-state and come to work (1986: 16). Even after the manager runs fearfully for the door, Gregor continues to chase after him in order to try and reason his way out of the dilemma.

Gregor also ignores the horror his family feels at the sight of him, hoping instead that his relationship with them will continue as it was before. After becoming a vermin, he persists in thinking that he must provide for the family, believing he will pay off their debts. The narrator explains, 'Gregor was still here and hadn't the slightest intention of letting the family down' (1986: 11). Even though he has become a vermin, Gregor believes that his relationship with his family will not change. He is also confused at their reactions toward him. He does not understand why they are horrified and why his father treats him aggressively. He believes that his father chases him with a cane because he is confused rather than because Gregor is a vermin (1986: 18). Later, his sister enters his room, and he seems annoyed at the fact that she is frightened of the sight of him. When his sister notices him hiding under the couch, she slams the door in fear. Gregor then thinks, 'God, he had to be somewhere, he couldn't just fly away' (1986: 23) – as if her fright is unreasonable. Thus, despite his condition, Gregor continues to hope that the world will provide meaning and purpose. But, as Camus suggests, hope is a delusion grounded in misguided logic. Gregor's hope is a diversion, blinding him to the facts of his situation. He is not a travelling salesman. He is not calm and rational. He is not the provider for his family. He can no longer attain this meaning from the world. Yet he continues to act as if the world actually does contain such meaning for him. It is interesting to note that, on Camus' analysis of Kafka and his works, Gregor's steadfast hope in the face of this tragic and bizarre condition is no surprise. As Camus remarks, 'the more tragic the condition described by Kafka, the firmer and more aggressive that hope becomes' (1991b: 133).

But, as the internalisation of his metamorphosis unfolds, Gregor eventually begins to realise that the world will not offer him the meaning he believed it would, and loses his hope, abandoning the attempt to respond to the Absurd by eliminating the world-condition. Instead, following Kafka's invitation to witness the internalisation of the struggle with the Absurd, in Part II we find that Gregor has adapted to his vermin-state, feeling 'an almost happy absent-mindedness' (1986: 32): he depends less on reason and more on vermin qualities; he feels comfortable in hiding places (1986: 23); he is fond of walking on the ceiling and walls (1986: 31–2); he relies on his antenna (1986: 21). By Part III, Gregor almost completely relies on instinctive actions, nearly abandoning his capacity for reasoning entirely. His social relationships and interactions undergo a radical paradigm shift. He completely gives up on the idea that he can work in his current condition, and no longer ponders working or providing for his family. He becomes more irritable, pretending to attack the cleaning woman in order to scare her away (1986: 45). He stops listening to his family's conversations, and takes little interest in others: 'lately he was showing so little consideration for the others; once such consideration had been his greatest pride' (1986: 48). He also takes little interest in other tasks, as 'his indifference to everything was much too deep for him to have gotten on his back and scrubbed himself clean against the carpet, as once he had done several times a day' (ibid.).

With Gregor's apparent acceptance of his vermin-state condition, Kafka offers us a glimmer of 'hope' that Gregor will be his Sisyphus: the Absurd hero who is ready to confront the Absurd and face his unceasing struggle against it with revolt, freedom and passion. This glimmer is rooted in one relationship that remains special to Gregor: that with his sister. Upon hearing his sister playing the violin, passion stirs within him. He ponders:

> Was he an animal, that music could move him so? He felt as if the way to the unknown nourishment he longed for were coming to light. He was determined to force himself on until he reached his sister, to pluck at her skirt, and to let her know in this way that she should bring her violin in to his room, for no one here appreciated her playing the way he would appreciate it. He would never again let her out his room – at least not for as long as he lived; for once, his nightmarish looks would be of use to him; he would be at all the doors of his room at the same time and hiss and spit at the aggressors. (1986: 49)

Here, we see Gregor's situation akin to Sisyphus. As if Gregor is condemned to be a vermin, he confronts the Absurd, prepared to eternally guard his bedroom doors and protect Grete so that she can flourish as a violinist. Rather than hope that somehow meaning will be restored in the world, Gregor is no longer in denial. Although he questions whether an animal could appreciate music, he accepts that he is a vermin and even plans to use his new vermin abilities to scare away aggressors. Like Sisyphus, he sees a way to confront the Absurd – rather than escape it – and so is filled with revolt against the meaninglessness of the world. He has an Absurd freedom, as he is living for the appreciation of this moment, and not for unattainable future human purposes or goals. And he lives with passion insofar as he has the 'most living' in his relationship with his sister. Like Sisyphus's rock, Gregor's relationship to his sister 'is his thing' and so gives him a 'silent joy', allowing us, the readers, to consider the possibility that Gregor may be happy.

But Kafka does not allow for such a life-affirming conclusion to his narrative, opting instead to emphasise the Camusian idea that experiencing the Absurd is an 'unceasing struggle'. Gregor's plan to become the Sisyphean Absurd hero is only a dream. Immediately, we find that the new tenants (who his family invited to sublet a room) see Gregor approaching Grete, upsetting her playing. They become angry as Gregor's father ushers them away from the sight of Gregor and an argument ensues. Gregor eventually makes his way back to his room. After Grete's pronouncement that 'things cannot go on likes this' and 'we must get rid of it [Gregor]', Gregor finally gives up his desires completely. The narrator explains, 'his conviction that he would have to disappear was, if possible, even greater than his sister's' (1986: 54). With his sister's rejection, Gregor turns to his final response: suicide. Unable to eliminate the world-condition and unwilling to continue the unceasing struggle, he chooses to eliminate the human-condition, himself, thereby finalising his escape from the Absurd. As Gregor realises that he will not find any meaning in the world and that his human purposes and goals are lost to him, he eventually gives up on living a human life altogether.[8] Losing all human desires and even seeming to give up on life as a vermin, Gregor stops eating. As if he were confessing that life is too much for him, Gregor's 'head sank down to the floor, and from his nostrils streamed his last weak breath' (ibid.).

Though the reason for Gregor's death is ambiguous enough to be open to several interpretations, we suggest that his death – whether it was literally the result of suicide or not – metaphorically connotes Camus' idea of physical suicide in response to the Absurd.[9]

Even if Gregor does not physically commit suicide, his death suggests that he gives up on any desire for meaning or purpose in life. He ceases to seek meaning through his work, through his relationship with his family and through his identity as a calm rational human being. In essence, Gregor's death constitutes the elimination of the human-condition and so the elimination of the Absurd. Though Gregor had a chance to become the Absurd hero, Kafka's internalisation of the struggle with the Absurd shows us that his demise entails the method of escape and the confession that life is not worth living.

III. SETH BRUNDLE AND THE EXTERNALISATION OF THE ABSURD

Inspired by 'The Metamorphosis', Cronenberg adapts the Kafkaesque portrayal of the Absurd through his cinematic piece, *The Fly*. In this unique free-adaptation, we follow Seth Brundle, an eccentric scientist who is developing the first teleportation system, referred to as 'telepods'. After a series of setbacks allowing him to only teleport inanimate objects, Brundle finally achieves the ability to teleport organic beings. But a botched experiment occurs where he and a fly are simultaneously teleported, leaving Brundle and the fly to become unified at the molecular-genetic level. Analogous to 'The Metamorphosis', the film unfolds as we witness Brundle's transformation and adaption to becoming the 'Brundlefly'.

The narrative schemas presented by both Kafka and Cronenberg are nearly identical: there is a human being that transforms into a vermin (more specifically, a fly for Cronenberg); the metamorphosis into the vermin includes the gradual adaptation to the vermin-body, the diminishment of reflective reasoning and the prominence of instincts; the new human/vermin hybrid undergoes stages of confusion and delusion and becomes disconnected from the world around him; he further loses all social ties to those he loves; and, finally, the story culminates with his death. While both pieces have identical key narrative tropes, there are at least two essential dissimilarities between 'The Metamorphosis' and *The Fly* – dissimilarities that, we argue, help Cronenberg to 'give flesh' to the Kafkaesque portrayal of the Absurd through the cinematic experience. That is, Cronenberg provides us with the visual experience of watching Brundle's transformation externalised through his bodily changes and his superficial reactions. As pointed out by Cronenberg (2014), the first striking difference is between the characters of Gregor and Brundle. While Gregor lives a mundane life and becomes representative of everyman, Brundle is living anything but the normal life. Alone and entrenched in his scientific project, he lives in his laboratory, with apparently no connection to the outside world. Likewise, Brundle is far from everyman. He is quirky but perspicacious; and while, at this point, he is an unknown in the scientific community, he is intently focused on completing his work that will 'change the world and human life as we know it'. As Cronenberg explains: 'Unlike the passive and helpful but anonymous Gregor, Brundle was a star in the firmament of science, and it was a bold and reckless experiment in transmitting matter through space (his DNA mixes with that of an errant fly) that caused his predicament' (2014: 14).

The second, and more prominent distinction between Kafka and Cronenberg's works concerns the perspective the author and director offer the audience. As mentioned above, Kafka offers us an internalisation of the struggle with the Absurd through the third-person limited point of view of Gregor. There, we are given direct (though limited) access to Gregor's personal thoughts and feelings, his mental reactions to the world around him and his emotional predilections through the voice of the narrator. As such, we become familiar with, and can come to identify with, Gregor and his challenges. Kafka is able to show us Gregor's condition through Gregor's internal dialogue, which explains his thoughts, feelings and reflections about his condition. Unlike Kafka's tale, however, we are not given access to the internal workings of Brundle's mind. In order to follow the style of the novella, Cronenberg would have to include a voice-over in the film which explains Brundle's thoughts and feelings. However, this technique would most likely be less effective and limiting to the cinematic medium. That is, Cronenberg provides us a perspective of the struggle rooted in the literary third-person objective point of view: in this point of view, the audience views the story through a third-person neutral narrator. The narrator is outside of the story and has no special knowledge of the characters' thoughts or feelings. As a film, *The Fly* offers us the moving image of the transformation into the insect and, in so doing, Cronenberg allows us to visualise the metamorphosis as an outsider. Unable to be privy to the internalisation of Brundle's struggle, we are permitted to only witness the struggle from an external perspective or point of view. That is, we see more of Brundle's physical changes and superficial reactions than we see his thoughts. This view is emphasised all the more by the character of Brundle. Reticent by nature and used to working and being alone, Brundle is often left to his own thoughts, leaving the viewer wondering what he is thinking. As his love interest and new assistant, Veronica Quaife, tells him while videotaping a failed teleportation of a baboon, 'We've got to do this, Seth. Talk to the tape. Get in the habit. The world will want to know what you're thinking.' As such, the film, as a moving image, rounds out Kafka's portrayal, by giving us the external visual of the struggle with the Absurd.

As Seymour Chatman explains, 'in its essential visual mode, film does not describe at all but merely presents; or better, it *depicts*, in the original etymological sense of the word: renders in pictorial form' (1980: 128; emphasis in original). Kafka can affectively describe Gregor's condition through his thoughts and feelings. Cronenberg can only present Brundle's condition through pictures and sound. Another example of the difference between the presentation of the two characters dealing with the Absurd is in how their transformations begin. Gregor awakens as an almost fully formed vermin without any explanation as to how or why this transformation occurred. He slowly gains use and comfort of his vermin body, and his rational capacity diminishes over the course of the narrative. Kafka uses the description of the narrator to show Gregor's transformation and disconnect from his former life. As mentioned already, Gregor often thinks back to his work and his relationship with his family before his transformation, explaining his thoughts and feelings during the time when he had a human body. Meanwhile, turning to the cinematic medium, we find that Cronenberg would have a challenge translating the narrator's function in 'The Metamorphosis' to film. As Chatman points out:

> The central problem for film adapters is to transform narrative features that come easily to language but hard to a medium that operates in 'real time' and whose natural focus is the surface appearance of things – hence film's traditional difficulties with temporal and spatial summaries, abstract narratorial commentary, representations of the thinking and feeling of characters, and so on. (1990: 162)

Rather than attempt to traverse the difficulties of representing Brundle's internalised thoughts and feelings, Cronenberg creates a reticent character. As such, we need to experience Brundle's transformation from the outside. *The Fly* begins with a completely human Brundle, immersed in his human life. Contrary to Gregor's metamorphosis, we learn of the meaning and purpose of Brundle's transformation, as we watch the metamorphosis take place, primarily focusing on the physical aspects and his outward reactions.

Together, these two distinctive marks help to enhance Kafka's rendition of the Absurd by offering the viewing audience a different angle or perspective of the human experience of the Absurd. To begin, following Camus' philosophy, we find that like Gregor, Brundle's journey leads to the experience of the Absurd. While Gregor's human-condition, or meaning and purpose in life, is characterised as providing security and stability for his family, Brundle's human-condition is defined in a more grandiose and far-reaching fashion: namely, to complete his teleportation system and 'change the world and human life as we know it'. For Brundle, as he explains to Veronica, this purpose will be achieved through the visual and physical presentation of his own teleportation: 'And the book will end with me transporting myself fifteen feet through space from one telepod to another. That's what's really missing.' Since we can experience Gregor's internal dialogue, we can see his connection to human meaning through his thinking and reminiscing about his familial relationships. Without such an internal dialogue for Brundle, we observe his connection to humanity through the importance he places on changing the world and human life. He makes this statement to Veronica at the start of the film. However, we get an even deeper sense of his connection to human meaning later, when his human body transforms into the body of a fly. He creates the Brundle Museum of Natural History, storing his shed body parts for science and humanity. Both Gregor and Brundle find their human lives important and monumental to who they are, and this depicts the first aspect of their relationship with the Absurd. It depicts their desire for human meaning. But we are shown this desire in two different ways based on the different mediums used.

Although Brundle and his human condition has the potential for making him a famous individual with a historical groundbreaking scientific advancement, Cronenberg shows us that his lot is the same as the everyday travelling salesman. Like Gregor, Brundle must experience the Absurd when the world-condition – the condition that the world is meaningless – reveals itself. Further, like Gregor, Brundle experiences the world-condition through the metamorphosis. Although Brundle is able to achieve his goal of transporting himself from one telepod to another, he does so at the cost of becoming an insect, thereby emptying his goals of changing the world and human life of any meaning or value.

Furthermore, through the third-person objective point of view, we are able to witness the visual metamorphosis of Brundle into the Brundlefly, which allows us to experience the struggle of the Absurd in a whole new way. With the cinematic depiction on the screen, we are able to experience the struggle with the Absurd as an outsider looking in. We, the viewers, are wrought with horror and anguish as observers watching Brundle's physical transformation take place, as he develops coarse insect-like hair on his back, displays super-acrobatic strength and endurance, gruesomely loses his fingernails, oozes puss, vomits and grows bumps over his face and body, until his eventual complete transition to a human-size fly. From his erratic, aggressive and energetic reactions, to his violent outbursts and abusive handling of Veronica, we are filled with confusion as we see his emotional and mental transformation unfold. Here, we can view another difference between Kafka's and Cronenberg's depictions of the characters responses to the Absurd. Both Gregor and Brundle feel a loss of control of their human emotions as they transform into vermin. However, in 'The Metamorphosis', the narrator simply tells us about Gregor's outrage. As noted previously, he explains that the hissing sound his father makes leads Gregor to 'lose his head completely'. We are then left to imagine the feeling of Gregor's inner loss of control. Cronenberg, on the other hand, shows us Brundle's loss of control through his angry actions and outbursts. We can watch this loss of control rather than imagine it as with the character of Gregor. As such, Cronenberg's film enhances our experience and understanding of Kafka's portrayal of the struggle with the Absurd.

The cinematic third-person objective point of view further enhances this experience and understanding of the struggle through Brundle's responses to the Absurd. Though Brundle does not offer us a glimpse of the choice of the Absurd hero, like Gregor, he attempts to escape the Absurd through both philosophical and physical suicide. First, following Kafka's novella, Brundle's initial response is one of hope. Brundle attempts to eliminate the world-condition by having faith that his metamorphosis into the Brundlefly allows him to transcend the meaninglessness of the world by deifying himself in the Camusian sense. He believes that his metamorphosis will change him in such a way so that the world, itself, will have meaning. As Cronenberg explains, 'certainly my Brundlefly goes through moments of manic strength and power, convinced that he has combined the best components of human and insect to become a super being, refusing to see his personal evolution as anything but a victory even as he begins to shed his human body parts, which he carefully stores in a medicine cabinet he calls the Brundle Museum of Natural History' (2014: 15). Brundle sees his strength and agility as human enhancements rather than deformities. It does not occur to him that these 'enhancements' are actually non-human qualities that can destroy his goals. With these qualities, he gains newfound stamina and energy, becoming, what he considers, a super-scientist and a super-lover. His goals of changing the world and having a relationship with Veronica seem *more* attainable to him, not less attainable. In this sense, Brundle sees himself as transcending the two necessary conditions of the Absurd insofar as he is a superhuman fly and, as such, the world can offer him meaning and purpose.

Both Gregor and Brundle deal with the Absurd through hope, but they do so differently. We see Gregor's hope by his willful ignorance of his condition. As noted previously, at the start of the story, Gregor repeatedly ignores his transformation and thinks about getting out of bed, getting dressed and going to work. Gregor's hope is shown through his internal dialogue. Cronenberg cannot explain Brundle's thoughts in the same way as Kafka can in the novella. Instead, Brundle's hope appears through his exhilaration at his super-human abilities. The story continues as we watch Brundle do pull-ups, flips, hand stands, etc. Here, we see Brundle's hope through his exhilaration and through the testing out of his new abilities. Again, both characters depict hope in face of the Absurd, but we are able to have a different experience of that hope through the separate mediums used. Like Gregor, Brundle's meaning will include the escape from exile by having an intimate connection to the one he loves. While Gregor was primarily tied to his sister, Brundle is tied to Veronica. In order to achieve a meaningful life, Brundle believes that Veronica must go through the teleport system just as he did, so that they can share the same experiences. Brundle wants Veronica to be just like him. Despite several invitations, Veronica continuously rejects the idea. This is where the cinematic third-person objective point of view becomes prominent once again. Here, we the audience can understand Veronica's vehement rejection as we can literally *see* the horrors of the metamorphosis. Whether it's the boils growing on Brundle's face and body, his aged and withered stature as he attempts to use a walker to stand like a human being, or even his mutated body that walks on the ceiling and walls, we are repulsed by the image and so identify with Veronica's response. The visual personification of the human-insect believing he can co-exist with others in this world and live a meaningful life allows us to see the delusion of having such hope that Camus had warned us about. Cronenberg picks up on this frame of mind, as he suggests that Gregor, Brundle and even he, himself, undergo this experience: 'our reactions, mine and Gregor's, are very similar. We are confused and bemused, and think that it's a momentary delusion that will soon dissipate, leaving our lives to continue as they were' (2014: 9). But we, the viewers, see the hope exposed for what it is through the moving images of Brundle's transformation – that is, Brundle's attempt to ignore or resist the Absurd.

The disconnect between these characters' desire for meaning and their inability to obtain meaning, can be seen further through their different inabilities to communicate. Gregor literally cannot speak. At the start of 'The Metamorphosis', he is just barely understandable. He makes a great effort to call through the door to his parents. But as the story continues, he completely loses his ability to speak. It would be difficult in a film to have a main character who cannot speak, and Brundle is able to speak throughout most of the film. However, like Gregor, he is also unable to *communicate*. Brundle's main goal after beginning his transformation is to persuade someone to transform with him. He tries to explain to Veronica how exhilarating his transformation is, but he cannot get his thoughts and feelings across to her. She refuses to go through the telepods.[10] Neither Brundle nor Gregor are able to communicate to the people they care the most about and who connect them to human life.

Another example where the film and novella are able to depict the characters' disconnect with human meaning in different ways is through Brundle's and Gregor's strange food preferences. Gregor's sister brings him a bowl of milk and he runs over to it, ready to consume it all. However, the narrator explains that Gregor quickly pulls back from the milk, disgusted by it, even though it used to be his favourite drink (1986: 21–2). Later, his sister brings him 'old half-rotted vegetables; bones left over from the evening meal, caked with congealed white sauce; some raisins and almonds; a piece of cheese, which two days before Gregor had declared inedible' (1986: 24). Gregor explains that he eats all the old rotten foods, but not the fresh ones. He is now disgusted with foods he loved and likes rotten foods he previously deemed inedible. Here, the disconnect between Gregor and his human life is growing as he loses his humanity. Brundle has a similar experience with food. However, we think, this is one place where the film is able to show the character's disconnect with the human world more effectively than the novella. First, Brundle heaps piles of sugar into his coffee, which Veronica points out casually. But later, as he becomes more transformed, he invites Veronica over and while sitting in front of her regurgitates onto his food, like a fly. She gasps, horrified, with tears in her eyes, and leans away, repelled by Brundle. Brundle looks at her with a confused expression, but then realises, 'Oh, that's disgusting.' Chatman explains: 'Though the visual imagination may be less stimulated by a film than by a novel, the conceptual imagination may be very much stimulated by, say, a face filled with emotion that goes unexplained by dialogue or diegetic context' (1990: 162). Although there is sound from the characters with Veronica's gasp and with Brundle's statement, this scene illustrates Chatman's point, as it demonstrates exactly what both Kafka and Cronenberg are trying to get across – the growing disconnect between these characters and their previous human lives. Like Veronica, the audience is repelled by Brundle, but more importantly, Brundle is initially confused by this reaction, and his confusion is almost as horrifying as his actions. He is swiftly losing his understanding of human emotions, and with it, his own humanity.

The power of the moving picture continues as we watch Brundle's transition from hope to suicide. As he becomes more and more fly-like, losing his humanity and gaining insect-like instincts, he realises that he is not becoming a superhuman. He is becoming something other and as such cannot attain his previous goals. His awareness of the Absurd, in the meaninglessness of the world, begins to surface as his exile from human life becomes more apparent. Unable to convince Veronica to join him, a fully transformed Brundlefly attempts to force Veronica into a telepod so that he and Veronica can be physically unified at the molecular-genetic level. However, once again, Brundle's experiment goes awry. Instead of fusing with Veronica, he fuses with the telepod itself. Now, part human, part fly and part machine, Brundle physically personifies the realisation that his hope was simply a delusion and that, ultimately, the world will always be void of meaning and purpose. Like Gregor, it is when Brundle is completely disconnected from the one that he cares the most for that he finally realises he has no hope for meaning in the world. Aware of this hopelessness, Brundle points Veronica's shotgun at his head, thereby suggesting to Veronica and the audience that he now chooses suicide to eliminate the human-condition and, thereby, the Absurd. Even though Brundle goes through another transformation here, he does so because he is attempting to transform Veronica, so that she can be like him. Thus, his reason for wanting death is his realisation that he is completely disconnected from the person he cares for, and from humanity. Gregor also chooses to give up on his life because of the loss of his family and his growing disconnect from his human life. This is the last instance where Brundle and Gregor have a similar reaction to the Absurd, but through experiences that are more appropriate for their differing mediums. We experience Gregor giving up on his life through his thoughts about disappearing. We experience Brundle giving up on his life through his action of holding the gun barrel to his head. Both of the characters' final choices in response to their conditions are reflected through the media in which they are presented. Gregor thinks, and Brundle acts.

IV. WRITTEN AND CINEMATIC PORTRAYALS OF THE ABSURD

Cronenberg creates a visual portrayal of 'The Metamorphosis' with *The Fly*, demonstrating Kafka's narrative of the Absurd, and in so doing, Camus philosophy. Kafka depicts the Camsuian Absurd through Gregor's metamorphosis into a monstrous vermin. Moreover, the way in which Gregor deals with the Absurd follows Camus' three responses to the Absurd. In *The Fly*, following Kafka, Cronenberg also depicts the Absurd through Brundle's transformation into a fly. Brundle, too, responds to the Absurd with philosophical suicide and then physical suicide. But he never reaches Absurd heroism. Although both the novella and the film depict similar character arcs with Brundle and Gregor, they are unique in their portrayal of the Camsuian Absurd. That is, 'The Metamorphosis' shows the internal struggle with the Absurd, while *The Fly* shows the external struggle. As such, they each allow the reader or audience to access this struggle with the Absurd in different ways. Although both characters go through a mental and physical transformation, Kafka focuses on the mental struggle, while Cronenberg focuses on the physical struggle.

In 'The Metamorphosis', we experience Gregor's internal dialogue. We are aware of his thoughts and feelings as his mind slowly transitions into that of a vermin. When Gregor awakens in the novella, he has already completely changed into a vermin. We do not see that process occur. However, his mind remains that of a human being. With the third-person limited point of view, Kafka is able to give the reader access to Gregor's mind as he loses his job, his family and his rational capacity. We can follow Gregor's thought process and feelings as he first turns to hope as a response to the Absurd, has a fleeting moment with Absurd heroism, and eventually succumbs to physical suicide. In *The Fly*, we watch as Brundle transforms into a fly, experiencing the transformation from the outside rather than the inside. We do not have access to Brundle's thoughts and feelings. Instead, we see Brundle's physical transformation. We watch his body slowly deteriorate as he becomes more and more fly-like. Together they can provide a better understanding of Camus' philosophy of the Absurd. Although human beings do not metamorphose into vermin, Camus' argues that we each are confronted with the Absurd. Both 'The Metamorphosis' and *The Fly* demonstrate the confusion, horror and feeling of homelessness that accompany that confrontation. They also show the various responses one can have towards the Absurd and how such feelings can lead to those responses. We get Gregor's actual thoughts and feelings of this confusion, horror and loneliness. We do not get the internal dialogue from Brundle, but we do get to watch these same feelings as we watch his deterioration into a fly. We experience the confusing, horrifying and lonely confrontation with the Absurd through Brundle's physical struggle. Thus, each medium is able to portray the Absurd in a way that better suits the format of that medium. On the one hand, the novella portrays the internal struggle with the Absurd by allowing the audience access to a character's horror from his own mind; on the other, the film portrays the external physical struggle with the Absurd by allowing the audience to see the character's horror through moving images. Together they can provide a deeper understanding of the confusion, horror and loneliness – in short, the experience – that accompanies the confrontation of the Camusian Absurd.

NOTES

1. While it is true that Gregor continues to have human aspects, such as the capacity for thought and general consciousness, throughout the novella, these elements are overshadowed by Kafka's emphasis on the transformation into the monstrous vermin. For a further discussion of Gregor's psychological indeterminacy that is created by his possessing a private psychological interiority with a seemingly rational consciousness, while at the same time exhibiting insect-like behaviour, see Sweeney (1990) and Corngold (1973).
2. Strictly speaking, Cronenberg's film is an adaptation of George Langelaan's 1957 short story, *The Fly* (also adapted to film in 1958). Although it is officially based on Langelaan's story, we suggest that it is arguably closer to Kafka's story; see Cronenberg's article for his discussion on his film, Langellan and Kafka (2014).
3. Shimon Sandbank (1989) explores the philosophical worldviews and understandings of the Absurd offered by Kafka and Camus. There, he acknowledges Kafka's influence upon Camus, as well as the existential philosopher, Jean Paul Sartre.
4. In this respect, Camus is wondering 'if there is a logic to the point of death?' Furthermore, while 'it is always easy to be logical … it is almost impossible to be logical to the bitter end'. In other words, Camus suggests that suicide is an act that culminates, not with a logical line of reasoning, but with 'emotional inclination' (1991a: 9).
5. Moreover – the transformation itself is meaningless, reasonless and purposeless. This leaves the condition of the reader, desiring meaning in a meaningless transformation, in one's own predicament of confronting the Absurd.
6. Roy Pascal refers to Kafka's use of the narrator as the 'non-personal narrator' in that the narrator is subordinated to the main character, Gregor, so that the narrator 'identifies himself almost completely with Gregor' (1982: 32–3) thereby allowing us direct access to Gregor's consciousness.
7. As the narrative progresses, we see the truth of this statement. Without his job and the other goals that are important him, Gregor will not live.
8. One may argue that he not only gives up on the human life, but also on living at all.
9. Kevin W. Sweeney suggests that there are at least three interpretations, each related to different views of personal identity in 'The Metamorphosis'. According to the duelist view, Gregor commits suicide by starving himself to death 'because he realizes the hopelessness of the situation'. Meanwhile, the materialist view holds that Gregor dies of natural causes, as the 'change in eating habits and death indicate … the course of the vermin's life cycle, exacerbated by the infected wound from the apple thrown by the father.' Finally, the social constructionist view holds that with the loss of his relationship to his family, and the loss of his job, Gregor 'emotionally and socially starves to death' (1990: 33–4).

10 We can also view Brundle's inability to communicate with Veronica through his confusion at her disgust when he regurgitates on his food in order to eat it like a fly. In this scene, he cannot comprehend her human emotions, and as such, their ability to understand one another becomes even more of a struggle.

BIBLIOGRAPHY

Camus, Albert (1991a [1942]) *The Myth of Sisyphus and Other Essays*, trans. Justin O'Brien. New York: Vintage Press.
____ (1991b [1951]) *The Rebel: An Essay on Man in Revolt*, trans. Alfred A. Knopf. New York: Vintage Press.
Chatman, Seymour (1980) 'What Novels Can do that Films Can't (and Vice Versa)', *Critical Inquiry*, 7, 1, 121–40.
____ (1990) *Coming to Terms: The Rhetoric of Narrative in Fiction and Film*. Ithaca, NY: Cornell University Press.
Corngold, Stanley (1973) *The Commentators' Despair: The Interpretation of Kafka's Metamorphosis*. Port Washington, NY: Kennikat Press.
Cronenberg, David (2014 [1996]) 'Introduction: The Beetle and the Fly', *The Metamorphosis*, Franz Kafka. New York: W. W. Norton, 9–17.
Kafka, Franz (1986 [1915]) *The Metamorphosis*, trans. Stanley Corngold. New York: Bantam Books.
Langelaan, George (2005 [1957]) 'The Fly', in Stephanie Harrison (ed.) *Adaptations: From Short Story to Big Screen: 35 Great Stories That Have Inspired Great Films*. New York: Three Rivers Press, 176–203.
Pascal, Roy (1982) *Kafka's Narrators: A Study of His Stories and Sketches*. Cambridge: Cambridge University Press.
Sandbank, Shimon (1989) *After Kafka: The Influence of Kafka's Fiction*. Athens, GA: University of Georgia Press.
Sweeney, Kevin. W. (1990) 'Competing Theories of Identity in Kafka's *The Metamorphosis*', *Mosaic*, 23, 4, 23–35.

'THIS IS NOT NOTHING': VIEWING THE COEN BROTHERS THROUGH THE LENS OF KAFKA

IDO LEWIT[1]

In March 2004, the *Washington Times* published excerpts from a 'promotion-talk' between filmmakers Joel and Ethan Coen and Tom Hanks, the star of their then-upcoming feature *The Ladykillers* (2004):

> Mr. Hanks: Didn't you guys want to do something on Kafka at some point? Didn't I read a script on Kafka?
> The Coen brothers (in unison): No.
> Joel: Steve Soderbergh did.
> Mr. Hanks: I know there was that, but I think I read something else of yours, like three and a half years ago.
> Ethan: When we're bored…
> Joel: Yeah, when we're writing, we sometimes decide to take a Kafka break.
> (Anon. 2004)

The term 'Kafka break' was mentioned by the brothers on several other occasions. In another interview, included in the DVD commentary for *The Big Lebowski* (1998), they state that 'usually, if we haven't done it by page 70 [of the screenplay], we arbitrarily throw in a "Kafka break"'. Later in the same interview the brothers recall the scene of the Dude's hallucination in *The Big Lebowski* as an example of a 'Kafka Break'. The term is also mentioned in the DVD commentary on *The Man Who Wasn't There* (2001), where they explain the decision to omit an alien encounter dream sequence because it is 'too much of a "Kafka break"'. Judging by these instances it seems that a 'Kafka break' is an unrealistic or hallucinatory scene that does not refer specifically to any literary work by Franz Kafka.

Still, one can detect affinities to Kafka's oeuvre throughout the Coen Brothers' filmography. The early scene in *The Big Lebowski*, in which a couple of thugs break into the protagonist's apartment and demand the repayment of an alleged debt, mistaking him for a different man by the same name, is somewhat reminiscent of the opening of Kafka's *Der Prozess* (*The Trial*, 1925). In *A Serious Man* (2009) the name of the protagonist's neighbour, Mrs. Samsky, evokes Samsa from 'Die Verwandlung' ('The Metamorphosis', 1915). When asked where her husband is, Mrs. Samsky replies that 'he travels' – indeed, Gregor Samsa is a travelling agent. In *The Man Who Wasn't There*, the legal system is described as hopelessly inconsistent and mindlessly bureaucratic, which brings *The Trial* to mind. Moreover, the film's title is evocative of the English translation of Kafka's first novel *Der Verschollene* (*Amerika: The Man Who Disappeared*, 1927).

These Kafkan allusions, however, are sporadic and carry little substantial weight. The Coen Brothers seem to have read little of Kafka,[2] and as they reply to Tom Hanks they probably never meant to make a film on him. Nevertheless, in this essay I suggest that a profound affinity between the works of Kafka and the Coens can be extracted by scrutinising the ways both make use of the possibilities of their respective media in addressing the same existential predicament – an epistemological crisis and its effect on human agency.

After introducing the epistemological crisis in Kafka and the Coens, I will address the former's linguistic choices using two methodological approaches which can be designated – using Jakobsonian terminology – as *referential* and *metalingual*. While both approaches assume, implicitly or explicitly, the exclusiveness of literary expression, I will show that distinctively Kafkan tropes have respective cinematic parallels in two recent Coen films: *A Serious Man* and *Inside Llewyn Davis* (2013).

I. THE EPISTEMOLOGICAL CRISIS

Kafka's work is all about failure: from his failure to complete and publish his stories and novels through his characters' failure to fulfil their aims, to his commentators' despair. Within his narratives, failure predominantly takes the form of an epistemological crisis, a futile struggle to know and understand.

Samsa – and the reader – is kept perceptually at bay from the mystery of his transformation, Josef K. from the enigma of his guilt and K. the land surveyor from the secret of the castle (see Sandbank 2007: 139). This detachment is first and foremost the result of an intrinsic failure of rationality. Whether it is the philosopher who busies himself with a spinning top in order to achieve 'the understanding of all things' but ends up trotting 'like a top under a clumsy whip' (Kafka 1971:

444); the burrower whose underground maze – 'the outcome of intense intellectual ... labor' (1971: 327) – ultimately fails to serve its purpose and provide security; or the nightwalker whose inability to choose one of several equally plausible explanations for the actions of two passers-by who run past him results in paralysis (1971: 388). In Kafka's world the failing of reason inevitably results in the failing of action, and reason is like 'the true way' (*der wahre Weg*) that goes 'along a rope that is not spanned high in the air, but only just above the ground. It seems intended more to cause stumbling than to be walked along' (1991: 13–14).

As in Kafka's oeuvre, the epistemological condition that informs the Coens' corpus is the incapacitation of reason, resulting in uncertainty, misunderstanding and failed action. This account is evident as early as on the opening of the Coens' first feature, *Blood Simple* (1984), where a voice announces over shots of a West Texan vast and bare landscape that 'nothing comes with a guarantee' and that 'something can always go wrong'. This germinal 'broad, bare and lifeless' landscape (Coen and Coen 2002: 3) seems to echo the impenetrable, opaque nature that Stanley Corngold calls 'the bare *factum brutum* of a material world' in Kafka's snow-blanketed *The Castle*' (1973: 37).

More than two decades later, *No Country for Old Men* (2007) echoes *Blood Simple* as it opens with a West Texas landscape, serving as the backdrop to the voice of Sheriff Ed Tom Bell who expresses profound failure to fathom evil: 'I don't know what to make of that. I surely don't.' Sheriff Bell's words also resonate with the ending of *Fargo* (1996), where Police Chief Marge Gunderson concludes while driving through a snow-covered wasteland: 'I just don't understand it.' The Coens' preoccupation with the limited capacity of reason is evident in their films' frequent realisation in archetypical knowledge-based institutions such as courts of law, universities, the CIA and the police. The films present these institutions and their 'masters of commentary' (lawyers, professors, agents and police detectives) as barren, generating nothing but false interpretations.

The dominance of randomness in a chaotic existence that defies reason is the source of epistemological failure in the Coens' films. It is introduced at the beginning of *The Big Lebowski* with the metaphor of a tumbleweed rolling along the streets of Los Angeles, powerless to resist the blind forces that carry it along (see Douglas and Walls 2012: 147–8), as well as in *No Country for Old Men* with Anton Chigurh's habit of forcing his quarry to gamble on their lives with a coin toss. Their film characters commonly protest against this. In *Miller's Crossing* (1990), for example, mob boss Johnny Caspar demands compliance with ethical codes after, due to the selling of information on his fixed boxing fights, he finds himself in the vexing situation where 'you can't even trust a fixed fight'. Similarly, in *The Big Lebowski*, Walter Sobchak demands that a bowling opponent adhere to the rules: 'This is not 'Nam, this is bowling. There are rules!' – a demand acceded to only after Walter pulls out a loaded gun. For both Caspar and Sobchak rules and regulations distinguish culture from chaos, but the irony in these violent situations, where a gangster advocates ethics and a bowler enforces fair-game at gunpoint reveals these strivings to be self-defeating.

In such a chaotic universe any planned action is destined to fail. Indeed, the unhinging of human plans is probably the narrative element most commonly associated with the Coens' films. In *Fargo*, for example, Jerry Lundegaard's plan to have his wife kidnapped so he can pocket the ransom money is violently thwarted by unexpected twists; in *The Big Lebowski*, the Dude's plan to be compensated for the soiling of his rug launches a rollercoaster of deceptions and counter-deceptions; while in *The Man Who Wasn't There*, Ed Crane's wish to change his tedious life by partnering in a dry-cleaning venture goes terribly awry due to a series of deadly misinterpretations. In these and other Coen films, characters fall short of their aims, or wildly overshoot them, because any action performed triggers violent plot swings and any attempt to restore things to 'normal' only makes things worse.

II. THE REFERENTIAL FUNCTION: A CODELESS MESSAGE

'Thinking things over is the advice of the serpent', Kafka tells Max Brod, only to retract immediately: 'But it is also good and human. Without it one is lost' (Brod 1995: 165). As it is both 'the advice of the serpent' and 'good and human', the cycle of trial and failure in the quest for understanding by 'thinking things over' can never break, be it by achievement or withdrawal. It can only end (contingently and meaninglessly) in death. Respectively, despite repeated failures, the Kafkan characters never quit their quest for understanding, never lose faith in rationality, never fully realise the absurdity of their situation. The situation of the Kafkan protagonist is therefore bound with the indispensability and incapability of rationality.

The unsustainability of belief systems and schools of thought is a common theme in Kafka's world. In such stories as 'Josefine, die Sängerin, oder Das Volk der Mäuse' ('Josephine, the Singer, or the Mouse Folk', 1924) and 'Forschungen eines Hundes' ('Investigations of a Dog', 1931), and novels such as *The Trial* and *Das Schloss* (*The Castle*, 1926), Kafka typically describes great interpretive traditions. The volatile blend of rationality's necessity and inevitable failure is especially pronounced in Kafka's 'Zur Frage der Gesetze' ('The Problem of Our Laws', 1931) where interpreting ancient laws 'has been the work of centuries' even though many suspect that 'these laws that we are trying to unravel do not exist at all' (1971: 437, 438).

Other stories explicitly provoke questions of meaning and interpretation. 'Prometheus', for example, offers four versions of the Greek myth: after the versions are rejected one by one, the story concludes with the 'unerklärliche Felsgebirge', 'the inexplicable mass of rock' (1971: 433), and adds that 'the legend tried to explain the inexplicable [but] had in turn to end in the inexplicable' (ibid.). Legends are incomplete interpretations, leaving behind them a substratum which defies explication, thus demanding further interpretation *ad infinitum*. Interpretation is destined to fail, though at the same time it is also an imperative.

Another engagement with the problem of interpretation is the polemics over the parable of the law in chapter nine of *The Trial*. After telling of the parable, the priest and K. embark on a lengthy polemics. The priest presents opinions by commentators who have been engaged with this parable without ever agreeing on its moral, and the labour of interpretation never reaches its destination: meaning. In the midst of their interaction the priest himself reflects on this mounting proliferation of interpretations and asserts that 'what is written is unchanging, and opinions are often just an expression of despair at that' (2009a: 157). In other words, we are free to refer, but bound to despair.

Thomas Kavanagh investigates the endlessly irresolvable *referential function* in Kafka in terms of code and message: 'a given enunciation does not exist as a message until it is understood in terms of a particular code' (1972: 244). The understanding – moreover, the constitution – of a message requires possession of a code (understanding of this sentence for example requires possessing the code of English language). The Kafkan epistemological crisis is, in Kavanagh's terms, 'nothing other than the absence of a code adequate to the various messages being emitted' (ibid.). But this conclusion actually fails to express the radical projection of Kavanagh's model. A condition in which messages cannot be deciphered because the code is unavailable seems different than the one in which the existence of messages as such is merely a delusion which warrants and perpetuates the supposition of the code. We can thus refine Kavanagh's designation: the Kafkan epistemological crisis is the condition where man lives *as if* there exists a hidden code (or *code absconditus*) – a condition which vindicates its search – while in fact there is not even a message.

Kavanagh views the adventure of Kafka's protagonists as the 'adventure of the mind, the adventure of the semiologist' (1972: 245) whose hope is to penetrate the code. This hope, along with the supposition or delusion that there *is* a code, that there are more than discrete, unrelated, meaningless facts, is what drives them to 'impart to every and any collection of possible differences the status of a sign' (ibid.). Kavanagh shows that as a meta-critical comment in *The Trial*, the parable of the law and its conflicting interpretations reveal that the impossibility of interpretation experienced by the discussants in the diegesis is duplicated on the level of the text itself: 'The "message" of both parable and text is that there is no message, that there is no universal code in terms of which all is able to "mean"' (1972: 252).

Finally, and particularly important for our discussion, Kavanagh takes on the function of the literary medium in Kafka's codeless universe. While spoken language requires prior knowledge of a specific code, literature's use of language (its poetic function in Jakobson's terms) activates secondary codes that convert what has been declared to something other than its immediate use in language (1972: 252–3). Kavanagh's analysis of *The Trial* shows the novel to be 'constructed as the systematic refusal of all access to any such secondary codes' (1972: 253). The Kafkan text presents itself as a message, but 'for all its tension, for all its straining, it unveils no code […]. Disguised as message, it reveals only the form of its disguise' (ibid.). In the spirit of Derridean *différance*, Kavanagh refers to the literary word as distinctively manifesting 'movement from signifier to signifier' (ibid.). This movement provides the literary medium its potential as 'an only apparent message forever changing, forever soliciting meanings, and forever redefining itself' (ibid.).

III. THE METALINGUAL FUNCTION: THE CREATION OF UNBEING

Looking into the referential function of language in Kafka reveals a fallacy in the chimera of the codeless message. But arguably, some of the richness of Kafka's uses of language may be lost when viewed from the referential perspective alone, hence the need for addressing the *metalingual function* as well. I have noted earlier the threefold failure in Kafka's oeuvre: unfinished writings, failing characters and despaired commentators. But this threefold failure is itself a failed failure. The failure of his stories to be completed and published was itself 'failed' by the ambiguity of his famous last request.[3] Similarly, the inability of many of his protagonists to fulfil their aims is itself incomplete (as in 'Der Bau' ['The Burrow', 1931] and *The Castle*) precisely because the narrative never concludes. Even his commentators' despair is never complete, as it does not derive from inability to interpret, but from the inability to *stop* interpreting.

One should read Kafka's (first) marriage proposal to Felice Bauer (probably the weirdest ever made) to fathom the depth of retraction and indecisiveness in both Kafka's life and texts. As a master of his medium, indeed as an artist who sees himself *as* his medium ('It is not that I am interested in literature. I am literature', he writes to Felice [quoted in Corngold 1986: 161]), Kafka infuses this failed failure into the very core of his writing, both epistemologically in the form of incessant hesitation, and ontologically in the form of impossible interlacing of being and nonbeing.

Complete avoidance of any decisive statement or factual commitment is articulated by Kafka's stylistic choices. As shown by Shimon Sandbank, by qualifying statements using phrases like 'it appears' and using the modal auxiliaries *können* (can) and *müssen* (must), most famously in the opening sentence of *The Trial*, Kafka replaces commitment with fallible perspective and withdrawal from facts (1981: 390). Likewise, by avoiding names, definite pronouns and all identifiable reference, Kafka remains at a theoretical level of description and 'stops short of an implication of existence' (1981: 389).

'Vermin is born of the void', Kafka notes in *The Blue Octavo Notebooks* (1991: 51). Indeed, Gregor Samsa's metamorphosis into an *ungeheueres Ungeziefer* ('monstrous vermin') constitutes an ontological impossibility. The term *ungeheueres Ungeziefer* does not designate any natural being (see Corngold 1973: 32), it cannot stand for anything but the impossibility of linguistic signification. 'As reader of etymologies', Stanley Corngold notes, Kafka 'knew what depth of *unbeing* underlies this phrase' (1973: 32; emphasis added).

Many of Kafka's crossbreeds – the lamb-cat, the monkey-academician, the dog-musicians, the singer-mouse and other ambiguous creatures – are also such unbeing-beings. Tuvia Ruebner's study of Kafka's metaphors presents the creature from 'Eine Kruezung' ('A Crossbreed', 1931) – a half-lamb, half-cat who is neither – as a self-contradicting linguistic figure (1996: 127). While common fictional figures can be imagined as living persons or animals, Kafka's crossbreeds cannot even exist conceptually, since they are flawed metaphors, annulled assertions, linguistic contradictions that exist only thanks to their incapacity to exist (Ruebner 1982: 22).

Sandbank's, Corngold's and Ruebner's studies point at the metalingual aspect of Kafka's referential fallacy: it is not simply, as suggested by Kavanagh, a *poetic* 'constant movement of signifiers' in the spirit of *différance*, but rather a sign system whose very referentiality is its own incompetence. To keep pace with Kafka's constant retraction language must subvert itself. In *Beschreibung einer Form* ('Description of Form', 1961) Martin Walser uses the Hegelian term *Aufhebung* (sublation) to refer to a typical Kafkan mode of expression: a spiral movement of affirmation and denial in which every assertion made is immediately renounced in a process that is, to use Adorno's words, 'constantly obscuring and revoking itself' (1981: 247). This mode can be seen as a process whereby 'language brings about its own doom' and 'the medium is … prior to anything else, a way of "performing" this linguistic failure' (Biderman 2008: 189).

Given this self-destructive function of language, it comes as no surprise that Kafka has been seen as essentially confined to written language, widely considered unadaptable to visual media (see Ruebner 1996; Nicolin quoted in Brady and

Hughes 2002; Gilman 2005).⁴ Indeed it might seem that the filmic image, by virtue of its indexical nature and the blunt presence it discloses, is essentially unable to reproduce Kafka's contradictory ontology and radical uncertainty. Similarly, Kavanagh's referential perspective also suggests that literature, with its lingual nature and poetic potential to stir the movement of signifiers, is the most appropriate medium for articulating Kafka's systematic refusal of all access to secondary codes and the absence of code at the very level of the literary signifier (1972: 253). In what follows, however, I present two Coen Brothers' films as effective cinematic counterparts to Kafka's medial engagement with the epistemological crisis. I approach *A Serious Man* from the referential perspective, focusing on the problem of code and message and the creation of an indecipherable text, and *Inside Llewyn Davis* from the metalingual perspective, focusing on the level of the signifier and the creation of narrative conundrums and cinematic unbeings.

IV. 'NAILING IT DOWN. SO IMPORTANT'

Misinterpretation and deductive failure are common to the films made by the Coen Brothers. Despite being engaged in laborious interpretation, the Coenesque character cannot elicit any operative rule, any operative code. In *The Big Lebowski*, after realising that everything thus far has been a sham – the millionaire has no money, the kidnapping of his wife is a ruse and the ransom briefcase empty – Sobchak deduces that Jeffrey Lebowski must be faking his disability. He therefore lifts Lebowski from his wheelchair, certain he will stand up on his feet; however, Lebowski slumps on his face, refuting Walter's refutation of reasonability – turning his realisation of ultimate interpretive failure into a failure.⁵

Another example for the total absence of code is *Fargo*'s introduction of Police Chief Marge Gunderson. In the whitewashed North Dakota plains, Marge deciphers the signs left at a murder scene – footprints, traces – and records in a dead police officer's notebook. Upon leaving the scene, Marge tells her partner a joke about a guy who changed his name to J3L 2404 because he couldn't afford a personalised plate. In the joke the man's name is substituted in order to provide the plate signification. This imposition produces a decodable string, but the code – and that is the punch of the joke – has been predetermined by the manufacturer. Consequently message and code are trapped in a closed loop and decoding is unable to produce new knowledge. Presenting the joke just after Marge's decoding of the signs (specifically the suspects' license plate) implies that regardless of Marge's deductive reasoning abilities her interpretation will never be more than the imposition of meaning on essentially meaningless facts, and alludes that, at best, crime may be solved but never truly understood.

The film that deals most profoundly with the absence of a code in the Coens' oeuvre is *A Serious Man*. Set in 1967, it depicts two weeks in the life of Larry Gopnik, a Jewish professor of physics who teaches – how appropriate – Heisenberg's Uncertainty Principle. Larry suffers a string of unpredictable misfortunes: his wife Judith asks for divorce; his brother Arthur is arrested; Judith and her intended husband, Sy Ableman, ask him to leave the house; and, although Judith has emptied their bank account, when Sy dies in a car accident Larry is asked to pay the funeral expenses. Meanwhile he suspects a mysterious student who tried to bribe him for a passing grade is responsible for anonymous letters sent to the head of his department urging that his application for tenure is denied. Larry tries to understand those events, but of course to no avail.

We have seen that Kavanagh views the Kafkan necessity and futility of interpretation as the mind's desperate grasping for code in a codeless world. In *A Serious Man* as well, the inability to assign meaning to facts is central to the narrative. One of the countless examples for this is the dialogue between Larry and his student Clive Park, during which Larry presents Clive with the money-filled envelope that was found on his desk after their previous meeting, where Clive had pleaded for a passing grade:

> Larry: Well... then, Clive, where did this come from? This is here, isn't it?
> Clive: Yes, sir. That is there.
> Larry: This is not nothing, this is something.
> Clive: Yes sir. That is something. ... What is it?
> Larry: You know what it is! I believe. And you know I can't keep it, Clive. [...] I'll have to pass it on to Professor Finkle, along with my suspicions about where it came from. Actions have consequences.
> Clive: Yes. Often.
> Larry: Always! Actions always have consequences! In this office, actions have consequences! [...] Not just physics. Morally. [...] And we both know about your actions.
> Clive: No, sir. I know about my actions.
> Larry: I can interpret, Clive. I know what you meant me to understand.
> Clive: Meer sir my sir.
> Larry: Meer sir my sir?
> Clive: (*careful enunciation*) Mere... surmise. Sir. Very uncertain.
> (Coen and Coen 2007)

Apparently Larry and Clive can agree that there is 'something' before them, but any interpretation of this as a sign, a 'meaningful something' (like bribery) is, as

Clive says in appropriate incomprehensibility, a 'mere surmise'. Thus, the envelope remains as inexplicable as the 'mass of rock' in 'Prometheus'. The scientific model for this inherent interpretive failure is presented by Larry in his physics class early in the film: Erwin Schrödinger's famous thought experiment that concludes with the inability to determine whether a cat is dead or alive. Variations on this theme recur throughout the film: the inability to determine whether Rabbi Groshkover is a Dybbuk, whether the envelope indicates attempted bribery; and whether Larry's brother is guilty of solicitation.

The film's most explicit treatment of the incapability to reveal *the* meaning of facts, to unearth the sought-after code, is the Parable of the Goy's Teeth. Confused and dejected, Larry turns to his rabbi for epistemological solace: 'What is *Hashem* [God] trying to tell me [...]? And, did I tell you I had a car accident the same time Sy had his? Is *Hashem* telling me that Sy Ableman is me, or we are all one or something?' Larry seems to (want to) regard his misfortunes as a divine message – he only lacks the code. In response, the Rabbi tells Larry a story: a Jewish dentist named Sussman prepares a plaster mould for corrective bridge work in the mouth of one of his patients, incidentally a 'goy' (gentile). When Sussman examines the mould he finds to his amazement Hebrew letters engraved on the patient's incisors: ה-ו-ש-י-ע-נ-י. Ho'shieni – help me, save me. Sussman tries to understand what this could mean: he decodes the message according to the Hebrew numerical system and as a seven-digit number has been formed he suspects it as a telephone number. He calls and reaches a grocery store. He drives there with tremendous anxiety, but the store is just as any other. Bewildered and helpless Sussman visits the Rabbi and asks:

> What does it mean, Rabbi? Is it a sign from *Hashem*? I, Sussman, should be doing something to help this *goy*? [...] Or maybe I'm supposed to help people generally – lead a more righteous life? Is the answer in Kabbalah? In Torah? Or is there even a question? Tell me, Rabbi – what can such a sign mean?

While Sussman articulates the basic questions of semiology, he also alludes to the absence of the code by suggesting that there might not even be any question – or law, to echo Kafka's short story – to begin with. Indeed, the parable demonstrates Kavanagh's conception of Kafka's codeless message. The message, if there is one, may be converted using any number of codes – letters, numbers, phone numbers – but these never lead to an interpretation that provides a sense of resolution, of relief.

The entire scene bears remarkable resemblance to Josef K.'s meeting with the prison chaplain in *The Trial*. Both the film and novel bring together a protagonist with a cleric; both clerics tell a parable; both parables comment on the entire text; and in both cases immediately after being told, the parable's meaning, if any, becomes the object of reflection and debate between the two characters, ending up not only as indecipherable, but as pointing at its own indecipherability. In both, the code is being shifted or reproduced from the signified world to the signifying medium. That is, it is lacking both in the signified *and* in the signifier. While the 'Parable of the Goy's Teeth' is a prime example of the Kafkan quest for an absent code at the level of its story, its employment of the cinematic medium is equivalent to Kafka's unique application of the literary medium to create the 'systematic refusal of all access to ... secondary codes' (Kavanagh 1972: 253) thus replicating the absence of the code on the level of the cinematic signifier. To discern this replication we must pay careful attention to the stylistic choices employed in the rendering of the parable.

The parable is presented as a visualisation of Sussman's tale accompanied by the rabbi's narration. The depicted events are muted while the dialogues are dubbed by the rabbi. 'What is seen' and 'what is heard' are presented as separate, though synchronised tracks. In order to analyse this unique filmic approach, we should return to a short scene presented several minutes earlier. In this scene Larry's son Danny prepares for his Bar-Mitzvah recital with the help of a recording while the television is on and muted. When his sister Sarah enters the room the two begin to quarrel. On its visual track, the scene begins with a close-shot of the TV screen, presenting in centre frame a huge brain in a fluid receptacle next to two uniformed men typical of 1960s science-fiction imagery. Next, two guards enter, dragging a man in front of the brain. Once the camera tracks back from the screen it reveals the quarrelling siblings. On the audio track the scene begins with Danny's Torah recitation, moving to Sarah's entry, and ending with the quarrel. The audio track completely corresponds to the muted action on TV, providing it with fitting dubbing. This segment demonstrates how an accidental, unintended situation can be conceptualised as interpretable when the correspondence of media (sound and image in this case) forms a coherent text. Although completely meaningless, the viewer-listener cannot but perceive the sequence as bearing a message.

Stylistically, the short TV-dubbing scene is therefore closely linked with the parable, as both manipulate the relations between the audio and video tracks, creating a rupture between cinema's two most basic elements: 'what is seen' and 'what is heard'. They are also linked thematically as both not only present a codeless message (the goy's teeth, the TV dubbing) but also refer to a divine code. The biblical portion recited by Danny (Leviticus 25:1–26:2) is unique in that it states explicitly at the outset (as recited by Danny) that the laws it presents have been delivered to Moses by God on Mount Sinai – the moment when the transcendental code for deciphering existence is given to man.

The stylistic and thematic interlinking of the two scenes allows us to view them as complementary. The parable's rupture of sound and image directs attention to the means by which cinematic meaning is constructed. This is further supported by the conspicuous use of other cinematic communication channels: sharp camera movements, unusual camera angles, expressive lighting and noticeable editing mark this scene as 'explicitly cinematic' compared to the rest of the film. Complementarily, the TV-dubbing scene's engagement with the sound-vision rupture demonstrates the fallacy discussed in the parable, as in the entire film – the detection of ostensibly meaningful patterns that actually carry no meaning – by manifesting the medium's ability to entice viewers to form interpretable patterns from random concurrences of sound and image. In turn, this demonstrates what Kavanagh refers to as Kafka's 'apparent message' (1972: 253), forever soliciting meanings while denying all access to secondary codes.[6]

V. 'IT WAS NEVER NEW, AND IT NEVER GETS OLD'

While *A Serious Man* cinematically executes the *referential* fallacy of the Kafkan codeless universe, it is *Inside Llewyn Davis* that manifests the Kafkan *metalingual* incapacitation of the medium itself. Set in the early 1960s, the film depicts several days in the life of folk musician Llewyn Davis. Despite being clearly talented and motivated Llewyn fails in the music business, as well as in all friendly and intimate relationship.

Inside Llewyn Davis's systematic deception of its audience is exceptional even within the Coen's filmography. This is achieved mainly by restricting narration to the protagonist's knowledge, thereby reproducing his misconceptions on the level of spectatorship. For example, when Llewyn plays an old seamen's song to his ailing father, a former sailor, the viewers share his perspective on the old man's facial expression and interpret it as deep emotional engagement sparked by the sentimental gesture, but as it turns out the demented old man has simply soiled himself. Similarly, when Llewyn finds a ginger cat that looks just like his friends' cat, the one he has lost, we share his misrecognition only later to be disappointed together with Llewyn.

The film's most extreme deception is carried out by a series of similarities and differences between the opening and closing scenes. Very similar to Kafka's narratives that 'arrest the reader and subject him to a game of deception with no redemptive catharsis' (Beicken 1977: 404), these differences withhold narrative comprehension, lead the audience to continuous retractions and culminate with the impossibility of constructing a coherent diegesis. To delineate this cinematic manoeuvre I will rely on David Bordwell's (1985) cognitive model of narrative comprehension. Bordwell conceives film viewing as a dynamic psychological process that involves perceptual capacities, prior knowledge, experience, and of course the material and structure of the film itself (1985: 32–3): 'When information is missing, perceivers infer it or make guesses about it. When events are arranged out of temporal order, perceivers try to put those events in sequence. And people seek causal connections among events, both in anticipation and in retrospect' (1985: 34). As films put to work 'devices and forms that elicit the spectator's activity' (1985: 48) the cognitive process by which comprehension is achieved involves narrative *schemata* and *hypotheses*. Schemata are 'cognitive maps' or 'organised clusters of knowledge' (1985: 31) essential for arranging information in familiar templates: from the construction of a three-dimensional space and face recognition to the causal and temporal organisation of plots. Thus, familiar schemata help viewers recognise such recurring formulas as 'bank robbery' and 'Depression era', as well as arrange events chronologically when presented one after another, but concurrently if presented using cross-cutting. Based on schemata spectators 'define narrative events and unify them by principles of causality, time, and space' (1985: 39). The spectator applies schemata to incoming cues in order to 'make assumptions, draw inferences about current story events, and frame and test hypotheses about prior and upcoming events'; as the film unfolds some inferences will be revised and some hypotheses suspended (ibid.). Bordwell uses the Russian Formalists' terms *fabula* and *syuzhet*, and adds the term *style*, to describe cognitive narrative construction. *Fabula* is the action as a 'chronological, cause-and-effect chain of events occurring within a given duration and spatial field'; it is 'a pattern which perceivers of narratives create through assumptions and inferences ... the result of picking up narrative cues, applying schemata, framing and testing hypotheses' (1985: 49). While the *fabula* can only be inferred and is 'never materially present' (ibid.), what is encountered by the spectator is *syuzhet*, or the 'actual arrangement and presentation of the *fabula* in the film ... as a blow-by-blow recounting' (ibid.). While *syuzhet* patterning is independent of medium, it is *style* that constitutes the medium-specific tools which carry out the *syuzhet*. Thus, based on *syuzhet* patterning and *style* configurations film spectators apply schemata that help them infer about the *fabula* in order to attain the central goal of 'the carving out of an intelligible story' (ibid.).

Bordwell's model will help me present *Inside Llewyn Davis* as encumbering the process of narrative comprehension by preventing viewers from determining the course of the *fabula* and thereby constructing a coherent diegesis.[7] The fallacies used for that purpose are achieved using cinematic devices that solicit viewers to adopt conflicting narrative schemata as well as by introducing inconsistencies in *fabula*, *syuzhet* and *style* between the film's opening and closing scenes.

The film opens with a performance by Llewyn in Gaslight, a New York club. He performs the song 'Hang Me', after which he walks offstage, talks to the manager and goes outside to meet 'a guy in a suit' that is said to be waiting for him. In a dark alley outside the club a mysterious man socks the bewildered Llewyn. The next scene presents Llewyn as he wakes up at his friends' (the Gorfeins) apartment when their cat Ulysses leaps on his chest. He gets up, peers down the hall, makes breakfast, leaves a note and when he leaves the apartment the cat slips out as the door shuts behind, forcing Llewyn to take it with him.

The spectator organises these events into a *fabula* using a simple chronological schema which assumes that the order of the presentation is the order of occurrence: Llewyn ends his performance with 'Hang Me', then he is assaulted, and the next day he wakes up in a friends' apartment. The assault is constructed as a riddle within a narrative schema of 'mystery', arousing curiosity and generically promising eventual clarification.[8] As the film unfolds this line of investigation is neglected, frustrating the expectation that this mystery will be central in the narrative. Instead the film follows the penniless Llewyn as he roams Manhattan accompanied by a ginger cat, sleeping on occasional couches, losing the cat, trying to borrow money, finding the wrong cat and offending the Gorfeins, going on a surreal ride to Chicago for a failed audition, losing the second cat and returning to New York to fail in his attempt to resume his career as a seaman. With no other place to stay, Llewyn spends the night with the Gorfeins and finds out that Ulysses has found his way home. The next scene presents Llewyn waking up in a manner that evokes the film's opening scenes.

Llewyn wakes up at the Gorfeins' apartment to find Ulysses on his chest. He gets up, peers down the hall, leaves a note and when leaving, makes sure the cat does not escape. Next, Llewyn walks down the street and his attention is caught by a poster of Walt Disney's *The Incredible Journey* (1963). Next, in the film's last scene Llewyn is in the club playing 'Hang Me', but this time before getting off stage he plays another song, 'Fare Thee Well'. Then he walks offstage, talks to the manager, and goes outside to meet 'a guy in a suit', who proceeds to sock him.

Two common narrative schemata will help us analyse the complex relations between the opening and closing scenes. By *circular fabula schema* I designate a narrative structure that ties the opening of the *fabula* with its ending. In such narratives the events presented in the end follow the events presented in the beginning, but evoke them stylistically and thematically. This schema is common to circular journeys and homecoming narratives such as *The Odyssey, The Wizard of Oz* (1939) or Disney's *The Incredible Journey*. The structural closure in such stories commonly represents the equilibrium regained as well as the journey's educational value in the tradition of the *Bildungsroman* ('there's no place like home'). By *circular syuzhet schema*, however, I designate a narrative structure that ties the opening of the *syuzhet* with its ending by presenting the exact same event(s) at the beginning and end. This schema, identified mostly with film noir, is common to themes of futile journeys, fatalism and helplessness.

When Llewyn wakes up in his friends' apartment towards the end, the similarities to the second scene raise the assumption that this is the same scene and therefore the relevant schema is the circular *syuzhet* schema. However, when Llewyn prevents Ulysses from escaping the spectator must revise this assumption. Upon realising that the scenes are not identical but merely similar, the spectator applies the circular *fabula* schema. This is supported by the cat's name and recent homecoming (both disclosed on the previous scene), as well as *The Incredible Journey* poster. However, when we are next presented with Llewyn's gig and his encounter with the mysterious man we must reapply the circular syuzhet schema and to rearrange our *fabula* construction to locate the events of the first scene (Gaslight gig) after, and not before, those presented in the second (waking up).[9]

In jolting the spectator between those two schemata (as a kind of spectatorial sublation) the film frustrates the spectator's efforts to form a coherent *fabula*. This frustration is coupled by the inability to construct the film as coherent diegesis due to a series of inconsistencies in *fabula*, *syuzhet* and style between the opening and closing club scenes, as detailed in the table below.

	Opening Scene	**Closing Scene**
Syuzhet (inside club)	Upon finishing 'Hang Me', Llewyn walks offstage.	Upon finishing 'Hang Me', Llewyn plays 'Fare Thee Well' and only then walks offstage.
	While talking to the manager Llewyn seems to be looking at something but we do not get to see what.	We see Llewyn's respective point of view: he is looking at a young man preparing for his own gig.[10]
	The talk with the manager cuts to Llewyn's exit from the club to the back alley.	Between talking to the manager and exiting Llewyn's look lingers on the young performer.
Style (outside club)	The scene in the back alley is mostly focalised internally by Llewyn.	The scene in the back alley is mostly focalised externally, from an objective perspective.
	Llewyn is presented mostly in close-up and medium-shot.	Llewyn is presented mostly in long-shot.

	The sounds of Dylan singing 'Fare Thee Well' from the club are barely distinct.	The sounds of Dylan singing 'Fare Thee Well' from the club are clearly heard.
Fabula (outside club)	As he exits the club Llewyn scratches his face.	As he exits the club Llewyn does not scratch his face.
	Llewyn asks the mysterious man: 'who are you?'	Llewyn does not ask the mysterious man: 'who are you?'
	Llewyn's reply to the mysterious man is 'I'm sorry, what?'	Llewyn's reply to the mysterious man is 'what?'
	The mysterious man says: 'Had to open your big mouth, ha, funny boy?'	The mysterious man says 'Had to open your big mouth?'
	The intonations of the mysterious man's utterances are different.	

The various differences and inconsistencies in the three levels carry out different functions. On the level of *syuzhet* the closing scene reveals two pieces of information missing in the first scene: Llewyn played a second song before walking offstage, to be replaced by the young Bob Dylan. The differences in *syuzhet* patterning thus reveal the medium's ability to mislead, to easily convince the audience that 'Hang Me' was the final song in Llewyn's concert whereas in fact it was followed by 'Fare Thee Well'; and to withhold significant information, such as the pop legend's first concert in the Gaslight in winter 1961.

In fact, Dylan's deceptively minor disclosure is of great significance, as it suggests a comparison between the two young musicians (supported by the fact that all letters in 'Dylan' are found in 'Llewyn Davis'). This comparison is most explicitly presented by the choice to have the two musicians play songs that highlight the words 'fare thee well'. Given Llewyn's hitherto exhibited talent and motivation this comparison begs the question: why does Dylan become a success while Llewyn keeps failing? The disparity grows even more poignant in light of the musicians' dissimilar cinematic representations: Llewyn is given screen time to play an entire song that is heard for the second time in the film and is presented in flattering expressive close-shots using agreeable lighting that amplify the emotional attachment of his powerful diction. Dylan on the other hand plays a rather unfamiliar song ('Fare Thee Well'), his boyish unpolished voice muddled by sounds from the audience and the street, and he is given scant screen time from a restricted point of view. It seems as if the film tries to point at the peculiarity in the contrast between the careers of the two musicians.

Thus, by disclosing Dylan the differences in *syuzhet* seem to highlight Llewyn's failure as an anomaly. Meanwhile, however, the differences in style (the shift from subjective to objective focalisation and from close to long shots, and Dylan's amplification in the soundtrack) reveal an abandonment of Llewyn in favour of Dylan. This culminates at the very end of the film when a black screen wipes off Llewyn and the soundtrack further amplifies Dylan's song to accompany the film's end-credits. Finally, the inconsistencies in *fabula* prevent the construction of a coherent diegesis: since a given event cannot take place one way or another, the inconsistencies detailed in the table above prevent the viewer from treating the two scenes as representing the same event, while the fact that they are nearly identical prevents these events from being treated as separate.

It can be said that the differences in *syuzhet* present the general expectations in the film (Llewyn should succeed) and the differences in style refute them. The differences in *syuzhet* and style thus join to present the conundrum of Llewyn's failure while the differences in *fabula* complement this conundrum with an inability to generate a coherent diegesis that can contain the depicted events within a logical and consistent story-world. In fact the inconsistency of this story-world provides the preconditions for Llewyn's failings – an inconsistent world, like Kafka's 'true way', 'seems intended more to cause stumbling than to be walked along' (Kafka 1991: 13–14). The failing of action as a result of the failing of reason is, as discussed, a shared motif in Kafka's and the Coens' work. Similar to Kafka who 'involves the reader in an unintelligible and paradoxical world where the fate of his heroes remained inexplicable' (Beicken 1977: 399), *Inside Llewyn Davis*'s frustration of narrative comprehension mirrors the protagonist's failings and intrinsic misinterpretation of reality. If, as Bordwell notes, the spectator's central goal is 'the carving out of an intelligible story' (1985: 39), then what *Inside Llewyn Davis* offers is, to recall another Kafka aphorism, 'a way of hesitation' (1991: 23).

We have seen that Kafka's avoidance of any decisive statement or factual commitment is impressed into his language by means of incessant retraction (Walser), fallible perspective (Sandbank) and the creation of ontological impossibilities (Corngold) and literary unbeings (Ruebner). The narrative rhetoric of *Inside Llewyn Davis* can be said to introduce on the level of spectatorship cinematic parallels to these linguistic and literary techniques: Kafka's systematic retraction finds a counterpart in the film's continuous solicitation to revise narrative schemata; fallible perspective is achieved in restricting narration to the protagonist's knowledge; and ontological contradictions find their parallel in the film's construction of an intrinsically subverted diegesis.

Walser's, Sandbank's, Corngold's and Ruebner's studies point to Kafka's medium as performing its own referential failure. The power of literature as a medium is its ability to contain and communicate this failure. Indeed, Kafka's linguistic 'impossibilities' are possible as language, which is to say that while they cannot signify they can be *expressed*. They work well as language, as signifiers, even if they cannot signify anything. While the crossbreeds, the *ungeheueres Ungeziefer*, and the annulled assertions may be impossible to conceptualise they can be linguistically expressed – this is their unique existence as literary unbeings, which 'exist only thanks to their incapacity to exist' (Ruebner 1982: 22). Something similar happens in the impossible relationship between the beginning and ending of *Inside Llewyn Davis*. Logically the beginning and ending of the film are mutually exclusive, their coexistence is absurd. And yet filmically, as visual and auditory signifiers, they seem to work well. Like Kafka's crossbreeds they may be impossible to conceptualise, but can be expressed. In this aspect the film image – its existence as phantom, as a ghost conjured from a past that had long ceased to exist and is yet so vivid – may function as the ultimate Kafkan medium.

This essay rethinks obstacles to a cinematic rendering of Kafka. It uses two methodological approaches to present a profound affinity between Kafka and the Coen Brothers. Naturally, Kafka's use of language comprises of much more than the two perspectives – the referential and metalingual – discussed here. Accordingly, this essay should not be taken to imply that Kafka's language, let alone other aspects of his fiction, is entirely adaptable to film. What it does highlight is the productiveness of *thinking* cinema through Kafka's lens.[11]

NOTES

1. Some of the discussions in this essay are elaborated on ideas first suggested in previous articles by the author (2011, 2015). I wish to thank Maria Luise Caputo Mayr for her permission to use this material.
2. In an interview Joel Coen states that he 'devoured' 'The Metamorphosis' in his university days and adds that he did not read *The Castle* or 'In the Penal Colony' (see Allen 2006).
3. Brod argues that Kafka would have appointed another executor had he really intended his writings to be burned (1945: 198).
4. Günther Nicolin notes that nothing is gained by rendering Kafka visually; rather, 'attention is wrenched away from Kafka's diction' (quoted in Brady and Hughes 2002: 228); Ruebner contends that only language, metaphorically improper, with its silences and contradictions, can express his paradoxical linguistic-image

(1982: 11, 22; 1996: 132); and Sander Gilman states that 'Kafka's world was a visual world even though (or exactly because) it was one that could not be represented' (2005: 144).

5   In its frustration of any deduction the scene is reminiscent of Kafka's 'The Trees' (1971: 382). In this fragment, after appearance turns out to be misleading, the correction turns out to be just as misleading (see Sandbank 1974: 39).

6   'The Parable of the Goy's Teeth' itself also solicits viewers to form interpretable patterns from random concurrences of sound and image in at least two instances: in narrating that Sussman's clinic is called Great Bear exactly when closing up on his chubby-cheeked face; and in the dubbed dialogue between Sussman and the clerk in the 'Red Owl' grocery store where, after being asked about the goy the clerk asks 'who?' in an 'owly' manner while a drawing of a red owl is visible behind him.

7   Bordwell does not use the term diegesis, but the distinction between coherent and incoherent diegesis is essential to discussing narrative miscomprehension. The sentence 'the orphan child went to school after he had breakfast with his parents', for example, exemplifies coherent fabula and *syuzhet*, but presents a logical contradiction denying coherent diegesis.

8   In terms of Roland Barthes' *S/Z*, this schema functions within the narrative's hermeneutic code.

9   It is still unclear to me whether even this organization of events is exclusive. By systematically refuting assumptions and constructions, the film leaves several scenes in a 'fabula limbo', so that they can be indiscriminately inlaid in different parts of the story as in a multiple choice puzzle.

10 Spectators will recognise this young man as Robert Zimmerman, just before his soaring career under the name Bob Dylan.

11 I would like to thank Kata Gellen for her helpful advice about this essay.

BIBLIOGRAPHY

Adorno, Theodor W. (1981) 'Notes on Kafka', *Prisms*, trans. Shierry Weber and Samuel Weber. Cambridge: MIT Press, 243–71.

Allen, William R. (ed.) (2006) *The Coen Brothers: Interviews*. Jackson: University Press of Mississippi.

Anon. (2004) 'Remakes and Kafka Breaks', *The Washington Times*, 25 March 2004; available at:http://www.washingtontimes.com/news/2004/mar/25/20040325-103703-1488r/?page=all (accessed 10 July 2015).

Barthes, Roland (1974) *S/Z*, trans. Richard Miller. New York: Blackwell.

Beicken, Peter (1977) 'Kafka's Narrative Rhetoric', *Journal of Modern Literature*, 6, 3, 398–409.

Biderman, Shlomo (2008) *Crossing Horizons: World, Self, and Language in Indian and Western Thought*, trans. Ornan Rotem. New York: Columbia University Press.

Bordwell, David (1985) *Narration in the Fiction Film*. Madison, WI: University of Wisconsin Press.

Brady, Martin, and Helen Hughes (2002) 'Kafka Adapted to Film', *The Cambridge Companion to Kafka*, ed. Julian Preece. Cambridge: Cambridge University Press, 226–41.

Brod, Max (1945) 'Epilogue' in Kafka, Franz, *The Trial*, trans. Willa and Edwin Muir. New York: Schocken, 196–200.

____ (1995 [1947]) *Franz Kafka: A Biography*, trans. G. Humphreys Roberts and Richard Winston. Boston: Da Capo Press.

Coen, Ethan and Joel Coen (2002) *Collected Screenplays Volume 1: Blood Simple, Raising Arizona, Miller's Crossing, Barton Fink*. New York: Faber & Faber.

____ (2007) *A Serious Man: Screenplay by Joel Coen and Ethan Coen*; available at: http://www.coenbrothers.net/scripts/aseriousman.pdf (accessed 10 July 2015).

Corngold, Stanley (1973) *The Commentators' Despair: The Interpretation of Kafka's Metamorphosis*. Port Washington, NY: Kennikat Press.

____ (1986) *The Fate of the Self: German Writers and French Theory*. New York: Columbia University Press.

Douglas, Matthew K. and Jerry L. Walls (2012) '"Takin' 'er Easy for All Us Sinners": Laziness as Virtue in *The Big Lebowski*', in Mark T. Conard (ed.) *The Philosophy of the Coen Brothers*, updated edition. Lexington, KY: University Press of Kentucky, 147–62.

Gilman, Sander L. (2005) *Franz Kafka*. London: Reaktion.

Kafka, Franz (1971) *The Complete Stories*, ed. Nahum N. Glatzer. New York: Schocken.

____ (1991 [1954]) *The Blue Octavo Notebooks*, ed. Max Brod, trans. Ernst Kaiser and Eithne Wilkins. Cambridge, MA: Exact Change.

____ (1999 [1937]) *Schriften, Tagebücher, Briefe: Kritische Ausgabe*. Frankfurt am Main: S. Fischer.

____ (2004 [1927]) *Amerika: The Man Who Disappeared*, trans. Michael Hofmann. New York: New Directions.

____ (2009a [1925]) *The Trial*, trans. Mike Mitchell. Oxford: Oxford University Press.

____ (2009b [1926]) *The Castle*, trans. Anthea Bell. Oxford: Oxford University Press.

Kavanagh, Thomas M. (1972) 'Kafka's *The Trial*: The Semiotics of the Absurd', *NOVEL: A Forum on Fiction*, 5, 3, 242–53.

Lewit, Ido (2011) 'The Kafkaesque Cinematic Language of the Coen Brothers' *A Serious Man*', *Journal of the Kafka Society of America*, 33/34, 29–38.

____ (2015) 'Orson Welles's *The Trial* and the Problem of Interpretation after the Holocaust', *Journal of the Kafka Society of America*, 36/37, 115–26.

Ruebner, Tuvia (1982) 'Can One Illustrate Kafka's Cockroach (Remarks on Kafka's Metaphoric Language)', *Kafka Symposium, March 1981*, ed. D. Hanegbi. Tel-Aviv: Sifriat Poalim, 7–26. [Hebrew]

____ (1996) 'Some Remarks Concerning Kafka the Jew', in Hans-Jürgen Schrader, Elliott M. Simon and Charlotte Wardi (eds) *The Jewish Self-Portrait in European and American literature, Vol. 15*. Berlin: Walter de Gruyter, 125–34.

Sandbank, Shimon (1974) *The Way of Wavering: Forms of Uncertainty in Kafka*. Tel Aviv: Hakibbutz Hameuchad. [Hebrew]

____ (1981) 'Uncertainty as Style: Kafka's *Betrachtung*', *German Life and Letters*, 34, 4, 385–97.

____ (2007) 'Postscript to The Octavo Notebooks', in Franz Kafka, *The Octavo Notebooks*, trans. Shimon Sandbank. Tel Aviv: Am Oved. [Hebrew]

Walser, Martin (1961) *Beschreibung einer Form: Versuch über Franz Kafka*. Munich: Carl Hanser.

THE FACE: K. AND KEATON

OMRI BEN-YEHUDA

THE TALKING HUMAN AND THE MOVING BODY

One of Kafka's later works, 'Erstes Leid' ('First Sorrow', 1924), tells the story of a trapeze artist who suddenly feels uneasiness after a long stoic career of equilibrium (quite literally). Suddenly he wishes – a strange wish for a second trapeze – to act for the sake of a goal, for which he undertakes a dialogue with his impresario. This dialogue should be followed by reaction, implications and outcomes. This sudden emotional arousal makes the artist cry, and when he finally sleeps, the impresario – after trying to put his mind at ease – notices the first pain on the artist's face: 'how the first wrinkles began to etch themselves into the trapeze artist's smooth, childish forehead' (2002: 125).

A change in the trapeze artist is signified on his face, but apparently this description of face is a rare exception in Kafka's work. We don't know what Josef K. looks like, we only know his age and gender. In the case of his successor, K. the land surveyor, we know only the latter. Franz Kafka took figurative language and even description as such with the utmost seriousness, and judiciously tried to avoid it as much as possible (in a diary entry from 6 December 1921 Kafka also proclaims his reservation from metaphors). In both *Der Prozess* (*The Trial*, 1925) and *Das Schloss* (*The Castle*, 1926), the storyteller rarely elaborates on the feelings and personal attributes of his characters, not even his protagonists, preferring to focus almost exclusively on action and dialogue. The exclusive focus on action, while avoiding any attempt to come to terms with its mental impressions or emotional consequences, also informs the art of one of silent film's most innovative masters: Buster Keaton.

Although Keaton was active in film from 1917 to his death in 1966, his most famous and original films were created between 1920, when producer Joseph Schenck gave him control of a production unit of his own, and 1928, when talking film emerged and quickly led to the demise of slapstick comedy. In this period Keaton's films centred on his virtuoso bodily abilities and the outrageous physical situations his figure endures. The fact that all the while he keeps a deadpan facial expression has earned him the nickname The Great Stone Face.

Keaton's art is much more than just slapstick, however. He is philosophical in using his gags to stage a distinct human condition. This human condition is twofold, as it is informed by both a futile human struggle against undefeated, and sometimes completely indifferent opponents, and by the immersion of the human within the mechanical. The idea of a futile fight by a single individual against overwhelming odds is articulated repeatedly in Keaton's struggles against the forces of nature (*One Week*, 1920; *Steamboat Bill Jr.*, 1928) as well as in being chased by preposterous masses – be it cops (*Cops*, 1922) or women (*Seven Chances*, 1925). The reification of the human through his immersion in the mechanical informs some of Keaton's most famous images: his merging with the locomotive in *The General* (1926), with the steamer's paddle-wheel in *Daydreams* (1922), or with the cinematic apparatus itself in *Sherlock Jr.* (1924).

In many ways, much like Kafka's works, Keaton's films anticipate the existential notion of the absurd, as it would appear later in the twentieth century in the works of Albert Camus, Samuel Beckett and others.[1] As shown in this essay, this is far from being the only commonality between Kafka's and Keaton's art.

As already observed by Rudolf Arnheim (2005: 56–7), the distinction between silent and sound film may be illustrated by the human figure: in the former case it is part of its surroundings, while in the latter it is the uniqueness of the talking man that stands in the foreground of artistic creation. Speech took man away from things and destroyed his equality with them, leading to a complete dichotomy in the way we understand the art of both motion picture media: action and gesticulated narration and performance in the silent film led to words and to a more restrained kind of acting that supported psychologically developed characters in the talking film.

These aspects are also at the core of Adorno's 'Notes on Kafka', where he refers at length to the author's opposition to psychology that has special implications for movies, and particularly the silent ones which naturally had to rely much more on gestures. For Adorno, the most important process in Kafka's prose is the dismantling of the individual's inner soul by perceiving him as an object among objects, or a body among bodies. It is a process of becoming-a-thing (*Verdinglichung*), by which the world of objects takes over the place of the abstract subject. Adorno refers to Kafka's literature as a study of what would happen if psychoanalysis manifested itself not in the mental sphere but in the body itself – if 'the results of psychoanalysis were to prove true not merely metaphorically but in the flesh' (1983: 251).[2] If it lost its metaphoric condition to become lively, that is, liveable, then Adorno himself uses figurative language when stating: 'The flight through man and beyond into non-human – that is Kafka's epic course' (1983: 252). By 'non-human', Adorno refers both to Kafka's many animalistic figures and to his fascination with objects as such, and there are cases that are a perfect hybrid of the two, as is Odradek's in 'Die Sorge des Hausvaters' ('The Cares of a Family Man', 1919), who/which is both a living creature and an object. The 'course' referred to here (*Bahn*, in German) is both a rail or track, and a motivation or fascination, and so this 'epic motivation' is also a narrative move in the course of which (that is, its movement, or flight) makes the human inhuman.

It appears therefore that Adorno's and Arnheim's depictions are complementary oppositions: in literature, the movement is from the elaborate mimesis of psychological individuals in the talkative mode (of the Western novel for example) to the world of reification found in Kafka's depiction of man (with and among the non-human). In film, it is the movement from a mimesis of action, a vibrant dynamics between man and the objects around him, to the talking film that emphasises psychological development. As we shall see, this metaphor is in complete accord with Keaton's fascination with machinery as a consolidation of his narrative motivation. This crucial conceptualisation of Keaton is most clearly evident in his famous feature film *The General*, which serves as a fitting illustration of Adorno's metaphor because it is all about the railway.

I. INDIFFERENCE: BETWEEN SPACE AND FACE

Another quote from Adorno can be useful for my next argument: 'It is not the horrible which shocks, but its self-evidence' (1983: 248).[3] This banality of the shock experience was similarly applied by Gabriel Moked, who devoted an entire book to Kafka's 'Die Verwandlung' ('The Metamorphosis', 1915):

> Gregor's entire new body is meticulously depicted and only his face is never mentioned. True, Gregor cannot see his own face and in his room there is no mirror. It is clear that everyone can see his face but the entire metamorphosis is being told from his point of view, or at least from the point of view of someone who identifies with him. This is why we are not told what others see. (1959: 18; my translation)

Only when Gregor Samsa starts looking at the four familiar walls of his room, does he become aware of his metamorphosis. The adjectives Kafka uses here – 'human', 'regular', 'quiet' and 'familiar' – are incommensurate with a nightmare. This banal appearance of the room becomes starkly clearer as Gregor's gaze passes over his furniture and belongings.

Moked's evaluation of the story's famous opening plays down nuances to point to an important general phenomenon. The room's depiction is not entirely banal, since Kafka uses a very peculiar way of describing it, thereby creating something that is at the same time banal and haunting – *uncanny* to use Freud's poignant concept. He refers to it as the 'human-room' (*Menschenzimmer*) – actually not a word in common German usage, but more of a neologism (see Hubel 2005: 21). But the crucial point is that while there is no description of the face, body and space are carefully depicted with all their uncanniness.

This mode of description is exactly what enables the shock effect referred to by Adorno, because using it turns our attention away from the monstrous metamorphosis itself and towards the terrifying indifference with which the author (and his protagonist) deal with it. This indifference, I argue, is a by-product of Kafka's choice to focus on space rather than on the face, synecdochic of his aforementioned general tendency to avoid description of emotions and reactions. Just like the face of the Keaton figure, Gregor does not react: he just acts. It is this lack of reaction on the protagonist's part that makes for the Kafkaesque horror effect and affect, which in turn also enables comedy, for if the terrifying fails to generate shock or any other affective reaction, for that matter, our entire perception goes off the rails.

The faces of figures in Western literature, and especially in the realistic novel, are primarily what makes them human, unique in both their physical and mental properties. They make them individuals, a word that connotes distinction from what is common, and which represents one of the most crucial concepts of Adorno's philosophical heritage. For example, famous female protagonists such as Emma Bovary or Tony Buddenbrook are depicted through their minutest facial features as individuals *reacting* emotionally to what unfolds before them. Eyebrows, cheeks, the forehead, lips and chin, and, of course, the nose and eyes – not to mention the skin itself – are of tremendous importance in Western mimesis. This is also true of film with its countless emotionally powerful close-ups on both female and male protagonists, such as Keaton's most famous contemporary, Charlie Chaplin's tramp.

'The Metamorphosis' is therefore a paradigmatic case for my argument, since the avoidance of the individual face and the emotions it embodies and the privileging of the common space that surrounds it are to be found not only in the extreme case of Gregor the monstrous vermin, but also in the depiction of K., the common (and even bourgeois, in the case of Josef K.) man, in *The Trial* and *The Castle*. Clearly evident in all three is the tension between a faceless, indifferent or transparent subject and the careful attention devoted to his physical surrounding. This focus on space rather than the individual is, as we shall see, one of the strongest parallels between Kafka and Keaton.

Moreover, recall that previous to the confrontation with the quiet room, the narrator in 'The Metamorphosis' focuses on Gregor's new body, particularly describing his stomach and the many new tiny legs that brought physical difficulties upon him. Alongside the description of the space around him, Gregor's physical travails, his successes and failures, form the core of the narrator's view. Body, objects and movement go hand in hand.

In a similar vein, Noël Carroll emphasises that the comic effect in Keaton's movies derives from his failures to meet our expectations of bodily intelligence, mainly because of his absentmindedness (2007: 7). For our present purposes, we can see in this absentmindedness a link and source of indifference, since while events in the protagonist's environment are met with indifference (no real reactions or consequences follow the action), absentmindedness is what initiates them in the first place. Thus, human agency is lacking on both the proactive and reactive ends of the filmic action. As I will show, the Keaton figure embodies a blend of activity and passivity that is unique both in comparison with some of Keaton's contemporary silent-film comedians and in its relation to Kafka's figures.

In many of his films Keaton's figure is focused on a specific (mostly romantic) goal: *Sherlock Jr.*, *The General*, *College* (1927) and *Steamboat Bill Jr.* are some examples where the narrative is based almost entirely on the protagonist's physical activity in pursuit of that goal. But this physical agency is discrepant with Keaton's facial and emotional passivity. As already intimated, Carroll's main argument concerns the body, as he identifies the Keatonesque almost as a study of how the body collides with the material world around it (2007: 10), reminiscent of Adorno's scrutiny of Kafka and his focus on the body. This behaviour, or intelligence, whether with objects or with the body itself, can be shown to us only by placing the *process* itself (meaning the mechanism, the means without necessarily having any ends) that is at the core of fictional representation, in film and literature alike. Even compared to Chaplin – whose fascination with objects such as the feeding machine in *Modern Times* (1936) is clearly very present – Carroll states that the process itself is more evident in Keaton (2007: 126). However convoluted, what Chaplin's tramp does is always imbued by what Carroll identifies as an individualistic romantic view that makes him an outcast of society who always sees things differently (2007: 133). Accordingly, one can argue that even in Chaplin's films, processes have their motivations and ends.

Carroll's reference to Keaton's contemporary Harold Lloyd suggests insights on the differences between Josef K. and K. the land surveyor. In Carroll's view, the motivation behind Lloyd's action is his ambition – 'success in its popular clichés'; he does not have extraordinary physical skills or inexhaustible energy but he continues to wring out one last ounce of energy in order to throw his wearied body into the breach one more time (2007: 141–2). We cannot find this kind of constant ambition in Keaton, but we can certainly find it, for example, in K.'s struggle in *The Castle*: to accomplish his goal he is willing to retire from his position as land surveyor and become a school janitor. But can we associate Josef K. with constant ambition too? Much like Gregor Samsa, he is involved in a (quite physical) struggle that comes upon him from the outside, from the circumstances of his surroundings.

Facial passivity combined with physical agency can be also explored through Keaton's relation to Harry Langdon, whom Carroll identifies as a character who lacks both intelligence and physical ability: 'In *The General* we find a character that makes things happen and we find gags about how he makes things happen. Such agency is beyond the developmental capability of baby Harry' (2007: 150).

In order to benefit more from these comparisons, however, we have to place Keaton just between these extremes: in relation to Lloyd, Keaton is passive, but in relation to Langdon he seems active. The same goes for his childish attributes: Keaton seems to lack these attributes compared to Langdon, but compared to someone like Lloyd – who shares what all adults (and even children, but certainly not babies) share, ie effort designed to achieve something concrete – he seems lost and completely agentless. This 'passive activity' is accomplished through the conflict between Keaton's body and face: he ceaselessly acts and he is involved in extremely physical situations, but his indifferent face creates the impression that he is reluctant to accomplish anything.

I find that Carroll somehow misses those important nuances that shed light on both Keaton and Kafka's two K.s. My argument is that Keaton is unique precisely because he combines these traits of passivity and physical intelligence. Keaton's face hovers above in indifference as if in complete nirvana, and from this indifference comes his alleged passivity.

In many ways, this hyphenated existence of being both passive and active is what makes both K.s, Gregor Samsa, and to some extent all of Kafka's characters so remarkable. Kafka subjects his protagonists to an enactment that is completely imposed from the outside, one that never has its own motivation or ends. These representations of the human resemble in a way the accused in *The Trial*, who are drawn into the courthouse by their own guilt, as is Josef K. when he arrives at a hearing apparently of his own will but in a way that seems much more decreed from above. To some degree, this is also true of K. the land surveyor, whose entire struggle to remain in the village, despite being so degraded by its inhabitants, places a huge question mark on his human ability to re-act. Like Keaton and Josef K., he only acts. It is as if one can imagine his quarrels with Frieda, the two innkeepers, Momus and practically everyone else in the novel, unfold while his face remains completely devoid of any visible emotion.

II. SPACES: BETWEEN PASSIVITY AND MOVEMENT

North-African French critic Robert Benayoun dedicated a brief chapter in his book *Le regard de Buster Keaton* (*Buster Keaton: Der Augenblick des Schweigens* ['The Look of Buster Keaton'], 1983) to a comparative study of Kafka and Keaton. The German translation made this connection more explicit by adding the word 'silence' to the book's title *Buster Keaton: The Look of Silence*. It is the silent look that inspired Benayoun to explore the comparison with Kafka, as he noted in the two epigraphs to the chapter: one by Walter Kerr referring to Keaton as the most silent moviemaker of silent movies, and the other by Max Brod referring to Kafka's Prague nickname, 'the quiet one'.

But what does it mean to be silent, or the most silent? Clearly, it has nothing to do, as with the 'silent' film adjective, with sounds themselves. This muteness is a personality attribute, possibly alluding to some kind of mystery. But referring to the eyes or the gaze that are all about expressiveness as 'silent' is referring precisely to their lack of expression, and by extension to a more general passivity or indifference. Benayoun's study of Kafka and Keaton is highly impressionistic, and so this quietness that he attributes to Kafka after Brod is more of a biographical anecdote about his reception by his contemporaries. Still, his observations are valuable and I would like to dwell shortly on some of them.

In describing Kafka's protagonists (mostly Josef K. and Gregor Samsa) and Keaton, Benayoun uses the following adjectives, among others: their 'indecisiveness' unravels life to them as blows of destiny, violent and rapid; they are 'naive' and 'stubborn' and share the same fear of authorities and an ongoing sense of guilt (1983: 54). Of course one can question each of these traits, especially with regard to Keaton, whose sense of guilt is entirely doubtful and of a different register than that of Kafka's K.s. But this reference to indecisiveness and naivety combined with stubbornness represents a very astute observation, since as we have seen (especially in the case of K. the land surveyor), passivity combined with activity is very evident in the description of these figures as they are always in the process of acting without *reacting*. Moreover, the ability to react is the essence of agency, since someone who just acts constantly and monotonously without really interacting with the environment is apathetic or even catatonic, hence the muted gaze. We can find constant guilt in someone who simply always acts, constantly in the process of doing something, and perhaps even has desires, but all while his face and look are reluctant to reveal any of this. When faced with someone, Keaton's body constantly acts, but face does not budge – we gain the impression of naivety and guilt. He is not really calm, only his face is, rendering his effort suspicious. One can feel this tension especially in Keaton's interaction with other men, whose masculinity and ability are superior to his, as he is constantly in pursuit to try and please his girl, while all manner of terrible humiliations do not seem to leave any mark on him.[4]

Generally the energetic or hyperactive person is motivated by the desire to please (even if they are actually only pleasing themselves). A remarkable illustration of this may be found in the proverb mentioned by the merchant Block in *The Trial*, addressed to Josef K.: 'For a suspect, movement is better than staying still, for someone who is still can always, without realizing it, be in the scales and be weighed with his sins' (2009a: 138). While it is unclear what exactly Benayoun means by 'guilt', it is clear that those industrious beings that are never in the position of sitting calmly, these bodies of movements, are in the end bodies of the accused. By referring here to the face, I hope to illustrate this notion of Block's, for unlike Block, whose trembling body and appearance are carefully depicted in the novel, Keaton – as well as Kafka's protagonist – are in motion, but at the same time frozen, giving the impression that they too are being weighted on the scale.

The full sense of the term *klidas* – Kafka's nickname among his Czech-speaking acquaintances referred to in Benayoun's chapter – is 'the silent giant' (*stummer Koloss*; see Löwy 1992: 82) – clearly not referring to Kafka's physical character, particularly as in German the meaning of the word has generally more to do with structure than with stature. Referring to an entire structure that has silent presence captures a lot of what I have intimated after Adorno on space, the body and its relation to objects.

When Kafka does linger on descriptions, he deals with a peculiar structure in space, such as the appearance of Gregor's room after the metamorphosis. To that we can add the voluminous description of the machine in 'In der Strafkolonie' ('In the Penal Colony', 1919) or the innkeeper's dresses in *The Castle*. Two other examples will make this point and its relevance to Keaton clearer. One of Kafka's most peculiar creatures is the abovementioned Odradek in 'The Cares of a Family Man'. It is a story that is almost entirely devoted to the description of that creature that, on the whole, seems to look like a 'flat star-shaped spool of thread' (1988: 469), whatever that means. The author continues to question the properties of the *Gebilde* (like *Koloss*, this word means form or structure), that moves constantly and rapidly, and has infantile attributes because of its small proportions. What interests me is the outcome of the narrator's interaction with the creature:

> But it is only the kind of laughter that has no lungs behind it. It sounds rather like the rustling of fallen leaves. And that is usually the end of the conversation. Even these answers are not always forthcoming; often he stays mute for a long time, as wooden as his appearance. (1988: 470)

After a short dialogue between them, Odradek laughs, but it seems that this expression is so minor that it is more likely to produce almost no sound at all. That creature dwells in all the contours of the house, resembling in a way Keaton's movements in interiors as in *The Electric House* (1922), and seems to be ultimately an integral part of its objects: he is himself a piece of wood (1988: 469). After this it seems that to accurately define Odradek would be to argue that he is a 'tiny giant', and that this tendency to be marginal, minor and almost invisible, is actually what stands behind Kafka's Czech nickname.

But then, in the next and final paragraph of the story, comes a very interesting observation by the narrator on the creature's immortality: 'Anything that dies has had some kind of aim in life, some kind of activity, which has worn out; but that does not apply to Odradek' (1988: 470.). So Odradek's very minor but also very hectic activity is without end, what makes him/it immune to death, and thereby indifferent to human agency.

The second example is informed by Lisa Trahair's work on the Keatonesque, which is based largely on her conception that Keaton's film mastery is at its finest when he is able to use a single prop to construct both his entire plot and his gags, such as the train in *The General*, the movie camera in *The Cameraman* and the steamboat in *Steamboat Bill, Jr.* (2007: 64). This fascination with machinery, the operational aesthetic, is invoked by the machines that make cinema – the camera and projector – and thereby finds an end in itself, fascination without purpose (2007: 69). After Daniel Moews' analysis, Trahair offers *The General* as an example of where the film's spatial and narrative lines emerge and coincide in the railroad line that animates the collision between Johnny the protagonist and his rivals the northerners.

This offers a wonderful starting point for comparing the machinery narrative that Trahair finds in Keaton with Kafka. Kafka can even be said to exceed Keaton in that regard, in a story where the structure itself *is* the antagonist. I am referring to one of Kafka's most astonishing achievements: the long fragment novella 'Der Bau' ('The Burrow', 1931). It is a novella centred on only one figure – a mole-like animal which is also the narrator – and its space, the underground structure it has built throughout its entire life. Description dominates the story. It is all about architectural description of burrows and tunnels, squares and entrances, and when not, it is about hushed noises leading to a build-up of some state of light paranoia, driven by the creature's complete solitude. The construction, which is also the story's title (given by Brod after Kafka's manuscript),[5] becomes an entity which the protagonist addresses in the second-person speech, and sometimes unravels to us in parts, such as the Castle Keep (*Burgplatz*) or the different burrows themselves, as it addresses them in the plural. The space itself becomes its friend and at times its rival.

I want to examine a passage that is not entirely devoted to description, and not entirely to these dialogues with spaces, but one that shares both, and clearly echoes my notions on 'The Metamorphosis'. After establishing a kind of uplifted wall around the Castle Keep, the narrator is in a state of rapture:

> What a joy to lie pressed against the rounded outer wall, pull oneself up, let oneself slid down again, miss one's footing and find oneself on firm earth, and play all those games literally upon the Castle Keep and not inside it; to avoid the Castle Keep, to rest one's eyes from it whenever one wanted, to postpone the joy of seeing until later and yet not have to do without it, but literally hold it safe between one's claws. (1988: 374)

Those up and down movements recall of course Samsa's intense physical arousal from climbing the walls of his 'regular' room. Here it is even clearer that what is experienced is a kind of sexual intercourse that derives from the precise quality Odradek displays, of recursive movement, or traffic (*Verkehr*, one of the German words for intercourse).

Most important for my purposes, this game is anything but instrumental. That a place or object can be transformed into a partner, in many ways literally a live partner, is also an example of one of the important features Trahair finds in the relation between the Keaton figure and its objects: their 'metamorphos-ability' (2007: 92). This can happen much more easily when objects do not have purposes. In other words, Keaton and Kafka rob objects of their objectives for the purpose of pure movement.

One can find examples of this all throughout Trahair's book, but there is an important difference between Keaton and Kafka when it comes to this incongruous manner in which objects transform their senses. While in Keaton it is only processes that deal with objects – as in *The Navigator* (1924), where while diving underwater Keaton puts up a barricade with the sign 'men at work', and washes his hands with a bucket – in Kafka, processes (as clearly alluded by the German title of his famous novel) play a role of their own. The incongruity in

Kafka is in fact a lack of decorum, and has much to do with *social* processes, where the entire realm of speech acts (as in fact in the example of 'men at work') is completely distorted.⁶ An accusation is not an accusation and the same applies to arrests, trials, hearings, petitions or investigations (especially in *The Trial* and *The Castle*).

III. THE GESTURE AND THE HUMAN

Kafka's biographer Reiner Stach claims that Kafka was the first author to ever deal at length with total alienation and dehumanisation in industrialised companies. Stach compares Karl Rossmann's encounter with his uncle's factory in *Der Verschollene* (*Amerika*, 1946) and Chaplin's *Modern Times* (2002: 198). Let us examine parts of this encounter:

> His uncle opened the first of these doors and in the glaring electric light Karl saw an operator, quite oblivious to any sound from the door, his head bound in a steel band which pressed the receivers against his ears. His right arm was lying on the little table as if it were strangely heavy and only the fingers holding the pencil kept twitching with inhumanly regularity and speed. [...] Through the hall there was a perpetual tumult of people rushing hither and thither. Nobody said good day, greetings were omitted. (1946: 43)

Here, too, Kafka provides a lengthy and elaborate description – using careful depiction of eye contacts and gestures – of an apparatus that is mute as much as tumultuous. Stach emphasises that Kafka actually depicts the lack of any nuances in human behaviour and that in doing so he surpasses Chaplin:

> In this respect Kafka went beyond Chaplin: the human disposition no longer expresses anything per se; it either becomes a function or withers away. Not only do people stop saying hello to one another, they also stop looking one another in the eye or exchanging hand signals, or showing even the most basic tolerance of uncertainty, ambiguity and redundancy. (2005: 183)⁷

I suggest that what Stach does not find in Chaplin can actually be found in my analysis of Keaton. It is indifference that makes human gestures inhuman and it is this inhumanity that distinguishes Keaton from Chaplin.

Interestingly, like many others, Stach does not see the link between these inhuman movements and the poetics of gestures that became a prominent aspect in Kafka's interpretations since Walter Benjamin in the 1930s. These gestures are unique because of their 'pictorial quality that resists on their surface appearance and thereby refuses any meaning "behind", "beyond" or "beneath"' (Mladek 2003: 232); they are physical, pictorial and totally refuse *human* interpretation. This resistance to interpretation was cunningly perceived by Benjamin (2007: 120), who described Kafka's literature as antinomy between the call for interpretation made by its parabolic quality and the refusal thereof by its symbolic quality in the form of these obscure gestures.

Can this antinomy be found in Keaton? It is difficult to tell. Clearly the gestures are similarly evident in his work because of their incongruity. Perhaps the answer may be found in the Keaton figure itself that is even more abstract than Chaplin's tramp: the Keaton figure does not even have a nickname and one can hardly characterise it as 'vagabond' or 'uprooted'. Like Josef K. and K. the land surveyor, it has only the signifier of its author – Kafka, Keaton, K. – rather than a given name: only a signifier, no name.[8] The biographical attachment Kafka and Keaton share makes it even more striking: the filmmaker's given name was Josef Frank Keaton, which resembles so many of Kafka's much beloved abbreviations, such as F. K., F., K. and, of course, Josef K.

Let us now proceed to more obvious similarities. Klaus Mladek's brilliant study of the performance in Kafka's fiction and its relation to the court of law carefully scrutinises the observations also made by Adorno and Benjamin. Mladek shows how fascinated Kafka was with postures, gestures and their enactments in performance and imitation. In the end, the court is nothing but plain conventions:

> The more 'senseless' the demands of the court officials, the more compelling is their performative force. The tautological pronouncement that the 'law is law' paradoxically proves to be the most 'convincing rhetoric the court can employ'. Kafka's *The Trial* shows convincingly that interiority and the soul – among the most powerful cultural concepts in our modern philosophical tradition – do not proceed corporeality, but rather that they are cooriginary and coexistent with their expression. (2003: 228)

The interiority of the human – his psychological aspect in Adorno's words – is left barren, only the body and its actions remain, with no 'behind' or 'above'. The questioning of the legal *process* unfolds precisely by these gestures that are deprived of any continuity, coherence, or congruity. Herein also lies the importance of the speech acts in Kafka and Keaton as a continuation of these traits that Benjamin was able to detect. The signifier K. is again the one that only acts and does not leave any impression, thereby rendering life's conventions, be they verbal or physical, traceless and therefore senseless.

The bending of the upper body is perhaps the most familiar gesture in *The Trial*, shared by all parties, prosecutors and defendants alike. It is somewhat similar to one of Keaton's most famous frames in *The General*, in which the Keaton figure sits on the locomotive's coupling rod, bending with his head on the machine, and thus in this act of full indulgence immerses itself as part of the object: Keaton and the engine become one as it starts moving and they both coalesce in movement. The human indulges in complete passivity so that the gesture arises as such, with no purpose.

Benjamin's understanding of the human gesture is also informed by his eruptive dialogue with his friend Franz Rosenzweig and the latter's *Der Stern der Erlösung* (*The Star of Redemption*, 1970). In this book, Rosenzweig uses Jewish and Chinese examples to define a state of purity that is enabled by its plainness, its lack of any characteristics: 'Chinese feeling is without the least relation to character, without any relation, as it were, to its own bearer; it is purely *objective*. [...] Of Lau-tzu, however, it is said that he wanted to remain nameless. It is this "concealment of the self"' (1970: 75; emphasis added). Examining Chinese poetry, philosophy and theatre, Rosenzweig is fascinated by this elevation of the plain (also by Confucius): a pureness of being that lacks everything other than being itself, without even having a name. In order to achieve this purity, poetry has to learn to be mute:

> It [poetry] would itself have to bring forward a configuration; it will have to become gesture. For only gesture is beyond word and deed [...]. This is accomplished on our festival of redemption by that prostration which is the ultimate gesture of all mankind; this prostration bursts every space and erases all time. [...] A word forgets itself and has to be forgotten; it wants to perish in the answer. The power of the glance, however, does not perish with the moment. (1970: 371, 372)

In a way, Rosenzweig's poetic vision is to dismantle poetry of its dependence on time – to make the spoken word almost non-referential, something that has nothing to do with communication; no speech or action as means to any end, but a gesture for itself. That is why he talks of poetry but prioritises the glance over the word. The look acts for itself without continuation, it does not imply reaction.

It is not clear which gesture Rosenzweig refers to when he talks about 'prostration', but one can assume it is the general movement made by Jewish worshippers, bending forward or to the sides while folding the knees slightly. It has great cultural and historical significance with regard to the way Jews were seen in Europe during the first half of the twentieth century.

This essay has suggested several similarities and connections between Kafka's literary heritage and Keaton's filmography. Of course, the face and the look have many philosophical implications that deserve further elaboration. For Emmanuel Levinas, for example, the face is a constant call for political recognition of the Other, a constant and inherently *passive* acceptance that creates a kind of alertness among people (2004: 185). The wrinkles on the trapeze artist's forehead in 'First Sorrow' lead to the psychological realm of the ego. It is precisely the lack of description (as in Jewish literature from the Hebrew Bible onwards), the lack of a face, that enables awareness of the Other, who stands precisely in an equal relation to Me, since both the I, much like its Other, do not possess the individual face for which humanism calls. As I have intimated, Kafka is not inclined to literary description, and when he does dwell on it, it is for the sake of a unique space or apparatus, rather than a human emotion. I would go even further and say that with the exception of the trapeze artist in 'First Sorrow', there is no face in Kafka.[9]

NOTES

1   Hence it comes as no surprise that in his short cinematic piece *Film* (1966), Samuel Beckett casts the seventy-year-old Keaton in the lead role.
2   'Die Flucht durch den Menschen hindurch ins Nichtmenschliche – das ist Kafkas epische Bahn' (Adorno 1977: 262).
3   'Nicht das Ungeheuerliche schockiert sondern dessen Selbstverständlichkeit' (Adorno 1977: 258).
4   This is particularly evident in *The Cameraman* (1928), in which his rivalry with the other man is most extreme, since he has only one main antagonist, who in fact abuses him, as, for example, in the scene where he is left exposed in the rain during a long ride – that, too, does not leave any mark on him.
5   As in English, the original title 'Der Bau' (the building), means both the act and its outcome.
6   The speech act is completely understudied in the Kafka literature and literary studies in general. John Hillis Miller, in his *Speech Acts in Literature* (2001) and in his chapter 'The Breakdown of Community and the Disabling of Speech Act in Kafka's *The Trial*' is an exception.
7   'Noch entscheidender aber ist – und hier greift Kafka weit über Chaplin hinaus – dass das menschliche Habitus nichts mehr ausdruckt sondern entweder Funktion wird oder untergeht. Abgeschafft wird … jeder art von Unbestimmtheit, Mehrdeutigkeit und Redundanz' (Stach 2002: 199).
8   Some of the protagonists in Keaton's feature films do have a name, but otherwise the generic Keaton is referred to just as 'Buster'.

9   I thank the editors, Shai Biderman and Ido Lewit, for their help and advice.

BIBLIOGRAPHY

Adorno, Theodor W. (1977 [1953]) 'Aufzeichnungen zu Kafka', *Gesammelte Schriften T. 10.1*, ed. R. Tiedemann. Frankfurt am Mein: Suhrkamp, 254–87.

____ (1983) 'Notes on Kafka', *Prisms*. Cambridge: MIT Press, 243–71.

Arnheim, Rudolph (2005 [1957]) 'The Artistry of Silent Film', in Thomas E. Wartenberg and Angela Curran (eds) *The Philosophy of Film: Introductory Texts and Readings*. Malden, MA: Blackwell, 50–8.

Benayoun, Robert (1983) *Buster Keaton: Der Augenblick des Schweigens*. Munich: Bahia.

Benjamin, Walter (2007 [1934]) 'Kafka: On the Tenth Anniversary of his Death', *Illuminations*, trans. Harry Zohn. New York: Schocken, 111–40.

Carroll, Noël (2007) *Comedy Incarnate: Buster Keaton, Physical Humor, and Bodily Coping*. Malden, MA: Blackwell.

Hubel, Monika (2005) 'The Implications of Translations: Franz Kafka's Voice and its English Echo', *Translation Review*, 69, 1, 17–25.

Kafka, Franz (1946 [1927]) *Amerika*, trans. Edwin Muir. New York: New Directions.

____ (1988) *The Complete Stories*, ed. Nahum Glatzer. New York: Schocken.

____ (1993) *Selected Short Stories of Franz Kafka*, trans. Willa and Edwin Muir. New York: The Modern Library.

____ (2002) *Kafka's Metamorphosis and Other Writings*, ed. Helmut Kiesel. New York: Continuum.

____ (2009a [1925]) *The Trial*, trans. Mike Mitchell. Oxford: Oxford University Press.

____ (2009b [1926]) *The Castle*, trans. Anthea Bell. Oxford: Oxford University Press.

Levinas, Emmanuel (2004) *Autrement qu'être, ou-delà de l'essence*, Paris: Livre de Poche.

Löwy, Michael (1992) *Redemption and Utopia: Jewish Libertarian Thought in Central Europe: A Study in Elective Affinity*. Stanford, CA: Stanford University Press.

Miller, Joseph H. (2001) *Speech Acts in Literature*. Stanford, CA: Stanford University Press.

____ (2011) 'The Breakdown of Community and the Disabling of Speech Act in Kafka's *The Trial*', in *The Conflagration of Community: Fiction Before and After Auschwitz*. Chicago: University of Chicago Press, 67–101.

Mladek, Klaus (2003) 'Radical Play: Gestures, Performance, and the Theatrical Logic of the Law in Kafka', *Germanic Review*, 78, 3, 223–49.

Moked, Gabriel (1956) *Franz Kafka's Die Verwandlung: A Critical Study by Gabriel Moked*. Tel Aviv: Mahadir. [Hebrew]

Rosenzweig, Franz (1970) *The Star of Redemption*, trans. William W. Hallo. New York, Chicago and San Francisco: Holt, Rinehart and Winston.

Stach, Reiner (2002) *Kafka: die Jahren der Entscheidungen*. Frankfurt am Main: S. Fischer.
____ (2005) *Kafka: The Decisive Years*, trans. Shelley Frisch. Orlando, FL: Har-court.
Trahair, Lisa (2007) 'The Machine of Comedy, Gunning, Deleuze, and Buster Keaton', in *The Comedy of Philosophy, Sense and Nonsense in Early Cinematic Slapstick*. New York: SUNY Press, 59–85.

TRANSLATING KAFKA INTO ITALIAN: KAFKAESQUE THEMES IN ELIO PETRI'S FILMS

FERNANDO GABRIEL PAGNONI BERNS
AND LEONARDO ACOSTA LANDO

A man kills his mistress and then leaves the crime scene, but he does so leaving ample clues of his identity. Why does he do that? Because he wants to prove that he is above all suspicion and, sure enough, nobody seems to connect him with the crime. This is the premise of *Indagine su un cittadino al di sopra di ogni sospetto* (*Investigation of a Citizen Above Suspicion*, 1970), an Elio Petri film that ends with a line from Franz Kafka's 'Vor dem Gesetz' ('Before the Law', 1915). The film's message is clear: law, as an institution, rather than searching for the truth, uses its bureaucratic mechanisms to separate the guilty from the innocent. This message rings particularly true in a country such as Italy which, in the 1970s, saw the extreme-left movements trying to shatter all forms of institutional representation that is intrinsically associated with oppressive fascist movements (see Vighi 2006: 96).

This is not the only one of Petri's films manifestly influenced by Kafka. Many of his multi-genre outputs, from thrillers through science fiction to horror, present Kafkaesque stories. This is more than just a matter of personal literary taste. During the 1960s and 1970s, Italy experienced an ongoing lack of coherence: in these years, Italy's post-war 'economic miracle', which had opened the country to the world, was fading, while terrorism intensified year after year. Italian society's self-perception was therefore fragmentary and obscure, elements easily recognisable as Kafkaesque. If this adjective means, among other things, 'anxiety-ridden' (see Gross 2002: 98) then the Italy of those decades certainly was.

Also Kafkaesque is the narrative of *Un tranquillo posto di campagna* (*A Quiet Place in the Country*, 1968), a surrealist horror film that explores the ultimately elusive meaning of art; while the lesser-known *L'assassino* (*The Assassin*, 1961) foreshadows *Investigation of a Citizen Above Suspicion*. All these films are generously sprinkled with humour, an often ignored but clearly recognisable element in Kafka (see Deleuze and Guattari 1986: 41).

This essay examines Kafka's presence in Petri's films through intertextual analysis of his work. The purpose of this analysis is thus to articulate literary influence, social context and film discourse in the works of Elio Petri.

I. LAW IN *INVESTIGATION OF A CITIZEN ABOVE SUSPICION* AND *THE ASSASSIN*

Kafka's influence on Petri's oeuvre is explicit in *Investigation of a Citizen Above Suspicion*. It ends with a quote from Kafka's parable 'Before the Law', where the author expresses the impossibility of having recourse to any kind of primordial source of law: 'Whatever he may seem to us, he is yet a servant of the Law; that is, he belongs to the Law and as such is set beyond human judgment.' With this line, Petri signals a clear separation between what law is – corruptible, fallible, bureaucratic, capriciously arbitrary and rigidly structured – and some kind of 'essential' notion of law, one that precedes (and exceeds) human practice. If this latter notion of law truly exists, it is inapprehensible to humans. In this scenario, laws are cultural constructions and culture a prolonged denial of humanity, glossed over by rules and norms inextricably linked to ideology.

In the same vein, Kafka's 'Zur Frage der Gesetze' ('The Problem of Our Laws', 1931) offers a transparent political reading of the nature of power that denounces 'Law' as merely a euphemism for 'hegemony' (see Dodd 2002: 145). 'The Problem of Our Laws' is a short story about a community governed by secretive nobility, which claims exclusive access to knowledge of the law and its mechanisms, and keeps all other social groups ignorant of its truth. As in 'Before the Law', knowledge of the law is denied. But in 'The Problem of Our Laws' this knowledge is denied to common citizens. Thus, law as an institution – and Kafka 'was fascinated by institutions' (Robertson 2004: 67) – connotes hegemony and the ideology that supports it. Those who uphold it, are 'pushed quite out of question' (Tester 1993: 82) and do not have to answer for the true status or origin of their power and capacity of judgement. Law and the mechanisms that support it are a theme both Kafka and Petri return to time and again. For both, it is an extraneous set of bureaucratically applied rules and norms which have become increasingly detached from human intellect.

Petri's *Investigation of a Citizen Above Suspicion* is based on the idea that thanks to their class or status, some citizens are above suspicion. An unnamed chief homicide inspector kills his lover, Augusta Terzi, seemingly only to make the point that he is above suspicion: as a senior detective, nobody will connect him with the crime even if he left ample clues behind, including finger- and footprints all over the crime scene. Moreover, he leaves a large sum of money in a highly visible place so that investigators will discard robbery as a motive. He even deliberately leaves a loose thread of his purple tie entangled in one of the dead woman's nails. Before leaving the crime scene, he makes an anonymous tip to the police, without faking his voice and with his characteristic commanding tone unmasked. Finally, when he leaves the building after the murder, he does not take any particular precautions to conceal his presence: in the front door, for example, he engages in a brief and unnecessary dialogue with a male stranger who is entering the building. This exchange is deliberate, intended to secure a witness who sees him leaving the building just minutes after the murder.

When the culprit returns to Augusta's apartment, now as a chief inspector in charge of the investigation, he again touches everything. This way, his absolute power is doubled: he is now both the killer and the coroner. In both capacities, and as opposed to ordinary citizens, he has the 'right' to touch everything. The inspector cover-ups the killer. This is retroactively anticipated in one of the inspector's many flashbacks recounting his days with Terzi: when he enters her apartment unannounced, she states that only 'cops or criminals' can do that.

The inspector is not the only citizen above suspicion in the film. In the apartment next to Terzi lives a famous doctor, one that the cops do not bother to question because he is also deemed beyond reproach. The law is thus a machine that identifies and targets its suspects, culprits, innocents and citizens above suspicion *a priori*, with little or no attention to the realities of each case. The analogy with a machine is thus far from superfluous. In a key scene, the inspector is introduced to a machine that can allegedly identify suspects even given very little leads. The machine is fed with names of those suspected of criminal activities – in this case, affiliation with politically subversive movements. After a few seconds, it spits out a name – Antonio Pace, the man who had accidentally seen the inspector leave the crime scene. The machine heralded by its operators as bringing progress to Italy, ironically pinpoints an innocent man. Note that the machine is fed with names of those with leftist political agendas rather than citizens who have previously been involved in murders. The boundaries between the different kinds of crimes are blurred and law seems unable to sustain a logic that helps separate the guilty from the innocent.

Thus, guilt is not constructed by transgression but by the pure power of law to designate any act as criminal, and suspects are moulded to fit predetermined parameters grounded in social status, race or ideology. Thus, Nicola Panunzio, one of the inspector's men, is chastised because his brother works for the Communist party, while Terzi's ex-husband is interrogated from the very beginning just because the inspector argues that 'ex-husbands are always guilty'. Furthermore, Terzi's ex-husband is homosexual, which makes him more suspicious by definition since some of the usual murder suspects produced by law are those who live on the fringes of society, such as gays. Terzi's ex-husband is brutally interrogated, not in order to refute suspicion, but to force a confession. He will be released only after the inspector, the embodiment of the law, pronounces his innocence.

Nobody links the inspector with the crime, even when investigators and witnesses make the right conjectures. Terzi's ex-husband tells about a man who had been harassing him by phone and describes him as someone of authority, probably a police officer (indeed, the inspector did make the calls). An unnamed witness who recognises the inspector as the real murderer changes his mind after a brief encounter. He does so not out of fear of reprisal but rather because, once faced with the inspector, he cannot recognise a killer in the face of the law, even when both look the same.

The inspector's actions become Kafkaesque when he explains that interrogated suspects become children and he, in his role of torturer, is the father of them all. In Kafka's texts, the figure of the father becomes a kind of primordial law (see Corngold and Wagner 2011: 54), a vacant space that reveals something about the authority of its discourse, but nothing about its content. The reference to the primordial is not incidental, since it is hidden to modern eyes, denying the modern common citizen any possibility of understanding where law obtains its legitimacy.

As noted by Asja Szafraniec (2007: 43), 'Before the Law' tells about the condition of its own possibility, working as a meta-language, since it places *en abyme* things usually considered external to works of literature such as the author, the reader, the experience of reading and so on. In this sense, Petri's film is a free play on generic conventions widely familiar in Italy, borrowing narrative devices and aesthetics from two of the most popular subgenres in the 1970s: the *giallo* and the *poliziotto*. The former means 'yellow', and is 'the metonymic term given to a series of mystery novels that the Milanese publisher Mondadori began producing in the late 1920s' (Koven 2006: 6). Soon enough, the term began to encompass any film mystery involving highly stylised crimes and amateur detectives as core narrative devices. The latter subgenre refers to mysteries based on procedural investigation 'where the police are the protagonist. Despite the differences between the *giallo* and the *poliziotto* film, both focus on the hunt for a serial killer' (Koven 2006: 7). Often these two subgenres are difficult to tell apart. From the *giallo*, Petri borrows the stylised murder of a beautiful woman and the visual motive of the spiral staircase as a symbol of the distorted criminal mind (the inspector has to walk up such a staircase up to Terzi's apartment) – one of the subgenre's most common motifs. From the *poliziotto*, he borrows the procedural investigation.

However, Petri disarms both subgenres in a series of deconstructive metalinguistic moves highly reminiscent of Kafka (see Thiher 2008: 47): Terzi makes her first appearance reading a yellow book, in a clear reference to the film's genre. Furthermore, she and her lover play highly complex sexual games in which she stages her own death and poses as a corpse. When the real murder is committed, it does not differ that much from the false murders reconstructed in the perpetrator's flashbacks. In turn, the *poliziotto* is deconstructed from the very start: this subgenre's essential plot movement is the search for the killer's identity, while keeping the audience guessing. Here, the audience knows the culprit's identity *ab initio*, and the procedural investigation is manifestly ineffective in that sense because the investigators overlook the ample clues connecting the inspector with the murder. This way, Petri uses displacement and estrangement to cast the audience in the role of the omniscient spectator. The film is not a murder story but a tale that utilises law just like Kafka does: as a poignant critique of power (see Dodd 2002: 136) and as a way of depicting the workings of hegemony.

By the end of the film, the inspector is formally accused of the crime, but not before practically giving himself away. If he is apprehended in the end, it is only thanks to his own last-minute contribution to the investigation, otherwise he would have been proved correct: some citizens, especially those who represent justice, are above it, and can escape judgement because they are part of the obscure mechanisms, largely invisible to ordinary citizens, which produce both culprits and innocents.

The process of interrogation has been a key point in *Investigation of a Citizen Above Suspicion*. In *The Assassin*, the process of interrogation and trial constitutes the entire plot. A socialite is murdered and her playboy lover and gigolo, Alfredo Martelli, is brought in for questioning, while the police are eager to convict him.

Unlike *Investigation of a Citizen Above Suspicion*, *The Assassin* does not make any explicit reference to Kafka. Still, Kafka's influence and the presence of the law as a sphere that structures its subjects are clearly present in the film (see Nowell-Smith et al. 1996). Especially clear is the film's reference to *Der Prozess* (*The Trial*, 1925), where Joseph K., a chief bank clerk, is unexpectedly arrested by two unidentified agents from an unspecified agency for an indefinable crime. Petri's film mirrors the novel's premise: Martelli is picked up by the police in his apartment without any apparent justification. In the precinct, he slowly discovers what the investigation is about as the audience learns details about his life. From the very beginning, Martelli insists on being told the cause for his arrest, but repeatedly receives only evasive answers. Furthermore, the police have no arrest order or indictment or at the very least, do not consider him important enough to peruse them.

Robert Burns characterises the opening scene of *The Trial*, where Joseph K. is similarly arrested without being told why, as 'at the same time ominous and ridiculous' (2014: 8). *The Assassin* echoes that duality: Martelli's arrest is ominous, since the bullying police officers deny him any information about his fate; but it is also humorous: Martelli insists he would not be taken to the police station, even by force, before a cut takes us to the station only to see a grumpy Martelli entering the interrogation room. There, he waits for long stretches of time without any clue. This situation once again invokes a Kafkaesque character – the man waiting indefinitely at the doors of the law to enter in 'Before the Law'.

In charge of Martelli's interrogation is Palumbo, a commissioner who resembles the Joseph K's inspector. The latter is 'helpful' in the sense that he 'liberates' Joseph K. and, in the film, the former constantly reassures Martelli that everything is fine. And like in *The Trial*, Martelli decides to go along with anything to speed things up. In the novel, Joseph K. asks to call a friend who can help him. The commissioner tells him this makes little sense. In *The Assassin*, Martelli asks to call someone who can help him, his rich lover Adalgisa De Matteis. The inspector lets him make the call, which proves pointless as De Matteis has been murdered and Martelli is being interrogated in relation to her death.

The Assassin is not a direct adaptation of any particular work, but the influence of *The Trial* pervades the entire plot. Martelli is a nasty person: an antiquarian who swindles sellers, and a man who uses the favours of wealthy women to climb up the social ladder. Still, he is innocent of De Matteis's murder, rendering the entire legal procedure an oppressive mechanism exercised by the powerful against the powerless. Martelli is locked in a cell while Palumbo slowly spins the web of guilt around him. In that, Palumbo acts much like the unnamed inspector from *Investigation of a Citizen Above Suspicion* when he managed to place the blame on the victim's ex-husband, if only momentarily.

In the end, Martelli is released once the real culprit is found (ironically, this time it really is the victim's ex-husband). Again, in some aspects the end mirrors *The Trial*: both Joseph K. (after the initial interrogation) and Martelli (at the film's end) are free, but the process continues to haunt them. Despite his innocence, Martelli cannot shake off his sense of guilt, and in the last scene he calls himself 'the murderer', assuming the role of the culprit. Thus, the judicial process and the law ultimately succeed in creating a culprit where there is none. Instead of catching the real criminal, the law makes an innocent man guilty.

In Petri's films, the interrogation process is depicted as a method designed not to extract some truth but to gradually construct a culprit. Being interrogated is itself proof that one is guilty, at least of something. *Investigation of a Citizen Above Suspicion* has a second (and peripheral) interrogation scene. When the inspector celebrates his promotion from chief of the homicide unit to the head of the department, he enters a room where an interrogation is taking place, interrupting it. The interrogated man is briefly forgotten by everyone. As glasses are raised to toast the inspector's promotion, even the interrogated man timidly raises his glass. In other words, the accused adopts his torturers' perspective, even if briefly.

The theme of the law as an institution which does not discern truth from falsehood, and which constructs culprits, is familiar in the Italian context. Importantly, Elio Petri was involved with the Communist Party and had written for the communist daily *L'Unitá* at the time when communists were persecuted, so he personally understood the capacity for the law to make culprits of people who attempt to construct a political alternative.

From the late 1960s, Italy experienced a period of socio-economic turmoil known as the *anni di piombo* ('years of lead'). This period was marked by a wave of terrorism that began with the assassination of police officer Antonio Annarumma and the Piazza Fontana bombing, both in 1969. These events were attributed to the far-right, the far-left and the secret services, depending on the source. In fact, the terror campaign was conducted by extremists on both sides of the political map and lasted through the 1970s (see Killinger 2002: 165). Throughout the *anni di piombo*, the situation was highly volatile, particularly since there was no one group that could be singled out as the culprit. Citizens lived in constant fear and anguish. Against this backdrop of uncertainty and oppression, Petri's penchant for the Kafkaesque and paradoxical makes perfect sense.

II. THE ALIENATED ARTIST IN *A QUIET PLACE IN THE COUNTRY*

While both films discussed above utilise Kafkaesque themes to deliver Petri's political message and criticise their volatile and violent social context, *A Quiet Place in the Country*, the director's only horror film, can be read as an expansion of the Kafka-cinematic canon. Taking cues from Kafka's vision of art, Petri's surrealist and fragmentary film uses the artist's alienation as its main plot and theme.

A talented, imaginative painter, Leonardo Ferri is having trouble completing any of his paintings because of painter's block. His matron and lover Flavia arranges for him to stay at a quiet villa out in the country. Instead of getting any work done there, however, he becomes obsessed with the story of a beautiful and promiscuous 17-year-old girl who was mysteriously killed at the villa during World War II. As Naomi Ritter explains, Kafka sees 'the artist as permanently excluded from normal living' (1989: 71); indeed, Leonardo seems to be incapable of living among common citizens. The very title of the film – *A Quiet Place in the Country* – refers to the need artists have of a place far from the quotidian and its distractions.

The film's first sequence foreshadows the plot: it is an oneiric moment in which Leonardo dreams of himself vulnerably naked and tied to a chair. He is visited by Flavia, who chatters incessantly about the marvels of the city and modernity, miracles embodied in a series of electrical appliances that she has bought. Cut to a shower scene in which she repeatedly stabs Leonardo while reminding him of his business engagements, each stab symbolising a boring meeting with art dealers. She is his lover, but also his link to the capitalist world that he so desperately wants to flee. Later in the film, one of Leonardo's benefactors mentions that he believes in the artist because of his youth: 'Young horses always win', he says, implying that he buys youth and future, rather than talent, individual expression or ideas. Leonardo, from this capitalist perspective, is just another young artist to manage, not an individual personality.

The artist as a solitary, anguished man can be seen, following Henry Sussman, as a product of modernity, which is embodied in the film's dream sequence in the endless parade of electric appliances: 'since the outset of the broader modernity, the ideology of artistic production has been couched in terms of unique and brilliant creativity, a transcendental attribute, inhering to the individuated artist' (2002: 144). But Sussman continues: 'this ideology has been undermined by the disposition and canonisation of artworks according to (collective) contractual understandings of what "works," that is, what answers fundamental epistemological and ontological questions under particular socio-cultural formations' (ibid.), i.e. what has market potential. This short-circuit is what prompts Leonardo to seeks a quiet place outside the urban areas so intoxicated with modernity. In another of Leonardo's dreams, the city is seen as a nightmarish space, a grey and dreary landscape where he sees himself being pushed along by wheelchair through the streets. The city as an icon of modernity thus mirrors Leonardo's sense of displacement and echoes Kafka's approach to urban space as 'the location for the disappearance of the alienated individual in the lonely crowd' (Goebel 2002: 42). Alienation is even more marked when the alienated are artists, particularly prone to falling ill with masses.

Escaping modernity and the city, Leonardo flees to a mysterious house in the country that he sees while travelling. Even so, the connection with both capitalism and Flavia is not clear-cut: she rents the house for Leonardo with her money, since the painter seems to always be broke. In Kafka's vision, the artist frets at practical constraints and defends his integrity against external pressures to conform. One of the best-known examples is 'Ein Hungerkünstler' ('A Hunger Artist', 1922), which tells the story of an obsessed man whose profession and art is fasting. In this story, the artist is also facing the anxieties caused by the intervention of impresarios who simply do not understand his art as such, but rather as entertainment. After forty days of fasting, he is ready to be released from his self-imposed cage and be fed. But he chooses to extend his fasting indefinitely to produce the ultimate artwork.

Kafka's hunger artist and Petri's Leonardo are both powerful examples of men who, in their preoccupation with their ego and personal objectives, have become irrevocably estranged from their community and the life around them. Leonardo desperately needs to work away from the city and its crowds. But his alienation will only be exacerbated his new country home. Just hours upon arriving at the new house, Leonardo senses a ghostly presence within him. Soon he learns the story of the little countess who used to live in the house before World War II, when she was killed in an air-raid. Leonardo becomes increasingly anxious with the ghost haunting him and eventually learns that other locals (especially the men) are equally obsessed with her ghostly presence.

The film stages a hallucinatory *mise-en-scène* in which it is difficult to know what is truly taking place in the real world as opposed to Leonardo's mind. He apparently kills Flavia, but that action is revealed, in the film's climax, to be imaginary. Leonardo's argument for killing her is that the ghost hates Flavia. But there is very little evidence that a spectre is actually haunting the house. Rather, Leonardo's many attempts (real or imaginary) to kill Flavia are a more direct reflection of the artist's desire for freedom from the constraints of the art market embodied in the countess, thus achieving true art.

A Quiet Place in the Country ends with another scene reminiscent of Kafka's tale, where the artist achieves a remarkable fasting but nobody takes notice: he has become invisible since he is no longer 'a young horse', so to speak. Leonardo also becomes invisible in the end: he has been admitted to a psychiatric hospital, where nobody sees him as anything more than a patient. Even so, his art has achieved the highest degree of perfection. Flavia is obtaining Leonardo's art, now for free, and presumably selling it for a handsome profit. If 'A Hunger Artist' can be read as a joke – consider its final 'punchline' (see Cervo 2003: 60), which reveals that the artist chose to fast not because of some ideal of art, but because he couldn't find any food he liked – then Petri's film argues that Leonardo has achieved the peace that he so desperately needed within the asylum and even more, that his new and perfect source of inspiration are porn magazines. Indeed, his new artistic iconography is suggestive of the female sex organ. He has attained higher art through inspiration, not from ghosts or houses in the country, but through nude photographs. His entire Eros is sublimated in marketable pornography. Both Kafka and Petri know how to paint their horrors with comic strokes.

Finally, we can identify an additional link between Kafka and Petri. Both authors have to struggle with an audience always open to realistic fiction but cautious in the face of experimental art. Realism in the conventional sense was not of interest to Kafka (see Troscianko 2014: 113), while Petri made Kafkaesque films in a country famous for its neo-realism. The Italian Communist Party heavily promoted Socialist Realism as the only acceptable genre. That is why Petri, even under Kafka's influence, chose to keep at least one foot in realism. If modernists such as Kafka 'reduce social reality to nightmare, as angst-ridden and absurd, thus depriving us of any sense of perspective' (Butler 2010: 82), then *A Quiet Place in the Country*, Petri's more experimental film, is an oneiric critique of bourgeois assessments of art, and the 'genius' artist in particular. Kafka's fiction usually contains a rendering of both realistic and dreamlike passages, a clash that provokes unease in the reader. It is this desire for a Kafkaesque world that inspired Elio Petri to use a fragmentary narration that oscillates continuously between reality and dream, nightmare and hallucination. Thus although Petri's horror film is the least influenced by a particular work of Kafka, it is arguably the most Kafkaesque in its narrative.

CONCLUSION

Kafka has been considered a hermetic modernist (see Dowden 1995: 94). Petri, in turn, 'uses the mystery genre to reveal certain features of the functioning of capitalist society' (Liehm 1986: 210) – a narrative device conducive to communist ideology. Even so, a Kafkaesque narrative permeates much of Petri's oeuvre: in the films analysed in this essay and others such as *I giorni contati* (*His Days Are Numbered*, 1962) or his science-fiction opus *La decima vittima* (*The Tenth Victim*, 1965), ideas, characters and situations recalling Kafka's world run through the Italian director's oeuvre.

In the highly volatile context of Italy at the end of the 1960s and 1970s Petri's use of Kafka's ideas with respect to law as an abstract concept is perhaps unsurprising. 'Kafka is, of course, the one European author who most intensely portrayed – indeed, suffered through – the anguish caused by laws seemingly not made by humans and for humans' (Testa 2002: 130). In this sense, the inspector of *Investigation of a Citizen Above Suspicion* makes his entry as an agent of the law, but an agent who has no need of it precisely because he is its agent. Law, rather than the search for truth, moulds its own truth, especially in the *anni di piombo*, when being communist was equivalent to being an anti-social criminal. Thus, the inspector and the commissioner of *The Assassin* are doppelgängers. Both choose among the usual suspects to construct a perfect culprit that fits the requirements of the law.

Kafka's interest in artists and their world is also central to Petri's films. Whereas *Investigation of a Citizen Above Suspicion* refers to 'Before the Law' and 'The Problem of Our Laws', and *The Assassin* refers to *The Trial*, then *A Quiet Place in the Country* takes some cues from 'A Hunger Artist' and mirrors Kafka's complicated vision of the art world. The complex relationship between artist and community is illustrated in the latter case in a horror tale of ghostly presences which are ultimately not embodiments of repressed eroticism but rather of a desire for freedom from constraints. Elio Petri even takes up Kafka's sense of humour and his films can be seen as dark comedies.

With clear references to Kafka, or simply a penchant for Kafkaesque characters and situations, Petri's work calls for re-examination of the various ties that bind national cinema, literature, authorship and European social contexts.

BIBLIOGRAPHY

Burns, Robert (2014) *Kafka's Law: 'The Trial' and American Criminal Justice*. Chicago: University of Chicago Press.
Butler, Christopher (2010) *Modernism: A Very Short Introduction*. New York: Oxford University Press.
Cervo, Nathan (2003) 'Kafka's "A Hunger Artist"', *Franz Kafka*, ed. Harold Bloom. Broomall, PA: Chelsea House, 60–1.
Corngold, Stanley and Benno Wagner (2011) *Franz Kafka: The Ghosts in the Machine*. Chicago: Northwestern University Press.
Deleuze, Gilles and Felix Guattari (1986) *Kafka: Toward a Minor Literature*. Minneapolis, MN: University of Minnesota Press.
Della Porta, Donatella (2006) *Social Movements, Political Violence, and the State: A Comparative Analysis of Italy and Germany*. Cambridge: Cambridge University Press.
Dodd, Bill (2002) 'The Case for a Political Reading', in *The Cambridge Companion to Kafka*, ed. Julian Preece. Cambridge: Cambridge University Press, 131–49.
Dowden, Stephen (1995) *Kafka's Castle and the Critical Imagination*. Columbia, SC: Camden House.
Goebel, Rolf (2002) 'The Exploration of the Modern City in *The Trial*', *The Cambridge Companion to Kafka*, ed. Julian Preece. Cambridge: Cambridge University Press, 42–60.
Gross, Ruth (2002) 'Kafka's Short Fiction', *The Cambridge Companion to Kafka*, ed. Julian Preece. Cambridge: Cambridge University Press, 80–94.

Kafka, Franz (1979a [1922]) 'A Hunger Artist', *The Basic Kafka*, trans. Willa and Edwin Muir. New York: Pocket Books, 80–90.

____ (1979b [1931]) 'The Problem of Our Laws', The Basic Kafka, trans. Willa and Edwin Muir. New York: Pocket Books, 154–6.

____ (1979c [1915]) 'Before the Law', The Basic Kafka, trans. Willa and Edwin Muir. New York: Pocket Books, 174–81.

____ (2009 [1925]) *The Trial*, trans. David Wyllie. New York: Dover.

Killinger, Charles (2002) *The History of Italy*. Westport, CT: Greenwood Press.

Koven, Mikel (2006) *La Dolce Morte: Vernacular Cinema and the Italian Giallo Film*. Toronto: Scarecrow Press.

Liehm, Mira (1986) *Passion and Defiance: Italian Film from 1942 to the Present*. Berkeley, CA: University of California Press.

Nowell-Smith, Geoffrey, James Hay and Gianni Volpi (1996) *The Companion to Italian Cinema*. London: Cassell.

Ritter, Naomi (1989) *Art as Spectacle: Images of the Entertainer since Romanticism*. Columbia, MO: University of Missouri Press.

Robertson, Ritchie (2004) *Kafka: A Very Short Introduction*. Oxford: Oxford University Press.

Sussman, Henry (2002) 'Kafka's Aesthetics: A Primer: From the Fragments to the Novels', *A Companion to the Works of Franz Kafka*, ed. James Rolleston. Rochester, NY: Camden House, 123–48.

Szafraniec, Asja (2007) *Beckett, Derrida, and the Event of Literature*. Stanford, CA: Stanford University Press.

Testa, Carlo (2002) *Italian Cinema and Modern European Literatures, 1945-2000*. Westport, CT: Greenwood Press/Praeger.

Tester, Keith (1993) *The Life and Times of Post-Modernity*. New York: Routledge.

Thiher, Allen (2008) 'The Judgment' and 'The Metamorphosis', in *The Metamorphosis*, ed. Harold Bloom. New York: Infobase, 47–62.

Troscianko, Emily (2014) *Kafka's Cognitive Realism*. New York: Routledge.

Vighi, Fabio (2006) *Traumatic Encounters in Italian Film: Locating the Cinematic Unconscious*. Bristol: Intellect.

EPILOGUE

A PERSONAL QUEST INTO THE CINEMATIC KAFKAESQUE

MAGIC, MYSTERY AND MIRACLE: RE-SPIRALLING MARKER AND KAFKA

DAN GEVA

> One of the most effective means of seduction that evil has is the challenge to struggle.
>
> – Franz Kafka (1946: 87)

> Miracles die with their witnesses. A second struggle begins.
>
> – Chris Marker (*Description d'un combat*, 1960)

Early in his life, Kafka confronted the question of the essence of his art, fiction writing, probing the nature of the spirituality of this existential experience. His response formed a triptych: 'magic, mystery and miracle' (Sokel 1987: 98). Let us consider another art – documentary filmmaking – and ask: what is the nature of its creative powers? What emotional and spiritual sense does filming a documentary evoke in great artists such as Chris Marker?[1] Such a comparative analysis is diabolically difficult. However, in 1960, Marker alluded to Franz Kafka's earliest surviving story, 'Beschreibung eines Kampfes' ('Description of a Struggle', 1912; hereafter 'BK') with a film-essay on Israel bearing the same title, *Description d'un combat*. Hence, following Marker's innovative spiralling with Kafka, the first question to be addressed here is: can we re-spiral Kafka and Marker in order to provide insights into the spiritual relations between the artist and his artwork? Another problem explored in this essay is the extent to which we can establish magic, mystery and miracle as a descriptive basis for the enduring, lifelong struggle of authors and metaphysicians such as Kafka and Marker.

For Kafka (as for *the documentarian*) insofar as he is a discursive function, questions of truth, the nature of one's art and the artist's epistemic role and ontological nature are fundamental.² In *The Blue Octavo Notebooks*, Kafka writes:

> Art flies around truth, but with the definite intention of not getting burnt. Its capacity lies in finding in the dark void a place where the beam of light can be intensely caught, without this having been perceptible before. [...] Knowledge we *have*. Anyone who strives for it with particular intensity is suspect of striving against it (1991: 39; emphasis in original).

In 1963, Chris Marker reacted to the age-old problem of the limitations of knowledge, specifically in the realms of documentary, insofar as this art form claimed a general truth (see, for example, Nichols 1991; Winston 1995). Marker challenged that claim, encapsulated in the often misused idiom *cinéma-vérité* (see Isari 1971 for a historical overview). Catherine Lupton sums it up nicely:

> Faced with [Jean] Rouch's label *cinéma-vérité* with its troublesome connotation of some general truth discovered through cinema, Marker is credited with promptly rephrasing it as '*ciné ma vérité*' ['cinema my truth']. (2005: 84).

A broader consideration of Kafka and Marker's intellectual trajectory suggests that both reacted instinctively and vigorously to the elusive possibility of capturing truth on their respective creative media (see Udoff 1987 for Kafka). Moreover, both stated, in their artwork as well as writings (Kafka; Brady and Hughes 2002) and interviews (Marker; for example, Douhaire and Rivoire 2003; Alter 2006), the possibility of truth's non-existence, *ex-hypothesi*. Obviously, this triadic locus is the crux of 'the Kafkaesque'. From a bird's eye-view, however, it is also the *locus classicus* of the fundamental, still often denied, *arche* of documentary metaphysics. Put in this context, Marker is positioned and viewed here as a sincere emblem to the challenge that Kafka sets for artists and commentators alike.

In this essay I evoke Kafka's timeless notions, expressed in his early letters, regarding the nature of the act of literary writing as magic, mystery and miracle, with the goal of examining their relevance to Marker's own sense of 'writing in film'.³ I take pains to show how Marker's unification of literary and visual signification in *Description d'un combat* creates an intimate correlation with the *archai* of Kafka's contemplative self-analysis. Furthermore, I extend my critical reflection through a discussion of my filmic response to Marker's *Description d'un combat* and Kafka's 'Beschreibung eines Kampfes': the documentary *Description of a Memory* (2006).⁴

I. A DESCRIPTION OF THREE DESCRIPTIONS

'Description of a Struggle' is the earliest posthumously preserved Kafka story.[5] It is also the title of an early Chris Marker film-essay classic about the young and re-emerging State of Israel. The latter, largely forgotten because it was pulled from distribution and prohibited from public screenings by Marker after the 1967 war in the Middle East, was revisited in my personal film-essay *Description of a Memory*.

Kafka's 'BK' relates the events of a long and unexpected midnight walk along the frozen Petřín hill (Laurenziberg) in Prague. The nameless, mysterious narrator/protagonist struggles to describe in detail the unexpected relationship he forms with an anonymous acquaintance. This acquaintance is partly imposing his company on the narrator, and partly seduced by the latter into wandering through the night and listening to his stories, thus becoming part of his nightly mishaps. Nora Alter reads this story as 'the complex relationship between a victim and a victimiser and the narrow boundary between the two roles' (2006: 61).

The story alternates between a concrete sense of actual and physical reality that unfolds through a linear and cohesive narrative, and a surreal, impenetrable representativeness, drowned by its obsessive struggle to tell itself. The story contains two dialogues: 'Conversation with the Supplicant' and 'Conversation with the Drunk'. After riding on his acquaintance's back like a horseman, and then meeting a very fat man carried on a litter, the narrator is smashed to the ground and hit on the head, only to continue walking through the wintry night. When the two finally sit down to rest, the acquaintance, without any warning – and worse, for no apparent reason – stabs his arm with a knife. The narrator then tells him: 'You have wounded yourself for my sake. You are in such a good position' (1971: 51). With this unresolved statement, addressed later in my discussion, they continue what had begun as an unexplained and unexpected walk for both. The acquaintance's last words are 'Oh God!' (ibid.). The story ends with a description of their surroundings: lights, shadows, walls, broken branches, snow and tree trunks – all leading nowhere, and much reminiscent of Jean Epstein's analysis, as discussed by Jacques Rancière: 'Life is not about stories, about actions oriented towards an end, but about situations open in every direction. Life has nothing to do with dramatic progression, but is instead a long and continuous movement made up of an infinity of micro-movements' (2006: 2).

My second account addresses Chris Marker's *Description d'un combat*. The film unfolds like a jigsaw puzzle: an impressionistic mosaic of the twelve-year-old State of Israel. The narrator – an omniscient time traveller[6] – remains anonymous and disembodied throughout his observation, a position that amounts to an act of both monstration and narration.⁷ This stubbornly invisible audible narrator inhabits the diegesis by means of a calm, certain and persistent voice, allowing both his cinema camera and his stills camera to freely roam the land while scavenging for visual signs waiting to be interpreted on their way to 'coming home to roost' (see Lupton 2009). The narrator's all-knowing and yet mysterious voice is in itself a sign of hyper-perceptiveness. It notices and immediately translates geographical, human and cultural perspectives, which to him are all simply signs only waiting to be deciphered. Among them are a burnt tank's skeleton; iconic road signs; camels; advertisements; a synagogue and a university library to mention just a few.⁸

By means of its dominantly semiotic presence and corporeal absence, *Description d'un combat*'s narrator creates a sense of an engaged meta-subjectivity, obsessively immersed in the works of a description of the decryption. For Marker, this description is not only of the land's plethora of iconic, symbolic and indexical signs, but, more important, of its meta-sign-structure – *the langue of the land* – the governing system that allows all signs to appear as a mystery awaiting decryption. This sought-after structure is, in Marker's view, none other than Israel's essence. Accordingly, the film's search is not for an accountable history of the land or its people. Rather, it pursues the hidden treasure, the 'Madeleine' of the Israeli people's spirit. Arriving at the end of his impressionist cinematic journey in Israel, the invisible narrator reaches at an enigmatic, still incontrovertibly prophetic conclusion about the fate of the young state: a nation that seemed to have mysteriously and miraculously emerged from its erased past. It is embedded in an image of a young girl. In the following sections I will look into Marker's concluding scene and argue that it encapsulates and demonstrates the deepest sense of Kafka's relations to miracle, mystery and magic.

In order to properly contextualise Kafka and Marker, I will now offer a third account, of my documentary *Description of a Memory* (hereafter, *Description*). Garnet C. Butchart notes that the film 'critically examines the appearances of the state of Israel as depicted in Marker's 1960 documentary *Description d'un combat* by the French filmmaker, Chris Marker' (2014: 27). With respect to *Description*, he further observes:

> The outcome of this reflective, visual-archeological project ... is a richly textured, dream-like description of what, on the one hand, was unforeseen in Marker's film at the time of its making ... and, on the other hand, what would have remained unforeseeable about its image content prior to the return and reappearance of it in *Description of a Memory*, namely new perspectives on the dream life of Israel's past that recurs to the expressions and experiences of her children in the future. (2014: 28).

Description opens with a Vertovian act of mischievousness.[9] Time and space are simultaneously turned upside down and reversed. *Description d'un combat*'s last image is shrunk (most of the frame is blackened) and is now viewed through the mechanical gate of a 35mm projector. We see it as an inverted and reversed image. This opening image is thus tied to the final statement of Marker's film, all the more so in the logical form of negative dialectics. The narrator's voice announces: 'I have no memory of the first time I saw your film. To recall the beginning, I'd have to rewind to the moment before it all began'. This statement regulates *Description*'s time and space as immanently dubious categories, at least from a naïve realist point of view whose conception of reality necessitates time and space as *a priori* conditions, by which logic any set of linear, still-contingent arrangements of historical events unfold and retrospectively validate its absolute temporal configuration. The cinematic reality of *Description* negates such presumptive linear clockwork temporality subordinated to an orderly continuum of historical events. From here on, the act of cinematic remembering and trans-temporal memorising constitutes itself as 'non-place' and 'non-time'. The essential sign for this metaphysical position is 'before it all began' – surely an oxymoron – a mystery induced by a miracle, realised by a feat of magic. In effect, what is pronounced here is a mythical view, echoing Genesis 1:1 in its logical and theological difficulty: 'In the beginning…'

Moreover, the opening line of *Description* constructs no less than its own formal language. According to this logic, all realistic contents presented to cognition are subjugated to an imaginary order that, in turn, is not preceded by any concrete realistic disposition. This statement not only stands out as a direct dialogical response to Marker's *Description d'un combat*, but also draws on Kafka's 'BK'. At least this is so in the sense in which June Leavitt describes Kafka's attempt to pierce 'the veil': 'there are many signs in the opening scenario of section 1 in "Beschreibung eines Kampfes" that the fabric of reality is about to tear' (2012: 50).

Henceforth, *Description* depicts thirteen memories hauled up from the profundity of the forgotten/repressed wells of Marker's struggle to forge an idiosyncratic cinematic description of Israel's essence. Each cinematic memory is strung to Marker's original footage according to a recurring dreamlike logic wherein facts are subordinated to the order of remembrance, dis-remembrance and non-remembrance of whatever any victorious people ought to remember when they re-write their history. Marker's *Description d'un combat*, like the rest of his gigantic oeuvre, stands as both a philosophical and a historical warning against the vanity of the modern individual and modern peoples. In the same breath, it warns against the dangers of the fragile moment in which a nation re-invents itself by re-writing its triumphant narrative. Triumphant over what?

Over whom? *Description* confronts these existential questions in the same manner as Kafka's 'BK' and Marker's film. It immerses itself in the struggle for a description insofar as it is a duty of the rational mind – admittedly a devilish seduction.

In order to appreciate *Description*'s relevance to the dialogical ontology of Marker's response to Kafka, note how it elicits a spiral structure in which the first image of the film is already marked as a sign that is doomed to re-appear in the end.[10] Thereupon it will be recast into the eternal abyss of what Charles Sanders Peirce calls *semiosis*: 'an infinite regression', whereby 'the interpretant is nothing but another representation to which the torch of truth is handed along; and as representation, it has its interpretant again' (1974: 171; see also 1955: 275). In this process, the opening visual image is finally revealed in its true dimensions: a bait for future generations' duty to pursue the task of signification, doomed to reach no firm land beneath their feet, or to experience what Kafka calls 'a seasickness on land' (1971: 33).

II. KAFKA AND MARKER: MAGIC? MYSTERY? MIRACLE?

On 6 September 1903, Kafka wrote to his friend Oscar Pollack and claimed that from the beginning his writing was connected with magic. Walter Sokel notes: 'In one of his earliest letters, Kafka refers to his writing as to "Wunderdingen" (miracle things) … sorcery, Satanism and magic' (1987: 98).[11] Leaning on Kafka's contemplation and Sokel's observation, we can ask: in what sense are these incommensurable, all-the-more-authentic Kafkaesque sensations about the nature of the creative act of writing immanent to and productive for an enquiry into Chris Marker's notion of what one of his principal muses, Dziga Vertov, calls 'writing-in-film'? (see Marker 2006).

To better frame this sought-after perspective, one must refer to Michael Chaiken and Sam Diiorio's comment that 'any separation of Marker the filmmaker from Marker the writer would be false' (2003: 42). Following Lupton's insightful conception of Marker as 'the eye that writes' (2005: 217), I further ask: how should we understand these five feats of metaphysical matter – description, struggle, magic, mystery and miracle – in Marker's case? After all, in the eyes of too many, he was an enigma, an elusive embodiment of the human capacity to exist simultaneously as a singular known individuality as well as a cultural sign of an enigmatic hero. In more than one way, Marker qua persona and author is, like Kafka, a human personification of magic, mystery and miracle. Critics and friends alike compete for the most accurate metaphor by which to describe what and who Marker is – to begin with, an individual resistant to the conventional tyranny of the symbolic order. He has been variously crowned as 'an image scavenger', 'a free radical', 'a magic-marker' and 'a time traveler' (see Gross 2012). In particular, Roger Tailleur's succinct account stands out:

> It's simple: Chris Marker is a writer/image-hunter, a contemplative traveler, a world citizen who expresses himself in French, a revolutionary prophet, a dreamer-poet, a serious humourist, a humanist member of the Society for Protection of Animals, a musical documentarian, a dialectical idealist. Alain Resnais was right the day he remarked that cinema, to which Marker eventually devoted himself, had snagged itself a rich acquisition. So many mixed-up tendencies – enough to worry the critic who has the task of encompassing them all. (2007: n.p.)

A rarely discussed historical fact relating to the origin of Marker's *Description d'un combat* deserves mention here. Marker did not initiate a film project based on a personal creative desire to translate or transform Kafka's story to the screen. Michal Friedman tells us that

> Marker was invited to Israel to direct the film that would finally release local documentary production from its heavily propagandist and didactic shackles. Such was the intention of his hosts, Lia and Wim van Leer who, as pioneers of the cinema culture in this country, had set up the first film clubs. […] They equipped him with a little-known short story by Kafka … and a scooter he used for traveling all over the country, returning from these jaunts with over a thousand snapshots. (2011: 25)[12]

Hence, our subject of study does not simply correspond to what critics call 'screen adaptation'.

After finishing his work on two film-essays in China and Siberia, Marker picked up on the van Leers' invitation, came to Israel, and after roaming the country for two months, decided to accept their proposal about linking his project to a dialogue with 'BK'. In what follows, we will trace evidence of shared consciousness and poetic allusions linking the young Kafka to the adolescent filmmaker Marker, and both to *Description*.

III. RE-SPIRALLING KAFKA AND MARKER

Two chapters in 'BK' – 'Ride' and 'Walk' – are described by Sokel thus:

> A strikingly literal and prophetic illustration of the insight which Freud

incidentally formulated eight years after Kafka's tale was written. In these sections the first person narrator performs feats of magic omnipotence, and the world obeys his orders. (1987: 101).

In 'BK' Kafka writes:

> The stones vanished at my will and the wind disappeared. [...] Because I love pinewoods I went through the woods of this kind and since I like gazing silently up at the stars, the stars appeared slowly in the sky, as is their wont. [...] This sight, ordinary as it might be, made me so happy that I, as a small bird on a twig of those distant scrubby bushes, forgot to let the moon come up. (1971: 22)

Sokel argues that 'this blissful domination of nature by itself is art'. He traces the German root of 'arts' in the expression 'to be able to', which, according to his interpretation, is no different than 'magic' in the sense that it 'elevates its practitioner to divine highest'. He then concludes: 'Kafka sought to reach the infinite power and happiness of such magic in his writing' (1987: 98, 99).

Marker's filmic and written oeuvre presents similar sensitivity. In what follows I propose a hypothesis along the lines of Kafka's and Sokel's approach to prose writing, this time on Marker's genuine interpretation of the art of documentary making. His rhetoric in the opening lines of *Description d'un Combat* is, like Kafka's, more poetic than prosaic. The omniscient traveller is represented in the film by a consistently invisible, steadfast voice. A few seconds after the appearance of the first visual-image on the screen, a contemplative, crystal-sharp voice says, in a meditative tone:

> Signs.
> This land first speaks to you in signs.
> Signs of land.
> Signs of water.
> Signs of man.
> Signs.

To understand how this poetic hexagon functions in the service of re-spiralling Marker to Kafka's world, the present discussion unfolds by way of focusing on the study of the omniscient presence of magic, miracle and mystery – only in the first and the last visual images and corresponding voice narrations of the film.

It opens with an image of a burnt-out object. At first blush it seems like a rusty and seriously decaying, unidentified object, presented to the eye and mind as a desolate and deformed unknown-known. The near-centre framing of the object is no arbitrary choice, given Marker's rigid aesthetic approach. The very first glance suffices to convince us that it is no less than a concise epistemological positioning by the renowned French cinematographer Ghishlain Cloquet, who worked with Marker on this project, as well as a bold ontological argumentation from the auteur's perspective. The frame's composition suggests that what Marker is offering to our cinematic field of vision is not a mid-sized, everyday realistic object. Rather, the unidentified thingness of the presented thing invites contemplation of humans' fragile ocular perception. Even more, it illustrates how our perception can contain a certain degree of bleariness prior to alerting the mind that it is irritated by an uncanny object that has just invaded the field of vision. Is this not exactly what magic is about? Does not every magician attempt to lead the viewer astray to the point where doubt is planted in one's mind as to the trustworthiness of one's perceptions?

This aspect of Marker's opening visual statement only begins to tap the complexity of his conclusive cinematic statement. Let us consider it further. The monstrous object, much reminiscent of a metamorphosed insect, possesses another critical virtue: its appearance triggers a magical shrinkage of the object from its actual real-life enormous proportions, into a minuscule cinematic object, placed in the context of the vast desert surrounding it. In this way Marker re-constitutes the relations between the real-life size of the object on the one hand and its infinite circumambient space on the other – highlighting nature's grandeur. It is somewhat reminiscent of Hans Holbein's anamorphic skull in *The Ambassadors* (1533), only in the form of a dark stain, plucked from a bright sand palate stretching toward an infinite horizon. Marker's oblique visual strategy forces one to doubt the obvious signification attributed to any recognisable object qua object. In this process one is inescapably led to ask, for example, 'Should I not in the first place have visually recognised "the thing" prior to naming it a tank?' Or is it? Perhaps it is an asteroid, a message from outer space? From another time? The obscure referential quality of this metamorphosed object in space, added to its blurred temporal quality, reinforces its magical, mysterious quality. In effect, it is the interpretational perspective of the world traveller (narrator) that secures the non-thing-ness of 'that thing' and marshals its turning into an invitation for an adventure: lo and behold, *a semiotic adventure*. Marker invites us for a walk through the most dangerous route in the uncharted, infinite desert of language, insofar as it is an ancient form of a prayer, much in the same manner as Kafka invites his two protagonists to initiate their magical nocturnal walk away from any social order (see Sokel 1987: 100).

As for the narration accompanying the opening image, note that in prayers, at times, a single word signifies wholeness. It serves as a metonymy for the whole process. A case in point is the universal word 'amen' or the concluding utterance 'Oh God!' pronounced by the acquaintance in 'BK'. In *Description d'un Combat*, too, Marker's opening enunciation encrypts the entire film through the use of a single word – 'signs', to which Italo Calvino (1974) refers throughout *Invisible Cities* as a mystery in its own right. A close scrutiny reveals that Marker's narrator says 'signs' only a split second after the appearance of the first visual image. It would be reasonable to argue that the entire film is encapsulated in this word. The infinite semantic field that creates the philosophical and cultural atmosphere of 'signs' precedes and overwhelms all optional embodiments of contingent screen occurrences. That is to say, it overshadows any potential signification that might be drawn from succeeding actual, real-life events presented on the screen, insofar as these indexical happenstances might be referred to as truth. In many senses, then, Marker's choice of opening word ('signs') is closely linked to the final words of 'BK' – 'Oh God!'

At this point we can already determine with some confidence that the governing law of Marker's proposed semiotic adventure is mysterious, magical and miraculous on account of its diminished, hard-core realistic line of representation. The Land of Israel, insofar as it is an object of gaze for the world traveller Christian-François Bouche-Villeneuve (known as Chris Marker), is not in any way about to be historicised on a factual basis. If information is presented, it is always with a distinct Markerian wink – it becomes a monstration of the magic of unknown-ness.[13] This is even truer if, in the case of Kafka's story, the narrator meets a supplicant along the way. Here, then, in Marker's interpretation of the Kafkaesque *struggle*, the narrating voice acts, from the outset, as a sign for Kafka's supplicant.

Marker, the world traveller, speaks and pleads for the ancient land – that which 'first, speaks to you in signs'. By means of his distinctly detached poise, Marker is at once one with the land, yet separated from it.[14] What is it that he supplicates? His object of desire is the universal and archaic unconsciousness of the land and its people. Throughout the journey, it is the unspeakable *desire* on the author's part to grasp at what the land and its people will never be able to plead for with their own conscious, earthly voice.

In that moment of crude and utter separation between the land and its universal observer, the struggle commences. It is the struggle between the desire to linger infinitely on the interpretation of the land's infinite sign structure, and at the same time reach out to its finite decipherment. Description, then, becomes both the means and the end: a site of decryption and desperation; a site of short-lived and short-sighted triumph and preordained defeat.

The following shot only triples Marker's magical mystery tour with respect to the earlier mentioned Vertovian concept 'writing in film'. The screen-object that occupied centre frame in the first shot is now thrust to the rear left corner. It is re-introduced, only this time out of focus. The object is presented in a confusingly oppositional perspective to its previous form of monstration. In the foreground is now placed another 'metamorphosed insect'. The new object is similar yet utterly foreign to the previous one. The quantitative as well as qualitative doubling of the estranged and de-familiarised objects strikes doubly hard. This is true especially with respect to the fact that the two shots are taken in broad daylight. Marker's introduction of the Land of Israel is deliberately a bright, sunny day. Unlike Gregor Samsa, whom Kafka traps in the hell of indoors, and also unlike the two nocturnal travellers in 'BK' who are desperately dependent on the fog of night for their victim/victimiser relations, Marker brings his struggle into the light. To echo Plato, he pulls the slave out from the cave and forces him to look into the sun.[15] By doing so, Marker undermines the presumptuous human belief in the powers of visual perception to arrive at the supposedly perfect condition supported by broad daylight inasmuch as it is both a realistic emblem of true vision and a conceptual metaphor for truth.

Further analysis supports the idea that Marker's strategy is reminiscent of Kafka's opening gesture in 'BK'. Consider, for example, how the first encounter between Kafka's protagonist and the acquaintance destabilises the established social foundations presumed to anchor social norms. The acquaintance approaches the narrator; but it soon becomes obvious that they somehow already know each other – a mystery that remains unresolved throughout the story (see Leavitt 2012: 50–1). Marker does nothing less and nothing different, but he does it on dissimilar terms. In a poetic sense, he binds the visual images to the acoustic signifier of the narration, introducing them as if they knew one another, prior to matching them on the screen, yet in a mysterious way. Marker forces the images to surrender to the almighty power of the spoken word – a magical feat in its own right. Similarly, the following images in his film shadow and obey the divine act of creating a world through the spoken word. As in the Book of Genesis, in Marker's magical theme park the world is created by the power of the word spoken by the omniscient commentator. Even though from a production point of view the visual-image was captured prior to the later added narration, when we examine the diegetic screen we find the former trailing behind the latter. Hence, Marker constructs the viewer's path toward a meaningful process of signification by means of a strategy based on injecting counter-implications into the image's ambivalent connotative plain. Thus, counter-commonsensical relations between words and images are becoming dialectically opposed to one another.

However, a minor – but still critical – difference distinguishes the biblical attitude toward the relation between words and objects from Marker's Kafkaesque interpretation of the mystery of creation. Recall that in Genesis, what is created is the world itself: flesh and blood. In contrast, in Marker's universe, what is being created is *the sign*. We hear the words 'Signs of land', and only then does the film cut to the next shot. In parallel, the screen's visual plain presents a long shot of the Dead Sea. To those who do not know it, it is an image of the end of the world. The next cut leads to an image of a small, unidentified rural settlement. As simple as this syntagm appears to be to the innocent eye, it still requires scrutiny. Marker's opening and blunt argument is that 'this land first speaks to you in signs'. Plainly speaking, it is a metaphor. However, we are here invited – as always with Marker – to be deeply suspicious of the content's presumed naïveté (see Arthur 2003). Lo and behold 'the land', whispers the voice, 'is first speaking to you'. Who is that 'you'? On the one hand, we are tempted to apply the normative grammatical rule according to which second-person singular refers to anyone; to the inhabitant, acquaintance, of both the land and the movie theatre. I suggest, however, reading this as a soliloquy of the manic traveller-artist who wishes to gain divine powers to create the magic of his documentary art. These are, as Sokel argues, the narcissistic powers of the artist, a supplicant, a lunatic lost in the desert, talking to himself in second-person singular. The 'you' is actually a repressed 'me': 'This land, first speaks to *me* in signs.' Marker would never have used that kind of a language. I use it now only to contend that there is no simplified 'me' in the Markerian or Kafkaesque universe.

This certainly invites thinking through other frameworks – Jacques Lacan's, for example. We can think of the narrator's relations with the gazed-at land and its people in terms of 'impossibility and inability' (Lacan 1975: 16). What is left for the traveller is a desperate, tragic attempt to achieve some degree of comprehension, a promised land never to be reached. This lonely man then speaks in person to the silent land, and this speech is the foundation of the intimate dialogue Kafka was seeking in 'BK'. In place of the diabolic relations between Kafka's narrator and an acquaintance, Marker's *struggle* is to structure a *description* of relations between a lost, mad traveller (an authentic documentarian) and a land that speaks to him in mysterious tongues: magical signs.

The circle is completed: the narrator and the land, in parallel a victim and a victimiser – or equally vice versa? In that context, the first sentence of Marker's film becomes a confession about a magical state of affairs in which he, much like Moses, is standing at the entry gate to the land, hearing the land speaking to him in the most mysterious if not divine language of signs, knowing he would never enter it. The 'you' turns into a 'me', offering us a new understanding of the speech: 'This land first speaks to *me* in signs.' And these signs obey my will – the will of the observer's gaze, much reminiscent of Kafka's acquaintance. The inner voice of the narrator then says without words: 'I look here and I see land,

I cut the film and I see water. I cut as I please and I see "man".' Reality obeys the observer, in turn surrendering to the image.

In contrast to the magical, mysterious nature of the opening sequence, the final sequence in Marker's *Description d'un combat* has a quasi-salvific function. The young swan girl, deeply immersed in performing her narcissistic act of painting, presents herself as the sign of all signs. Her slim shoulders are doomed to carry the burden of two thousand years of Jewish and Christian guilt. So strong and precise is her image that for Marker she is the emblem of all preceding signs. She is 'The Sign', she is everything, because signs and the process of *semiosis* mark the eternal enslavement to the task of infinite meaning-seeking. This, then, is the root cause for *Description of a Memory* to open and conclude with a dialectic analysis of that girl's mysterious image.

Much as the act of her painting remains mysterious to Marker, so does Kafka's protagonist's destiny remain unresolved. Earlier I mentioned that in the last phase of Kafka's description of the night walk, the acquaintance stabs himself in the arm. The narrator then makes the most surprising of all announcements: 'My dear, my friend. You have wounded yourself for my sake. You are in such a good position' (1971: 51). Later in the twentieth century, this all-encompassing willingness to care for the other will become a trademark of Levinasian thought, but in the meantime the primordial Kafkaesque victim/victimiser relations take another surprising turn as the narrator dials up his wild imagination another notch:

> You're surrounded by well-meaning friends, you can go for a walk in broad daylight when any number of carefully dressed people can be seen far and near among tables or on mountain paths. Just think, in the spring we'll drive into the orchard – no, not we, that's unfortunately true – but you with your Annie will drive out at a happy trot. Oh yes believe me, I beg you and the sun will show you off to everyone at your best. Oh there will be music, the sound of horses from afar, no need to worry, there'll be shouting and barrel organs will be playing in the avenues. (Ibid.)

If the first part of the closing pronouncement speaks of the ultimate sacrifice and redemption through self-sacrifice, this last part of the monologue can be traced in Marker's return to the theme of the Holocaust, with the swan girl as the image to carry his film's closing message.

> Miracles die with their witnesses. A second struggle begins. To become a nation implies the right to selfishness, conceit. But Israel's history cries out against power for its own sake. Strength, power are merely signs. The greatest

injustice may well be denial of the right to be unjust. Look at her! There she is! Like Israel! We've to understand her, remind her that injustice on this land weighs heavier than elsewhere, this land, the ransom of injustice. The threats that surround her, to which she gave no cause. Yes, look at her. A vision that defeats the eye as words endlessly repeated. Amongst all the wondrous things, most wondrous is their being there like a cygnet, a signal, a sign.

However, Marker, the cosmonaut of human memory, understood this only partially. Indeed, miracles die with their witnesses. Moreover, as he claims, a second struggle begins. Nonetheless, that struggle also dies, and a new struggle begins. New miracles are performed and new witnesses die again. There is an element of a Nietzschean eternal return put to work here, as long as the image is kept alive. In retrospect, Marker understood that well, as late in his life he told me that the images do not belong to anyone, but to their own (private communication; Paris, December 2006). In the opening scene of *Description*, I evoke such a determination:

> And I wanted to be like you. But he who ventures out with a camera in his own land is doomed to recall nothing but the pictures he had taken. And, perchance, I am asked whether things really happened, I will not recall, and no one will believe that those things did indeed happen, unless, at the end of the voyage, I myself will say: look at her. Look at her like an enigma for more than the images and the words you left haunt me, they stand before me. Silent. Cryptic. Which one holds the clue to that girl's fate?

Marker's swan girl died insofar as she was captured as a pre-fixed sign in the bubble world of a world traveller, a compulsive scavenger of images of beautiful women around the world. She died a second time the minute she left her country to live in England. There, far away from home, she dedicated her real and actual life to painting houses from all over the world. In *Description*, the narrator concludes his journey:

> The girl who had the privilege of leaving a home and making a home away from home has since been painting houses of the whole world. You film a girl painting, and ask us to look at her until she becomes an enigma as if she were Israel itself. Half a century later she no longer lives in Israel and already has a daughter of her own.
> Now she sees the end getting closer…
> And if she looks at herself again, the one you said would never again be Anne Frank.

> Will she recognise herself in herself?
> Look at her.
> Look at her.
> Until, amongst all the wondrous things in this world, the most wondrous of all is
> Her being here before us.
> Like a cygnet.
> Like a signal.
> Like a sign.

Kafka signs off with a transcendental pitch: 'Oh God!' sighs the self-wounded acquaintance. Marker, on the other hand, locks his ultimate girl-sign in pitch darkness. His last frame obscures itself to black – the unknown future of this land. In the final analysis, *Description* struggles to propose its own description by forming a dialectical response to the works of the masters. While gazing at the now-woman girl, painting in her home in England, the film cuts to a surprise party that her Israeli friends are giving her, in Israel, after she has been away for over thirty years. In the room the now-woman girl, called Illana, is putting on a slide presentation with images from her life. The principal image is her image as a girl in Chris Marker's film. The narrator repeats her words to her friends: 'Here Chris Marker filmed me for his *Description d'un combat*.' She points with her index finger at her mirror image on the screen. The camera captures this indexical image of an image of an image and freezes it. The narrator is contemplating:

> And if her pictures could speak
> Not in picture-language
> But in human language
> They might have said:
> Look at me.
> Look at me until amongst all the wondrous things in this world, the most wondrous of all is my being here again.
> Before you.
> Not like a picture.
> Not like a cygnet.
> Not like a signal.
> Not like a sign.
> Like a human being.

At the same time that the concluding text of *Description of a Struggle* calls to emancipate the human from the tyranny of inhumane sign-hood, the accompanying image freezes full screen – desperately surrendering to the ghostly still, eternal monarch of images. The message cannot come across entirely. However, the thinking is clear: with their power, images will remain beyond our fragile and senseless sustainability. Images, beyond humans, pass on to future generations the struggle to describe our struggle. That is why Kafka's story ends with an image of nature's eternal beauty. That is the magic. This is the mystery. Those are the miracles yet to be performed. This is the struggle worthy of both present and future descriptions. And yet, in the final analysis, Kafka's words of magic, mystery and miracle, in which I have placed myself following Marker's advice to whomever feels compelled to interpret him to write as if one was sailing down the Nile while being drunk, are more than worthy of repeating: '*One of the most effective means of seduction that evil has is the challenge to struggle.*'

NOTES

1   Born Christian François Bouche-Villeneuve, 1921. 'Information regarding the early life of Chris Marker ... is scarce and conflicting. The year to which his movies, videos, and multimedia projects are dated depends on which source you use, and in which country you live' (Christley 2002). For a detailed filmography and bibliography of Marker see Nora M. Alter (2006: 151–83).
2   These issues are notably addressed, for example, by scholars such as Bill Nichols (1976, 1985, 1991) and Michael Renov (1986, 2004).
3   The term was originally coined by Dziga Vertov (1984: 132).
4   My motivation for re-spiralling Kafka and Marker needs to be explained. When making *Description of a Memory*, I met with Chris Marker for several conversations from 2004 to 2011. Though Marker was very clear about his intention not to take any active role in the creative process of *Description of a Memory*, he was all the same more than generous in welcoming me to his studio apartment in Paris for long conversations about cinema and filmmaking. However, like Nora M. Alter, a prominent Marker researcher who said she had never even dreamt of asking Marker to allow her to record their conversations, I, too, saw no purpose in doing so. Jaime Christley tells about one such experience by another artist who collaborated with Marker: 'When Mikkel Aaland ... who wrote about meeting with Marker during the early '90s ... wanted to record on tape his talks with the multimedia artist, he was told, "No interviews. Instead, if you must write something, use your imagination. Place us on a boat on the Nile. We are drunk. It's your story"' (2002). And so here we are, 'on the Nile', listening to my story about Kafka and Marker.
5   It was written in two versions, presumably over 1904 and 1905, and then further edited by Kafka until 1910. Bianca Theisen dates its first publication to 1912 (2006:

546). For a detailed account of the history of the original publication see Sokel (1987).

6   Howard Hampton ventured to describe Marker using a series of questions that included: 'A Zone poet stalking the inner life of history? Nature documentarian tracking that most elusive of endangered species – subjectivity? Is Marker the late, semilamented twentieth century's most pitiless coroner, or its last partisan?' (2003).

7   Garnet C. Butchart defines 'monstration' as 'a showing without the narrative telling of a story' (2014: 41). William Brown defines it as 'the moment when the film does not make sense, when the film exists before us as presence and image, as opposed to as absence and text' (2012: 414). André Gaudreault defines it as 'that which calls for conscious reflection' (see Butchart 2006: 42); see also Gaudreault (1987: 29–36).

8   For a detailed account of the film's production, see Friedman (2011). The facts mentioned in this report have been confirmed to me by Marker (private communication, Paris, 25 April 2005), as well as by Lia Van-Leer (private communication, Jerusalem, 13 January 2005).

9   For an analysis of Dziga Vertov's metaphysical disposition, see Petric (1978) and Michelson (1972).

10   This narrative gesture is inspired by and alludes to Marker's *La Jetée* (1962) and *Sans Soleil* (1983).

11   The following discussion of 'sorcery' in documentary is inspired by Dziga Vertov's *The Man with the Movie Camera*, 1929, and Joris Ivens and Marcelline Loridan's *Une Histoire de Vent* (*Tale of the Wind*, 1988).

12   This information was confirmed to me by both Lia Van-Leer and Marker (private communications, Jerusalem, 3 January 2005 and Paris, 24 May 2006, respectively).

13   For example: 'The Huleh region was sheer marshes, complete with malaria and gunfire. [...] What is a swamp good for? One said: "All we need is a miracle", which at once put everyone at ease. If little was known of agriculture, the Jews knew all about miracles' Or: 'To grownups, the young are a wonder. They search for the missing link, between them and the ghetto ghosts'; *Description of a Struggle*.

14   This position was critiqued in the opening verse of my response to Marker's film: 'Like all travellers here before you, you came to see for yourself – a state reborn after 2,000 years, a miracle. You filmed, left, never to return'; *Description of a Memory*.

15   Marker revisited Plato's Cave Allegory in his 'Mythology' (1989).

BIBLIOGRAPHY

Alter, Nora M. (ed.) (2006) *Chris Marker*. Urbana, IL: University of Illinois Press.

Arthur, Paul (2003) 'Around the World with Chris Marker: Part II: Time Regained: Kino-Eye: The Legacy of Soviet Cinema as Refracted through Chris Marker's Always

Critical Vision', *Film Comment*, 39, 4; available at: http://monoskop.org/images/d/d1/Marker_Chris_Around_the_World_with_Chris_Marker_Part_II_Time_Regained.pdf (accessed 10 July 2015).

Brady, Martin and Helen Hughes (2002) 'Kafka Adapted to Film', *The Cambridge Companion to Kafka*, ed. Julian Preece. Cambridge: Cambridge University Press, 226–41.

Brown, William (2012) 'Monstrous Cinema', *New Review of Film and Television Studies*, 10, 4, 409–24.

Butchart, Garnet C. (2014) 'Haunting Past Images: On the 2006 Documentary Film *Description of a Memory* in the Context of Communicology', *American Journal of Semiotics*, 30, 1/2, 27–52.

Calvino, Italo (1974) *Invisible Cities*, trans. William Weaver. San Diego, New York and London: Harcourt Brace.

Chaiken, Michael and Sam Diiorio (2003) 'Printed Matter: The Author behind the Auteur', *Film Comment*, 39, 4, 42–3; available at: http://search.proquest.com/docview/1702393?accountid=14765 (accessed 10 July 2015).

Christley, Jaime N. (2002) 'Chris Marker', *Senses of Cinema*, 21. Available at: http://sensesofcinema.com/2002/great-directors/marker/ (accessed 10 July 2015).

Douhaire, Samuel and Annick Rivoire (2003) 'Marker Direct: A Rare Interview with One of Cinema's Most Secretive Filmmakers', *Film Comment*, 39, 3, 38–41; available at: http://www.filmcomment.com/article/marker-direct-an-interview-with-chris-marker (accessed 10 July 2015).

Friedman, Michal R. (2011) 'Between the Essay and the Midrash: *Description d'un Combat* by Chris Marker', in Sandra Meiri, Boaz Hagin, Raz Yosef and Anat Zanger (eds) *Just Images: Ethics and the Cinematic*. Newcastle: Cambridge Scholars.

Gaudreault, André. (1987) 'Narration and Monstration in the Cinema', *Journal of Film and Video*, 39, 2, 29–36.

Gross, Larry (2012) 'Time Traveler', *Film Comment*, 48, 5; available at: http://fiaf.chadwyck.com/fulltext/indexFullText.do?id=004/0407436&area=index&fromHistory=fullrecord&jid=006/0000127 (accessed 10 July 2015).

Hampton, Howard (2003). 'Remembrance of Revolutions Past', *Film Comment*, 39, 3, 33. Available at: http://search.proquest.com/docview/210280031?pq-origsite=gscholar (accessed 10 July 2015).

Isari, Ali (1971) *Cinéma Vérité*. Ann Arbor, MI: University of Michigan Press.

Kafka, Franz (1946 [1933]) 'Reflections on Sin, Pain, Hope, and the True Way,' in Max Brod and Hans J. Schoeps (eds) *The Great Wall of China*. London: Secker and Warburg, 87–100.

____ (1991 [1954]) *The Blue Octavo Notebooks*, ed. Max Brod. Cambridge, MA: Exact Change.

____ (1971 [1912]) 'Description of a Struggle', *The Complete Stories*, ed. Nahum Glatzer. New York: Schoken, 9–51.

Lacan, Jacques (1975) *The Seminar of Jacques Lacan, Book XX*. New York: W. W. Norton.

Leavitt, June O. (2012) *The Mystical Life of Franz Kafka: Theosophy, Cabala, and the Modern Spiritual Revival*. Oxford: Oxford University Press.

Lupton, Catherine (2005) *Chris Marker: Memories of the Future*. London: Reaktion.

____ (2009) 'When Signs Come Home to Roost', *Vertigo*, 4, 2; available at: https://www.closeupfilmcentre.com/vertigo_magazine/volume-4-issue-2-winter-spring-2009/when-signs-come-home-to-roost-dan-gevas-description-of-a-memory/ (accessed 10 July 2015).

Marker, Chris (2006 [1967]) 'Let Us Praise Dziga Vertov', in Nora M. Alter (ed.) *Chris Marker*. Urbana, IL: University of Illinois Press, 135–6.

Michelson, Annette (1972) 'Man with a Movie Camera: From Magician to Epistemologist', *Artforum*, 10, 7, 60–72.

Nichols, Bill (1976) 'Documentary Theory and Practice', *Screen*, 17, 4, 34–8.

____ (1985) 'The Voice of Documentary', in Bill Nichols (ed.) *Movies and Methods: An Anthology, Vol.2*. Berkeley, CA: University of California Press, 258–73.

____ (1991) *Representing Reality: Issues and Concepts in Documentary*. Bloomington, IN: Indiana University Press.

Peirce, Charles S. (1955) *Philosophical Writings of Peirce*. New York: Dover.

____ (1974) *Charles Sanders Peirce: Collected Writings Vol. 1* (8 vols.), eds Paul Weiss, Arthur W. Burks and Charles Hartshorne. Cambridge, MA: Harvard University Press.

Petric, Vlada (1978) 'Dziga Vertov as Theorist', *Cinema Journal*, 18, 1, 29–44.

Rancière, Jacques (2006) *Film Fables*, trans. Emiliano Battista. Oxford: Berg.

Renov, Michael (1986) 'Re-Thinking Documentary: Towards a Taxonomy of Mediation', *Wide Angle*, 8, 3/4, 71–7.

____ (2004) 'Surveying the Subject: An Introduction', *The Subject of Documentary*. Minneapolis, MN: University of Minnesota Press, ix–xxix.

Sokel, Walter H. (1987) 'Kafka's Beginnings: Narcissism, Magic and the Function of Narration in "Description of a Struggle"', in Alan Udoff (ed.) *Kafka and the Contemporary Critical Performance*. Bloomington, IN: Indiana University Press, 98–110.

Sterritt, David (2015) 'Level Five', *Cineaste*, 40, 2. Available at http://search.proquest.com/docview/1658782674?accountid=14765 (accessed 10 July 2015).

Tailleur, R. (2007 [1963]) 'Markeriana: A Scarcely Critical Description of the Work of Chris Marker', *Rouge*; available at: http://www.rouge.com.au/11/marker.html (accessed 10 July 2015).

Theisen, Bianca (2006) 'Simultaneity of Media: Kafka's Literary Screen', *Modern Language Notes*, 121, 3, 543–50.

Udoff, Alan (1987) 'Introduction: Kafka's Question', in Alan Udoff (ed.) *Kafka and the Contemporary Critical Performance*. Bloomington, IN: Indiana University Press, 1–16.

Vertov, Dziga (1984 [1935]) 'My Latest Experiment', *Kino Eye: The Writings of Dziga Vertov*, ed. Annette Michelson, trans. Kevin O'Brien. Berkeley, CA: University of California Press, 132–7.

Winston, Brian (1995) *Claiming the Real: The Griersonian Documentary and Its Legitimations*. London: British Film Institute.

TRANSCRIBING KAFKA INTO FILM: A TORTUOUS LOVE-STORY

HENRY SUSSMAN

I. A FAMILY AFFAIR

My complicated relationship to Franz Kafka – as well as to the very possibility of transposing literary invention to the screen – goes back to Mother's Day, 1962, when I had the crazy idea of bringing my mother and my older sister along with me to see Orson Welles's *The Trial* (1962). To this day, conceiving how I could have possibly orchestrated this experience as an excuse for my mother's annual Mother's Day present remains beyond me. The scene of this filial as well as social faux pas was the World, the centre-city Philadelphia film-*boîte* with the most consistent slate of foreign film offerings, though welcome surprises were also to be encountered just blocks away, at venues including the Fox, the Goldman and the Trans-Lux.

Even in its grainy, black and white presentation, Welles's cine-adaptation remains, insofar as I am concerned, absolutely contemporary. It is so, among other things, by dint of its jarring cuts, the play of Welles's signature 'long' and extreme wide-angle shots retrofitted for the occasion perfectly to bureaucratic spaces. Welles, as always strapped for cash, had nonetheless dragged cast and crew to Belgrade, to give that immense, open-office panorama early in the movie just the perfect *soupçon* of Soviet 'totalitarianism'. The casting achieved for this film was nothing less than genial, with Anthony Perkins, already coded for incipient psychosis of the paranoid persuasion by his work in Alfred Hitchcock's *Psycho* (1960), in the role of Josef K. The protagonist's chief love-interest, Frl. Bürstner, is played, with just the degree of completely cynical sexual world-weariness that one would expect of Kafkan romance, by a Jeanne Moreau, who was just at that juncture, with her near-simultaneous pivotal role in the love-triangulation of *Jules et Jim* (*Jules and Jim*, 1962), the very icon of feminine radiance and interiority in French cinema. (At an oblique angle, we will recur to this particular film-treasure below.) Moreau would be joined in the Kafkaesque role of holding the fort for femininity in Welles's *Trial*-adaptation by Romy Schneider, playing Lawyer Huld's nurse-companion, Leni; and by Elsa Martinelli in a powerful cameo appearance as the Court attendant's wife. Schneider, at that moment of her career, was a screen-icon of just a slightly different gauge: the very queen of advanced Euro-sexual *savoir-faire*. Sex, if it had to persist under the administration of the Kafkan imaginary, could only be a matter of remorseless disillusionment and political decay. In Frl. Bürstner's early cameo appearance in the proceedings, Moreau's rumpled trench coat says just about all; but then, Welles was also no slouch in devising the webs between Leni's fingers, a symbol of the overgrowth that textual exegesis holds in common with corruption.

My mother and sister, disoriented both by Kafkan disaffection and Welles's cinematic antics, left the World after fifteen minutes while I, in a state of morbid fascination, stayed on – as I have throughout the intervening decades. Nothing will ever redeem the self-absorption that could have allowed me to stick with this still-disturbing film while my family members, upset and mildly miffed, sought more hospitable climes. More than other cineastes, Welles's radicality of style and delivery is infused by an exquisite literary sensibility. Uncannily, he knows just where to go for literary inspiration. Cervantes,[1] the Shakespeare of *Othello*, *Macbeth* and the Henry plays,[2] Booth Tarkington (of *The Magnificent Ambersons*, 1942), and the still largely unknown Kafka make up an odd and incompatible assortment of dominant literary influences. Yet if I'm arguing here for a history-perforating contemporaneity to Welles's film-production, it is surely rooted, among other factors, in the acute sympathetic vibrations by which the auteur relates to the literary forerunners of his film projects. (The only other film that works on me exactly as it did on the day on which I saw it is Stanley Kubrick's cine-adaptation of Anthony Burgess's *A Clockwork Orange* [1971]. And in this latter case, it is the architectural settings, including the Korova Milk Bar and the modern house in which Alex and his *droogs* savage its occupants, which could have been erected yesterday.) Cinema, in its constant self-placement at the cutting-edge of verisimilitude, is thus radically endowed with the capability to puncture and perforate history and the succession of real time. Cinema is in this respect the flowering of that 'plank' of modernist experimentation militating for radical time-travel via the vehicles of the inexhaustible art-experiments of all times: Baroque painting and drama for Walter Benjamin; Greek and Chinese poetry and the troubadour lyric for Ezra Pound.

II. WELLES, TRUFFAUT, GODARD AND RESNAIS: GOING FOR BAROQUE IN *CINÉMA NOUVEAU*

The focus of the present comments is the fortunate elective affinity through which the aesthetics (or even better, the *idiom*) of the French cinema nouveau became the perfect vehicle for the adaptive transcription not only of the Kafkan sensibility but for, in one instance after the next, specific Kafkan innovations in the spheres of narrative, characterisation and mood. The multifaceted blockbusters from the heyday of the French New Wave, whether François Truffaut's *Les Quatre Cents Coups* (*The 400 Blows*, 1959), *Tirez sur le pianiste* (*Shoot the Piano Player*, 1960) and *Jules et Jim* or Jean-Luc Godard's *À bout de souffle* (*Breathless*, 1960), *Bande à part* (*Band of Outsiders*, 1964), *Alphaville* (1965) and *Masculin Féminin* (1966) literally explode with improvisations and revisions to classical film history ultimately implicating a prime suspect in the domain of aesthetics that can only be Kafka. Surely among these innovations have to number jarring discontinuities in narration and perspective; also disjunctions between image and soundtrack. And if we began our discussion with Welles, it is because his unique personal trajectory in theatre and radio before cinema bequeathed a vast legacy of moves and tonalities to the French auteurs of the late 1950s and beyond. To inject one final personal note: cinema nouveau as comprehensive film-idiom became so intertwined with my very understanding of the medium that I entered a state of mourning as its dominance as *the* operating language of cinematic production began slowly to wind down at the very end of the last century. (This was, of course, only a symbolic mourning for a cinematic idiom and way of being that like Godard himself, joined by the likes of Volker Schlöndorff, Claire Denis and Michael Haneke, remains very much with us.) If cinema nouveau became the very generator for the filmic dialectical image (as christened by Benjamin in Convolute N of his *Passagen-Werk* [*The Arcades Project*]), that very hardy sea-craft plies on.[3]

With the possible exception of Charles Baudelaire, no author was more decisive to the emergence of Benjaminian critical tact and touch than Kafka himself. And it was Benjamin who discerned in baroque allegory – a scene of rare continuity and follow through between constative and performative linguistic dimensions in the synthesis of striking figurative imagery – something utterly prophetic and quintessential both to Kafkan innovation and such twentieth-century 'complex culture games' as Surrealism. It is indeed the discernment of a powerful forerunner to the major 'aesthetic contracts'[4] of modernist improvisation that was a major driving force behind Benjamin's failed 'Habilitationsschrift', *The Origin of German Tragic Drama*.[5] Yet Benjamin's appeal, in his *Trauerspiel*, both to the major (Calderón, Shakespeare) and the minor (Lohenstein, Gryphius) dramatic programmers of the seventeenth century hardly exhausted itself in the name of historical comprehensiveness. He saw himself as mining in these fields something crucial if lost, something emblematic of language-usage at it had emerged in the speeded up commerce and sociological collisions of nineteenth-century Paris, in the shorthand staccato characteristic of such twentieth-century media as newsprint and radio.

One more Benjaminian link interposing itself here may temper any red alerts set off by the constellation I am positing between Kafka, Welles's 1962 screen-adaptation of the latter's most formally coherent novel, and the crystallisation of a radical new and comprehensive (as in *gesamt*) film idiom by the French cinema nouveau. And I am teasing it out here not only for the sake of 'going baroque'. I refer to François Truffaut's explicit reliance, in his scenario for *Jules et Jim*, on Henri-Pierre Roché's semi-autobiographical novel of the same title from 1953. The polymorphous, sexually volatile marital arrangements that Roché depicted in his novel happen to have been based on his own prior contacts with the couple consisting of Franz Hessel, Benjamin's co-translator of Proust, and his wife, a notable journalist and fashion critic in her own right, Helen Grund Hessel. Indeed, Franz Hessel's book, *Spazieren in Berlin* (1929), transposing nineteenth-century Parisian *flânerie* to the Berlin scene of the following century, could almost have been *commissioned* by the Benjamin who had already by the 1920s emigrated, on the virtual plane, to the capital of his imagination. Helen Grund, for all the emancipation of her lifestyle, would remain one of Benjamin's stalwart Parisian supporters as times increasingly toughened throughout the 1930s. It cannot be entirely coincidental that the *lives* of the intellectuals who most acutely and creatively registered the shocks, disruptions and anomalies of advanced urban modernity that Benjamin traced back to its glimmerings in the Arcades became the very *fabric* out of which cinema nouveau fashioned its moral and not-so-moral parables.

Unlikely though it is that Welles could have ever encountered the Benjaminian *Trauerspiel*, an unmistakable post-baroque aesthetic surrounds Josef K.'s remorseless perambulations through the bureaucracy in his film adaptation of *Der Prozess* (*The Trial*, 1925). This is not only a question of mood, as when K. quickly grows disenchanted with Lawyer Huld's pep talks regarding his case's prospects. It is a matter of the soundtrack, in which Albinoni's *Adagio in G Minor* plays a disproportionate role. Indeed, until Josef K.'s life is truncated by the slapstick deliberations of henchmen wearing trench coats with an aura of Stalinist fatality about them and wielding dynamite rather than a dagger, the course of the film may be described as a *retrospective descent into baroque melancholia*.

I leave the debate as to whether Alain Resnais counts as a bona fide member of the French cinema nouveau to film-scholars of higher pedigree than myself.

But it can surely be not entirely coincidental that when Resnais authors a film, *L'Année dernière à Marienbad* (*Last Year at Marienbad*, 1961), almost concurrent to Welles's *Trial*-adaptation – whose task is in part to gauge the difference between European culture's (writ large) pre-World War II and post-war experiences of itself – he also draws on the baroque, emblematically as well as musically, as the dominant cultural *environment* to the narrative's *system*.[6] Albeit circuitously, via the agency of baroque aesthetics and language theory, the trend-setting *Last Year at Marienbad* accords Kafka definitive centrality within the deliberations of French cinema nouveau; it embeds his signature and aesthetics within this idiom's progressive contractual negotiations.

Last Year at Marienbad, along with *Hiroshima mon Amour* (*Hiroshima My Love*, 1959), assures Resnais a role of enduring splendour within the creative achievement of post-War European cinema. Whether this has been brokered by Resnais' familiarity with Welles's overall oeuvre or not, Kafka remains a crucial 'secret sharer' in Resnais' landmark achievements. When it came time for me to score my own commentary on Resnais, I could only do so in verse – distantly following in the footsteps of Jean Epstein. In a series of experiments known as Screen-Memories, I inscribed my reactions to the films that had formed me in a writing-medium as truncated and compressed as film-editing itself. The following extract from *Screen-Memory # 5*, on Resnais, explains the uncanny resonance between Kafkan aesthetics and the practices of cinema nouveau with greater exigency than I could manage in prose:

                     In very

thinnest bas-relief
setting COMPLEXITY
bounding and enriching
possibility, tenor of a day, desire's dusky
flavor, twilight
falling, Hausmannian boulevard,
big in grain & very bad focus
(first of Rohmer's moral fables).

                     Nothing

yielding what we want of it, nothing
panning out – only unbounded pan
orama
Alain Resnais sweeps
through least likely setting of tur
bulent

passion, Baroque spa-spot
teeming ceiling to floor
w arab
esques thoroughly useless, dis
tracting ornament.

                                    Detail
left over, undisclosed
prior moment, submerged forever,
maybe pre-War, archaeological
remains, dispersed
Euro-elite class,
dinosaurs! Not only im
plausible,
BO-RING--
big time!

                              What compelled Resnais
configuring THIS fiction-world?
Xpressly 2 unpack un
tried cine idiom, launch un
paralleled run--
thru & thru
entire terrestrial habit

ation,
very language of film, medium
of experience in *fragrant*
delit of simul
cast unrolling.

Marienbad: how contrived, artsy
fishal, 2 point, un
bashed seat-squirming, alienation, that is
just the joint!

                                So it began,
cine idiolect, still speak it,
as we submit 2 darkened cave, out
& out

COMPLEXITY!

                                        w Frank
appealing in name of lost time,
hyperthyroid memory 2 last
year's playmate
known to us as "Delphine," un
realized infatuation, Frank
unleashing every trick & stratagem in male play
book so she plays @ being
she, projection, plaything, captive
2 male fantasy & public im
agination as stands,
ON THE RECORD!

                                        Exquisite
excruciating self-correcting
full declination, all pos
sible tenses, postures, in stereo:
on right, classic matinee-idol Romeo; left, sleek
French brunette ingénue,
lingering legs stork
like in grace, allure reaching all extreme
ities, *petite chemise noir* doesn't hurt. Endless

                                        infatuation
under watchful eye,
keeper may be a hubby,
player-king @ game, odds & propriety,
all cards in his hand

                                        amid trap
pings: Euro-refinement @ X
treme of expression qua ornament,
revision, *N*th level,
crit sensibility.

                                        Where ges
ture *is* substance, sole mea
sure, proportion & plausibility,

reducing (or elevating?) char
acters: level, indexical ci
phers (B4 we might have
discerned them, flickering art).

        Ciphers,

gesticulating contrived shadow
grams,
done up, exaggerated
formal garb, hairdo,
especially super
fluous, irrelevant to post
War environment, when
edifice, W. Civil
ization first allows self
'nother deep breath? These char
actors trundled out, 2 what
essential drama

        other than the story,

con
jugugal conjunction,
waiting 2 B born?
Baroque stage-set, Euro
lifestyle gone by, against all
strictures, polite & refined society
legislated under mono
gamy's meta
physics

        &

set
2 extended dirge,
soundtrack,
full-stop organ
reminder, grim burden,
melancholy & theatre
to bear. "Melancholy
betrays the world for the sake of
knowledge," writes Benjamin,

fated *Habilitationsschrift*,
Baroque tragic page
ant. "But in its tenacious
self-absorption it embraces dead
objects in its contemplation, in
order to redeem them." Self-
contained gesticulating characters, *Marienbad*,
traversing stage-set,
fluff-fragments, distant age,
under
scoring strang
eness. Melancholy arising,
not merely
@ throttled sex
pression,
rage @ stifled life,
dislocated, specters of War.
"The only pleasure
the melancholic permits himself, and it is a pow
erful one, is
allegory."

                              So again, Walter,
and again: "The word 'history' stands
written on the countenance of nature in char
acters of transience. The allegorical physiognomy
of the nature history . . . is present in reality
in the form of the ruin. In the ruin
history has physically merged
in the setting. And in this guise history
does not assume the form of the pro
cess of an eternal life so much as that
of irresistible decay. Allegory
thereby declares itself
to be beyond beauty. Allegories
are, in the realm of thoughts, what ruins
are in the realm of
things."

                                    Châ

teau: Marienbad, Friedrichs
bad, whatever, dis
membered
architectural index,
allegorical setting,
film's post-War
drawing
room,
travesty
desire stunted, hyper-mannered
CONTRIVANCE, story, costume, gest
ure, scene, cardgame
ESPECIALLY synch,
image, music & voice.
World: cascading, mutual
reinforcing artificialities. So it began:
cine-eye relent
lessly cataloguing endless
hallways, funereal saloons, lamps giving forth
overbearing crystal,
ornatest tracery, protoscript
mouldings o'ergrown ceiling 2
wall, rain-forest
profusion; utterly inept
setting, film-patois, utter
DISrespect 4 BIG WAR
back-story
(that battle
Renais fought, *Night*
& Fog).

                                                  Rad
ically artificial
code & zone, post-War
film declaring indy
pendence,
set allegiances, af
FIRMations
'mid multiple exaggerations,
empty-headed (through dressed 2 gills)

cast, *Marienbad*.

        So when film's
female object of allure
(trussed into
 bird costume, splayed
"dead" while keeper
shoots target practice)
protests & denies
anything resembling last year's
dalliance

        OBSTINATE LOVER
marshals every shard,
INCRIMINATING evidence: above all
NOTOR
ious photo, THE WOMAN, mug
ging, garden-bench,
mechanically reproducible (as in whole drawer
full), cine
artifact digresses
historical ex
igency,
2 critique
tornado-heap, cultural
THINGS history deposits
@ our feet.

        Me
mori problem here to be sure,
not simply SEXUAL misunder
standing; fannying out, broader
considerations: CAPACITY,
not just sexual:
how much
can Euro civil society
handle?
Its own recent memory,
muddled, intense
moral lapses, compromises,

deft denial, BAROQUE
PRESTIDIGITATION
@ very core
of post-War
WONDER?

                                                       In garden
not of forking paths,
perfectly con
ical trees, spherical
bushes, pop
ulated‑‑
mildly ominous men in tuxedos,
poses of "mobile rigidity,"
the Surreal
encounters history & sex,
no obvious winner.

                                                      Soundtrack
switches off
'twixt lugubrious
organ accompaniment, dunning din,
Frank's sexual drone,
 – and the jingle of fashion-show
come-on,
promise, gallic Roe
mance.

So streiten
two musical voices, modes
over mood,
Baroque costume
drama: what's it
gonna take for the X-
PRESSION,
sexual yearning &
DEE-SIRE
(*jawohl*,
even in lady's POV!) under
New Prevailing

Operating System
(preeminent
house-organ:
CINEMA!)

      Yes, it's music
we're left with: film
indexes, appeals,
EVERY artform. Twists of nar
rative betraying voice, image,
terrible freedom common to art & sex, me
andering where
ever. "In *Last Year
@ Marienbad*, image and text
play a sort of game of hide-
&-seek in which they give
each other passing
caresses," so Christian
Metz. & no other film
so utterly taken & given by this ca
ress, dancing it, embroidering it
in song, than *Hiro
shima mon Amour*.

      How not be enraptured,
reverie, adult
openeyed, freegiven love,
digging out the double-war, one
splayed out, extremities,
sun's weary & dis
consulate path, mirrored
orgies of becoming-death,
far reaches,
systemic global overload.

      Transfiguring
dialogue (thanks, Marguerite Duras!)
keyed perfectly,
demands of moment & imagery
(not character or story),

run-on poem, of this could only be,
soundtrack flying free,
everything but our impressions:
Magnificently paired lovers
unearthing shrapnel of Real
as persistent, 2 wars;
peace tribunal, Hiroshima,
cinema-style negotiation,
fourteen years post
Big Bang.

                                    Never

screen woman so primed,
embracing unbridled
intimacy, Emmanuelle
Riva this rhapsody. Never
so perfectly accompanied--
fleeting love at best risky business--
Eiji Okada, husky
French bass to her
openmouthed
discovery.

                                      Even

in view,
checkered history,
crimes--visual contempt & violence against women in film,
eloquently pressed,
Laura Mulvey.

                                    Beneath skin/

skin intimacy
picked up, camera in full
texture, intertwined
skeins,
war stories knot
increasing nearness, complexity. Pelts,
female hair archived,
Hiroshima War Museum, detached from owners
full atomic blast,

rhymes w humiliation
visited upon enemy-lovers,
(as our heroine was),
eighteen year-old,
War's end, You
rope, his loss THE signature
trauma. Joyous bike
jaunts, tufted
fields around Nevers,
illicit lover, most pastoral land.
scapes (by far)
gathering in
New Wave's art
gallery.

       Song of Nevers

this film, anthem's incongruity
soaring outward from brute facts,
never resolved, poetry's song
unabsorbed by film, however rich
visual treasury.
Nevers return
losses incurred by war,
above all social empathy,
Nevers, gorgeous *Qi*
pouring out livelong night,
full-throttled love abutting
@ dawn, *Nevers* hope
radiating, *petit rayon vert*,
cusp, Realest disaster.
Remains for us
to say we made good,
life-
line tossed us by Resnais.

III. INTO THE FORTRESS OF KAFKAN SCREEN-MEMORY

Unpredictably, with two major adaptations of Kafka's most philosophical, least finished novel-project, *Das Schloss* (*The Castle*, 1926), the 1990s witnessed a stampede into the virtual space of the Kafkan Imaginary. A 1997 sombre, made-for-TV version in black and white by Michael Haneke strove for (and achieved) high fidelity to Kafka's meandering and speculative novel. The director, in anticipation of his *tour de force* in *Der Weisse Band* (*The White Ribbon*, 2009), pressed his uncanny sense for the temperamental climate prevailing in isolated and dank villages into the service of this adaptation. K.'s remorseless wanderings from one end of the Castle village to the other in a double-barrelled quest for sense and affirmation are shot in absolutely level horizontal *verité*. This does not begin to exhaust what is levelheaded about Haneke's adaptation. K. is a bit jaded and at the end of his tether, as we would expect a drifter in the middle of life's road to be. There is a great performance by Frieda (Susanne Lothar), K.'s primary love-interest and his only living link, a sexual one, to *administrator absconditus*, Klamm. The film offers everything in the way of slapstick idiocy on the part of messenger Barnabas and assistants Artur and Jeremias that Kafka fans everywhere rightly demand. An impressive tribute to Kafka's most enigmatic extended work, the Haneke adaptation performs public service as well: at a consistently high level of artistic specs, it presents the novel, accurately and plausibly, to the broader public.

Three years earlier, and in the wake of the Soviet Union's demise, Aleksei Balabanov, in *Zamok* (*The Castle*, 1994), implanted every bit as firmly as Haneke in the Castle's virtual domain, had mounted a distinctively different adaptation strategy – looser in fidelity, wilder in improvisation, and more open in its splicing in of tangential motifs. Balabanov remains bolder in setting Kafka's Castle in the Russian counterparts to its 'natural' and architectural settings. Indeed, Haneke curtails the 'outside' to deliberations on K.'s part that are first and foremost bureaucratic and domestic. What we see mostly of the outside in Haneke's version is characters bracing themselves against onslaughts of snow. The most extended outdoors scene is in the courtyard of the Herrenhof Hotel: K. waits there in futility, hoping to snag Klamm as he hops into his sled. Haneke does not even venture an image of the Castle from afar, although Kafka's nuanced description of this pile is one of the great narrative triumphs in his ouevre.

Balabanov's framing of the Castle in its natural environment is striking indeed. His shots of the surrounding countryside are exquisite. The Russian Castle village echoes Kremlin architecture, and in this sense references the Eisenstein classics, whether *Ivan the Terrible* (*Pt. I*, 1945; *Pt. II*, 1958) or *Alexander Nevsky* (1938). At transitional moments in the film, Balabanov foregrounds the Castle in long shots of volatile water whose current is no more liquid than it is solid. In their indeterminate turmoil, the menacing swells echo K.'s predicament.

The first chapter of *The Castle* specifies that in age, K. has reached the plateau of 'thirty-something'. In contrast to Haneke's K., the masterful Ulrich Mühe,

Nikolai Stotsky, Balabanov's protagonist, is as youthful an actor as could possibly be imagined for this role. Under Balabanov's direction, K., and the novel he dominates, works in the interest of an implied youth movement, perhaps the generation being called upon to galvanise and redirect Russia in its post-Soviet phase. The expectation of Balabanov's K. from the get-go – that he is, authoritatively, to employ and direct Barnabas and the assistants in their tasks – takes on a theatre of the absurd cast.

Perhaps the most substantial difference in the approaches to adaptation taken by Haneke and Balabanov is that the latter's adaptation filters back to us through the active mediation of Walter Benjamin – and not only the Benjamin of the groundbreaking retrospective on Franz Kafka, 'Kafka: On the Tenth Anniversary of his Death' (1934). The most remarkable torque that Balabanov applies to Kafka's plot may well be that the master-craftsmen with whom K. interacts, Barnabas's aging and discredited father and *his* former assistant, Brunswick, are no longer master cobblers but manufacturers of music cylinders (as in player pianos and similar devices). This single plot-twist opens the film to a wild and proliferating showcase of outmoded mechanical technologies of reproduction – in the visual as well as audio sphere. In its artistic design and décor, the film becomes a Benjaminian phantasmagoria (and 'Antique Road Show') of way stations on the road to advanced tele-technic verisimilitude. If endless waiting and hovering indecision form the 'steady state' of K.'s existential predicament, this open-ended deferral becomes an occasion for meditating on the crisis of mediation, *its* endless quest for 'purer' and more advanced forms, for 'higher fidelity' realism. It is in this way that Balabanov's Castle adaptation becomes a carnivalesque and parodic quest for the *ultimate* modality of 'technological reproducibility'. It is a master-stroke as well that Balabanov names K.'s love interest who replaces Frieda amid the steady fast-forward that the novel prescribes for all human interactions (this in opposition to bureaucratic procedures) 'Milena' instead of 'Pepi'. This act of renaming enables Balabanov, improbably, to loop Kafka's life-story into his adaptation. In Kafka's later years, a liaison largely by correspondence with Milena Jesenska supplanted his tortuous on-again off-again engagement to Felice Bauer.

In a way that would be much appreciated by Mikhail Bakhtin, Balabanov transforms *The Castle* from existential travesty precisely into carnival – without departing from the virtual and aesthetic landscapes established by the Castle and its domains. In this dimension of the iteration, implausibly, Federico Fellini joins the cast of the film's cinematic forbears. Resolute in his quest, K. is almost never afforded the luxury of being alone with his thoughts. K.'s struggle not only to reach and confront Klamm but with the unavoidable crowds into which he is constantly thrust comprises a central element in the film's social satire.

Periodically, the 'madding crowd' that K. has been forced to join forms a chorus, breaking out into song and dance routines whose preeminent quality is their mechanical stutter-step. (An appropriately eerie and marvellously variegated soundtrack by Sergey Kuryokhin accompanies the visuals.) Along with the film's showcase of outmoded mechanical technologies, the film's musical 'numbers', especially when performed by its chorus of children, reference an early nineteenth-century aesthetic, the mechanical possession periodically overwhelming E. T. A. Hoffmann's major characters. If the trappings surrounding K.'s personal predicament and existential quest derive from an aesthetic of the Romantic grotesque, the costumes designed for the film, perhaps in keeping with its architecture, tend to hover in the late Middle Ages, on the cusp of Modernity. This menacing, strictly black attire recalls an age of social anomie and violence constantly on the verge of reemergence.

Balabanov's *The Castle* evolves into a romp from one rural medieval outpost *à la Russe*, from one Kafkan love-impasse, and from one technology of 'mechanical reproducibility' to the next. It is, in the world of film adaptations, as loose and fanciful as Haneke's is faithful and *de rigeur*. Balabanov's *The Castle* is not afraid to run away where Kafka contented himself with spare one-liners. As Frieda clears the taproom where she works as barmaid so that she may deepen her intimate ties to K., the narrator compares her to Circe. In Balabanov's version, a flock of very tangible swine unpredictably romps through cine-space at all the wrong moments. Balabanov unlocks *The Castle*; he springs the novel's embedded absurdities, even while maintaining his version of tight fidelity to plot, theme and mood.

Perhaps the ultimate coup that Balabanov pulls off in his 'loose-construction' adaptation of the Kafka classic is inserting, toward the end of K.'s drama in the village, a Faustian pact by which Brunswick, the music cylinder master, assumes the interloper's identity in exchange for his wife. (She is the unusually dainty 'girl from the Castle' that K. spots early on in his village rounds. Balabanov has set K.'s infatuation for her in his film somewhat higher than it plays out in the novel.) Through this added role-reversal, the tangential novelistic character, Brunswick, reaps all the recognition and reward ultimately accruing to K., though only in Balabanov's retelling. This definitive 'so near but so far' final plot-twist only reinforces the futility of K.'s position. His fate remains very much the one that Kafka had programmed for him: a slacker with much to commend him in his common sense and basic instinct for justice – doomed, however, to being thwarted by the inevitable blind-spots and *méconnaissance* in his vision.

This film employs colour and set-design to great effect. It evokes notable performances, above all by Svetlana Pismichenko (Frieda), Igor Shibanov (Brunswick), Andrei Smirnov (Teacher), Vladislav Demchenko (Barnabas),

Bolot Bejshenaliev (Mayor), Vladimir Kuznetsov (Hans Brunswick), Svetlana Sviroko (Olga) and Svetlana Serval (Amalia). Kafka himself could only marvel at how far his striking images have travelled; how well his scenarios of systematic insult, bureaucratic deferral and instinctual thwarting fare in a radically distant socio-cultural 'frame'; how much his inaugural fictive forays into media and technology ended up suggesting.

NOTES

1   From 1955 until his death in 1985 Welles was working on his never finished film adaptation of Don Quixote.
2   In *Chimes at Midnight*.
3   I could only be referring here to such a statement as the following one that Benjamin crystallizes in Convolute N of *The Arcades Project* – this particular section his methodological apotheosis, set in prose aphorisms, of his lifelong labour on Paris as the incubator of advanced urban and industrial modernity: 'What matters for the dialectician is having the wind of world history in his sails. Thinking means for him: setting the sails. What is important is how they are set. Words are his sails. The way they are set makes them into concepts' (1999: 473). For a treatment of how the theoretical aphorisms of *The Arcades Project* arise from the radical democracy of the diverse materials that Benjamin assembled for his panoramic Parisian overview, see my 'Theory on the Fly: Critical Synthesis under Conditions of Material Pirating and Borrowed Time', in *Playful Intelligence: Digitizing Tradition* (Sussman 2014).
4   This is a term I devised and floated in my *The Aesthetic Contract: Statutes of Art and Intellectual Work in Modernity* (1997: 165–205).
5   The brief passage that follows is one of several indicative of how Benjamin marshalled baroque allegory in service to a modern/postmodern recalibration of writing both as an overarching, 'smart' medium and inscriptive science: 'Considered in allegorical terms, then, the profane world is both elevated and devalued. [...] For allegory is both: convention and expression; and both are inherently contradictory. However, just as baroque teaching conceives as history as created events, allegory in particular, although a convention like every kind of writing, is regarded as created, like holy scripture. The allegory of the seventeenth century is not convention of expression, but expression of convention. (1977: 175)
6   With a strong nod in the direction of systems theory, I'm implying here, in the sense of Niklas Luhmann, that baroque trappings in *Last Year at Marienbad* play surround, or 'environment', to the more 'central' drama (or 'system') as to whether 'Frank' consummated an affair with 'Delphine' during some past Marienbad saison (Luhmann 1995: 16–17, 24, 26).

BIBLIOGRAPHY

Benjamin, Walter (1977) *The Origin of German Tragic Drama*, trans. John Osborne London: New Left Books.

____ (1999) *The Arcades Project*, trans. Howard Eiland and Kevin McLaughlin. Cambridge, MA: Harvard University Press.

____ (2007 [1934]) 'Kafka: On the Tenth Anniversary of his Death', *Illuminations*, trans. Harry Zohn. New York: Schocken, 111–40.

Burgess, Anthony (1962) *A Clockwork Orange*. London: Heinemann.

Hessel, Franz (1968 [1929]) *Spazieren in Berlin*. Berlin: Rogner & Bernhard.

Kafka, Franz (2009 [1926]) *The Castle*, trans. Anthea Bell. Oxford and New York: Oxford University Press.

____ (2009a [1925]) *The Trial*, trans. Mike Mitchell. Oxford: Oxford University Press.

Luhmann, Niklas (1995) *Social Systems*, trans. John Bednarz, Jr. with Dirk Becker. Stanford, CA: Stanford University Press.

Roché, Henri-Pierre (1979 [1953]) *Jules et Jim*. Paris: Gallimard.

Sussman, Henry (1997) *The Aesthetic Contract: Statutes of Art and Intellectual Work in Modernity*. Stanford, CA: Stanford University Press.

____ (2014) 'Theory on the Fly: Critical Synthesis under Conditions of Material Pirating and Borrowed Time', *Playful Intelligence: Digitizing Tradition*. London and New York: Bloomsbury, 167–202.

INDEX

À bout de souffle see Breathless
Absurd   19, 236–55, 256n.n.3,5; Absurd freedom   246; Absurd hero/heroism   237, 240, 242, 245–7, 255; *see also* Camus, Albert and suicide
Accident on the Dock, The   82
Acousmatics   112; de-acousmatisation   114–17, 120, 127n.7
acoustic effects   111, 113; non-identical   111; *see also* sound
Adams, Jeffrey   13, 15, 21n.14, 183–4
Adorno, Theodor W.   1, 7, 9, 14–16, 20n.5, 70, 84, 158n.9, 160n.17, 191, 204, 264, 280–3, 286, 290, 292n.2
Aeroplane in Brescia, Die see Airplanes in Brescia, The
aesthetics   131, 133, 298, 331, 333; film aesthetics   193; of modernism   193; noir   184
After Hours   14
Agamben, Giorgio   55, 58, 65n.3
Airplanes in Brescia, The   77
Alexander Nevsky   344
Allen, Woody   15, 21n.15

alltägliche Verwirrung, Eine see Common Confusion, A
Almendros, Néstor   13
Alone at Last   82
Alphaville   331
Alter, Nora   125–126n.2, 311
Alt, Peter-André   10, 48–49n.1, 85, 99
America   89, 104, 106, 130–5, 137–8, 140–9, 152, 156, 157n.2, 157–158n.3, 158–159n.n.n.4,9,11, 159–160n.14, 160n.15, 183, 186, 201–2, 222–3; American aesthetics   131, 133; American culture of masculinity   145; American dream   89, 132; American hero   152, 156; American values   131; democracy   138, 147, 160n.16
Amerika see Amerika: The Man Who Disappeared
Amerika: The Man Who Disappeared   3, 10, 11, 20n.4, 51n.19, 84, 89, 130, 157n.1, 158–9n.11, 159n.13, 160n.17, 186, 195n.2, 199, 201–2, 229, 289

Amerika: The Missing Person see *Amerika: The Man Who Disappeared*
Aneignung 46
animation 3, 4, 14, 16
anni di piombo 301
anti-Semitic discourses 215
anti-televisual television 191
Aquaviva, Seraphine 53, 54
Arcades Project, The 331, 237n.3
archaism 30, 31
Arendt, Hannah 149, 203
Arnheim, Rudolf 280–1
Arrival of a Train at La Ciotat Station, The 7, 35
Assassin, The 296–301, 305
auteurism 37, 188–9, 317, 330; and adaptations 184, 188, 193; French auteurs 331; script 192

Balabanov, Aleksei 20, 344–6
Balázs, Bela 87, 108n.2
Bande à part see *Band of Outsiders*
Band of Outsiders 331
Bau, Der see Burrow, The
Bauer, Felice 5, 47, 181, 263, 345
Baum, Oskar 30, 50n.11
Bazin, André 117n.2, 194
Beckett, Samuel 280, 292n.1
Beetle and the Fly, The 210, 211–17, 210
Before the Law 12, 14–15, 38, 146, 182, 184, 195n.4, 222, 295–6, 298, 300, 305
Beim Bau der Chinesischen Mauer see While Building the Chinese Wall
Bell, Anthea 12
Benayoun, Robert 285–6
Benjamin, Walter 7–9, 18, 29, 30, 68, 71–2, 82, 84–5, 91, 126n.4, 131, 135–41, 144, 146–8, 158n.n.n.6,8,10, 182, 186, 191, 199–200, 204, 207, 213–14, 289–91, 330–2, 336, 345, 347n.n.3,5
Benny's Video 189, 191
Benson, Peter 12
Bericht für eine Akademie, Ein see *Report to an Academy, A*
Beschreibung eines Kampfes see Description of a Struggle
Betrachtung 88
Biderman, Shlomo 204
Big Lebowski, The 258–61, 265
BK 313–16, 318–20
Blade Runner 72
Blood Simple 260
Book of Genesis 319
Blue Octavo Notebooks, The 264, 310
Bordwell, David 127–128n.13, 164, 269–70, 274, 276n.7
Borges, Jorge Luis 12
Bouche-Villeneuve, Christian-François see Marker, Chris
Boy who Sank out of Sight, The see *Amerika: The Man Who Disappeared*
Breathless 331
Bresson, Robert 184–5, 190–1, 193
Brod, Max 1, 2, 4, 20n.n.1,2, 30, 32, 39, 40, 56, 81, 84, 97–100, 107, 157n.2, 199, 211, 229, 261, 275n.3, 285, 288
Buber, Martin 194
bugwriters 225, 228
Burgin, Victor 72
Burroughs, William 210–11, 226–8, 231
Burrow, The 17–18, 111–25, 126n.3, 127n.9, 163–72, 174–6, 263, 287
Buster Keaton: The Look of Silence 285
BuzzFeed 38; see also rumourology

Cabinet des Dr. Caligari, Das see Cabinet of Dr. Caligari, The
Cabinet of Dr. Caligari, The   164
Cabiria   77
Calvino, Italo   318
Cameraman, The   287, 292n.4
Camus, Albert   19, 237–47, 250–2, 254–5, 256n.n.3,4, 280
Cares of a Family Man, The   281, 286
Carroll, Noël   177n.2, 283–4
Castle, The (1926)   12–14, 19, 31, 60, 62, 64, 66n.6, 84, 89, 91, 160n.17, 181, 188, 261, 229, 260 –1, 263, 275n.2, 279, 283–4, 286, 289, 343
Castle, The (tv adaptation) (1994)   20, 344–6
Castle, The (tv adaptation) (1997)   18, 20, 185, 188–91
Castle Keep   288
Catholicism   222
Cavell, Stanley   18, 131, 133–5, 137, 142, 158n.6, 159n.13
Cervantes, Miguel de   9, 330
Chaplin, Charlie   16, 18, 84, 145, 158–159n.11, 198–207, 282–3, 289–90, 292n.7; *see also* Kafkaesque
Character in Need of Support, A   14
Chatman, Seymour   249, 253
Chion, Michel   113–16, 120, 125n.1, 204
Chosen People   59–60
Chronicle of Anna Magdalena Bach   193
Chronik der Anna Magdalena Bach see Chronicle of Anna Magdalena Bach
cinema nouveau *see* French cinema nouveau
cinematic adaptations   10–11, 13, 18, 176
cinematic comedy   199
cinematic image   5, 8, 83, 206
cinematic remembering   313

Cinematograph   2, 34, 35, 97–9, 107; *see also* Lumière, Auguste and Louis
Cinematographic Theatre   98
cinematographic writing   48–49n.1, 55, 60–1
cinéma-vérité   310
circular journeys   271
Citizen Kane   184
City Lights   147, 159, 158, 202, 203, 205–6, 207n.1
cityscape   94, 99; *see also flâneur/ flânerie*
Class Relations   18, 181, 185–7, 192, 194
Clockwork Orange, A   330
Cloquet, Ghislain   317
Codeless Message   19, 263, 267, 268
Coen, Joel and Ethan   16, 19, 21n.15, 258–75, 275n.1
Coetzee, J. M.   115, 116, 119–20, 122–3
Cohen, Hermann   30
Cold War   183, 223
College   283
Common Confusion, A   13, 15
Communism   14, 45, 304–5;
  Communist Party   298, 301, 304
confusión cotidiana, Una see Everyday Confusion, An
Conversation with the Drunk   311
Conversation with the Supplicant   311
Cops   280
Corngold, Stanley   1, 2, 7, 12, 165, 177n.5, 212, 224, 229–31, 256n.1, 260, 263–4, 274–5, 298
Country Doctor, A   14–15, 19, 217–25, 233, 233n.2
Countryman and the Cinematograph, The   34
Cronenberg, David   16, 18–19, 210–33, 233n.1, 236–7, 247–50, 251–5, 256n.2
crossbreeds   264, 275

dark comedy 200, 233
daydream 4, 68–79, 92–4, 205, 280;
    and déjà vu 70
Daydreams 280
decima vittima, La see Tenth Victim, The
Deleuze, Gilles 13, 79, 93, 296
Description d'un combat 309–16, 318,
    321, 323
Description of a Memory 20, 310–12,
    321, 324n.4, 325n.14
Description of a Struggle 6, 20, 85, 192,
    309, 311, 323, 325n.13
Dichter und das Phantasieren, Der *see*
    Poet and Daydreaming, The
dogdom 122
Dolar, Mladen 115–19, 127n.n.7,9
Dorfschullehrer, Der *see* Village
    Schoolteacher, The
double negation 12
drawings 2–4, 182
Dreyer, Carl Theodor 184
dual-natured 11
Dylan, Bob 273–4, 276n.10

early cinema 16–17, 29– 43, 83–4, 91
Edison, Thomas A. 2
Electric House, The 287
Emerson, Ralph Waldo 134–5, 140,
    146, 158n.6, 159n.13
Emperor's Panorama 83
Epstein, Jean 311, 333
Erstes Leid *see* First Sorrow
Eternal Jew 217
Everyday Confusion, An 13
expressionism 4, 15; *see also* German
    expressionism
extra-diegetic 172
Eye-man 5, 98, 100

fabula 270–4, 276n.n.7,9

Fahrgast, Der *see* On the Tram
Fare Thee Well (song) 271–3
Fargo 260–1, 265
Fellini, Federico 11, 345
F for Fake 184
film adaptation 13, 21n.12, 169, 174,
    188, 332, 346, 347n.1
filmic writing 17, 89, 99
film sound 17, 114, 120
Fire Down Below 72
first-person narrator 85, 88, 121, 125,
    127n.12
First Sorrow 279, 292
flâneur/flânerie 6, 85–8, 92–4, 332
flickering images 83
Fly, The (1957) 210
Fly, The (1958) 210, 256n.2
Fly, The (1986) 19, 210, 211–17, 220–1,
    232, 233,n.1, 236–7, 247, 248–50,
    254–5
Forschungen eines Hundes *see*
    Investigations of a Dog
400 Blows, The 331
Freiheitsstatue *see* Statue of Liberty
French cinema nouveau 330, 331–43
French New Wave 331
French Revolution; *see also* Great Fear
Freud, Sigmund 17, 68–9, 71, 73–4,
    76–8, 113, 218–19, 282, 315
Friedland 5, 35, 83
Funny Games 188

Gandelman, Claude 2–3
geishas 97–100, 107, 108n.1
General, The 280–1, 283–4, 287, 291
German expressionism 15, 184; *see also*
    expressionism
German-Jewish symbiosis 59
Gerücht 41, 43
Gesellschaft 92

gestus   19, 82–3, 140
giallo   298
Ginsberg, Allen   228
Godard, Jean-Luc   331–44
Goebel, Rolf J.   6–7, 85–6, 302
Gold Rush, The   198
Golem, How He Came into the World, The   164–5, 177n.4
Golem, wie er in die Welt kam, Der see Golem, How He Came into the World, The
Goy's Teeth   267–8, 276n.6
Great Dictator, The   198
Great Fear   36–7, 40, 46, 49n.6, 50n.12, 51n.16
Great Stone Face, The   19, 280
Grund, Helen Hessel   332
Guattari, Félix   79, 93, 296
Gunning, Tom   33–4
Gutiérrez Alea, Tomás   13
GWBP   131, 133–7, 142, 148–52, 155–6

Haneke, Michael   18, 20, 181–94, 331, 344–6
Hang Me (song)   *271–3*
Heart of Darkness   225–6, 232
Heidegger, Martin   40
Heine, Heinrich   203
Heller, Heinz-B.   98, 99, 107, 108n.2
Hessel, Franz   332
Hilsenrath, Edgar   200
Hiroshima mon Amour   333
His Days Are Numbered   304
hissing   111, 116, 166, 169, 172, 175, 243, 251
Hitchcock, Alfred   329
Hitler, Adolf   59, 60
Hochzeitsvorbereitungen auf dem Lande *see* Wedding Preparations in the Country

Hoffmann, E. T. A.   87, 346
Hoffmeister, Donna   15
homoeroticism   92, 227–8, 230–1
homosexuality   92, 93, 229, 298
Hotel Occidental   101–2, 104, 141, 144, 146, 159, 160n.15
House, The   92
Huillet, Danièle   18, 181–95, 195n.8
humour   201, 212–13, 216, 233, 296, 305; dark humour   200; surreal humour   183
Hunger Artist, A   217, 233–234n.3, 303, 305
Hungerkünstler, Ein *see* Hunger Artist, A

I giorni contati see His Days Are Numbered
I heard it from X   38
image-language   43
image-making   152
imagistic thinking   2–3
Immigrant, The   202–3
Imperial Message, An   222
impure   194; *see also* Bazin, André
Incredible Journey, The   271, 272
Indagine su un cittadino al di sopra di ogni sospetto see Investigation of a Citizen Above Suspicion
inhumanity   230, 289
Inside Llewyn Davis   19, 259, 265, 269, 270, 274–5
Intervista   11
Interzone   225–32
In the Penal Colony   7, 68, 75, 223–5, 230, 233, 275n.2, 286
Investigation of a Citizen Above Suspicion   295–7, 299–301, 304–5
Investigations of a Dog   122–5, 261
Invisible Cities   318
Ivan the Terrible   344

Jackals and Arabs   193–4, 195n.8
Janouch, Gustav   3, 5, 83, 98–9, 107, 195n.6, 198
Jewish Pariah   200, 203
Josefine, die Sängerin oder das Volk der Mäuse *see* Josefine, the Singer or the Mouse People
Josefine, the Singer or the Mouse People   114–15, 126n.5, 261
Joseph Kilian see Character in Need of Support, A
Joubert, Joseph   36, 37
Jude, Der (journal)   194
Jules et Jim   330–2
Juráček, Pavel   14
Kafka (1991)   15
Kafka (1992)   15
Kafka break   258
Kafka Goes to the Movies   4, 6
Kafkan/Kafkaesque   7, 9–20, 20n.8, 21n.n.13,14, 30–1, 33, 38, 46, 48, 181–5, 187, 194, 199–201, 204, 207, 211, 216, 222, 227, 236, 247–8, 259, 261–4, 266, 268–9, 275, 282, 295, 298, 300, 301, 304–5, 307, 310, 314, 318–21, 329, 330–1, 333–4; *see also* Chaplin, Charles and Welles, Orson
Kafka Problem, The   1
kaiserliche Botschaft, Eine *see* Imperial Message, An
Kaiserpanorama   5, 20n.6, 35, 193
Kapferer, Jean-Nöel   38, 49–50n.10
Kavanagh, Thomas   262–9
Keaton, Buster   16, 19, 279–92, 292n.n.1,8
Kid, The   158–159n.11, 198, 201
Kierkegaard, Søren   36, 44
Kinematographentheater *see* Cinematographic Theatre
Kinetoscope *see* Edison. Thomas A.

Kinobuch   98
Kino-Debatte   98
Kittler, Friedrich   69, 72, 113, 118
Klassenverhältnisse see Class Relation
Kracauer, Siegfried   8–9, 85, 163, 176n.1
Kurtág, György   194

Lacan, Jacques   159n.12, 320
Landarzt, Ein *see* Country Doctor, A
Langelaan, George   210 , 256n.2
langue of the land   312
L'Année dernière à Marienbad see Last Year at Marienbad
L'Arrivée d'un train en gare de La Ciotat see Arrival of a Train at La Ciotat Station, The
L'assassino see Assassin, The
Last Year at Marienbad   333, 347n.6
Latin charlatanism   43
Lazar, Bernard   203
Legende, Die   38
Lesson of the Abyss, The   57
lezione dell'abisso, La see Lesson of the Abyss, The
L'Homme révolté see Rebel, The
Little History of Photography   85
Lloyd, Harold   284
locked gate   62
Lolotte   82
Lukács, Georg   137
Lumière, Auguste and Louis   2, 7, 35
Lumpen   45, 47, 48

Macbeth   330
machinery   77, 97, 99, 100–1, 104–5, 287
Mack, Max   98
magic   309–24
Magnificent Ambersons, The   330
male gaze   90–1, 93

mammoth mole   40–2, 44; *see*
    Riesenmaulwurf
Mann, Thomas   1, 30
Man Who Wasn't There, The   258–9, 261
Marker, Chris   16, 19–20,
    309–14, 314–24, 324n.n.1,4,
    325n.n.n.n.n.6,8,10,12,14
Masculin Féminin   331
Maulwurf   43–6; *see* mammoth mole
McLuhan, Marshall   213, 221, 222, 224
meaningfulness condition   59–62
medium: cinematic medium   2, 5, 17,
    20n.7, 32, 68, 73, 83, 176, 204, 206,
    220, 248, 249, 268, 334; cross-
    medium methodology   2; impure
    medium   194; literary medium   2,
    19, 263, 268; mass medium   32, 37,
    47; new medium   30, 31, 34, 55,
    98–100; silent medium   172 smart
    medium   247n.5; visual medium
    18, 169, 212; writing-medium   333
Méliès, George   2
meta-language   298
metaphor   7, 11–12, 43, 55, 73, 75–6,
    118, 127n.9, 165, 181–2, 188,
    192–3, 210, 212–15, 217, 220,
    224–7, 229, 233, 238, 243, 247, 260,
    264, 275–276n.4, 279, 281, 314,
    319, 320
metamorphosis   14, 19, 93, 140, 141,
    171, 212, 214–16, 219–21, 225,
    229, 232, 236–7, 241–2, 245,
    249, 250–1, 254, 281, 282, 286;
    backwards metamorphosis   215;
    horrors of the metamorphosis   252;
    metamorphosis of the metaphor   12,
    224; metaphor of the metamorphosis
    243; monstrous metamorphosis
    213, 247, 264, 282; postmodern
    metamorphosis   215; sexual
    metamorphosis   211; *see also* humour
Metamorphosis, The   4, 6, 11–13,
    18–19, 64, 127n.9, 163–76, 177n.7,
    200, 210–12, 215, 217, 226, 230,
    232–3, 236–7, 241, 247–9, 251–2,
    254–5, 256n.9, 259, 275n.1, 281–3,
    288; *see also* Absurd
Metamorphosis, The (1975)   14
metteurs-en-scène   185
Miller's Crossing   260
mirror: mirror image   63; mirror-image
    identities   59, 191, 203, 323; mirror-
    reading   63; mirror-writing   63, 65;
    two-way mirror   152; *see also Truman
    Show, The*
mise-en-scène   86–7, 164, 184, 188, 190,
    303
Mladek, Klaus   290
Moby Dick   156
modernism   125–126n.2, 200; aesthetics
    of modernism   193; hermetic
    modernist   304; postmodernism
    228; post-war modernism   183
modernity: discourse of modernity
    7; post-modern and noise   114;
    postmodernity   218, 222, 233; vision
    of modernity   233; urban modernity
    332, 347n.3
Modern Times   198, 201–3, 283, 289
Moked, Gabriel   281–2
Mole, Bigger Than Anyone Has Ever
    Seen, A *see* Village Schoolteacher
monster   165, 171, 174, 223, 228
Moreau, Jeanne   329–30
Mouchette   193
moviegoer   4, 61, 68, 72, 81, 85, 97, 99;
    see also flâneur/ flânerie
Murnau, F. W.   86, 164, 177n.3
Muybridge, Eadweard   84
My Cousin's Corner Window   87

Mythe de Sisyphe, Le see Myth of Sisyphus, The
Myth of Sisyphus, The 237

Naked Lunch 19, 210–11, 225–33
Naremore, James 13, 21n.13, 182, 194
narrative: of the Absurd 254; filmed narrative 172; Kafkaesque narrative 304; machinery narrative 287; mono-perspectival 9–10, 89, 93; narrative rhetoric 17, 274; narrative space 163, 167–70, 176; third-person narrative 89
narrator 19, 29, 37, 44, 47, 86, 88, 114–16, 119, 120, 128n.14, 166, 169, 174, 191, 192, 216, 241, 243–53, 256n.6, 283, 287–8, 311–13, 318–23, 346; anonymous narrator 204; first-person narrator 85, 121, 123, 127n.12, 316; invisible audible narrator 312 ; meta-subjectivity 312 ; narrator in film 121, 127–128n.13; narrator/protagonist 311; narrator/victim 233–234n.3; non-personal narrator 256n.6; off-camera narrator 194; third-person neutral narrator 248; voice-over narrator 173–4; world traveller narrator 317
Nature Theater of Oklahoma 48, 101, 103–4, 106, 108n.3, 130, 138–42, 145, 148–9, 152, 157n.2, 158n.n.4,8, 202
Navigator, The 288
Nazi and the Barber, The 200
Nazi und der Friseur, Der see Nazi and the Barber, The
Nemec, Jan 14, 16, 177n.7
Nicolin, Günther 11, 182, 264, 275–276n.4

night dreams 69–70, 74
No Country for Old Men 260
noir 15, 183–4, 272, 335; see also *Trial, The* and Welles, Orson
noise 64, 101, 111–25, 125–126n.6, 288; non-localisability 115, 119
non-diegetic music 184
non-diegetic sound 120–3, 125, 128n.14; see also Acousmatics
Nosferatu, a Symphony of Horror 164
Nosferatu, eine Symphonie des Grauens see Nosferatu, a Symphony of Horror
Notes on the Cinematographer 184

Odradek 281, 286–8
Old Penal Colony 233
On the Tram 6, 88
One Week 280
One Who Disappeared, The 48
ontological paradoxes 12
optical unconscious 68; see also Benjamin, Walter
Othello 330
Otherness 211, 225, 227
Othon 193

Passagen-Werk see Arcades Project, The
Passenger, The *see* Fahrgast, Der
Paul, R.W. 34
Petri, Elio 19, 295–305
phantasmagoria 68, 86, 119, 345
phantom 78, 79, 244, 275
Photographs Speak, The 2
Piano Teacher, The 190
Pinthus, Kurt 98
Poet and Daydreaming, The 69
point of view *see* POV
poliziotto 298–9
Pollack, Oscar 314
Porter, Edwin 2

Postava k podpírání see Character in Need of Support, A
Pound, Ezra   330
POV   17, 68–79, 173, 175, 177n.7, 340; third-person limited/objective point of view   241, 248, 250, 251–2, 255
Prague   14, 48–49n.1, 57–8, 81, 85, 89, 90, 97, 130, 164, 183, 230, 285, 311
Primal Noise   113, 118
Problem of Our Laws, The   261, 296, 305
Prolog vor dem Film   98
Prosessen (tv adaptation)   13
proto-cinema   17, 32, 43
Prozess, Der/Proceß, Der see Trial, The
psychoanalysis   69, 281
pure sonorous object   118

Quatre Cents Coups, Les see 400 Blows, The
Quiet Place in the Country, A   295, 301–5

Rancière, Jacques   311
realism   15, 16, 64, 66n.8, 68, 163, 164, 167, 177n.2, 282, 304, 345; empirical realism   15; Neo-realism 117n.2, 304; Socialist Realism   304
Rebel, The   238
Referential Fallacies   19
Report to an Academy, A   13
Report to an Academy, A   139
Resnais, Alain   315, 331–4, 343
Return to Zion   57
rhetoric of annulment   12
Riefenstahl, Leni   56–8, 61
Riesenmaulwurf (mammoth mole)   40, 45–6
Rilke, Rainer Maria   113, 118, 125–126n.2
Roché, Henri-Pierre   332
Rosenzweig, Franz   291

Ruebner, Tuvia   11–12, 264, 274–5, 275n.4
Rule of Rhythmic Presence and Absence, The   17, 97–107
rumour/rumourology   16, 29–48, 49n.n.n.n.6,7,8, 49–50n.10, 50n.n.12,14, 50–51n.15, 51n.16; gossip   32, 40, 215; mole-rumour 45
Rybczynski, Zbigniew   15–16
Rye, Stellan   83

sado-masochism   231
Sandbank, Shimon   1, 11, 12, 256n.3, 264, 274, 275, 276n.5
Schaeffer, Pierre   112, 113, 116, 118, 125n.1, 126n.3
Schakale und Araber see Jackals and Arabs
Scheherazade   136, 139, 141
Schenck, Joseph   280
Schloss, Das see Castle, The
Schmidt, Jan   14
Schmidt, Willy   13
Schrift   39, 41–2, 45
Scorsese, Martin   14, 16
Screen-Memories   333
Screen-Memory #5   333
Sebald, W. G.   17, 53–65, 65n.n.2,4, 65–66n.5, 66n.7
Selbstwehr (journal)   38
semiosis   314, 321
Serious Man, A   19, 21n.15, 259, 265–6, 269
Seven Chances   280
Seventh Continent, The   189
71 Fragmente einer Chronologie des Zufalls see 71 Fragments of a Chronology of Chance
71 Fragments of a Chronology of Chance 189

Shakespeare, William 155, 330, 331
Sherlock Jr. 280, 283
Shoot the Piano Player 331
Shadows and Fog 15
Shivat Zion see Return to Zion
Siebente Kontinent, Die see Seventh Continent, The
silence 12, 157–158n.3, 169, 172, 175, 206, 275–276n.4, 285; dimension of silence 172; rustle of silence 172; silent films 147, 172; *see also* Keaton, Buster
Simmel, Georg 113
Sisyphus 240–1, 246
slow cinema 184
Slaves of Gold 82, 88
Soderbergh, Steven 15, 258
Song of Myself 149
Sorge des Hausvaters, Die *see* Cares of a Family Man, The
sound 111–25; absence of sound 172; acousmatic sound 112–16, 120 125, 125n.1, 126n.3, 127n.11; film sound 17, 114, 120, 280; hissing sound 166, 172, 175, 251; history of sound 125–126n.2; non-diegetic sound 120–1, 123, 125, 128n.14; presence of sound 17; sound effects 15; sound-vision 269; synthetic sound 113, 118
soundtrack 274, 331–2, 336, 340, 342, 346
Soviet Union 113, 344; totalitarianism 329; post-Soviet 345; Soviet Cinema 325
space-time continuum 15
Starke, Ottomar 167, 212
State of Israel 311–13, 315, 318–19, 321–2
Statue of Liberty 89, 142, 158–159n.11, 202, 203; *see also* America

Steamboat Bill Jr. 280, 283, 287
stereoscope 5, 7, 35, 83, 193
stillness of reality 192–3
Strafkolonie, In der *see* In the Penal Colony
Straub-Huillet *see* Huillet Danièle and Straub, Jean-Marie
Straub, Jean-Marie 18, 181–95
Student of Prague, The 83
Student von Prag, Der *see* Student of Prague, The
style 270, 272
Sulla 73
Surrealism 68, 70, 86, 144–5, 217–19, 295, 301, 311, 331, 340; surreal humor 183
suicide 237, 239–41, 247, 254, 256.n.4,9; philosophical 240, 243, 254; physical 242, 247, 251, 254–5; *see also* Camus, Albert
syuzhet 270–4, 276n.7
Szafranski, Kurt 211

Tenth Victim, The 304
theriophany 45
three-dimensional 5, 7, 164, 193, 270
Tirez sur le pianiste see Shoot the Piano Player
Tolkien, J.R.R. 74
Trahair, Lisa 287–8
tramp 18, 145, 147, 158–159n.11, 198–207, 282, 283, 290; *see also* Chaplin, Charlie
tranquillo posto di campagna, Un see Quiet Place in the Country, A
Trauerspiel 331, 332
Trial, The 13, 19, 30–1, 38, 39, 64, 70, 83, 92, 127n.9, 181, 226, 229–31, 259, 261–4, 267, 279, 283, 284, 286, 289, 290–1, 292n.6, 299, 300, 305, 332

Trial, The (film)   10, 13, 14, 18, 20, 21n.n.13,14, 182–5, 190, 193, 329, 330, 333; *see also* Welles, Orson and noir
Tripp, Jan Peter   61
Triumph des Willens see Triumph of the Will
Triumph of the Will   56, 57
Truffaut, François   331–2
Truman Show, The   18, 112, 124–125, 130–6, 147, 150, 155
Truth about Sancho Panza, The   8
Tucholsky, Kurt   107, 211–12
Tyler, Parker   158–159n.11, 201–3

Unanständigen, die   33, 34, 45
Ur-Geräusch see Primal Noise
Urszenen   86, 89–91, 93
Urteil, Das *see* Judgment, The

van Leer, Lia and Wim   315, 325n.n.8,12
Varendonck, J.   76
Verdinglichung (becoming-a-thing) 280
vermin   11, 12, 15, 212, 213, 214–16, 242–7, 249, 255, 256n.9; becoming a   64, 224, 237, 251, 255, 264; human-sized   210; metamorphosed to a   200; monstrous vermin   165, 177n.5, 212, 236, 241, 254, 256n.1, 264, 282; salesman-vermin   11; vermin/extermination metaphor   210, 215, 233; vermin signifier   216
Verona   57–8
Verschollene, Der see Amerika: The Man Who Disappeared
Vertov, Dziga   313, 314, 318, 325n.11
Verwandlung, Die   14; *see also* Metamorphosis, The
Verwandlung, Die *see* Metamorphosis, The
Videodrome   19, 211, 217–25, 233

Village Schoolmaster, The   17, 49n.2
Village Schoolteacher, The   32, 37–40, 45–7
visual articulation   3
visual media   2, 11, 68, 264
voice of God   18
voice-over: voice-over commentary   174; voice-over creature   174; voice-over moving   175; voice-over narration/narrator   172, 173, 174, 177n.7; voice-over thoughts   173
Vor dem Gesetz *see* Before the Law
voyeurism   6, 88, 90, 91–2, 94, 230–1

Wahrheit über Sancho Pansa, Die *see* Truth about Sancho Panza, The
Walser, Martin   264, 274, 275
way of seeing   17, 68, 70
Wedding Preparations in the Country *see* Hochzeitsvorbereitungen auf dem Lande
Wegener, Paul   164
Weir, Peter   18, 112, 124, 130–57
Weisse Band, Der see White Ribbon, The
Welles, Orson   13, 14, 16, 18, 20, 21n.n.13,14, 177n.2, 181–93, 195n.4, 329–33, 347; *see also Trial, The* and adaptations
While Building the Chinese Wall   29
White Ribbon, The   344
Whitman, Walt   146, 149, 159n.13
widerlich   45
Widerwille   46
Wiene, Robert   164
Winnicott, D.W.   71, 74, 153
Wolff, Kurt   21n.10, 212
World War I/II   77, 183, 225, 302, 303; post-war   98, 183, 295, 333, 338, 340; European cinema   333, 338; pre-World War II   59, 333, 334

writing: bad writing 56; cinematic/ cinematographic/filmic 11, 16, 17, 48–49n.1, 55, 60, 61, 85–6, 89, 91, 93–4, 99, 314, 318; German-writing Jew 61; mirror-writing 63, 65; non-fictional writings 48–49n.1; orgasmic writing 227; torture-writing machine 68, 75; writing-as-cinematography 17, 55; writing-desks 143; writing in film 318; writing method ; writing in the third-person 241; word-writing-entity 2; *see also* Sebald, W. G. and Vertov, Dziga

Wunderdingen (miracle things) 314

Wyborny, Klaus 72, 73

X told me 38

Yamamura, Koji 14, 16

YouTube 37

Zamok see Castle, The (1994)

zeitgeist 131

Zischen see hissing

Zischler, Hanns 4–6, 48–49n.1, 56, 57, 60, 61, 65n.4, 81, 85, 97, 146, 177n.4, 193, 195n.6

Žižek, Slavoj 204–5

Zur Frage der Gesetze *see* Problem of Our Laws, The

GPSR Authorized Representative: Easy Access System Europe, Mustamäe tee
50, 10621 Tallinn, Estonia, gpsr.requests@easproject.com